Hippocrene Language and Travel Guide to

Ukraine

Hippocrene Language and Travel Guide to

UKRAINE

Linda Hodges
George Chumak

HIPPOCRENE BOOKS
New York

Acknowledgments

Our greatest thanks go to our computer guru, husband and friend, Laurent Hodges, whose ability to negotiate the interface between the Roman and Cyrillic alphabets made this work possible.

We also wish to thank all those who helped us in various ways. We are grateful for encouragement in the early stages to Professor Charles Gribble; for suggestions regarding language considerations to Robert De Lossa, Halyna Sydorenko, and Petro Matiaszek; for the reading and commenting on parts of the text to Alexandria Pecharska, Elaine Rook, Roman Pogranichniy, Sherry Sammons, and Diann Graham; and for help with the maps to Irina Tchoumanova. We also thank Sarah Doyle for her insights on Odesa and Alexander Litvenenko and Tania Diakiw O'Neill for their helpful information.

Special thanks go to our numerous friends on computer bulletin boards whose mutual interest in Ukraine have linked us together in a huge cyberspace network stretching from Kharkiv to Canada to California. They always had the answer.

All photographs in text and on cover by co-author Linda Hodges. Maps on pages 246, 260, 280 and 298 by co-author George Chumak.

For information, address:
HIPPOCRENE BOOKS, INC
171 Madison Avenue
New York, NY 10016

Library of Congress Cataloging-in-Publication Data available.
Hodges, Linda.
    Hippocrene language and travel guide to Ukraine / Linda Hodges, George Chumak.
        p.   cm.
    Includes index.
    ISBN 0-7818-0135-4 (pbk.)
    1. Ukraine—Guidebooks.   2. Ukrainian language—Conversation and phrase books—English.   I. Chumak, George.   II. Title.
    DK508.H63   1994
    914.7'710486—dc20   94-31081
                                                                            CIP

Printed in the United States of America.

Contents

PREFACE

This book fills a need for the traveler who regards Ukraine as a destination in itself, not a stopping point of a larger itinerary. It's for the traveler who is sensitive to the differences between national groups and who appreciates the distinctiveness of the Ukrainian language, history, and culture. This book is for the visitor to Ukraine who wants to speak to Ukrainians in their native tongue, who wants to learn more about their culture, and view the historical sights from a Ukrainian perspective.

The phrases are designed to cover the most basic situations that a visitor to Ukraine might encounter. They are expressed in up-to-date, idiomatic Ukrainian that should be understood by Ukrainian speakers anywhere in Ukraine. For those with no background in Slavic languages or the Cyrillic alphabet, the guide to pronunciation will take the mystery out of this highly phonetic language. For those who understand spoken Ukrainian but can't read it, the inclusion of the Cyrillic phrases with their phonetic rendition will improve their literacy.

Readers should be aware that they may encounter variations from the language presented in this book. In parts of Ukraine, Russian is heard in public more than Ukrainian, although Ukrainian may be spoken in more homes. We are hopeful that this book will encourage the use of the Ukrainian language and serve as a sign to native Ukrainians that the world still recognizes and values their native tongue.

Ukraine has been a buried nation for much of its history. Travel is now unrestricted and it's possible to find beautiful places where the friendly people still are unaccustomed to foreign visitors. One of the best pieces of advice we've heard from an enthusiastic visitor to Ukraine is "Go now before it's spoiled." Many of the relatively undiscovered, unspoiled places are discussed in the travel section along with the major tourist destinations. To enrich the travel experience, the book provides highlights of Ukrainian history and culture. It also answers the most-asked questions of those planning a trip to Ukraine.

Ukraine is also a country that, in the last few years, has experienced the most fundamental and radical changes on all levels and in all spheres of life. It has emerged from 300 years of colonialism and 70 years of totalitarianism to stand as an independent nation. There are continuing repercussions to the rapid changes and continuing adjustments to the repercussions. The way something is done today may not be the way it's done tomorrow.

While this guide presents what we consider the typical, we can't guarantee the particulars. Ukraine is a country of infinite variation. Each region has a distinct history. Even towns and cities within regions were subject to different influences. Also to be reckoned with is the legendary Ukrainian trait of individualism — the story goes that a committee of five Ukrainians will come up with six different plans. Add to that the blind-man-and-the-elephant phenomenon — the tendency of travelers to make generalizations and form opinions from limited experience, some giving positive interpretations, others making negative judgments — and we can't guarantee that your experiences in Ukraine will match our characterizations.

Linda Hodges
Ames, Iowa

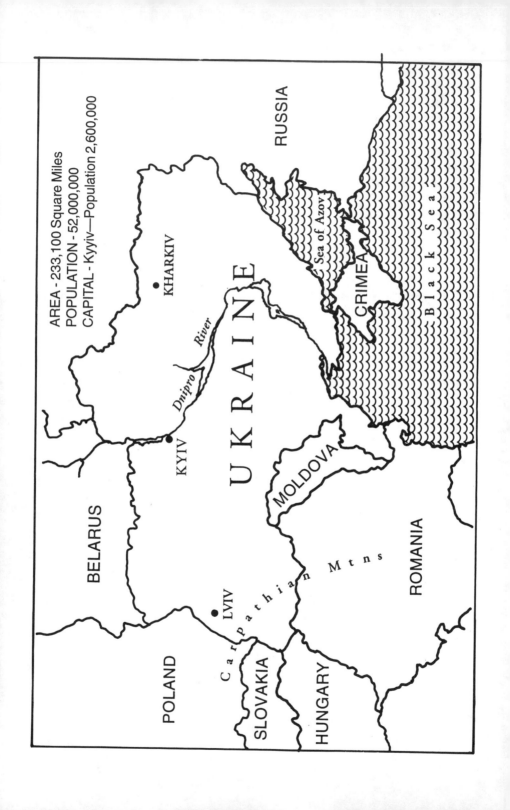

AREA - 233,100 Square Miles
POPULATION - 52,000,000
CAPITAL - Kyiv—Population 2,600,000

RUSSIA

BELARUS

POLAND

SLOVAKIA

HUNGARY

ROMANIA

MOLDOVA

UKRAINE

Carpathian Mtns

LVIV

KYIV

Dnipro River

KHARKIV

Sea of Azov

CRIMEA

Black Sea

CHAPTER 1. ABOUT UKRAINE

Certainly a visitor to a foreign culture can enjoy the pretty scenery and marvel at the architectural monuments without knowledge of the history and culture, but informed visitors will get so much more out of their experience. You can't visit Ukraine, for example, without walking upon a street named for Taras Shevchenko or noticing a monument to this famous Ukrainian son. If you know who Shevchenko was and what he did, you'll understand why his life and accomplishments personify Ukraine as a nation and thus why he is so great a popular hero. In order to make your trip a more valuable experience, we start with some background information.

With 233,100 square miles (603,700 sq. km.), Ukraine surpasses France to become the largest country completely in Europe. It's slightly smaller than the state of Texas.

Ukraine is a relatively modern country with a highly educated population that is two-thirds urbanized. Even so, traditional family values still prevail, including a strong work ethic.

Its population of 52 million is Europe's fifth largest, after Germany, Great Britain, Italy, and France. Ethnically, 73 percent of the population is identified as Ukrainian and 22 percent as Russian. The western and central oblasts are the most Ukrainian, while the eastern and southern oblasts are the most Russian. Minorities that number 100,000 or more are Jews, Belarusians, Moldovans, Poles, Bulgarians, Hungarians, and Romanians. Not surprisingly, the non-Ukrainian population tends to be concentrated around the borders.

To the north is Belarus; Russia is to the northeast and east; Moldova and Romania and Hungary are to the south and southwest; Slovakia and Poland border on the west and northwest. The southern border is on the Black Sea and Sea of Azov.

The country consists primarily of fertile steppeland with a forest-steppe area across the north and low-lying mountains along the western border. The Dnipro River, which flows down through the center and separates the country into east and west regions, has played an active role in the country's development from prehistoric through modern times. Ukraine's rich soil and moderate climate make it ideally suited to agriculture. Its huge coal reserves and deposits of iron and manganese ore have led to heavy industrial development, especially in the eastern part.

DEVELOPING A UKRAINIAN PERSPECTIVE

The adage that history is told by the winners is well-understood by those with roots in Ukraine. Without a Ukrainian state, Ukrainian history was handed down as a footnote, considered no more than a provincial expression of the dominant power. By an extension of stunted, simplistic logic, without a Ukrainian state, there was no Ukrainian identity. There ceased to be, for most of the world, not only a country with its own history, but a separate and distinct people who shared a unique language and a rich cultural heritage.

Thus, with the possible exception of the batik Easter eggs, nearly every aspect of Ukrainian history and culture was attributed to other groups. The mislabeling of things Ukrainian was carried to its logical absurdity in library card catalogs, encyclopedias, and history books. An example is the college-level history of civilization textbook that discusses the Kyivan-Rus legacy without once using the word "Ukrainian."

HISTORICAL HIGHLIGHTS

Ukraina means borderland. As a frontierland bridging the East and West, Ukraine was vulnerable to invaders from all sides. Among the early peoples who roamed across the steppes and navigated the Dnipro and Black Sea were Scythians, Greeks, Goths, Huns, and Khazars. After the establishment of the modern state, Ukraine was threatened by the shifting borders of the Grand Duchy of Lithuania, the Ottoman Empire, the Polish-Lithuanian Commonwealth, the Tatar Khanate, and Muscovy. For centuries various parts were under the Russian Empire, Poland, or Austria. The many foreign powers that occupied and ruled Ukraine sometimes enriched the country, but also brought exploitation and devastation.

As a nation that for most of its history was not in charge of its own destiny, Ukraine has over and over again been trapped between two bad choices, forced to choose the lesser of two evils. Ironically, fate has thrust upon Ukraine the opportunity to emerge from the shadows and stand as a free and independent member of the family of nations.

Here are a few highlights of Ukrainian history. Throughout this guide, we'll spell Ukrainian names in English according to the transliteration adopted by the United States Board of Geographical Names. While some of the equivalents may result in unfamiliar-appearing names, they are preferred by many scholars of Ukrainian history and language.

Kyiv Rus, the historical ancestor of Ukraine, was established by Vikings and peopled by various Slavic tribes. Kyiv was the center of this powerful princely state that dominated eastern Europe from the 10th through the 13th century. It was a center of trade, Slavic culture, and Byzantine Christianity. Internal dissention weakened the state and it ended with Mongol invasions in the mid-13th century.

Kozak Period. *Kozak* (Козак), often spelled Cossack in English, comes from a Turkish word meaning free man. The term was originally applied to refugees from serfdom and slavery who fled to the borderland that was Ukraine during the 15th to the 18th century. The term later was applied to Ukrainians who went into the steppes to practice various trades and engage in hunting, fishing, beekeeping, and collection of salt. The Kozaks set up democratic military communities and elected their leaders, who were called hetmans. From their island stronghold on the Dnipro, the Kozaks launched attacks against the Turks and Tatars and struggled against the Polish and Russians. Their establishment of an autonomous Ukrainian state is a high point of Ukrainian history.

During the mid-17th century, Poland controlled most of the Right Bank Ukraine (lands west of the Dnipro) while Muscovy controlled most of Left Bank. Ukrainian culture enjoyed a great revival during this period of ambiguous political status. Religious and educational activity flourished and there was a high rate of literacy.

By the late 18th century, however, 85 percent of Ukrainian land had fallen under Russian control, and Ukraine's window to the west was closed. It was a time of colonialism and Russification during which Ukrainian culture and language was suppressed.

The 20th century was a time of great turmoil and suffering in Ukraine. After the Bolshevik Revolution of 1917, Ukraine was engulfed in a chaotic civil war in which many different factions and foreign powers fought for control. A Bolshevik victory brought most of Ukraine under Soviet rule. The Ukrainian intelligentsia either was forced to move or perish. In 1932-1933 anywhere from four to seven million peasants were starved to death in a deliberately engineered famine designed to force them onto collective farms. During the Second World War, Ukraine bore the brunt of the Nazi drive to Stalingrad and the Red Army counteroffensive. Another 7.5 million people were lost, including almost 4 million civilians killed and 2.2 million taken to Germany as laborers. Cities, towns and thousands of villages were devastated.

National liberation struggles took place during the two wars, but Ukraine was not able to hold on to independence. In the second half of the century Ukraine's dissident movement thrived, but as a buried nation, the world paid little attention. With the collapsing Soviet Union, the Ukrainian Parliament proclaimed independence on August 24, 1991. On December 1, some 90 percent of the Ukrainian electorate supported the measure.

HEROES, POETS, AND PATRIOTS

In forging a new national identity, Ukraine is looking to its past and turning to its most durable symbols as a rallying point for patriotism. There's something appealing about a nation whose greatest hero is a poet and painter. Taras Hryhorovych Shevchenko (Тарас Григорович Шевченко), was born into a serf family in Moryntsi, a village that today is in the Cherkasy region. Orphaned as a teen, Shevchenko accompanied his master on his travels, serving as a houseboy. In St. Petersburg his talents as a painter attracted attention, and in 1838 a Russian painter helped him buy his freedom.

Shevchenko trained at the St. Petersburg Academy of Art where he had many contacts with Ukrainian and Russian artists and writers. His first collection of Ukrainian poems, *Kobzar* ("The Bard"), was published in 1840 and hailed as work of genius by Ukrainian and Russian critics alike. Drawing upon Ukrainian history and folklore, Shevchenko wrote in the Romantic style prevalent during his day. Soon his poems evolved from nostalgia for Kozak life to an indictment of rulers who abuse their power and a sympathy for oppressed people everywhere.

As a painter, Shevchenko was skilled in portraiture, landscape, and architectural monuments of Ukraine, but his most noteworthy paintings are the scenes of country life and historical events that are sympathetic to Ukraine and critical of its oppressors. For example, Shevchenko's tragic story of Kateryna, the Ukrainian girl who was seduced, impregnated, and abandoned by a Russian soldier, expressed both in ballad and later in a painting, are allegorical references to the fate of Ukraine under the Russian tsars who introduced serfdom.

Shevchenko's reputation as a leading Ukrainian poet and artist was already established when he came to Kyiv in 1846. There he joined the first modern Ukrainian organization with a political ideology, the Brotherhood of Sts. Cyril and Methodius. In 1847 brotherhood members were arrested, and Shevchenko was the most severely punished when the authorities discovered his unpublished collection of poetry satirizing the oppression of Ukraine by Russia. He was sentenced to ten years military service in a labor battalion in Siberia. Although Tsar Nicholas I himself stipulated, "under the strictest supervision, forbidden to write and sketch," Shevchenko managed during part of his term to write and paint clandestinely. After his release, Shevchenko was a broken man. He was not allowed to live in Ukraine, but permitted to visit. That led to his re-arrest and banishment to St. Petersburg where he remained under police surveillance until his death in 1861. His gravesite, monument, and museum in Kaniv are a popular tourist destination.

Even without his poetry, Shevchenko would be renowned for his art alone. His existing artwork numbers 835 paintings and engravings, with several hundred lost. His writings have a greater significance, however, not only for their literary merit but for the role they played in the development of the Ukrainian language. Shevchenko blended several Ukrainian dialects with elements of Church Slavonic, thus expanding the range, flexibility and resources of the Ukrainian language.

Elevating Ukrainian to a literary prose was equivalent to a literary declaration of Ukrainian independence, according to Orest Subtelny in his book, *Ukraine: a History*. Shevchenko showed that Ukrainians did not need to depend on the Russian language as a means of higher discourse because their own language was equally rich and expressive.

As a critic of tsarist autocracy and a champion of the universal struggle for justice, Shevchenko was exalted in the Soviet Union. His works were circulated and his memory honored in every republic. Even in Moscow there's a monument to him. But to Ukrainians, Shevchenko has a special meaning.   To Ukrainians, Shevchenko represents the right to *be* Ukrainian.   Ukrainians understood that when Shevchenko referred to Muscovy, he wasn't referring to a particular government, but to the Russian nation subjugating the Ukrainian nation. Ukrainians even knew which words in the official publications of Shevchenko's works had been changed to conceal his nationalistic intention.

Following independence, many more monuments were erected in Shevchenko's honor in Ukraine, often replacing statutes of Lenin that were torn down. The depiction of Shevchenko as an old man is stereotypical, as he died when he was only 47, and made his impact when he was much younger.

Two Kozak hetmans are important in Ukrainian history. Both were great leaders and statesmen and fought to free Ukraine from foreign domination.

Bohdan Khmelnytsky (1595-1657) headed the national uprising in 1648 that liberated a large part of Ukrainian territory from Poland. Khmelnytsky was recognized at home and abroad as the leader of a sovereign state. Under continual threat from Poland, a few years later he entered a pact with Muscovy. Ukrainians consider this a fatal turning point in their history. Moscow began its subjugation of Ukraine, turning an agreement of military and political union into an act of incorporation of Ukraine into Russia.

Today Ukraine looks to Ivan Mazepa (1639-1709) as a more appropriate hero. Mazepa wanted to unite all Ukrainian territories into a unitary state modeled after existing European states with features of the traditional Kozak structure.   At first Mazepa was allied with Tsar Peter I against foreign powers, but when he realized Russia intended to abolish the Kozak order and end Ukrainian autonomy, he sided with Charles XII of Sweden against Peter. After a disastrous defeat at the Battle of Poltava in 1709, Kyiv lost much autonomy and Kozak rule came to an end.

NATIONAL EMBLEMS AND ANTHEM

Trident. The trident (тризуб, *tryzub*) is the official coat of arms of Ukraine. It consists of a gold trident against an azure background. Archeological findings of the trident in Ukraine date back to the 1st century A.D. when it was apparently a mark of authority and a symbol of one or several of the various early tribes who inhabited Ukrainian territory and who later became part of the Ukrainian people.

As a state emblem, the trident dates back to the ninth century when the Rurik dynasty adopted it as their coat of arms. Prince Volodymyr the Great inherited the symbol. The design was engraved on gold and silver coins called "hryvni," as well as imprinted on official seals and on the portals of old Ukrainian cathedrals, palaces and tombs of nobility.

Some historians interpret the design as an abbreviation of a compounded Old Slavonic word, "Володимирстов" (*Volodymyrstov*), which means "Volodymyr on the throne." Or perhaps the design is an amalgam of the letters Я, В, and О, from the names of the prominent Kyivan rulers Emperor Yaroslav the Wise, Prince Volodymyr, and Queen Olha. Others suggest the symbol comes from a stylistic rendition of the Cyrillic letters В, О, Л, and Я, which spell the word *volya*, meaning "freedom." Or even more simply, the design may derive just from the letter "в" from "volya," written frontwards and in reverse.

To keep continuity with the past, Ukrainians adopted the trident as the official state symbol when they declared independence in 1917. Obviously, as a symbol of the struggle for Ukrainian sovereignty, the trident was forbidden under soviet rule for being "nationalistic." Not surprisingly, it was reprised as the national emblem when Ukraine finally achieved independence in 1991.

Flag. Many different flags have flown over Ukraine through the centuries; some represented foreign ruling powers, others were the choice of Ukrainian ruling groups, such as the flags of the Kozak period. Independent Ukraine's official flag is a rectangle composed of a horizontal blue and a yellow stripe. It was designed by Ukrainian leaders under the Austro-Hungarian Empire and first flown on June 2, 1848 by the Ukrainian delegation to a pan-Slavic congress held in Prague, Bohemia. It was used during the struggle for independence in 1917-1920.

Which of the two colors was on top sometimes varied and some of the earlier flags included a coat of arms emblem such as a lion or trident. On January 28, 1992 the Presidium of the Supreme Council of Ukraine adopted an unadorned blue-on-top and yellow-on-bottom flag as the official national flag. Why blue and yellow are the Ukrainian colors is not known; many believe the popular interpretation that blue represents the sky and yellow the golden wheat or sunflowers. The shades of blue and yellow are exactly the same as those used in the Swedish flag, but the link between the two is not exactly known.

National Anthem. Imagine the mixture of hope and desperation expressed in a national anthem that begins "Ukraine has not yet died." Although time and again in Ukrainian history, different regions adopted various patriotic songs as their anthem, the song that became the official anthem of the newly independent country is *Shche Ne Vmerla Ukrayina* (Ще Не Вмерла Україна).

Shche Ne Vmerla Ukrayina was published as a patriotic poem in 1863 by Pavlo Chubynsky, a Ukrainian ethnographer and civic leader. The music was written by V. Verbytsky and it was published with the score in 1885. Widely sung throughout Ukraine, it was recognized in 1917 as the anthem of the short-lived Ukrainian National Republic. It was replaced during the Soviet era, but again adopted after independence.

Ukraine is Not Yet Dead

Ukraine is not yet dead, nor its glory and freedom,
Luck will still smile on us brother-Ukrainians.
Our enemies will die, as the dew does in the sunshine,
and we, too, brothers, we'll live happily in our land.

We'll not spare either our souls or bodies to get freedom
and we'll prove that we brothers are of Kozak kin.

We'll rise up, brothers, all of us, from the Sain to the Don,
We won't let anyone govern in our motherland.
The Black Sea will smile yet, grandfather Dnipro will rejoice,
Yet in our Ukraine luck will be high.

Our persistence, our sincere toil will prove its rightness,
still our freedom's loud song will spread throughout Ukraine.
It'll reflect upon the Carpathians, will sound through the steppes,
and Ukraine's glory will arise among the people.

... adapted from a translation by Victor Ponomaryov

Ще Не Вмерла Україна

Ще не вмерла Україна, ні слава, ні воля,
Ще нам, Браття-українці, усміхнеться доля.
Згинуть наші воріженьки, як роса на сонці,
Заживемо і ми, браття, у своїй сторонці.

Душу й тіло ми положим за нашу свободу
І покажем, що ми, браття, козацького роду.

Станем, браття, всі за волю, від Сяну до Дону,
Вріднім краю панувати не дамо нікому.
Чорне море ще всміхнеться, дід Дніпро зрадіє,
Ще на нашій Україні доленька доспіє.

А завзяття, праця щира свого ще докаже,
Ще ся волі в Україні піснь гучна розляже.
за Карпати відіб'ється, згомонить степами,
України слава стане поміж гародами.

TO LEARN MORE ABOUT UKRAINE

We recommend the following sources whose help in compiling this guide we gratefully acknowledge:

Encyclopedia of Ukraine, Volumes I through V, University of Toronto Press, 1984, 1993. This is the largest, most comprehensive and authoritative source of English-language information on everything Ukrainian ever published, the product of 20 years of research and collaboration by writers, scientists, and scholars from around the world. Items are alphabetically arranged; discussion is in-depth and illustrated with photos and maps.

Ukraine: A Concise Encyclopedia, Vols. 1-2 (Toronto: University of Toronto Press 1963, 1971). This encyclopedia is a forerunner of the above one. The subject matter is topically rather than alphabetically arranged and it also is amply illustrated with photos, drawings, and maps.

Ukraine: A History, Orest Subtelny, University of Toronto Press, 1989, second edition 1994. This in-depth examination of Ukrainian history from Kyivan Rus through modern times is highly readable. It was selected by *Choice*, a journal of reviews for college libraries in North America, as one of the "Outstanding Academic Books of 1989/90."

Dilemmas of Independence: Ukraine after Totalitarianism, Alexander J. Motyl, Council on Foreign Relations Press, New York, 1993. This examination of the obstacles to nation-building confronting an independent Ukraine is lucid and insightful and should be required reading for all State Department Eastern Europe specialists.

Ukraine: The Land and its People, Ukrainian Media Centre, Toronto, Canada, is 55-minute-long video color travelogue, narrated in English. In a lively and upbeat manner, this excellent video shows all the major cities, dozens of historic sites, and the scenic beauty throughout the whole country. *Golden Kiev,* from the same producers, is an in-depth look at Ukraine's capital city. The videos cost under $30 each.

Ukraine: A Tourist Guide, Osyp Zinkewych and Volodymyr Hula, Smoloskyp Publishers, Kyiv, 1995. A region by region list of tourist attractions, hotels, shopping, and restaurants with many, many maps and photographs. This book is available in English or Ukrainian.

To keep up with current events, we recommend two weekly newspapers, both printed in English:

The Ukrainian Weekly, published by the Ukrainian National Association, Inc., 30 Montgomery Street, Jersey City, New Jersey, 07302 was founded in 1933 to serve a new generation of Ukrainian-Americans who did not always read Ukrainian. Yearly subscription rate is $60 ($40 for UNA members.) For copies or subscription, write the Ukrainian Weekly, P.O. Box 346, Jersey City, New Jersey 07302.

News From Ukraine, published since 1964 by the Ukraina Society, covers news, politics, and the arts in Ukraine. The cost of this weekly newspaper is $85 per year. Contact News From Ukraine, 35/37 O. Shmidt Street, Kyiv 254107.

IntelNews is Ukraine's oldest independent English language news agency. The service e-mails or faxes its subscribers, on a daily or weekly basis, the latest in economic, political, and parliamentary developments in Ukraine. *Economic Review* is a weekly magazine covering business in Ukraine. For subscription information, contact publisher Christine Demkowych, IntelNews, 6240B Bellona Ave., Baltimore, Maryland, 21212. Tel./Fax: 410-433-4941. E-mail: 0006240989@MCIMAIL.com In Ukraine contact IntelNews, 11/37 vulytsya Karla Marksa, Kyiv 252001. Tel./Fax. (380) 44-229-6485.

A very fine source of Ukrainian culture and history is Yevshan Book & Music Catalog, Yevshan Corporation, Box 325, Beaconsfield, Quebec, Canada, H9W 5T8. Tel. 1-800-265-9858. The Yevshan catalog lists books on Ukrainian history and culture, cookbooks, children's books, videos, cassettes, and compact discs.

Map Link, a map distributor at 25 East Mason Street, Santa Barbara, California, 93101, carries a very detailed map of Ukraine for $6.95 plus handling and shipping. Tel. (805) 965-4402; Fax: (800) 627-7768.

You can also find books, periodicals, and videos on Ukraine in gift and book shops and community centers in Ukrainian neighborhoods in cities with large Ukrainian populations.

CHAPTER 2. SO YOU WANT TO GO TO UKRAINE

EXPECT A FEW CHANGES

Hundreds of thousands of visitors come to Ukraine each year. They come for business, on academic and cultural exchanges, to provide expertise, to visit relatives.

Those who discover Ukraine for the first time are impressed by the richness of culture, the beauty of the cities and countryside, and especially by the warmth and hospitality of the Ukrainian people.

In the last few years, Ukrainians have experienced massive changes in every sphere of life. The birth of the country brought much joy: the opportunity to live in an independent, democratic nation — one of the largest in Europe — and the freedom to explore what it is to be Ukrainian.

Some responses to the new opportunities, while relatively inconsequential, have a bearing on visitors. For example, in many cities and towns, statues of soviet heroes have been toppled. Streets, avenues, and squares named for them have gone back to their historic names or, in many instances, been renamed after a new set of heroes.

Even when the names have not changed, public signs have. Ukrainian has replaced Russian as the official state language. As more and more textbooks and government documents are printed in Ukrainian, it gradually will move out of the schools and government offices and become the vernacular everywhere. Language is not uniform throughout Ukraine. While in the western part of the country, Ukrainian is the everyday language, as you go east, you'll notice less and less of it spoken publicly. In western Ukraine, a substantial number of names have been changed, while in eastern cities like Kharkiv, the changes are slower to take place.

Independence brought tremendous growing pains. Unemployment skyrocketed, run-away inflation put the necessities of life out of reach of most people, poverty became widespread. A fuel shortage all but ended domestic air flights. Cities were forced to cut their bus service and intercity buses stopped going to some of the off-the-beaten track tourist destinations. The consequent reduction in the numbers of tourists led to closing of restaurants in the more out of the way places. Thus the depression spiraled.

Ukrainians, however, have learned to endure hard times, to be resourceful, and to put up with inconveniences with patience and good humor. In this century alone, they've been through two world wars, foreign invasion from all fronts, an artificial famine, and severe political repression. Experience has taught them to trust first in themselves, then in family members, then in close friends. They don't trust institutions, especially the government, and are suspicious of even organized religion. When they need something, Ukrainians turn to those they can trust, avoiding official channels. Problems are solved in ingenious ways, whether finding a way for you to fulfill your itinerary when public transportation is full or improvising an impossible-to-get car part.

Chances are that during your visit to Ukraine you'll have an official host — either a friend, a relative, or a business contact. That responsible, caring person will see to all your needs, making it unnecessary to go through institutional channels. If you need a car with a driver, you might expect to first ask at your hotel service bureau, but that probably won't be necessary because your Ukrainian host will have a relative or friend with a car who'll be glad to serve as your driver.

Today in Ukraine, the reward for doing one's job will not support a family, so when a westerner comes bearing hard currency, some have trouble distinguishing the concept of "free enterprise" from that of "highway robbery." A generation that feels robbed of what was theirs now feels that it's their turn to take their due.

You might see evidence of corruption. Bribes were a common way of conducting business under the soviet system, and most public officials are holdovers from the former government. You may be expected to line the pocket of the customs official in order to cross the border hassle-free or to pay the conductor to squeeze you onto an already full train. Yes, dishonesty exists, but it's certainly not universal. Despite some desperate opportunism, Ukraine remains a nation of civilized, law-abiding people who are extremely hospitable to foreign visitors. There are few places where you'll feel unsafe, day or night.

Therefore don't hesitate to go to Ukraine. No one who goes regrets it. But don't take anything for granted, and don't count on anything working the way it works in the West or even the way it used to work in Ukraine. Be like the Ukrainians — be flexible, be willing to change your plans, and don't be afraid to try new ways of doing things.

OBTAINING A VISA

Visas are required for travel to Ukraine. To get a visa, first request an application from the Embassy of Ukraine in Washington, D.C. or from consular divisions in New York or Chicago. Complete and sign the application and return it along with a passport that will be valid through the entire period of your stay, a passport-sized photograph, an invitation or confirmation of tourist accommodations, and $30.

Residents of states not served by a regional consular division should apply to the consular office in the Embassy of Ukraine in Washington, D.C. The Embassy and Consulates in the United States are:

Embassy of Ukraine
Consular Division, 3350 M. Street NW, Washington, D.C. 20007
Tel. (202) 333-7507; -0606. Fax (202) 333-0817.

Consulate of Ukraine
240 East 49th Street, New York, New York 10017
Tel. (212) 371-5690; -5691. Fax (212) 371-5547
(Serves 9 Eastern states: Maine, New Hampshire, Vermont, Massachusetts, Connecticut, Rhode Island, New York, New Jersey, and Pennsylvania)

Consulate of Ukraine
10 East Huron Street, Chicago, Illinois 60611
Tel. (312) 642-4388. Fax (312) 642-4385
(Serves 10 Midwest states: Serving Illinois, Michigan, Indiana, Wisconsin, Iowa, Minnesota, Nebraska, Kansas, North and South Dakota)

In Canada, apply to Embassy of Ukraine, Consulate Division, 331 Metcalfe Street, Ottawa, Ontario, K2P 1S3, Canada. Tel. (613) 230-2961; Fax (613) 230-2400.

The visa takes nine business days to process. For double the fee, you can get rush processing (within three business days). For $100 you can get express (same-day, while-you-wait) service. Pay for your visa by money order, corporate or cashier's checks, or cash. No personal checks are accepted.

Your visa is valid for the period indicated on your invitation or tourist confirmation and will be stamped directly into your passport. If you expect to leave and re-enter Ukraine during your trip, apply for a dual-entry visa, which costs $60. Your invitation should include a request for dual entry. For frequent trips to Ukraine, apply for a multiple-entry visa. It costs $120 and is valid for a six-month period. A concurring telex from the Foreign Ministry in Kyiv is necessary.

Ukraine's visa procedure is rather restrictive; the invitation or tourist confirmation requirement discourages the casual tourist. Pending new legislation by the Ukrainian Parliament, a traveler requesting a "private visitor's visa" needs to produce an official invitation from a relative or friend made through their local OVIR (Ministry of Internal Affairs) office; a "business visa" requires a letter of invitation from a duly incorporated Ukrainian organization; a "tourist visa" requires a hotel confirmation showing that you've pre-paid your accommodations, along with a cover letter from a travel agency.

While purportedly designed to prevent the growing eastern European "mafia" from making quick trips for economic speculation, the regulations discourage the casual tourist who might want to include Ukraine on an Eastern European itinerary while encouraging the opportunity for bureaucratic corruption at the various border entry points.

Special visas can be issued at points of entry to Ukraine in emergency cases, under special circumstances, or to travelers who don't have a Ukrainian embassy or consulate in their country of origin. These visas are valid for only a 72-hour period. They cost $150 USD and require documentation certifying your intention to visit another country, such as a visa to another country. Travelers who stay beyond the terms of their visas will be fined as they exit Ukraine, but the 72-hour visa can be re-registered with the Ministry of the Interior in Kyiv.

Westerners traveling abroad who would like to add Ukraine to their itinerary are advised to go to the Ukrainian consulate in the country they are in and apply for a visa rather than try to get it at the border. The cost will be cheaper and the results more satisfactory. You will have to meet the same requirements as if you applied at home. The Ukrainian consulate in Moscow is at 18 Stanislavsky Street, in Warsaw at 7 Aleja Szucha, and in Vienna at 23 Naafgasse. However, it will be easier and more trouble-free to get the visas before you leave home, and you won't have to spend valuable business or vacation time waiting in bureaucratic lines.

Similarly, if you want to make a side trip to Russia, there's a Russian consulate in Kyiv that will issue visas to foreigners.

TRAVEL SERVICES

A number of travel agencies have long served the Ukrainian-American community by leading group tours to Ukraine. For their clients, sightseeing was a secondary reason for the trip. The big attraction was the opportunity to visit family members from whom they had long been separated or relatives they had never met. They came laden with suitcases and travel bags full of western consumer goods. They returned with embroidered linens and blouses, wooden and ceramic figurines, carved and inlaid wooden boxes, jewelry, and samovars. And most of all, with cherished memories.

Before the relaxation of the soviet system, travelers were restricted to the officially designated "open" cities. Their relatives came from towns and villages to meet with them either in the Inturyst hotels, or more commonly, outdoors, in nearby parks. Ukrainians, clutching photos of their relatives, didn't dare approach a foreigner unless they were absolutely certain of his or her identity. After the joyous reunion, many Americans disregarded the warnings of the travel agencies to stay in the official open cities and managed to find their way out to their relatives' villages to enjoy a few stolen hours in the home of their loved ones.

Today these agencies continue to serve the Ukrainian-American community with escorted package group tours. The partial group tour, combining sightseeing and lodging in the tourist areas with individual visits to the homes of relatives or friends, are especially popular among those who feel more comfortable with group travel. Going with a group offers the opportunity to meet interesting, congenial people.

The new freedoms in Ukraine have resulted in opportunities for more individualized travel. American travel agencies are no longer at the complete mercy of Inturyst, but rely on their own contacts in Ukraine to supply travel services they specify. Many agencies have re-oriented themselves to custom-designed travel (FIT or Foreign Independent Travel) for individuals, families, small groups, or businesspersons. They'll provide as much help as the client wants in getting around Ukraine, including making hotel reservations or finding lodging in a private home; arranging airport-pick-up; buying airline or train tickets for travel within Ukraine; providing cars with drivers and interpreters and guides for sightseeing. The more accommodating and creative agencies even provide auxiliary services such as delivering messages, parcels, or cash to your contacts in Ukraine.

Agencies differ in flexibility and in their orientation to group-versus-individual services or packaged versus customized travel. Before contacting an agency, it's a good idea to consider your needs and the amount of help you want. If a Ukrainian friend, relative, or colleague can arrange for your invitation, meet you at the airport, and provide lodging and local transportation, you may need an agency only to reserve your airline tickets. An agency that specializes in Ukrainian travel may also be very helpful in getting your visa from the Ukrainian consulate. Check if the agency has a representative in the part of Ukraine you'll visit, so you'll have somewhere to turn if something should go wrong. The following agencies specialize in travel to Ukraine. Their knowledge, experience, and contacts give them a big advantage over agencies without expertise in Ukrainian travel. They will be aware of current situations in Ukraine.

American Travel Agency (ATA)
2222 W. Chicago, Chicago, Illinois 60622. Tel. (312) 235-9322

Bravo International, Inc.
1320 Hamilton Street, Allentown, Pennsylvania 18102
Tel. 1-800-822-7286. Fax (215) 437-6982

Diaspora Enterprises, Inc.
220 South 20th Street, Philadelphia, Pennsylvania 19103
New Jersey: (201) 762-3090. Philadelphia: (215) 567-1328
Tel. 1-800-487-5324. Fax (215) 567-1792

Dunwoodie Travel Bureau
771-A Yonkers Avenue, Yonkers, New York 10704
Tel. (914) 969-4200. Fax (914) 969-2108

East-West Ventures, Inc.
PO Box 14391, Tucson, Arizona 85732.
Tel. (602) 795-5414.

Europe International Trade Enterprise, Inc.
2236 W. Chicago Avenue, Chicago, Illinois 60622.
Tel. (312) 489-3977 or (312) 489-9225. Fax (312) 489-4203.

Hamalia Travel Consultants
43 St, Mark's Place, Suite 6E, New York, New York 10003.
Tel. (212) 473-0839
Tel. 1-800-HAMALIA. Fax (212) 473-2180.

IBV Bed and Breakfast Systems
13113 Ideal Drive, Silver Springs, Maryland 20906.
Tel. (301) 942-3770. Fax (301) 933-0024.

Kobasniuk Travel, Inc.
157 Second Avenue, New York, New York 10003-5765
Tel. (212) 254-8779. Fax (212) 254-4005.

Landmark Opportunities, Ltd.
6102 Berlee Drive, Alexandria, Virginia 22312
Tel. (703) 941-6180 or 1-800-832-1789. Fax (703) 941-7587.

Lotus Travel Ltd.
475 Fifth Avenue, Suite 31112, New York, New York 10017
Tel. (212) 586-4545 or 1-800-998-6116.

Pallada International, Inc.
98 Second Avenue, 2nd Fl., New York, New York 10003
Tel. (212) 387-8683

Rahway Travel
35 E. Milton Avenue, Rahway, New Jersey 07065
Tel. (908) 381-8800 or 1-800-526-2786.

Scope Travel, Inc.
1605 Springfield Avenue, Maplewood, New Jersey 07040
Tel. 1-800-242-7267. Fax (201) 378-7903.

Shipka Travel Agency
5434 State Road, Parma, Ohio 44134
Tel. 1-800-860-0089.

Alternative Travel

During the "glasnost" era that characterized the final years of the Soviet Union, several organizations ran programs whose purpose was to foster friendship between westerners and Soviets through people-to-people contacts. Operating in several republics, they combined tourism with homestays. While they may lack the Ukrainian perspective of many of the above agencies, they do know their way around. These organizations are ideal for those who lack Ukrainian contacts but want to experience the people and culture as an insider.

Link Friendship House
1111 Willow Lane, Madison, Wisconsin 53705.
Tel. 1-800-484-1042; Tel. and Fax. 608/ 233-6979.
A non-profit, all-volunteer organization that leads several group tours per year to former soviet countries. Its Ukrainian specialties are Dnipro and Black Sea cruises.

American-International Homestays, Inc.
PO Box 7178, Boulder, Colorado 80306. Tel. 1-800-876-2048.
Formerly American-Soviet Homestays, Inc., this company began in 1988 with escorted packaged tours designed to offer a personal glimpse of life in the Soviet nations by interacting with families. It still offers both preplanned and customized group tours but has branched out into customized individual services.

Bolshoi Travel Adventures, Inc.
499 Mitchell Drive, Valley Cottage, New York 10989
Tel. 1-800-721-5159
Bolshoi offers homestays and services in Kyiv and can arrange group tours to pursue special interests such as folk music or history.

Ukrainian Travel Services

In the past, the western agencies listed above worked closely with the Inturyst, the All-Union company established in 1929 to handle foreign tourism in the Soviet Union. As the only travel service, its large, professional staff had complete control over all aspects of tourism, operating hotels, motels, camping grounds and arranging all tours and entertainment.

With the break-up of the Soviet Union, the Moscow-headed Inturyst also split up. The Ukrainian facilities fell under a special Ukrainian government body, Derzhcomintur, or the State Committee of Foreign Tourism. With almost ministry status, this company inherited the former Inturyst hotels, properties, and service bureaus on Ukrainian territory. It's headquartered in Kyiv: Derzhcomintur, 12 Hospitalna (Госпіґальна) Street, Kyiv, 252023.

Each of the regional capital cities has its own division of Derzhcomintur that apparently functions quite independently of the parent company. Look, for example, for something like "General Agency for Tourism in Poltava Region." The regional centers have their own hotels, service bureaus, and other facilities that formerly belonged to Inturyst. Many have dropped the Inturyst name. In Kharkiv, for example, the Inturyst Hotel changed its name to National Hotel. In Lviv, it's now Hotel George.

Recent travelers to Ukraine hold differing opinions of the Inturyst successors. Some find them not so well-organized and efficient as they formerly were. They also cite Inturyst's customary emphasis on group travel, its congenital lack of flexibility, and its unresponsiveness to individual wants and needs. Others, however, have had successful dealings with Inturyst and feel that the company still has more resources and can provide more services than its competition.

Suputnyk, the Bureau for International Youth Tourism, used to be the youth division of Inturyst but now serves travelers of all ages. It is a joint-stock company and has its own offices and hotels in tourist areas throughout Ukraine.

Ukrintur (Ukrainian Joint-Stock Foreign Tourism Company), 36 Yaroslaviv (Ярославів) Street, Kyiv, is a joint project of the State

Committee of Ukraine for Tourism and the Kyiv City Council. While Ukrintur can provide travel services, its main thrust is commerce.

State-owned and joint-stock tourism in Ukraine is in a state of transition, with continuous reshuffling. Much of the restructuring is prompted by government officials who are hoping to profit from the tourist industry. With the likelihood that Derzhcomintur, while motivated to keep its monopoly on the travel business, may become the state agency in charge of issuing permits to private companies, the business climate in Ukraine is not favorable for private agencies. Nevertheless, there now are private agencies that are more consumer-oriented than the state-run services. These provide what the client asks for rather than offering a package or setting an itinerary that the client can take or leave. Make pre-trip arrangements by writing, phoning, faxing, or e-mailing to Ukraine these fledgling companies that offer service with a more personal touch:

Ukrus
P.O. Box 10450, Kharkiv 231002 Ukraine
Telephone or fax: (011-7) 0572/47-9169.
E-mail: alex@ukrus.kharkov.ua
Ukrus (UKRaine + US) can book a hotel for you in Kyiv, arrange for guides and translators, local transportation, and theater tickets. Or if you prefer to stay in a private home, approximately $50 a day will cover accommodations, meals, guides and translators, local transportation, and entertainment. Homes are available in a number of cities. Ukrus also conducts relative searches and provides Ukrainian language lessons.

Travel Ukraine Agency, Pvt.
P.O. Box 5661, Lviv 290016 Ukraine
Fax: (+7) 0322/ 33-5342.
E-mail: IGOR@tuag.lviv.ua or 102477.1006@compuserve.com
Travel Ukraine Agency is run by former Inturyst workers who known the country thoroughly and are experienced in customizing itineraries for professionals and businesspersons and setting up religious and ethnic tours. TUA has several nice package tours but will customize them according to interest. TUA also arranges trips to ancestral towns in Ukraine for those of non-Ukrainian ancestry; for example, it works with certified genealogists from the US and Israel to help those of Jewish origin find their roots.

FLIGHTS TO UKRAINE

No U.S. carriers fly to Kyiv, but a number of European airlines make regular flights from North American gateway cities. These flights are not non-stop, but make a connection in the airline's home city. The layover may be as brief as a few hours or may be overnight. Lufthansa, for example, makes connections to Kyiv from either Frankfurt or Munich. Other European airlines that fly to Kyiv are Air France, Austrian Airlines, British Airways, Czech Air, Alitalia, Swissair, KLM, Balkan, Malev Hungarian, and Finnair. At this writing, only Lot Polish Airline flies into western Ukraine, with four weekly scheduled flights to Lviv. Odesa is served six times a week by Austrian Airlines. from Vienna and twice a week by Lufthansa from Frankfurt. These North American cities are gateways for the various airlines that fly into Ukraine: Atlanta, Boston, Chicago, Dallas/Fort Worth, Detroit, Edmonton, Los Angeles, Orlando, Ottawa, Miami, Minneapolis, Montreal, New York (JFK), Newark, Pittsburgh, San Francisco, Vancouver, and Washington, D.C.

Trans-Atlantic flights departing from the U.S. allow two suitcases per person, typically 60 pounds each, and one carry-on bag. There are some size limitations: the combined width, height, and depth of your first suitcase should not exceed 62 inches, the second, 55 inches, and your carry-on should be no more than a total of 45 inches, all dimensions. If you want to carry an additional suitcase, you'll be charged extra. Unless you're carrying irreplaceable gifts, it's worthwhile to ship your extra baggage over.

Air Ukraine. After the collapse of the Soviet Union, Ukraine became heir to all aircraft on its territory. Besides its 1,000 domestic aircraft, Air Ukraine purchased seven IL-62Ms from Poland for its trans-Atlantic fleet and is planning to replace them with Boeing aircraft in the near future. At first, Air Ukraine paid Aeroflot Russian International Airlines (the successor to Aeroflot Soviet Airlines) a percentage of its profits for use of its infrastructure — the offices, system of ticket sales, technical support, and pilot training with its Aeroflot past. The airplanes were painted the blue and yellow Ukrainian colors, sport a Ukrainian logo, and are manned by Ukrainian staff. Now, with its own facilities and toll-free phone number, reaching a friendly agent is very easy.

From New York, Air Ukraine has three non-stop flights to Kyiv per week, departing JFK on Tuesday, Friday, and Sunday at 3:55 p.m. From

Chicago, it flies direct to Kyiv every Thursday at 5:55 p.m, but during the summer months Air Ukraine from Chicago stops in Lviv first. There's an additional non-stop flight from Chicago to Lviv every Monday during the summer. In summer, Air Ukraine also adds a Wednesday flight from New York to Kyiv, stopping first at Ivano-Frankivsk in western Ukraine (135 km (84 miles) south of Lviv), for the benefit of Ukrainian-Americans who are visiting relatives in that area. Some Air Ukraine return flights to the U. S. refuel at Shannon International Airport in Ireland. Weight limits on Air Ukraine are 50 pounds per suitcase.

On the other side of the Atlantic, Air Ukraine has a subsidiary airline, Ukraine International Airlines, which has leased several Boeing 737-400s from Guinness Peat Aviation of Ireland. The Boeings fly regularly between Kyiv and Gatwick Airport in London. Ukraine International also has flights between Kyiv and Amsterdam, Berlin, Brussels, Frankfurt, Munich, Paris, and Vienna; and between Lviv and Frankfurt, London, and Amsterdam.

For ticket information call:

New York City: (212) 557-2300; fax (212) 557-3437.
551 5th Avenue, Suite 1002, New York, New York 10176

Chicago: (312) 640-0222; fax (312) 640-0154.
Suite 1740, 625 North Michigan Avenue, Chicago, Illinois 60611

All travel arrangements can also be made by calling 1-800-UKRAINE (1-800-857-2463).

In Kyiv, the Air Ukraine office is at 14 prospekt Peremohy (Перемоги); there's also a ticket sales and reservations office at the Kyivska Rus Hotel complex at 14 Hospitalna Street and at Borispil Airport.

WHAT TO PACK FOR A SUCCESSFUL TRIP

Pack light is the conventional advice given to travelers. Why then, the hordes of visitors going to Ukraine with multiple bulging suitcases?

Many are bringing scarce consumer goods to friends and relatives. Even allowing for the typical transatlantic baggage allowance of two 60-pound suitcases to be checked into the cargo hold and a carry-on case, some visitors are still willing to pay extra for the privilege of giving gifts. The approximately $108 per additional piece of luggage charged by the transatlantic carriers is worth it, they figure, compared to the $1 to $2 per pound cost of shipping packages overseas, and the two months' wait.

A list of useful gift items is below. Even keeping within the two-suitcase limit, you can fit everything you need for your own personal use for a 2-week to month-long trip into a single 26-inch-long suitcase, leaving the other suitcase for gifts.

While generally you can get by without a lot of clothes, what you do need depends on your itinerary. If you're just sightseeing and visiting friends or relatives, casual clothing will be acceptable. However, although you might find Ukrainians wearing casual clothing in their homes, when they go out for a special event, they dress up. Blue jeans and "California casual" style are not suitable for a night on the town. Ties for men and dresses for women are the standard. If you're going to be doing business or will be the invited guest for an occasion, dress appropriately. Women should pack one suit with several blouses and one lightweight, slightly-more-dressy outfit for evenings. Men should take a suit and wash-and-wear shirts. The rest of your travel wardrobe might consist of a pair of casual slacks and knit tops. Plan your wardrobe with layering in mind, in order to be prepared for weather changes. Plan separates to mix and match. Don't include any article of clothing that can't be worn with at least two other pieces.

There are rainy periods in Ukraine. A nylon raincoat, folding umbrella, and rain galoshes or shoes that won't be ruined when wet are a good idea. Well-padded athletic walking shoes are recommended. For women, comfortable low-heel shoes will come in handy when walking on cobblestone streets, uneven pavement, or dirt paths in rural areas.

Pack everything you think you'll need during the time you'll be in Ukraine to avoid the problem of not being able to find what you lack. Bring along all personal supplies required for your health, hygiene, and grooming: soap, shampoo, deodorant, toothpaste, sunscreen, razor and blades, tissues, feminine hygiene products, and contraceptives. Some necessities, such as toilet paper, are not the quality we're used to and in some places may be in short supply. Moist towelettes are useful for clean-up when you're on the road or rail and water is not available. Travel-sized containers of grooming aids are convenient, and your extra, unopened packages make ideal tips or small gifts for helpful Ukrainians you meet on your trip.

Be sure to pack an adequate supply of all medication and prescription drugs that you take regularly and carry them in their original containers. It's also a good idea to carry a copy of the prescription or a note from your doctor listing the generic name of the drug in Latin. Alka Seltzer, Pepto Bismol, and aspirin or non-aspirin pain reliever may come in handy. Take along a spare pair of glasses and a copy of your prescription for your glasses or contact lenses.

A small first aid kit containing adhesive bandages, sterile hypodermic needles, antiseptic cream, a thermometer, and insect repellent is also a good idea. Include in this kit a medical identification card that lists your blood type, your social security number, your allergies or chronic health problems, and your medical insurance information.

Travelers everywhere often find themselves on the road at mealtime. Consider some snacks that pack a lot of calories or nutrition for their size: peanut butter in plastic jars, dried fruits, and granola bars. Hot cocoa and soup mixes will provide a few calories as well as liquid. Instant coffee or a small plastic coffee caddy which allows boiling water to flow through a filtered coffee basket are a must for coffee drinkers in this land of tea lovers. Powdered milk or coffee creamer are also a good idea.

A small flashlight is essential. A Swiss Army knife which includes a bottle opener and knife will help you drink bottled water and eat your food while you're on the road or rail. A bottle stopper is necessary to recap the bottles with pop-off caps. A nylon sport bag or day pack is helpful for day excursions and a universal sink stopper may come in handy when washing out your clothes in the evening. Because hard currency is a common means of payment, a money belt is the most convenient and safest way to carry your wad of small denomination bills.

Don't forget some note pads for memos, letters, and recording impressions. If you don't have business cards, consider having some printed up with your name and address to give to those you'd like to keep in touch with.

Finally, Ukraine is a craft collector's paradise. If shopping is a priority, pack a large nylon shopping bag, some bubble wrap, and strapping tape.

Photography Equipment. A Polaroid camera is ideal for those you meet in chance encounters and with whom you don't care to correspond when you return home. It'll save you the trouble and expense of mailing back photos when you return home. A disadvantage of the Polaroid is the bulkiness of the camera and of its film packs. The easiest and most versatile camera to use is the "point-and-shoot," or fully automatic camera. Simpler ones have a single focal length, usually 35 mm. Be sure to pack more film than you think you'll need, and an extra battery for your camera.

Photographers sometimes have undeveloped film in their baggage ruined by exposure to excessive x-rays at airports. You may wish to buy lead-lined film pouches to protect your film, particularly if you use high-speed films or pass through many airports on your trip.

For a Successful Power Trip. The alternating current in Ukraine differs from that in the U.S. in two ways: it is 220 volts instead of 110 volts, and it has a frequency of 50 hertz instead of 60 hertz.

If you carry small American electrical appliances such as an electric razor, travel iron, portable hair dryer, or battery recharger, you'll need a converter to reduce the voltage from 220 to 110, or else your appliance will burn and blow out. Converters are available for about $20 and come in several sizes, some intended for low-power devices like electric razors and others for high-power devices like hair dryers.

In addition to the converter, you will need the proper inexpensive adapter plug, a simple device that allows you to plug the converter into a Ukrainian electrical outlet. The adapter needed in Ukraine as well as in other countries that were formerly part of the U.S.S.R. is the same as that used in most of Europe, including Austria, France, Germany, Italy, Poland, Scandinavia, and Spain, but it is different from that used in Great Britain. Look at electrical supply stores or travel shops for converters and adapters. An extension cord for the adaptor may come in handy.

Your power conversion problems may not yet be solved, however. Converters cannot be used with appliances that require a current with a frequency of 60 hertz instead of the 50 hertz standard in Ukraine. These may include some televisions, VCR's, movie cameras and projectors, and computers. If you want to use a computer, make sure it will work at 50 hertz or else bring a portable computer that can be run off batteries which are recharged using a separate battery recharger. Portable radios, cassette players, CD players, and TV's can also run on battery power.

Gifts. When considering gifts, a word about differences in lifestyle is necessary. Ukrainians have gotten along very well without disposable diapers, paper plates, adhesive bandages, convenience foods, and a legion of other consumer goods that Westerners have been convinced are essentials of modern life. Now that tremendous inflation is making it difficult for them to buy even basic necessities, it's more prudent (and kinder) to give something that's really useful. If socks seem too ordinary a gift, consider giving some of the more colorful and patterned socks on the market. Imagine the possibilities with women's lingerie!

While jeans and jean jackets make excellent gifts, you can give more if you fill your suitcase with lighter-weight necessities. Acrylic and nylon sports clothing, for example, are more practical to carry than jeans. Here are some gift suggestions:

> Children's clothing.
> Men's, women's, and children's underwear and socks.
> Pantyhose, cotton or woolen tights.
> Warm-up suits and sport shoes.
> Barbie dolls and clothes; Lego sets; coloring books and crayons.
> Nylon winter gloves and jackets.
> Coffee, loose tea, hard candies, canned meat or fish, jam.
> Vitamins, first aid cream, aspirin; children's aspirin.
> Hand and face cream, cosmetics, perfume, hair coloring products.
> Shopping bags, nylon duffle bags.
> Raincoats, folding umbrellas.
> Fabric, scissors, needles, thread, buttons, zippers.
> Fabric suitable for embroidering, such as Aida cloth, and embroidery floss.
> Garden seeds; open-pollinated varieties of common vegetables.
> Solar calculators.
> Portable radio, cassette players and tapes, CD players and compact discs.
> Batteries. Since batteries are hard to find in Ukraine, rechargeable batteries make a good gift. However, the recipient will need a battery recharger plus an adaptor to run it. The simplest, most elegant solution is to give a battery recharger that runs on solar energy. Real Goods, 966 Mazzoni Street, Ukiah, California, 95482-3471 (phone 1-800-762-7325)

has solar battery chargers ranging in price from $14 to $26 depending on the type of batteries they're designed to recharge. Earthsake, 1805 Fourth Street, Berkeley, California, 94710 (phone (510) 848-0484) also will mail order solar battery chargers in the $18 to $34 price range.

VCR and cassettes. If you wish to make a gift of a VCR, note that the standard U.S. and Canadian VCRs won't play on Ukrainian television, which uses a different format (SECAM). You must buy a VCR, such as a multisystem VCR, that is compatible with the SECAM format.

Blank cassettes make good gifts, as they can be recorded using Ukrainian equipment, but prerecorded American cassettes won't play on Ukrainian VCRs; similarly if you buy cassettes that have been recorded in Ukraine, they won't play on American VCRs.

Finally, don't forget to pack a few souvenirs of your home city and state. Postcards, label pins, insignia tee shirts, and picture books will be appreciated.

GO IN GOOD HEALTH

Check with your physician to see if your immunizations are up to date. If it's been ten years since you've gotten a diphtheria-tetanus booster, you should have another. Plan to see your physician at least a month before your departure so that you are not handicapped in case you should have a reaction; a sore arm could make it difficult to carry your luggage. It's also advisable that your dental care be up to date. For those planning an extended stay in Ukraine, carrying an official record or proof of vaccination is a good idea.

The demise of the Soviet Union has resulted in some health repercussions. There has been some break-down in the mass immunization programs and some parents are reluctant to have their children vaccinated for fear of contracting HIV. Consequently, a few diseases that were nearly eradicated are showing up again.

In the last few years the number of diphtheria cases reported in Ukraine has been dramatically increasing. Diphtheria is transmitted by airborne bacteria and can result in rapid death, but it can be avoided through proper immunizations. The incidence of infectious disease can change rapidly, however, and it's possible that diphtheria will again be under control during your trip while another disease presents a threat. For example, some incidents of cholera were reported in eastern Ukraine in 1995. Cholera, thought to have spread from central Asia, is a bacterial disease that's transmitted through water and causes severe gastrointestinal upset, even death. Cholera vaccine is effective only about 50 percent of the time. Water-borne hepatitis has also been reported, and a gamma globulin shot will offer protection for a limited time period.

Although the danger of contracting a water-borne disease in Ukraine is not very great, health officials are advising travelers to drink only bottled water or water that's been boiled for ten minutes. There are also iodine tablets on the market that can purify water. These are safe for short term use except for those with a thyroid condition or who are pregnant. It should be noted that even drinking perfectly purified, disease-free water can result in mild stomach or intestinal upsets in those who are not accustomed to the local microbes.

For the most up-to-date advisory on vaccination recommendations, disease outbreaks, or other precautions in traveling to Ukraine, check with the Center for Disease Control's 24-hour International Traveler's Hotline: (404) 332-4559. A touch-tone phone is helpful. If a staff member is not immediately available to answer your questions, you may punch in the information areas that interest you. If you still have questions after listening to the recorded messages, an operator will come on the line to help you. You may also leave your fax number and the information will be faxed to you. For general precautions about travel in Ukraine, check also with the 24-hour Citizens Emergency Center at the State Department, (202) 647-5225.

Travel Insurance. If you're concerned about your health, check with your insurance agent to see whether your policy covers medical help abroad. Many policies provide the same medical coverage overseas as they do at home. Because of severe shortages of medical supplies, medical treatment in Ukraine is not on par with that at home, so that the more useful insurance covers expenses incurred in leaving Ukraine for treatment elsewhere. If your policy doesn't provide for medical evacuation, consider one that does. The Ukrainian National Association, a Ukrainian-American fraternal organization can provide several short-term insurance package options, including medical evacuation. You needn't be a member of UNA to take out a short-term travel policy.

Financial Services UNA (Ukrainian National Association)
1-800-253-9862, ext. 58
in eastern Pennsylvania (215) 821-5800

Chornobyl. The world's worst nuclear power-plant accident took place on April 26, 1986 when one of the four reactors at the Chornobyl nuclear power station blew up, hurling nearly nine tons of radioactive material into the sky. The major fallout zones were to the north and west. Major parts of the Kyiv, Zhytomyr, Rivne, and Chernihiv regions were affected by radioactive contamination, amounting to 40 thousand square kilometers with more than 2,100 settlements inhabited by 2.5 million people. The Ukrainian government has made a massive attempt at clean-up or liquidation but simply is not equipped for the enormity of the job. Evacuation and rehousing of those in contaminated zones has been slowed by the switch from the planned to the market economy. Altogether close to 700,000 people remain in Ukrainian territory that's not fit for habitation.

Evaluation of the amount of radiation present in the contaminated districts is a continuing problem. While the cesium-137 and plutonium content in the soil can be measured, sufficient equipment and expertise is not available to continuously monitor the radiation in live animals, farm products, and forests throughout the affected areas. Even with the lasting horrors of Chornobyl and pressure from the world community, the Ukrainian government has balked at closing Chornobyl. In 1993 Parliament reversed itself and voted overwhelmingly to keep the Chornobyl station open as long as the life span of its reactors allow. The legislators were prompted by Ukraine's lack of fuel sources and its inability to pay the world market prices for gas and oil that Russia is asking. Ukraine depends on nuclear power for 33 percent of its energy and this desperate measure would allow a two percent increase of the amount of nuclear power available. With a 30-year life span the reactors will go out of service around 2010.

Chornobyl is 100 km (60 miles) north of Kyiv. Health experts agree that there is no danger whatsoever from the Chornobyl fallout to those visiting Kyiv for a short time. The effects on the health of long term visitors is yet unknown, although there is some concern for the residual effects from the radioactivity in the soil and in locally grown food.

CHAPTER 3. USING THIS BOOK

SOME FEATURES OF THE UKRAINIAN LANGUAGE

Of all the Slavic languages, Ukrainian is the second most commonly spoken. Usually it's classified as an Eastern Slavic language, together with Belarusian and Russian, but because of Ukraine's central location among the Slavic nations, the Ukrainian language is also historically connected to the West Slavic and the South Slavic languages.

Ukrainian has been a distinct recognizable language since the middle of the eleventh century. Then the Slavic languages began to diverge; Russian, for example, assimilated many words of Scandinavian and Tatar origin. While Ukrainian remained true to its Old Slavic roots, it was not able to develop freely over the centuries because of political conditions. Ukrainian was at best a subordinate language under occupying powers, at worst it was forbidden in print. These conditions discouraged a unified standard language and encouraged the growth of regional dialects and the assimilation of Russian words in the east and Polish words in the west. Nevertheless, there exists in Ukraine today a standard Ukrainian language that is taught in school and used in literature and understood by all Ukrainian speakers.

The Ukrainian language is written by an adaptation of Cyrillic, an old Slavonic alphabet named after St. Cyril, the ninth-century Christian missionary to the Slavs. In the 860's Cyril and his brother St. Methodius translated the Holy Scriptures into the language later known as Old Church Slavonic. In order to do this, they devised an alphabet based on Greek characters with adaptations from Hebrew. Various versions of that alphabet are used today by Russians, Belarusians, Bulgarians, Serbs, and Macedonians, as well as by Ukrainians.

A few letters of the Ukrainian alphabet correspond to certain English letters, both in appearance and in the sounds they represent, although the Ukrainian vowels have only a single sound and don't cover the range of the corresponding English vowels; examples are K, M, T, A, E, and O. Many Ukrainian letters have equivalent sounds in English but look quite different: Б is B, Г is H, П is P, Ц is TS, and Ч is CH, to name a few. Perhaps most confusing for those unfamiliar with the Cyrillic alphabet are the letters that look like Roman letters but in Cyrillic represent quite different sounds. Thus, B is V, C is S, P is R, and H is N.

The Ukrainian alphabet has 32 letters with sound values. Special note should be made of the difference between the Г (H) and Ґ (G). Since independence, linguists in Ukraine reintroduced the letter Ґ, which the Soviet government had dropped in order to make the Ukrainian language conform more closely to Russian. There are a relatively small number of Ukrainian words that contain the Ґ, and they're primarily of foreign origin such as гетто, ghetto. During the period in which the Ґ was banned, the letter Г (H), did double duty as replacement for G. As Ukrainians know which words are pronounced with a soft "H" sound and which take the hard "G" sound, some feel that the reintroduction of the infrequently-used character Ґ originated from political overreaction, the linguistic equivalent of changing the names of streets that had perfectly innocuous names.

Perhaps in due time the linguists will decide that the Ukrainian language can get along perfectly well without the Ґ character, and it will die a natural death. For the meantime, we are listing it in the alphabet. While it doesn't occur frequently, and is rarely found in printed materials in Ukraine, it's especially useful to a non-native-Ukrainian speaker who can't distinguish the H from the G sound in Ukrainian words. In this book, there are only a few words using the Ґ. The most common is the word for guide, ґід, which you should pronounce *geed* rather than *heed*.

Mastering the alphabet may be the most difficult part of learning to read Ukrainian because the pronunciation is simple and clear-cut. *The Ukrainian alphabet is absolutely phonetic: each letter has a single pronunciation in every usage.* A stress put on a vowel does not change its pronunciation.

We need mention only a few other points about the Ukrainian language: There is no pattern to accentuation; stress may fall on any syllable in a given word. However, Ukrainian tends to have only one stress per word. Ukrainian sentence construction is more flexible than English. The Ukrainian language is highly inflectional; endings of nouns, pronouns, and adjectives change according to gender and according to case.

TRANSLITERATION
When Ukrainian Cyrillic is Expressed in Roman Alphabet

If Ukrainian is a phonetic language, why are so many Ukrainian names unpronounceable when they're written in English? Why do they have so many "j's" and "w's" when the Cyrillic alphabet doesn't include these letters? Actually, it's more precise to say that some Ukrainian names are indecipherable, rather than unpronounceable, when they're written in English because they have been transcribed with a transliteration scheme that is not user-friendly to native English speakers.

Those who are not familiar with the Ukrainian language are often stumped by the various systems that linguists have devised to replace Cyrillic letters with their Roman equivalents. The Ukrainian character й, for example, sounds like the "y" that ends the words "boy" or starts the word "yet," but various transliteration systems express it with a "y," an "i," or a "j." Accordingly, the name Андрій (Andrew) is transliterated as Andrey, Andri, Andriy, Andrii, Andry, and the mysteriously confusing Andrij.

To a native English speaker "Andrij" is a puzzlement, but to a German or Scandinavian or Pole who pronounce *ja* as "ya" and *je* as "yeh," it makes a lot of sense. Similarly, the surname Вовк is pronounced "vovk" in any country in the world, even where it's spelled "Wowk."

In short, transliteration systems for Ukrainian reflect the sound values of particular Roman alphabet languages, and don't necessarily coincide with those given them by the English language. Linguists are now emphasizing the importance of transliterating Ukrainian into English using systems to which native English speakers can easily relate. One such system is used by the United States Board on Geographic Names (USBGN) in its work in translating Ukrainian place names.

In this guidebook, we use the USBGN system to transliterate Ukrainian words. According to it, the main street in Ukraine's capital, Хрещатик, is *Khreshchatyk,* and the beloved plant, калина, is *kalyna.* This transliteration should be helpful when you come across names in Ukrainian Cyrillic that you want to jot down in English. Simply replace the Cyrillic letter with the corresponding Roman one according to the list.

US Board on Geographic Names Transliteration System

Ukrainian Letter   *English Equivalent*

Ukrainian Letter		English Equivalent	
А	а	A	a
Б	б	B	b
В	в	V	v
Г	г	H	h
Ґ	ґ	G	g
Д	д	D	d
Е	е	E	e
Є	є	YE	ye
Ж	ж	ZH	zh
З	з	Z	z
И	и	Y	y
І	і	I	i
Ї	ї	YI	yi
Й	й	Y	y
К	к	K	k
Л	л	L	l
М	м	M	m
Н	н	N	n
О	о	O	o
П	п	P	p
Р	р	R	r
С	с	S	s
Т	т	T	t
У	у	U	u
Ф	ф	F	f
Х	х	KH	kh
Ц	ц	TS	ts
Ч	ч	CH	ch
Ш	ш	SH	sh
Щ	щ	SHCH	shch
Ь	ь	soft sign, not expressed in transliteration	
Ю	ю	YU	yu
Я	я	YA	ya

A shortcoming of the USBGN system is its heavy reliance on the letter "y." Y is used for the transliteration of several Ukrainian letters into English: both и and й are rendered as *y*; є is *ye*, ї is *yi*, ю is *yu*, and я is *ya*. Thus a proper name that ends with the adjectival -ий, such as Морський Вокзал (Sea Passenger Terminal) becomes *Morskyy Vokzal*. In the instance of the name of Ukraine's capital, Київ, the precise rendition is *Kyyiv*. The double y in the transliteration, while used by some mapmakers, has not been well received by many, especially by native Ukrainians. While it's difficult to predict at this point which transliteration of the Ukrainian name for the Ukrainian capital — *Kyyiv* or *Kyiv* — will stick as the replacement for the transliteration from the Russian name for the city, *Kiev*, we feel that the single-y spelling looks more appealing. Therefore, for this guidebook, we have chosen the alternative option of omitting one of the y's and spelling the city *Kyiv*.

PHONETIC GUIDE

For the Ukrainian phrases used in this book, we use a phonetic transcription designed to render an even closer approximation of their sound values than could be done with a transliteration. A phonetic scheme facilitates Ukrainian pronunciation for native English-speakers with no background in Slavic languages who cannot intuitively pick up the nuances of Ukrainian sounds and inflections. Among the advantages of using a phonetic scheme is that it indicates the stressed syllables. Thus a phonetic system would express the above examples like this: Київ as KIH-yeev, Хрещатик as Khreh-SHCHAH-tyk and калина as kah-LIH-nah.

The phonetic scheme we've devised for the *Hippocrene Language Travel Guide to Ukraine* is designed to approximate literary language that is standard throughout Ukraine. It will be understood everywhere despite foreign influences on dialect in certain regions.

Read the phonetic transcriptions as if they were standard English, putting extra emphasis on the letters that are capitalized. While stress may fall on any syllable, Ukrainian tends to have only one stressed syllable in each word, regardless of the length of the word.

Consonants

Ukrainian Letter	Transcription and Approximate Pronunciation		Example
Б б	b	like b in *b*at	без (behz)
В в	v	like v in *v*alve	він (veen)
Г г	h	like h in *h*at	гарно (HAR-no)
Ґ ґ	g	like g in *g*ot	ґанок (GAH-nok)
Д д	d	like d in *d*og	дім (deem)
Ж ж	zh	like ge in gara*ge* or s in plea*s*ure	жінка (ZHEEN-kah)
З з	z	like z in *z*oo	зуб (zoob)
Й й	ў	like y in *y*olk	його (YO-ho)
К к	k	like k in *k*it	кітка (KEET-kah)
Л л	l	like l in *l*ab	літо (LEE-to)
М м	m	like m in *m*ore	мама (MAH-mah)
Н н	n	like n in *n*o	ніс (nees)
П п	p	like p in *p*oor	під (peed)
Р р	r	like r in erro*r*	рада (RAH-dah)
С с	s	like s in *s*it	сад (sahd)
Т т	t	like t in *t*oe	там (tahm)
Ф ф	f	like f in *f*it	фірма (feer-mah)
Х х	kh	like ch in Scottish lo*ch*	хліб (khleeb)
Ц ц	ts	like ts in ba*ts*	церква (TSERK-vah)
Ч ч	ch	like ch in *ch*ip	час (chahs)
Ш ш	sh	like sh in *sh*ot	школа (SHKOH-lah)
Щ щ	shch	like sh ch in fre*sh ch*eese	ще (shcheh)

Vowels

А а	ah	like a in f*a*ther	там (tahm)
Е е	eh	like e in l*e*t	не (neh)
Є є	yeh	like ye in *ye*s	знає (ZNAH-yeh)
И и	ih	like i in *i*t or y in m*y*th	мити (MIH-tih)
І і	ee	like ee in m*ee*t	пісні (PEES-nee)
Ї ї	yee	like yie sound in *yie*ld	їм (yeem)
О о	o	like o in *o*ff, d*o*t	дорого (do-RO-ho)
У у	oo	like oo in b*oo*t	тут (toot)
Ю ю	yu	like the word *you*	любов (lyu-BOV)
Я я	ya	like ya in *ya*cht	моя (mo-YA)

Other Symbols

The Apostrophe. ь is the soft sign that sometimes follows the consonants д, з, л, н, с, т, and ц, and designates that these consonants are softened (palatalized).

′ is the apostrophe that sometimes occurs between the consonants б, в, м, п, ф and the vowels я, ю, є, ї. It denotes a distinct, separate articulation of the consonant and vowel.

In our phonetic scheme we use an apostrophe ′ to represent both of these Ukrainian symbols. In both instances, the apostrophe serves to add emphasis to the letters it separates.

For example, when скільки is transcribed as SKEEL′-kih, the apostrophe represents the soft sign ь and signals a soft pronunciation of the preceding consonant, the l. And when ім'я is transcribed as eem′YA, the apostrophe denotes an articulation of the *m* and *ya* sounds represented by the м and я.

Diacritical marks. In addition to the apostrophe, we use two diacritical marks to help clarify the pronunciation:

1. The ligature over the z͡h that represents the blended consonant sounds of ж distinguishes it from the two distinct and separate sounds required by the z and h when they occur in a word with a consecutive з and г. Thus in жінка, Z͡HEEN-kah, the zh representing the ж sounds like the *ge* ending in garage, but in згинути, zhih-NOO-tih, the z and the h representing the з and г are pronounced separately as in the phrase "jazz heaven."

While other characters of the Ukrainian alphabet represent a blending of two or more Roman alphabet characters, their pronunciation is obvious from context and they don't require a linking sign: х = kh, ш = sh, щ = shch, ц = ts, ч = ch.

2. A wedge is used over the transcription of the letter й (ў) to distinguish it from the "y" sound of certain vowels:

добрий   DO-briĥ

The Letter "H"   The frequent use of the letter "h" in our transcription serves a number of purposes:

"H" is the Ukrainian letter "Г".

An "h" after a vowel (ah, eh, ih, yeh) forces the vowel to remain a short vowel.   Thus невже is pronounced nehv-ZHEH and not neev-ZHEE and боець is bo-YEHTS' not bo-YEETS.   Note that the Ukrainian "o" is always a short vowel, but we do not use "oh" because that suggests a long o.

When the Ukrainian г follows a short vowel, the transcription will include a double h, which may or may not be separated by a dash, depending on the syllable break:

багато   bah-HAH-to

but   багно   bahh-no

CHAPTER 4. JUST ENOUGH GRAMMAR

Ukrainian grammar follows the Slavic language pattern. Here is a brief summary of the nuts and bolts of the language. Pronunciation is not given for the Ukrainian sentences, since it would detract from the explanation.

NOUNS

Ukrainian nouns have three genders — masculine, feminine, and neuter. It's necessary to know the gender of a noun in order to know which ending it should receive, to modify it with an adjective, or to form its plural. Ukrainian does not have a definite article (*the*) or indefinite articles (*a, an*) that indicate the gender of a noun; usually the gender is revealed by its ending.

Masculine nouns end with a consonant:
брат, brother   лікар, doctor   чай, tea

Feminine nouns usually end with -a or -я:
вода, water   кухня, kitchen   надія, hope

Neuter nouns usually end with -o, -я, or -e:
село, village   ім'я, name   море, sea

Nouns that end in -ь can be either masculine or feminine, but in most instances are masculine.
учитель (m.), teacher   сіль (f.), salt

There are exceptions:
Some masculine nouns end with -a or -o: тато, dad
Some feminine nouns end in a consonant: ніч, night

Plurals. Although there are exceptions, masculine and feminine nouns usually end in -и or -i in the plural:
газети, newspapers   вулиці, streets
столи, tables   хлопці, boys.

Neuter nouns usually end in -a or -я in the plural:
    міста, cities   поля, fields.

Some nouns change their internal spelling in the plural, so that they may be difficult to recognize:
    ніч, ночі — night, nights
    річ, речі — thing, things
    день, дні — day, days.

Declensions. Nouns change their endings according to their function in a sentence. In Ukrainian these functions are grouped into different categories called cases. There are six different cases in Ukrainian that are used for all nouns.

The nominative (N) case refers to the subject of the sentence. In Ukrainian dictionaries, nouns are always given in the nominative case. They refer to an object's existence.
    Це наш готель (N). This is our hotel.
    Де пошта (N)? Where is the post office?

The genitive (G) case indicates ownership or possession. It answers the questions whose or which and can usually be translated into English using the word "of" or the apostrophe plus an "s" ('s).
    машина чоловіка (G) — the car of the man, the man's car

The genitive case is also used in expressing the direct object of a negative sentence:
    Я не маю виделки (G). I don't have a fork.

Another use of the genitive case is to indicate an indefinite quantity of something:
    Я купила хліба (G). I bought some bread.

The accusative (A) case denotes the direct object of a verb.
    Я бачу річку (A). I see the river.
    Він знає точний час (A). He knows the correct time.

The dative (D) case is used to designate a person or thing to whom or to which something is done or given.
    Дай це своїй мамі (D). Give this to your mom.
    Я (тобі, *s.*) (вам, *pl.*) (D) допоможу. I'll help you.

The locative (L) case indicates the location or place of action. It answers the question "where?" The locative is always used with a preposition and is sometimes called the prepositional case. The most common prepositions used in locative case constructions are в (у) which means "in" or "at" and на which means "on," "at," and "in."

Він чекає в готелі (L). He's waiting at the hotel.

Вона лежить на пляжі (L). She's lying on the beach.

The instrumental (I) case answers the questions "by whom?" or "by what means?" In Ukrainian the preposition is not expressed:

Я пишу олівцем (I). I'm writing with a pencil.

Я поїду автобусом (I). I'll be going by bus.

The instrumental case is also used to denote a temporary or new condition or used with the verbs to be or to become:

Він був студентом (I). He was a student.

Вона хоче стати лікарем (I). She wants to become a doctor.

PREPOSITIONS

Prepositions determine the case of nouns. Some prepositions are followed by more than one case, depending on their use in the sentence. For example в (to) and на (on, at) are used with the accusative case when direction is involved, and with the locative to indicate simple position.

Іди в ту кімнату (A). Go into that room.

Він в музеї (L). He's at the museum.

Мій паспорт на столі (L). My passport is on the table.

Here are some of the most common prepositions, the cases they take, and their phonetic pronunciation:

across	напроти (G)	nah-PRO-tih
against	проти (G)	PRO-tih
around	навколо (G)	nahv-KO-lo
at	на (L)	nah
behind	за (A, I)	zah
between	між (I)	meezh
from	від, з, із (G)	veed, z, eez
in	в *or* у (A, L)	v *or* oo

in front of	перед (I)	peh-REHD
near	біля (G)	BEE-lya
on	на (A, L)	nah
over	над (I)	nahd
to, as far as	до (G)	do
to	на, за (A)	nah, zah
under	під (A, I)	peed
with	з, зі, (I)	z, zee

ADJECTIVES

In Ukrainian, adjectives change their endings to agree with the gender, number, and case of the noun they modify. Adjectives have masculine, feminine, and neuter forms. The plural form is the same for all genders:

a good boy	добрий хлопець	(masculine singular)
a good girl	добра дівчина	(feminine singular)
a good question	добре питання	(neuter singular)
good boys	добрі хлопці	(masculine plural)
good girls	добрі дівчата	(feminine plural)
good questions	добрі питання	(neuter plural)

Like nouns, adjectives are declined according to their use in a sentence. The table below shows the declension of nouns and adjectives using the phrases *hot tea, cold cereal,* and *tasty cookie*:

	Masculine *hot tea*	Feminine *cold cereal*	Neuter *tasty cookie*
singular			
N.	гарячий чай	холодна каша	смачне печиво
G.	гарячого чаю	холодної каши	смачного печива
D.	гарячому чаю	холодній каші	смачному печиву
A.	гарячий чай	холодну кашу	смачне печиво
L.	в гарячому чаї	в холодній каші	в смачному печиві
I.	гарячим чаєм	холодною кашою	смачним печивом

plural

N.	гарячі чаї	холодні каші	смачні печива
G.	гарячих чаїв	холодних каш	смачних печив
D.	гарячим чаям	холодним кашам	смачним печивам
A.	гарячі чаї	холодні каші	смачні печива
L.	в гарячих чаях	в холодних кашах	на смачних печивах
I.	гарячими чаями	холодними кашами	смачними печивами

PRONOUNS

Personal pronouns also change depending on their use in the sentence.

	I	*you (s.)*	*he, it*	*she*	*we*	*you*	*they*
N.	я	ти	він, воно	вона	ми	ви	вони
G.	мене	тебе	його	її	нас	вас	їх
D.	мені	тобі	йому	їй	нам	вам	їм
A.	мене	тебе	його	її	нас	їх	їх
L.	на мені	на тобі	на ньому	па ній	на нас	на вас	на них
I.	мною	тобою	ним	нею	нами	вами	ними

There are two ways to express the pronoun *you* in Ukrainian. Ти (*tih*), the familiar form, is used when addressing a close friend, a relative, or a child. Ви (*vih*) is for speaking to someone with whom you are not on close terms or someone in authority Ви is also the plural form, used when addressing more than one person, regardless of how close you are to them. Phrases in this guide that include both forms of the pronoun you give the familiar, singular form first, followed by the polite or plural form.

Possessive pronouns are declined like adjectives, agreeing with the noun in number and gender. Його (his and its), її (her), and їх (their) are not declined. Твій (your, *s.*) and свій (one's own) are declined exactly like мій (my):

	masculine	feminine	neuter	plural
N.	мій	моя	моє	мої
G.	мого	моєї	мого	моїх
D.	моєму	моїй	моєму	моїм
A.	мій, мого	мою	моє	мої, моїх
L.	на моєму	на моїй	на моєму	на моїх
I.	моїм	моєю	моїм	моїми

Наш (our) is declined like ваш (your, *pl.*):

N.	ваш	ваша	ваше	ваші
G.	вашого	вашої	вашого	ваших
D.	вашому	вашій	вашому	вашим
A.	ваш	вашу	ваших	ваші
L.	на вашому	на вашій	на вашому	на ваших
I.	вашим	вашою	вашим	вашими

DECLINING PROPER NAMES

The names of persons and places change their spelling according to the way they are used in a sentence. It may be difficult to recognize the various forms of a name that changes internally. Here, for example, are the different spellings for the city Lviv in its case inflections:

Nominative.   Це Львів. Львів є прекрасне місто.
This is Lviv. Lviv is a beautiful city.
tseh l'veev.   l'veev yeh preh-KRAHS-neh
MEES-to

Genitive.   Мій двоюрідний брат зі Львова.
My cousin is from Lviv.
meeў dvo-YU-reed-nihў braht zee L'VO-vah

Він має карту Львова.
He has a map of Lviv.
veen MAH-yeh KAHR-too L'VO-vah

Dative.   Львову майже 800 років.
Lviv is almost 800 years old.
(Literally, "To Lviv are almost 800 years.")
L'VO-voo MAHŸ-zheh vee-seem-SOT RO-keev

Accusative.   Я дуже люблю Львів.
I like Lviv very much.
ya DOO-zheh LYU-blyu l'veev

Instrumental. Я пишаюсь Львовом.
I'm proud of Lviv.
ya pih-SHAH-yus' L'VO-vom

Locative. У Львові багато чудових вулиць.
In Lviv there are many beautiful streets.
oo L'VO-vee bah-HAH-to choo-DO-vikh VOO-lihts'

VERBS

The infinitive form of Ukrainian verbs ends in -ти. Verbs are conjugated, that is, their endings change according to the gender and number of the subject of the sentence. There are three tenses, present, past, and future. Here are some common verbs conjugated in the present tense:

Person	мати (to have)	хотіти (to want)	робити (to do, to make)
я	маю (I have)	хочу	роблю
ти	маєш (you have, *s.*)	хочеш	робиш
він, вона, воно	має (he, she, it has)	хоче	робить
ми	маємо (we have, *pl.*)	хочемо	робимо
ви	маєте (you have)	хочете	робите
вони	мають (they have)	хочуть	роблять

"To be." The present tense of the verb to be (бути) is є for all persons, singular and plural. It's usually not expressed in Ukrainian.

Я голодний (голодна, *f.*).   I am hungry.
Хто там?   Who is there?

The past and future tenses of the verb "to be" are expressed:

Past: Я (ти) (він) був. (*m. sing.*)   I (you, *s.*) (he) was/were.
        Я (ти) (вона) була. (*f. sing.*)   I (you, *s.*) (she) was/were.
        Воно було.   It was.
        Ми (ви) (вони) були.   We (you, *pl.*) (they) were.

Future: Я буду.   I will be.
          Ти будеш.   You (*s.*) will be.
          Він, (вона) (воно) буде.   He (she) (it) will be.

Ми будемо.	We will be.
Ви будете.	You (*pl.*) will be.
Вони будуть.	They will be.

Past Tense. The past tense is formed from the infinitive by dropping the ending -ти and adding the appropriate endings to the stem: -в for the masculine singular; -ла for the feminine singular; -ло for the neuter singular; and -ли for plural in all genders.

думати (to think): думали (We were thinking.)

Aspects. Almost every verb in Ukrainian has two different forms, called aspects. The imperfective aspect is used when expressing continuous, repeated, or uncompleted action. The perfective aspect is used for expressing a limited action, a one-time-only action, or a completed action. Typically, it's formed by adding a prefix to the imperfective form. Almost all verbs have two or more infinitives — an imperfective infinitive (always given first in glossaries) and one or more perfective variations that express more specific or qualifying action:

бачити, imp. (to see)	побачити, perf. (to catch sight of)
говорити, imp. (to talk)	поговорити, perf. (to have a talk)
питати, imp. (to be asking)	спитати, perf. (to ask once)

When expressing the present tense, the imperfective aspect is used.

Future Tense. There are two ways to express the future tense in Ukrainian. For actions that are continuous or incomplete, combine the proper form of the verb "to be" with the infinitive of the imperfective verb:

Я буду іти.	I'll be going.
Ми будемо це читати.	We'll be reading it.

To express an action that will be completed in the future, use the present tense of the perfective aspect of the verb:

піти: Я піду. I'll go.
прочитати: Ми це прочитаємо. We'll read it through.

CHAPTER 5. ESSENTIAL PHRASES

Ukrainian Proverb: Мова — це душа народу.
                     MO-vah — tseh doo-SHAH nah-RO-doo
                     Language is the soul of a nation.

SOME BASIC WORDS

Yes	Так	tahk
No	Ні	nee
Maybe	Можливо	mozh-LIH-vo
Please	Будь ласка	bood′ LAHS-kah
	or Прошу	PRO-shoo

In the Lviv region, прошу *is more common, while* будь ласка *is used in eastern Ukraine. Both will be understood everywhere.*

Thank you.	Дякую.	DYA-koo-yu
Thank you very much.	Дуже дякую.	DOO-zheh DYA-koo-yu
Not at all.	Нема за що.	neh-MAH zah shcho
Excuse me.	Перепрошую.	peh-reh-PRO-shoo-yu
	or Пробачте	pro-BAHCH-teh

Перепрошую *is more common in the Lviv region, while* пробачте *is used everywhere.*

I can.	Я можу.	ya MO-zhoo
I can't.	Я не можу.	ya neh MO-zhoo

QUESTIONS

Who?	Хто?	khto
Which?	Який? (яка, яке)	yah-KIHY̆ (yah-KAH, yah-KEH)
Where? (place)	Де?	deh
Where? (direction)	Куди?	koo-DIH
When?	Коли?	ko-LIH
Why?	Чому?	cho-MOO
What?	Що?	shcho
What's that?	Що це?	shcho tseh

What do you call this?	Як ви це називаєте?	
	yak vih tseh nah-zih-VAH-yeh-teh	
Where is, are ...?	Де є ...?	deh yeh
How?	Як?	yak
How much/many?	Скільки?	SKEEL'-kih
How long?		
(How much time?)	Як довго?	yak DOV-ho
How far is it?	Як далеко?	yak dah-LEH-ko
What time is it?	Котра година?	
	kot-RAH ho-DIH-nah	
Where can I buy ...?	Де можна купити ...?	
	deh MOZH-nah koo-PIH-tih	
Where can I find ...?	Де можна знайти ...?	
	deh MOZH-nah ZNAHY̆-tih	

THIS, THAT, THESE, and THOSE

It is / this is / these are / those are	Це...	tseh
It isn't / this isn't / these aren't...	Це не ...	tseh neh
Is it ... ?	Чи це ... ?	chih tseh
That is ...	То є ...	to yeh
That isn't ...	То не є ...	to neh yeh
There isn't/aren't ...	Нема ...	neh-MAH
Here it is.	Ось тут.	os' TOOT
There it is.	Ось там.	os' TAHM

WANT AND NEED

A note about grammar: Adjectives agree in number and gender with the nouns they modify. Verbs in the past tense take either masculine, feminine, neuter, or plural endings in agreement with their subjects. Throughout this phrasebook, the masculine ending will be given first, followed by the feminine.

I want ...	Я хочу ...	ya KHO-choo
I'd like ...	Я би (хотів, *m.*) (хотіла, *f.*)...	
	ya bih (kho-TEEV) (kho-TEE-lah)	

We'd like ...	Ми би хотіли ...	mih bih kho-TEE-lih
What do you want?	Що ви хочете?	
	shcho vih KHO-cheh-teh	
I need ...	Мені потрібно ...	
	meh-NEE po-TREEB-no	
We need ...	Нам потрібно ...	nahm po-TREEB-no
to be ...	бути...	BOO-tih
to go ...	іти ...	EE-TIH
to have ...	мати ...	MAH-tih
I'm hungry.	Я хочу їсти.	
(I want to eat.)	ya KHO-choo YEES-tih	
I'm thirsty.	Я хочу пити.	
(I want to drink.)	ya KHO-choo PIH-tih	
I'm looking for ...	Я шукаю ...	ya shoo-KAH-yu

I can't find my way to ...
   Я не можу знайти дороги до ...
   ya neh MO-zhoo ZNAHÝ-tih do-RO-hih do

It's important.	Це важливо.	tseh vahzh-LIH-vo
It's urgent!	Це термiново!	tseh tehr-mee-NO-vo
Hurry up!	Поспiшаймо!	pos-pee-SHAHÝ-mo
Quickly.	Швидко.	SHVIHD-ko
It's dangerous.	Це небезпечно.	
	tseh neh-behz-PEHCH-no	
Watch out!	Обережно!	o-beh-REHZH-no

REQUESTS

May I?	Чи можу я?	chih MO-zhoo ya
	Чи можна менi?	chih MOZH-nah meh-NEE
May I have ..?	Чи можна менi	chih MOZH-nah mch-NEE
	мати?	MAH-tih

May we have ..?	Чи можна нам мати..?	chih MOZH-nah nahm MAH-tih
Please tell me ...	Прошу мені сказати ...	PRO-shoo meh-NEE skah-ZAH-tih
Please show me ...	Прошу мені показати ...	PRO-shoo meh-NEE po-kah-ZAH-tih
Please help me.	Прошу допомогти мені. PRO-shoo do-po-mo-HTIH meh-NEE.	
Please give me...	Прошу дати мені...	PRO-shoo DAH-tih meh-N EE
Please bring me ...	Прошу принести мені..	PRO-shoo prih-NEHS-tih meh-NEE
Where's a telephone?	Де знаходиться телефон?	deh znah-KHO-diht'-sya TEH-leh-fon
Where can I make a telephone call?	Де я можу подзвонити?	deh ya MO-zhoo pod-ZVO-NIH-tih
Where can I buy an English language newspaper?	Де я можу купити англійськи газети? deh ya MO-zhoo koo-PIH-tih ahn-HLEEY-s'kee hah-ZEH-tih	

QUANTITY

a little, few	трохи	TRO-khih
some, a few	декілька	DEH-keel'-kah
much, many, a lot	багато	bah-HAH-to
how much/many	скільки	SKEEL'-kih
so much/many	стільки	STEEL'-kih
more/less (than)	більше/менше	BEEL'-sheh/MEN-sheh
enough/too much	досить/забагато	DO-siht'/zah-bah-HAH-to
each, every	кожний	KOZH-nihў

COMMON DESCRIPTIVE WORDS

A note about grammar: The following adjectives are given in the masculine nominative case, that is, for when they modify a masculine gender subject of the sentence. In the nominative case, the masculine adjective ending is -ий, the feminine ending is -a, the neuter is -e, and the plural is -i.

beautiful	прекрасний	preh-KRAHS-nihў
ugly	страшний	strahsh-NIHЎ
better	кращий	KRAH-shchihў
worse	гірший	HEER-shihў
big, little	великий, малий	veh-LIH-kihў, mah-LIHЎ
cheap	дешевий	deh-SHEH-vihў
expensive	дорогий	do-RO-hihў
cold	холодний	kho-LOD-nihў
hot	гарячий	hahr-YA-chihў
light, dark	світлий, темний	SVEET-lihў, TEHM-nihў
easy, difficult	легкий, важкий	leh-KIHЎ, VAZH-kihў
fast	швидкий	shvihd-KIHЎ
slow	повільний	po-VEEL'-nihў
good, bad	добрий, поганий	DO-brihў, po-HAH-nihў
happy, sad	веселий, сумний	VEH-seh-liyў, soom-NIHЎ
near, far	близький, далекий	BLIHZ'-kihў, dah-LEH-kihў
new, old	новий, старий	no-VIHЎ, stah-RIHЎ
nice, nasty	гарний, поганий	HAHR-nihў, po-HAH-nihў
open	відкритий	veed-KRIH-tihў
shut	закритий	zah-KRIH-tihў
right	правильний	PRAH-vihl'-nihў
wrong	неправильний	neh-prah-VIHL'-nihў
tall, short	високий, низький	vih-SO-kihў, nihz'-KIHЎ
well (healthy), sick	здоровий, хворий	zdo-RO-vihў, KHVO-rihў
wonderful	чудовий	choo-DO-vihў
terrible	страшний	strahsh-NIHЎ
young, old	молодий, старий	mo-lo-DIHЎ, stah-RIHЎ

Colors	Кольори	**kol'-O-rih**
beige	бежевий	BEH-zheh-vihў
black	чорний	CHOR-nihў
blue (dark)	синій	SIH-neeў
blue (light)	голубий	ho-LOO-bihў

brown	коричневий	ко-RIHCH-neh-vihў
gold	золотий	zo-lo-TIHЎ
green	зелений	zeh-LEH-niyhў
grey	сірий	SEE-rihў
orange	оранжевий	o-RAHN-z͡heh-vihў
pink	рожевий	ro-Z͡HEH-vihў
purple	бузковий	booz-KO-vihў
red	червоний	cher-VO-nihў
beet red	бурячковий	boor-yach-KO-vihў
silver	сріблястий	sreeb-LYAS-tihў
turquoise	бірюзовий	beer-yu-ZO-vihў
violet	фіолетовий	fee-o-LEH-to-vihў
white	білий	BEE-lihў
yellow	жовтий	Z͡HOV-tihў
light-	ясно-	YAS-no-
dark-	темно-	TEHM-no-

EMERGENCY PHRASES

HELP!	Допоможіть	do-po-mo-Z͡HEETʹ
STOP THIEF!	зупиніть злодія!	zoo-PIH-neetʹ ZLO-dee-ya
WATCH OUT!	Обережно!	o-beh-REHZ͡H-no
POLICE!	Міліція!	mee-LEE-tsee-ya
FIRE!	Пожар!	po-Z͡HAHR

[While the Ukrainian word for fire, пожежа (po-Z͡HE-z͡hah), is used in normal conversation, in times of emergency, most Ukrainians will use the Russian word пожар.]

CHAPTER 6. ARRIVAL AND DEPARTURE

Ukrainian Proverb: Тихше їдеш, дальше будеш.
TIHKH-sheh YEE-dehsh DAHL'-sheh BOO-dehsh
The quieter you go, the farther you'll get.

Getting in and out of Ukraine quietly can be a bit of a challenge. Foreign visitors who stay more than three days are required to register their passports with local law enforcement authorities. Private visitors should have their hosts take them to the local office of the Ministry of Internal Affairs (VVIR) office. A $10 fee will be collected. The registration requirement is automatically met for tourists staying in hotels, for those doing business, or for students on an exchange program.

PASSPORT CONTROL

Passport control Паспортний контроль
PAHS-port-nihў kon-TROL'

Your passport and visa will be checked here. If you don't already have a visa, you won't see much of Ukraine. At the border you can get only a short-term (not exceeding 72 hours) visa for emergency situations. These conditions qualify for emergency visas: a serious health problem or death of a relative, participation in disaster relief operations and other urgent needs.

You can also get a transit visa that allows you to travel across Ukraine to another country. You will need some documentation to show the transitory nature of your travel, such as a visa to a neighboring country.

Is this passport control?
Це є паспортний контроль?
tseh yeh PAHS-port-nihў kon-TROL'

Here's my passport.
Ось мій паспорт.
os' meeў PAHS-port

Where can I get a visa?
Де я можу отримати візу?
deh ya MO-zhoo ot-RIH-mah-tih VEE-zoo

Where is customs?

Де знаходиться митний контроль?

deh znah-KHO-diht'-sya MIHT-nihў kon-TROL'

Where's the restroom?

Де знаходитьця туалет?

deh znah-KHO-diht'-sya too-ah-LEHT

Here are some possible questions you may be asked:

"What is the purpose of your visit?"	Яка ціль вашого приїзду? ya-KAH tseel' VAH-sho-ho prih-YEEZ-doo	
Business.	Бізнес.	BEEZ-nehs
Tourist.	Турист.	too-RIHST
In transit to ...	Проїздом до ...	pro-YEEZ-dom do ...
To visit relatives.	Відвідати родичів.	veed-VEE-dah-tih RO-dih-cheev
For a conference.	На конференцію.	nah kon-feh-REHN-tsee-yu
An exchange program.	Візит по обміну.	vee-ZIHT po OB-mee-noo
To study at ...	Навчатись в ...	nahv-CHAH-tihs' v ...
university.	університеті.	oo-nee-vehr-sih-TEH-tee
"Your passport please."	Ваш паспорт будь ласка . vash PAHS-port bood' LAHS-keh	
"How long will you stay in Ukraine?"	Як довго ви будете на Україні? yahk DOV-ho vih BOO-deh-teh nah oo-krah-YEE-nee	
One day.	Один день.	o-DIHN dehn'
One week.	Один тиждень.	o-DIHN TIHZH-den'
One month.	Один місяць	o-DIHN MEE-syats'
One year.	Один рік.	o-DIHN reek
Several days	Декілька днів	DEH-keel-kah dneev
(weeks)	(тижднів)	(TIHZHD-neev)
(months)	(місяців)	(MEE-syah-tseev)

BAGGAGE

Baggage   Багаж   bah-HAHZ̑H

Where do I claim my baggage?
Де я можу отримати мій багаж?
deh ya MO-zhoo ot-RIH-mah-tih meeў bah-HAHZ̑H

My flight number is ...
Номер мого рейсу є ...
NO-mehr MO-ho REHY̆-soo yeh

Where can I get a luggage cart?
Де я можу взяти возик для багажу?
deh ya MO-zhoo BZYA-tih vo-ZIHK dlya
bah-HAH-zhoo

I didn't get my luggage!
Я не (отримав, *m.*) (отримала, *f.*) мого багажу!
ya neh (ot-RIH-mahv) (ot-RIH-mah-lah) MO-ho
bah-hah-Z̑HOO

Where can I report missing luggage?
Де я можу заявити загубленний багаж?
deh ya MO-zhoo zah-ya-VIH-tih zah-HOO-blehn-nihy̆
bah-HAZ̑H

CUSTOMS

Customs   Митний контроль
                    MIHT-nihy̆ kon-TROL'

Tourists and those with business in Ukraine report little unpleasantness at entry. Some who are carrying large amounts of business or medical supplies are detained unless they are met by a Ukrainian counterpart who vouches for the legitimacy of their mission. Travelers are allowed to bring in most articles, exceptions being arms, ammunition, narcotics, explosives, toxic or radioactive materials, and materials that are racist, pornographic, or anti-Ukrainian. Upon arrival you'll be given an entry declaration form and asked to declare all personal valuables which you intend to take out with you. List total pieces of luggage, declare all currency, listing the traveler's checks separately. List valuable jewelry such as precious stones, gold, diamonds, and pearls. Don't forget to include your wedding ring. Declare also valuable high-tech equipment such as cameras, computers, and camcorders.

You do not have to declare valuables that you intend to give as gifts, since there's no duty or limit imposed on the quantity and value of gifts. You're also permitted to carry in and use or give away as much western currency as you wish, but you are required to declare all money — even that intended to be given away. In order to prevent any complications for the recipient, it's advisable to accompany a large donation with a statement from you notifying authorities of your gift.

Declare alcohol and tobacco. Each traveler 16 years of age or older is allowed to bring in 1 bottle of hard liquor plus 2 bottles of wine. You're allowed to bring in duty-free 1¼ cartons of cigarettes or 8¾ ounces of other tobacco. Duty may be collected on alcohol and tobacco in excess of these quantities. Goods, property, and equipment intended for commercial use is also subject to duty.

It's understood that many travelers to Ukraine are carrying large amounts of western currency in small bills to give away to relatives; be sure to wear a money belt at all times, and be especially careful in sleeping compartments of trains.

Here's my declaration form.
    Ось моя декларація.
    os' mo-YA deh-klah-RAH-tsee-ya

Where can I get a declaration form in English?
    Де я можу отримати бланк декларації по-англійськи?
    deh ya MO-zhoo ot-RIH-mah-tih blahnk
    deh-klah-RAH-tsee-yee po-ahn-HLEEY̌-s'kih

Here's my baggage.	Ось мій багаж.
	os' meeў bah-HAHZ̃H
Here's my suitcase.	Ось моя сумка
	os' mo-A SOOM-kah

You may be asked:

"Do you have	Чи ви маєте щось об'явити?
anything to declare?	chih vih MAH-yeh-teh shchos' ob'-ya-VIH-tih

Jewelry.	Ювелірні вироби.	yu-veh-LEER-nee
		VIH-ro-bih

A bracelet.	Браслет.	brahs-LEHT
A chain.	Ланцюжок.	lahn-tsyu-ZHOK
A necklace.	Намисто.	nah-MIHS-to
A ring.	Кільце.	keel'-TSEH
It's gold.	Це золото.	tseh ZO-lo-to
It's silver.	Це срібло.	tseh SREEB-lo
It's platinum.	Це платина.	tseh PLAH-tih-nah
It's diamond.	Це діамант.	tseh dee-ah-MAHNT
A camcorder.	Відеокамера.	
	vee-deh-o-KAH-meh-rah	
A camera with lenses.	Фотоапарат з об'єктивами.	
	fo-to-ah-pah-RAHT z ob'yehk-TIH-vah-mih	
A computer.	Комп'ютер.	kom-P'YU-tehr
Dollars.	Долари.	do-LAH-rih
Pounds.	фунти.	FOON-tih
Marks.	марки.	MAHR-kih
Money.	Гроші.	HROH-shee
... bottles of whisky.	... пляшка віскі.	
	... PLYA-shka VEES-kee	
... packages of cigarettes	... пачка цигарок.	
	... PAHCH-kah tsih-HAH-rok	

This is for personal use.
Це для особистого користування.
tseh dlya o-so-BIHS-to-ho ko rihs-too-VAHN-nya

"Please open this bag." Прошу відкрити цю сумку.
PRO-shoo veed-KRIH-tih tsyu SOOM-koo

"What do you have in there?" Що ви маєте там?
shcho vih MAH-yeh-teh tahm

"Do you have ...?" Чи ви маєте ...?
chih vih MAH-yeh-teh ...

weapons	зброю	ZBRO-yu
drugs	наркотики	nahr-KO-tih-kih
any food	які небудь продукти	ya-KEE neh-BOOD' pro-DOOK-tih
any animals	які небудь тварини	ya-KEE neh-BOOD' tvah-RIH-nih
any plants	які небудь рослини	ya-KEE neh-BOOD' ros-LIH-nih

"Do you have   Чи ви маєте інший багаж?
another bag?"   chih vih MAH-yeh-teh EEN-shihỹ bah-HAHZH

Where can I find a porter?
Де я можу знайти носильщика (*or* носильника)?
deh ya MO-zhoo znahỹ-TIH no-SIHL'-shchih-kah
(*or* no-SIHL'-nih-kah)

PORTER!   НОСИЛЬЩИК!   no-SIHL'-shchihk

Please take my baggage.   Прошу взяти мій багаж.
                                 PRO-shoo BZYA-tih meeỹ
                                 bah-HAHZH

I need to go to the ...   Мені треба до ...
                                 meh-NEE TREH-bah do

taxi stop	таксі	tahk-SEE
train station	поїзду	PO-yeez-doo
bus station	автобусу	ahv-TO-boo-soo
exit	виходу	VIH-kho-doo

How much do I owe you?
Скільки мені треба заплатити вам?
SKEEL'-kih meh-NEE TREH-bah zah-plah-TIH-tih vahm

DEPARTING IS SUCH SWEET SORROW ...

While in the past, entering Ukraine was a hassle for travelers, now departure is likely to be more trying. Many travelers are naturally wary of foreign customs and assume they'll be treated harshly or unfairly. Most instances of customs difficulties result from a misunderstanding. Usually the traveler simply is unaware of the regulations and attempts to exit with something that isn't allowed out. By familiarizing yourself with the regulations, you can avoid feelings of suspicion that might arise if your souvenirs are challenged.

Keep the customs declaration form you receive upon entry. When you leave you'll be given an identical declaration form that must be filled out and submitted along with the first form. By comparing the two, customs officials can determine if any of your purchases are not allowed out of the country, are subject to duty, or if your total purchases are greater in value than the amount of money you've declared upon entry. *Be sure to save all records of currency exchange and all shopping receipts.*

There is no restriction on consumer goods purchased with hard currency. You are not allowed to export arms, ammunition, narcotics, toxic or radioactive materials, or certain items of great artistic, cultural, or historical value, such as some paintings, sculptures, engravings, crystal, ceramics, icons, precious and semiprecious stones, relics, furniture, coins, books, and musical instruments. Those traveling with tour groups rarely encounter obstacles; frequent visitors to Ukraine may be more suspect.

Visitors to Ukraine usually can't resist the beautiful arts and crafts. There's no limit to the amount of inexpensive folk art craft items and souvenirs you can take out of Ukraine. If you buy them at a *Kashtan* or other store that accept hard currency, you should not have to pay duty on them. Simply show your receipts. If you prefer to shop with Ukrainian currency, you should not have to pay duty on the items you bought as long as you exchanged your money at a bank or an authorized currency exchange. Show your currency exchange receipt to the customs officials who will figure out whether the amount of hard currency you exchanged was sufficient to pay for the craft items you're declaring. If they suspect you've paid for your purchases with money exchanged on the black market, they can slap a one hundred per cent duty on them.

If you buy an original painting or art work, such as a new icon, ask the artist for a signed receipt or a permission form for taking it out of the country. Some valuable older works, including icons, are sold in special shops. These shops will provide a special permission form for you to export the work. If you happen to buy a valuable piece of art from a source that's not designated for selling it, or if you have any doubts about exporting any item you've bought, take it to the Ministry of Culture office. Your purchase will be inspected, and you'll be issued an export permit, and assessed duty based on its value. The fee for exporting an icon is typically $50 USD. In Kyiv, the Ministry of Culture is at 19 Ivan Franko Street (вулиця Івана франка, *vulytsya Ivana Franka).* In Lviv, a branch of the Ministry of Culture office is in the city hall building in Market Square (площа Ринок, *ploshcha Rynok*) in the city center.

Occasionally it happens that customs workers try to use their positions for personal gain. A customs worker, for example, might claim that an inexpensive souvenir is an antique and slap a large duty on it, which, of course, he or she has no intention of turning in to the government. What they are doing is illegal; while it is easier not to be intimidated if you're fluent in Ukrainian, you can nonetheless resist encouraging this unscrupulous practice by calmly refusing to give in. If you should find yourself in one of these situations, a few phrases will help you out: Produce your receipt for the item in question, proving that it isn't as valuable as the custom official claims.

Here is my receipt for this.	Ось мій чек.
	os' meeў chehk

Or if he or she persists in trying to fleece you, call their bluff by asking for a receipt for the duty you paid. Let your body language and your tone of voice imply that you will take this sham to the proper authorities:

I want a receipt for this.	Я хочу чек.
	ya KHO-choo chehk

As a last resort, you might try the following phrase:

I want to contact the American consulate.
Я хочу звіязатись з Американським консульством.
ya KHO-choo zvee-ya-ZAH-tihs' z ah-meh-rih-KAHNS'-kihm KON-sool'st-vom

If you're deadlocked at customs, and it appears you won't get your acquisition through without paying a fee you think is unreasonable, you might choose to leave it with the person who brought you to the airport and retrieve it another time.

When shopping in Ukraine, it's a good idea also to keep in mind how much your home country will allow you to import. U.S. Customs, for example, allows duty-free $400 worth of imports, including both purchases and gifts. Only 1 liter of alcoholic beverage can enter duty-free, but when faced with the opportunity to buy $2 bottles of fine cognac in Ukraine, travelers may opt to pay a small import duty at home. Note that the U.S. Department of Agriculture generally does not allow foreign foods to be brought into the U.S. unless they are canned.

MONEY

Money   Гроші   HRO-shee

Soon after independence, Ukraine decided to call its currency *hryvnya*, after a silver coin of various types used in the ancient Kyivan Rus state and again used as the primary currency when Ukraine last experienced independence in 1918. The unstable economic situation, however, prompted the government to place the *hryvnya* on hold and adopt a series of rationing coupons, called *karbovantsi* (карбованці) as the official Ukrainian monetary unit. Although it's legal tender, the *karbovanets* is considered a temporary currency to be used only until the country's economic situation stabilizes and the *hryvnya* is introduced. This could happen at any time.

Karbovantsi do not have coins. The banknotes, called coupons (купони), have been issued in denominations from 1 to 1,000,000. Because of the wildly escalating inflation, the lower denominations are worthless and by the time you make your trip, they may no longer be circulating.

BANKS

Banks   Банки   BAHN-kih

In 1989 Ukraine started on the long road toward a free-market economy by establishing commercial banks. At first these served mainly as credit societies, providing credit for their stock holders with special emphasis on short and medium-term loans in the trade and consumer goods industry with high return. By 1991, state-owned banks became public and were restructured with a vast network of branches throughout the country. There are now thousands of banks in Ukraine, but they do not provide all the services of banks in western Europe, such as transferring money from your bank back home. As a rule, try the main branch of a bank in a larger city if you are in need of more advanced banking service. In Kyiv, for example, the Eximbank at 8 Khreshchatyk Street will cash traveler's checks. All banks will change your money into Ukrainian currency, but it'll probably be more convenient simply to pay in dollars or use the currency exchange counter at a hotel or airport. Banking hours are 9 a.m. to 6 p.m.

CURRENCY EXCHANGE

Currency exchange   Обмін Валюти   OB-meen vah-LYU-tih

Ukrainian Proverb: Хто міняє, той і має.
khto mee-NYA-yeh toỹ ee MAH-yeh
Who changes money, has it.

Obviously, someone other than you is going to profit every time you exchange money. The reasons for NOT converting your hard currency into Ukrainian money are compelling. Some merchants accept only hard currency because of its greater stability. German marks and American dollars are particularly desirable. During your entire vacation or business trip to Ukraine, you can get along by paying for everything in dollars. If, during your stay, the Ukrainian government has set an artificial exchange rate, it'll be to your benefit to pay for goods and services with hard currency rather than use the official exchange counters. You should do very well with less than $200 US per week, plus whatever cash you will need to pay for internal airfare and hotel bills. The hotels in Kyiv average over $100 USD per night.

You should carry small bills. Be sure to have a good supply of fives, ones, and fifty-cent pieces and quarters. Paper currency in higher denominations than a US $20 will not be useful. Some places, in fact, may be reluctant to accept large denominations because of the fear that they may be counterfeit, or in the case of U.S. currency, will no longer be legal tender once the U.S. revises its paper currency. Paper currency should be clean, unmarked, and untorn. Crisp new bills, preferably issued 1992 or later, are less suspect of being counterfeit than old, worn ones.

The dollar route works best for the casual tourist in the center of the bigger cities. Long-term visitors, those going to less touristy areas, or those traveling around with Ukrainian relatives or friends may feel more comfortable in not calling attention to themselves by flashing foreign hard currency. And when you're spending local currency, you're less likely to be asked an outrageous price for a small purchase or service.

Personal checks are not accepted at this writing. The economic situation is fast changing, however, and with increasing private enterprise there are beginning signs of the acceptance of credit cards such as American Express and Diner's Club cards. However, it's not worth the effort to find a place that will take ersatz cash when the buying power of the dollar is so strong.

Currency Exchange Counters. If you wish to immerse yourself into the Ukrainian experience and convert your hard currency into Ukrainian money, there are numerous exchange counters located throughout the cities as well as in banks, airports, and hotels. The exchange rate will be about the same at all legal counters, although you may actually get a better rate for ten dollars than you would for fifty. Sometimes the official exchange counters don't have adequate *karbovantsi* to make the change, especially near the end of the business day. You'll need the declaration form you filled out at customs each time you change your dollars.

Since you're likely to receive Ukrainian currency as change when you make a purchase in dollars, it may not be necessary to visit an exchange counter. Watch, in fact, that you don't accumulate more than you can spend; you're not allowed to take Ukrainian money home as a souvenir of your trip and it may be impossible to cash it in for dollars before your departure.

In Kyiv alone there are hundreds of unlicensed money changers. These unlawful practitioners prefer to be known as "currency workers," (валютчики, *valyutchyky*) although they're commonly called "money changers" (міняйли, *minyayly*). The status of the unofficial currency workers is subject to the government's changing economic policies, particularly its attempt to control inflation.

The mobile currency bureaus have been tolerated to the point of near respectability in which the *valyutchyky* began to hold up signs listing their rates in dollars and Deutsche marks. Some even set up booths in the lobbies of large department stores. Then, when the government makes a drastic attempt to stabilize the currency, like pulling it out of the free market and setting an official exchange rate, it's likely to crack down on street changers, who are offering a better rate than the artificial official exchange. Add to their problems the fact that street changers often have to give protection money to gangs (рекетери, *reketery*) for their turf and occasionally have to pay off the police — on or off the books — for "foul language" or "minor hooliganism."

In short, if you see many street changers freely operating, they are being tolerated, which means that your rate may not be much better than at the official exchange. When there's a crackdown, you may get a much better deal, but you won't get the currency exchange receipt that will help you get your purchases through customs duty-free. And you run the risk of being short-changed or given counterfeit money. Even worse, you could be arrested.

Where can I change some money?
Де можна поміняти гроші?
deh MOZH-nah po-mee-NYA-tih HRO-shee?

Can you cash this traveler's check?
Чи ви можете обміняти цей дорожній чек на гроші?
chih vih MO-zheh-teh ob-meen-NYA-tih tseў
do-ROZH-neeў chehk nah HRO-shee

Can you change (Canadian) dollars (pounds) (marks)?
Чи ви можете поміняти (Канадські) долари (Фунти) (марки)?
chih vih MO-zheh-teh po-mee-NYA-tih
(kah-NAHDS'-kee) do-LAH-rih (FOON-tih) (MAHR-kih)

What is the exchange rate of (Canadian) dollars (pounds) (marks)?
Який обмінний курс (Канадського) долара (фунта) (марки)?
ya-KIHЎ ob-MEEN-nihў koors (kahn-NAHDS'-ko-ho)
do-LAH-rah (FOON-tah) (MAHR-kih)

How much commission do you charge?
Який процент ви берете за обмін?
ya-KIHЎ pro-TSEHNT vih beh-REH-teh zah OB-meen

Can you give me bigger/smaller bills?
Прошу, чи ви можете дати в більших/менших коп'юрах?
PRO-shoo chih vih MO-zheh-teh DAH-tih v
BEEL'-shihkh/MEHN-shihkh ko-P'YU-rahkh

Can you make change for this? [showing bill]
Чи ви можете розміняти це?
chih vih MO-zheh-teh roz-mee-HYsA-tih tseh

I think you made a mistake.
Я думаю що ви помилились.
ya DOO-mah-yu shcho vih po-mih-LIH-lihs'

CHAPTER 7. CONVERSATION

Ukrainian Proverb:
Слово не горобець, вилетить не спіймаеш.
SLO-vo neh ho-ro-BEHTS′ VIH-leh-tiht′ neh
speeў-MAH-yehsh
A word is not a sparrow, if it flies away, you won't catch it.

Using just the right words helps to make a good first impression. In languages that have both polite and familiar forms of the word "you," it's essential to use the polite form in initial meetings. Use the familiar when conversing with a family member, a friend, a classmate, or anyone else with whom you're on close terms.

Because this chapter deals with conversation among people who are generally not well acquainted, many of the phrases, especially those having to do with getting acquainted, give only the polite, *vy* (ви) form of the word "you." For other phrases in which both the *vy* and the familiar, *ty* (ти) forms are given, the familiar (and singular) is given first, followed by the polite (plural) form.

To address a person directly by name, use the first name plus the middle name, or patronymic. The patronymic is formed by attaching a suffix to the father's first name: females add *-ivna* and males add *-ovych*. Thus, if Oksana's father is Mykhaylo, you address her as Oksana Mykhaylivna and if Ihor's father is Vasyl, you call him Ihor Vasylovych. These forms are primarily for formal situations, such as student addressing teacher.

The Ukrainian language has forms of address equivalent to Mr., Mrs., and Miss. Mr. is *pan* (пан, pahn) Mrs. is *pani* (пані, PAH-nee), and Miss is *panna* (панна, PAHN-nah). While emigre Ukrainians commonly use these, in present day Ukraine they're mainly for addressing foreigners. Ordinarily, it's considered very impolite to address a person directly by their family name, so this form of address might be used at an initial meeting just to establish identity ("Are you Pan Melnyk?") or when referring to a person who is not present. A less official manner of address, that conveys both friendliness and respect, is the use of *pan, pani, panna* with the first name ("Hello, Pan Stepan and Panna Katerina.").

MEETINGS

My name is ...   Мене звати ...   meh-NEH ZVAH-tih

What's your (first name) (patronymic) (last name)?
Як (ваше ім'я) (вас по-батькові) (ваше прізвище)?
yak (VAH-sheh eem'-YA) (vahs po-BAHT'-ko-vee)
(VAH-sheh PREEZ-vih-shcheh)

Pleased to meet you.
Приємно познайомитись.
prih-YEHM-no poz-nah-ЎO-mih-tihs'

I'd like to present ....
Я хочу представити вам....
ya kho-CHOO pred-STAH-vih-tih vahm

my colleague	мого колегу	MO-ho ko-LEH-hoo
my husband	мого чоловіка	MO-ho cho-lo-VEE-kah
my wife	мою дружину	MO-yu droo-ZHIH-noo

This is my (acquaintance, *m.*) (boyfriend).
Це мій (знайомий) (друг).
tseh meeў (znah-ЎO-mihў) (drooh)

This is my (acquaintance, *f.*) (girlfriend).
Це моя (знайома) (подруга).
tseh mo-YA znah-ЎO-mah/po-DROO-hah

As in English, the words "boyfriend" and "girlfriend" have a romantic connotation. Ukrainians seldom use these terms because — short of marriage — it's not customary to reveal the nature of a male-female relationship. Instead they will introduce someone of the opposite sex as an "acquaintance," regardless of how intimate they are.

These are my (acquaintances) (friends).
Це (мої знайомі) (мої друзі).
tseh mo-YEE znah-ЎO-mee/mo-YEE DROO-zee

GREETINGS

Good morning.	Добрий ранок.	DO-brihў RAH-nok
Good day.	Добрий день.	DO-brihў dehn'
Good evening.	Добрий вечір.	DO-brihў VEH-cheer
Good night.	Надобраніч.	nah-do-BRAH-neech
Good-bye.		
(See you later.)	До побачення.	do po-BAH-chehn-nya
Hi.	Привіт.	prih-VEET
How are you?		
(familiar or sing.)	Як живеш?	yak z͡hih-VEHSH
(polite or plural)	Як ви живете	yak vih Z͡HIH-veh-teh
Very well, thanks,	Дуже добре,	DOO-z͡heh DO-breh
and you?	а (ти) (ви)?	ah (tih) (vih)
How's it going?	Як справи?	yak SPRAH-vih
Fine.	Добре.	DOB-reh
Not bad.	Непогано.	neh-po-HAH-no
So-so.	Так собі.	TAHK so-BEE
Bad.	Погано.	po-HAH-no
What's new?	Що нового?	shcho no-VO-ho
Nothing's new.	Нічого нового.	nee-CHO-ho NO-vo-ho

DO YOU SPEAK ...?

Do you speak ...?	Чи ви говорите ...?	chih vih ho-VO-rih-teh
English	по-англійськи	po ahn-HLEEЎS'-kih
Ukrainian	по-українськи	po oo-krah-YEENS'-kih

I speak only English.

Я говорю тільки по-англійськи.

ya ho-VOR-yu TEEL'-kih po ahn-HLEEЎ-s'kih

Does anyone here speak English?

Чи хто-небудь тут говорить по-англійськи?

chih KHTO-neh-bood' toot ho-VO-riht' po ahn-HLEEЎ-s'kih

I can understand Ukrainian but don't speak it well.

Я розумію по-українськи але погано говорю.

ya ro-zoo-MEE-yu po oo-krah-YEEN-s'kih ah-LEH
po-HAH-no ho-VOR-yu

Would you speak more slowly please?
Прошу говорити повільніше.
PRO-shoo ho-vo-RIH-tih po-veel'-NEE-sheh

Do you understand?
Чи ви розумієте?
chih vih ro-zoo-MEE-yeh-teh

I'm sorry, but I don't understand you.
Пробачте, але я не розумію вас.
pro-BAHCH-teh a-leh ya neh ro-zoo-MEE-yu vahs

I don't understand everything.
Я розумію не все.
ya ro-zoo-MEE-yu neh vseh

Would you please repeat that?
Повторіт це, будь ласка.
pov-to-REET tseh bood' LAHS-kah

What do you call that in Ukrainian?
Як ви це називаєте по-українськи?
yak vih tseh nah-zih-VAH-yeh-teh po-oo-krah-YEEN-s'kih

Would you spell it please?
Прошу написати це.
PRO-shoo nah-pih-SAH-tih tseh

Please write it down.
Прошу записати мені це.
PRO-shoo zah-pih-SAH-tih meh-NEE tseh

SAYING THANKS

Yes, thank you.   Так, дуже дякую.   tahk DOO-zheh
                                                    DYA-koo-yu

No, thanks.   Дякую, ні.   DYA-koo-yu nee

Thank you very much!   Дуже дякую.   DOO-zheh DYA-koo-yu

Thank you for all your help.
Дякую за (твою, s.) (вашу. pl.) допомогу.
DYA-koo-yu zah (tvo-YU) (VAH-shoo) do-po-MO-hoo

Thank you for your trouble.
Дякую за (твої, s.) (ваші. pl.) зусилля.
DYA-koo-yu zah (tvo-YEE) (VAH-shee) zoo-SIHL-lya

I'm very grateful to you.
Я дуже (вдячний, m.) (вдячна, f.) (тобі, s.) (вам, pl.).
ya DOO-zheh (VDYACH-nihỹ) (VDYACH-nah) (to-BEE)
(vahm).

Not at all.   Нема за що.   neh-MAH ZAH shcho

PARDON AND REGRETS

Excuse me!   Перепрошую!   peh-reh-PRO-shoo-yu

I'm extremely sorry. [an apology]
Я дуже вибачаюсь.
ya DOO-zheh vih-BAH-chah-yus'

I'm very sorry about that. [expression of commiseration or regret]
Мені дуже жалко.
meh-NEE DOO-zheh ZHAHL-ko.

That's too bad.   Шкода.   SHKO-dah

I apologize for being late.
Пробачте за запізнення.
pro-BAHCH-teh zah zah-PEEZ-nehn-nya

Please forgive me.
Прошу вибачити мене.
PRO-shoo VIH-bah-chih-tih meh-NEH

That's ok.   Нічого страшного.   nee-CHO-ho strash-NO-ho

BEST WISHES

Congratulations.   Мої вітання.   mo-YEE vee-TAHN-nya

I wish you all the best.
Я бажаю (тобі, s.) (вам, pl.) всього найкращого.
ya bah-ZHAH-yu (to-BEE) (vahm) VS'O-ho
nahỹ-KRAH-shcho-ho

I congratulate you on your ....
Я вітаю (тебе, *s.*) (вас, *pl.*) з ....
ya vee-TAH-yu (teh-BEH) (vahs) z . ...

birthday	днем народження	dnehm nah-ROD-zhehn-nya
engagement	обрученням	ob-ROO-chehn-nyam
marriage	одруженням	od-ROO-zhehn-nyam
new baby	народженням дитини	nah-ROD-zhehn-nyam dih-TIH-nih
success	успіхом	OOS-pee-khom

Get well soon.
(Виздоровлюй, *s.*) (Виздоровлюйте, *pl.*) швидше.
(vihz-do-ROV-l'yuў) (vihz-do-ROV-l'yuў-teh) SHVIHD-sheh

My deepest sympathy.
Мої співчуття.
mo-YEE speev-choot-TYA

I wish you ...	Я бажаю (тобі, *s.*) (вам, *pl.*) ... ya bah-ZHAH-yu (to-BEE) (vahm)
good luck	щастя SHCHAHS-tya
happy birthday	щасливого дня народження shchahs-LIH-vo-ho dnya nah-ROD-zhehn-nya
happy holiday	веселих свят veh-SEH-lihkh svyat
happy new year	щасливого нового року shchahs-LIH-vo-ho NO-vo-ho RO-koo

Happy Easter!   Христос Воскрес!   KHRIHS-tos vos-KREH
This greeting on Easter morning means "Christ is risen." The customary response is:
Indeed, he's risen.   Воістину Воскрес.
vo-EES-tih-noo vos-KREHS

Merry Christmas.   Христос Рождається.
khrihs-TOS nah-ROD-zhoo-yeht'-sya
This Christmas greeting means "Christ is born." The customary response is:
Already he was born.   Вже вродився.
vzheh vro-DIHV-sya

Another reply is:
We glorify him.   Славімо його.
slah-VEE-mo ўo-HO

Happy New Year!	З Новим Роком!	z NO-vihm RO-kom
Bon Voyage!	Щасливої Дороги!	shchahs-LIH-vo-yee
		do-RO-hih
Long Life!	Сто Літ!	sto leet

"Сто літ" means "100 years." Variations of it are popular throughout the Slavic countries for birthdays, anniversaries and other commemorative occasions. In Ukraine, "Сто Літ" is the preferred version of the "long life" toast, while Ukrainians in North America commonly say Многая Літа (MNO-hah-ya LEE-tah), a Church Slavonic phrase which is no longer popular in Ukraine.

At the dinner table, it's customary to wish your companions a good appetite and a pleasant dining experience. Two phrases are commonly used:

| "Смачного." | smahch-NO-ho. |
| "Приємного аппетиту!" | prih-YEHM-no-ho ahp-peh-TIH-too |

When making a toast, say "To your health:"
| "На здоров'я." | nah zdo-ROV'ya |

SAYING GOOD-BYE

Good-bye.	До побачення.	do po-BAH-chehn-n'ya
See you later.	Побачимось	po-BAH-chih-mos'
	пізніше.	peez-NEE-sheh
See you tomorrow.	Побачимось	po-BAH-chih-mos'
	завтра.	ZAHV-trah

I (we) had a wonderful time.
Мені (нам) було дуже приємно.
meh-NEE (nahm) BOO-lo DOO-zheh prih-YEHM-no

| Thanks for everything. | Дякую за все. | DYA-koo-yu zah vseh |
| All the best. | На все добре. | nah vseh DOB-reh |

When can we get together again?
Коли ми можемо зустрітись знову?
ko-LIH mih MO-zheh-mo zoos-TREE-tihs' ZNO-voo

Next time come and visit (me) (us).
Наступного разу приходіть до (мене) (нас).
nahs-TOOP-no-ho RAH-zoo prih-kho-DEET' do (MEHN-neh)
(nahs)

LET'S TALK ABOUT THE WEATHER

Ukraine has a moderate continental climate, that is, one characterized by
four distinct seasons, an annual snowfall, summers that are wetter than
winters, and a long, mild autumn. There are several climatic regions
according to average temperature and precipitation. Generally, annual
average temperatures decrease as you travel from south to north and from
west to east across Ukraine, with the exception of the Carpathian
Mountains in western Ukraine which are colder than typical for that part
of the country. The coldest areas are generally in the northeast; near the
Russian border in Kharkiv, for example, temperatures may drop below
freezing in the middle of October and persist through the end of March.
The warmest region lies along the coast of the Black Sea; in Odesa, the
winter lasts only from the middle of December until the end of February.
The very warmest region is the southern coast of the Crimea which has
a Mediterranean climate.

Even with these variations, Ukraine's climate is more temperate and
predictable than that of many parts of the U.S. Spring and fall are
especially pleasant; in summer your hosts may apologize for the
discomfort if the temperature reaches the low 80's. There are rainy
periods in Ukraine. Be sure to bring a raincoat, a folding umbrella, and
shoes that won't be ruined if wet.

How's the weather today?
    Яка погода сьогодні?
    ya-KAH po-HO-dah s'o-HOD-nee

What will the weather be like tomorrow?
    Яка буде погода завтра?
    ya-KAH BOO-deh po-HO-dah ZAHV-trah

What a beautiful day!
    Сьогодні чудова погода!
    s'o-HOD-nee choo-DO-vah po-HO-dah

Is it cold outdoors?
> Чи надворі холодно?
> chih nahd-VO-ree KHO-lod-no

Am I dressed warmly enough?
> Чи я (вдягнений, *m.*)(вдягнена, *f.*) достатньо тепло?
> chih ya (VDYAH-neh-nihў) (VDYAH-neh-nah) dos-TAHT-n'o
> TEHP-lo

I'm freezing.   Я змерзаю.   ya zmehr-ZAH-yu

Is it going to (rain) (snow) (today) (tomorrow)?
> Чи буде (дощ) (сніг) (сьогодні) (завтра)?
> chih BOO-deh (doshch) (sneeh) (s'o-HOD-nee) (ZAHV-trah)

Do I need to carry an umbrella?
> Чи буде мені потрібна парасоля?
> chih BOO-deh MEH-nee pot-REEB-nah pah-rah-SO-lya

It looks like a storm.
> Збирається на бурю.
> zbih-RAH-yeht'-sya nah BOO-ryu

It's raining cats and dogs.
> Л'є як із відра.
> l'yeh yak eez veed-RAH

What terrible weather!
> Яка погана погода!
> ya-KAH po-HAH-nah po-HO-dah

How long will it stay like this?
> Як довго буде така погода?
> yak DOV-ho BOO-deh tah-KAH po-HO-dah

How are the road conditions between here and the (village) (farm)?
> Який стан дороги звідси до (села) (ферми)?
> ya-KIHЎ stahn do-RO-hih ZVEED-sih do (seh-LAH)
> (FEHR-mih)

Weather Words

Today is	Сьогодні ...	s'o-HOD-nee
bright and sunny	сонячно	SON-yach-no
clear	ясно	YAS-no

hot and humid	гарячо і вологого	hah-RYA-cho ee vo-LO-ho
warm	тепло	TEHP-lo
cool and cloudy	холодно і хмарно	KHO-lod-no ee KHMAHR-no
foggy	туманно	too-MAHN-no
frosty	морозно	mo-ROZ-no
windy	вітряно	VEET-rya-no
It's raining.	Іде дощ.	ee-DEH doshch
It's snowing.	Іде сніг.	ee-DEH sneeh
cloud	хмара	KHMAH-rah
fog	туман	too-MAHN
ice	лід	leed
lightning	блискавка	BLIHS-kahv-kah
moon	місяць	MEES-syats'
rain	дощ	doshch
sky	небо	NEH-bo
snow	сніг	sneeh
sun	сонце	SON-tseh
thunder	грім	hreem
thunderstorm	гроза	hro-ZAH
wind	вітер	VEE-tehr

CHAPTER 8. FAMILY AND FRIENDS

Ukrainian Proverb:
Яка хата, який тин, такий батько, такий син.
ya-KAH KHAH-tah, ya-KIHЎ tihn, tah-KIHЎ BAHT'-ko,
tah-KIHЎ sihn
As is the house, as is the fence, so is the father, so is the son.

Even with a high degree of urbanization, a high educational level, and a low birth rate, family life in Ukraine still follows a traditional, close-knit pattern. The extended family regards itself as a unit, with adults remaining close to their siblings as well as to their parents. They also form close relationships with in-laws. Family members enjoy each others' company, not only on holidays or important occasions, but even in their leisure hours.

The immediate family is small, averaging less than two children. While children are doted on, they are not spoiled. "Seen but not heard" is the rule for children when adults get together. When visitors come, if there is not enough room at the table, younger people will fade into the background so that guests and older family members can socialize.

Children receive a well-disciplined upbringing and are expected to contribute to the family by helping out. This sense of responsibility carries over to adulthood; Ukrainians feel obliged to help their parents however necessary, especially caring for them in their old age.

The attitude of sharing and responsibility serves Ukrainians well in view of the housing shortage which results in three or even four generations living together in the same apartment. Young people live with their parents longer than in Western countries, even years after marrying and having children. Ukrainian homes are characterized by a great deal of cooperation and delegation of responsibility. Someone is always available to care for children and aged grandparents, while another family member takes care of the necessary shopping.

Household responsibilities are largely delegated according to traditional, gender-related roles: women provide the child care and kitchen work and men assume the heavier and maintenance jobs. The difficulties of modern life require flexibility and a sharing of tasks. Husbands and wives may take turns shopping, for example. The blurring of traditional roles is especially more noticeable among the younger generation in which women are as well educated as men.

Women are independent and do not consider themselves secondary to men; however, men are strong and refuse to be subject to women. The relationships between the sexes can be very interesting.

THE FAMILY

family	родина	ro-DIH-nah
aunt	тітка	TEET-kah
brother	брат	braht
brother-in-law	зять	zyaht′
1. sister's husband	чоловік сестри	cho-lo-VEEK sehs-TRIH
2. wife's brother	брат жінки	braht Z͡HEEN-kih
3. husband's brother	брат чоловіка	braht cho-lo-VEE-kah

cousin
The term for first cousin comes from prefixing the word for brother or sister with двоюрідн(-ий)(-на); it's common however to simply call a first cousin "brother" or "sister." You might also hear an approximation of the English word "cousin" (*kyzen, m., kyzena, f.*).

male first cousin	двоюрідний брат	dvo-YU-reed-nihy̆ braht
female first cousin	двоюрідна сестра	dvo-YU-reed-nah SEHS-trah
daughter	донька	don′-KAH
daughter-in-law	невістка	neh-VEEST-kah
father	батько	BAHT′-ko
father-in-law		
(husband's)	тесть	tehst′
(wife's)	свекор	SVEH-kor
granddaughter	онучка	o-NOOCH-kah
grandfather	дід	deed
grandmother	бабця	BAHB-ts′ya
grandson	онук	o-NOOK
husband	чоловік	cho-lo-VEEK
mother	мати	MAH-tih
mother-in-law		
(husband's)	теща	TEH-shchah
(wife's)	свекруха	svehk-ROO-khah

nephew	племінник	pleh-MEEN-nihk
niece	племінниця	pleh-MEEN-nih-tsya
parents	батьки	baht'-KIH
sister	сестра	sehs-TRAH
sister-in-law	зовиця	zo-VIH-tsya
1. brother's wife	братова	BRAH-to-vah
2. wife's sister	сестра жінки	sehs-TRAH ZHEEN-kih
3. husband's sister	сестра чоловіка	sehs-TRAH cho-lo-VEE-kah
son	син	sihn
son-in-law	зять	zyat'
uncle	дядько	DYAD'-ko
wife	жінка	ZHEEN-kah

GETTING ACQUAINTED

Note: In phrases in which the pronoun you is given or implied, the familiar, singular form is first, followed by the polite or plural form.

Like other cultures which have both a familiar and a polite form of "you," in Ukraine the familiar "ти" (tih) form is becoming more common with the increasing informality of social relations. However, you should be aware that the "ви" (vih) form of address still characterizes the majority of relationships and interactions. "Ви" is the norm among business associates and casual acquaintances. Even in many families, particularly those with rural roots, children address their mother as "ви."

Hello, my name is ....
  Добрий день, мене звати ....
  DO-brihў den' meh-NEH ZVAH-tih

I'm so glad to meet you!
  Мені дуже приємно зустріти (тебе, *s.*) (вас, *pl.*).
  meh-NEE DOO-zheh prih-YEHM-no zoo-STREE-tih (teh-BEH) (vahs).

I'm here for ... days (weeks) (months).
  Я тут на ... днів (тижднів) (місяців).
  ya toot nah ... dneev (TIHZHD-neehv) (MEE- sya-tseev)

Where do you live?

Де (ти живеш, *s.*) (ви живете, *pl.*)?

deh (tih zhih-VEHSH) (vih zhih-VEH-teh)

I'm staying at hotel ...

Я (зупинився, *m.*)(зупинилась, *f.*) в готелі....

ya (zoo-pih-NIHV-sya) (zoo-pih-NIH-lahs') v ho-TEH-lee ...

Is your family well?

Чи все добре в (твоїй, *s.*) (вашій, *pl.*) сім'ї?

chih vseh DOB-reh v (TVO-yeeў) (VAH-sheeў) seem'YEE

We have all been well.

У нас все добре.

oo nahs vseh DO-breh

My mother (my father) is well.

Моя мати (мій батько) почуває себе добре.

mo-YA MAH-tih (meeў BAHT'ko) po-choo-VAH-yeh seh-BEH DOB-reh.

My mother (my father) has not been well.

Моя мати (мій батько) не є дуже добре.

mo-YAH MAH-tih (meeў BAHT'ko) neh yeh DOO-zheh DO-breh

My parents are feeling their age.

Мої батьки відчувають вже вік.

mo-YEE baht'KIH veed-choo-VAH-yut' vzheh veek

I'm married.

Я (одружений, *m.*)(одружена, *f.*).

ya (od-ROO-zheh-nihў) (od-ROO-zheh-nah)

I'm single.

Я не (одружений, *m.*)(одружена, *f.*).

ya neh (od-roo-ZHEH-nihў) (od-roo-ZHEH-nah)

Are you married? (familiar, singular form of you)

Чи ти (одружений, *m.*)(одружена, *f.*)?

chih tih (od-ROO-zheh-nihў) (od-ROO-zheh-nah)

Are you married? (polite or plural form of you)

Чи ви одружені?

chih vih od-ROO-zheh-nee

I'm (he's) divorced. [for men]
Я (він) розведений.
ya (veen) roz-VEH-deh-nihў

I'm (she's) divorced. [for women]
Я (вона) розведена.
ya (vo-NAH) roz-VEH-deh-nah

Have you any children?
Чи (ти маєш, *s.*) (ви маєте, *pl.*) дітей?
chih (tih MAH-yehsh) (vih MAH-yeh-teh) dee-TEHЎ

How old are your children?
Скільки років (твоїм, *s.*) (вашим, *pl.*) дітям?
SKEEL'-kih RO-keev (TVO-yeem) (VAH-shihm) DEE-tyam

I have ...	Я маю ...	ya MAH-yu
a son (two sons)	сина (два сина)	SIH-nah (dvah SIH-nah)
a daughter	доньку	DON'-koo
two daughters	дві доньки	dvee DON'-kih
two children	двоє дітей	DVO-ych dee-TEHЎ
three children	троє дітей	TRO-yeh dee-TEHЎ
I'm (she's) pregnant.	Я (вона) вагітна.	ya (vo-NAH) vah-HEET-nah

AT HOME, IN THE APARTMENT

At home	Вдома	VDO-mah
In the apartment	На квартирі	nah kvahr-TIH-ree

Ukraine is almost 70 percent urbanized, and in cities and towns virtually all families live in apartments. Older apartments are usually more substantial and have larger rooms with higher ceilings than the newer apartments. Although some of the new apartment buildings may look drab or shabby on the outside, individual apartments are clean, tidy, and well-kept. There is no air conditioning, but homes are rarely uncomfortable because of the solid construction and temperate climate. Private ownership of apartments is increasing; in addition about ten percent of city apartment dwellers might own a very simple home or *dacha* (дача, DAH-chah) in the country where they go for rest and recreation.

In the countryside, Ukrainian homes are noted for their tidy, well-kept
and attractive appearance. They are often colorfully painted and accented
with patches of flowers. Because the houses may lack indoor plumbing,
the property might include a well, a small pool for rinsing clothes, and
an outhouse. Rural homes might also include a number of outbuildings
such as a woodshed, a greenhouse, and a summer kitchen. Heating is by
means of ceramic wood-burning stoves, which usually provide adequate
heat in the winter.

This is an attractive (home) (apartment).
    Це (чудовий дім) (чудова квартира).
    tseh (choo-DO-vihỹ deem) (choo-DO-vah kvahr-TIH-rah).

How long have you lived here?
    Як довго ви живете тут?
    yak DOV-ho vih zhih-VEH-teh toot

Do you mind if I ...?   Чи можна мені ...?
                           chih MOZH-nah meh-NEE

take a shower	прийняти душ	prihỹ-NYA-tih doosh
take a bath	прийняти ванну	prihỹ-NYA-tih VAHN-noo
turn on the radio	включити радіо	vklyu-CHIH-tih RAH-dee-o
watch TV	подивитись телевізор	po-dih-VIH-tihs' teh-leh-VEE-zor
open the window	відкрити вікно	veed-KRIH-tih veek-NO
close the window	закрити вікно	zah-KRIH-tih veek-NO

I'd like to take a short nap.
    Я би (хотів, *m.*) (хотіла, *f.*) подрімати трошки.
    yah bih (kho-TEEV) (kho-TEE-lah) pod-rih-MAH-tih
    TROSH-kih

When Ukrainians want to smoke at home, they usually go out for a walk
or step outside on the balcony deck. In some homes, smoking is
permitted in the kitchen only. If you must smoke, it's best to first ask:

Where may I smoke?
    Де я можу покурити?
    deh ya MO-zhoo po-koo-RIH-tih

Rooms in the home. Compact living conditions — by our standards —
result in rooms that are multi-purpose. The dining room is often

someone's bedroom and may also serve as the library or study. In Ukrainian homes, bathroom facilities are usually separated into two different rooms, the toilet in one and the bathtub in another.

Where's the toilet (bath), please?
    Перепрошую, де знаходиться туалет (ванна)?
    peh-reh-PRO-shoo-yu deh znah-KHO-diht'-sya too-ah-LEHT (VAHN-nah)

soap	мило	MIH-lo
toilet paper	туалетний папір	too-ah-LEHT-nihy̆ pah-PEER
towel	рушник	roosh-NIHK
water	вода	vo-DAH

How does the shower work?
    Як працює душ?
    yak prah-TSYU-yeh doosh

I'd like to wash out a few things.
    Мені треба випрати декілька речей.
    meh-NEE TREH-bah VIH-prah-tih DEH-keel'-kah reh-CHEHY̆

Bedroom	спальня	SPAHL--nya
bed	ліжко	LEEZ͡H-ko
blanket	ковдра	KOVD-rah
pillow	подушка	po-DOOSH-kah
sheet	простирало	pros-tih-RAH-lo
wardrobe	шафа для одягу	SHAH-fah dlya OD-ya-hoo

Good night. [Use this phrase only immediately before retiring.]
    Надобраніч.
    nah-do-BRAH-neech

Good morning.	Добрий ранок.	DO-brihy̆ RAH-nok

I slept very well.	Я (спав, *m.*) (спала, *f.*) дуже добре.	
	ya (spahv) (SPAH-lah) DOO-z͡heh DO-breh	

The bed is very comfortable.
    Ліжко дуже зручне.
    LEEZ͡H-ko DOO-z͡heh ZROOCH-neh

| Dining Room | столова | sto-LO-vah |

At meals in Ukrainian homes, many different dishes are placed on the table and the diners help themselves to what they want. Don't expect your hostess to pass the dishes to you.

That tasted delicious. Це було дуже смачно.
tseh BOO-lo DOO-zheh SMAHCH-no

Won't you give me the recipe for this dish?
Чи ви би не могли дати мені рецепт цієї страви?
chih vih bih neh moh-LIH DAH-tih meh-NEE reh-TSEHPT tsee-YEH-yee STRAH-vih

Living Room	жила кімната	zhin-LAH keem-NAH-tah
armchair	крісло	KREES-lo
bookcase	книжкова шафа	knihzh-KO-vah
		SHAH-fah
sofa	софа, диван	so-FAH, dih-VAHN
TV set	телевізор	teh-leh-VEE-zor

How does the television work?
Як працює телевізор?
yak prah-TSYU-yeh teh-leh-VEE-zor

Kitchen	кухня	KOOKH-nya
cold tap	холодний кран	kho-LOD-nihў krahn
hot tap	гарячий кран	hahr-YA-chihў krahn
garbage can	смітник	smeet-NIHK
kitchen sink	раковина	RAH-ko-vih-nah
stove	плита	plih-TAH
refrigerator	холодильник	kho-lod-DIHL'-nihk
washing machine	пральна машина	PRAHL'-nah
		mah-SHIH-nah

Gifting. It's customary to give your hostess a small gift, especially after an overnight stay. Gifting can be an art in Ukraine. If you're a guest for several days or more, smaller gifts given periodically are more gracious and pleasing than a single larger one at the end of your visit.

Thank you for your hospitality.
Дякую за (твою, *s.*) (вашу, *pl.*) гостинність.
DYA-koo-yu zah (TVO-yu) (VAH-shoo) hos-TIHN-neest'

Please accept this gift.
Прошу взяти цей подарунок.
PRO-shoo VZYA-tih tsehў po-dah-ROO-nok

INVITATIONS AND GOING OUT

Ukrainians are extremely hospitable and generous to guests and will not only offer visitors help with travel arrangements, but may want to host you in their home or out on the town where they may insist on picking up the check. Although casual clothes may be worn in the home, when Ukrainian women go out for an evening, they like to dress up.

Give me your address and telephone number.
(Дай, *s.*) (дайте, *pl.*) мені (твою, *s.*) (вашу, *pl.*) адресу і телефон.
(dahў) (DAHЎ-teh) meh-NEE (TVO-yu) (VA-shoo)
AHD-rehs-oo ee teh-leh-FON

Drop in to see (me) (us).
заходте до (мене) (нас).
zah-KHOD-teh do (MEH-neh) (nahs)

Do you want to go out with (me) (us) tonight?
Чи (ти хочеш, *s.*) (ви хочете, *pl.*) піти (зі мною) (з нами) сьогодні ввечері?
chih (tih KHO-chehsh) (vih KHO-cheh-teh) pee-TIH (zee MNO-yu) (z NAH-mih) s'o-HOD-nee VVEH-cheh-ree

With great pleasure.   О, з радістю!   o, z RAH-dees-tyu

I'm sorry, I have other plans.
Д'якую, але я маю інші плани.
D'YA-koo-yu ah-LEH ya MAH-yu EEN-shee PLAH-nih

Can we do it another time?
Чи ми можемо зробити це другим разом?
chih mih MO-zheh-mo zro-BIH-tih tseh DROO-hihm RAH-zom

Where shall we meet?
Де нам зустрітись?
deh nahm zoo-STREE-tihs'

When shall we meet?   Коли нам зустрітись?
ko-LIH nahm zoo-STREE-tihs'

I'll pick you up.
Я зайду за (тобою, *s.*) (ваму, *pl.*). [on foot]
ya zahў-DOO zah (to-BO-yu) (VAH-mih)
Я заїду за (тобою, *s.*) (ваму, *pl.*). [by vehicle]
ya zah-YEE-doo zah (to-BO-yu) (VAH-mih)

See you later.
Побачимося пізніше.
po-BAH-chih-mo-s'ya peez-NEE-sheh

Please, let me pay for this.
Я заплачу за це.
ya zah-plah-CHOO zah tseh

May I take you home?
Чи можу я провести (тебе, *s.*) (вас, *pl.*) додому?
chih MO-zhoo ya pro-VEHS-tih (teh-BEH) (vahs) do-DO-moo

I had a wonderful time.
Було дуже приемо.
BOO-lo DOO-zheh prih-YEHM-no.

When can I see you again?
Коли я можу побачити (тебе, *s.*) (вас, *pl.*) знову?
ko-LIH ya MO-zhoo po-BAH-chih-tih (teh-BEH) (vahs)
ZNO-voo

For a growing friendship, you might want to say:

I like you very much.
Ви мені дуже подобаєтесь.
vih meh-NEE DOO-zheh po-DO-bah-yeh-tehs'

Literally, this phrase means "You appeal to me." Don't use it in a casual
manner, but save it for a rather personal situation in which increasing
intimacy is the goal. If the sentiment is reciprocated, you will need to
switch from "ви" to "ти" in future conversations. And occasionally, no
phrase is more useful than:

I love you.   Я люблю (тебе, *s.*) (вас, *pl.*).
                       ya lyu-BLYU (TEH-beh) (vahs).

The meaning and occasion for using the phrase "I love you" are exactly
the same as they are in English. It's used primarily for lovers and family
members. The familiar form of you is usually appropriate when saying
"I love you," but a child might use the polite form when speaking to an
adult.

CHAPTER 9. AT THE HOTEL

Ukrainian Proverb:

Добре їсти, гарно спати, Бог здоров'я мусить дати.
DOB-reh YEES-tih HAHR-no SPAH-tih, boh zdo-ROV'-ya
MOO-siht' DAH-tih
Eat well, sleep well, God has to give health.

In Ukraine, a hotel (готель) is more than a place to spend the night. It's a travel agency, a bank, a restaurant, a bar, a beauty parlor, and a ticket window. Traditionally run by Inturyst for the convenience of foreign tourists, hotels theoretically offer all the services a traveler might desire. Now accustomed to the influx of businesspersons and other well-heeled travelers, hotels no longer consider tour groups special, and the changed attitude shows up most in the dining experience.

Through joint ventures, a few luxury hotels have opened up in major Ukrainian cities and tourist destinations. A night's lodging may be no more than an Inturyst hotel — which in Kyiv is now well over $100 per night — but the ambience, service, and meals are more in line with that in top European or American hotels.

Availability of rooms varies with the season and location. In Kyiv, it's easier to get a hotel room in the winter, while in smaller towns that are off the beaten track, hotel rooms are almost always available, even without advance reservations.

If you're traveling as an individual and want to get into one of the better hotels, consult a travel agency that specializes in Ukrainian travel. Unless you have an invitation from a Ukrainian business colleague or relative, you'll need to have a hotel reservation preconfirmed and prepaid in order to get a visa. Hotels generally want payment in hard currency only, but the larger tourist hotels accept credit cards, and those in the out-of-the-way places, coupons.

A word of caution about large tourist hotels. The flow of hard currency in them attracts muggers and prostitutes. Try to look as inconspicuous as possible to avoid security problems. Leave expensive jewelry at home. It's risky to leave your valuables in your room, and safety deposit boxes are not usually available or are unsafe.

CHECKING IN

Upon checking in, you'll be asked to turn over your passport to the desk clerk who will return it in a day or two. You'll be issued a "hotel card" which is your identification for entry into the hotel, for picking up your keys, and for being served breakfast. Be sure to ask the desk for the phone number of your room; there may be no hotel switchboard so that your room phone is on a direct city line. When you go out, leave your keys either at the front desk or with the floor monitor.

My name is	мене звати	meh-NEH ZVAH-tih
I made a reservation	Я (замовляв, *m.*) (замовляла, *f.*) номер	ya (zah-mov-LYAV) (zah-mov-LYA-lah) NO-mehr
two days ago	два дні назад	dvah dnee nah-ZAHD
a week ago	тиждень назад	TIHZH-dehn′ nah-ZAHD
a month ago	місяць назад	MEE-tsyats′ nah-ZAHD
two months ago	два місяця назад	dvah MEE-sya-tsya nah-ZAHD
We have reserved two rooms.	Ми замовляли дві кімнати.	mih zah-mo-BLYA-lih dvee keem-NAH-tih
Here's the confirmation.	Ось підтвердження.	os′ peed-TVEHRD-zhehn-nya
"Fill out this form."	Заповніть цю форму.	zah-POV-neet′ tsyu FOR-moo
"Your passport, please."	Прошу, ваш паспорт.	PRO-shoo vash PAHS-port
"For how long do you need a room?"	На скільки вам треба номер?	nah SKEEL′-kih vahm TREH-bah NO-mehr?
We'll be here	Ми пробудемо	mih pro-BOO-deh-mo
one night	одну ніч	od-NOO neech
two days	два дні	dvah dnee
one week	один тиждень	o-DIHN TIHZH-dehn′
half a month	пів місяця	peev MEE-sya-tsya
Is the room ready?	Чи номер готовий?	chih NO-mehr ho-TO-vihy̆

In case you haven't got a reservation, these sentences may come in handy:

Do you have a room available?
Чи ви маєте вілъний номер?
chih vih MAH-yeh-teh VEEL'-nihÿ NO-mehr

I'd like a single room.
Мені треба номер на одного.
meh-NEE TREH-bah NO-nehr nah od-NO-ho

We'd like a double room ...
Нам треба номер на двох
nahm TREH-bah NO-mehr nah dvokh

with a bath	з ванною	z VHN-no-yu
with a shower	з душем	z DOO-shehm
with a balcony	з балконом	z bahl-KO-nom
facing the street	з вікнами на вулицю	
	z VEEK-nah-mih nah VOO-lih-tsyu	
facing the back	з вікнами на задній двір	
	z VEEK-nah-mih nah ZAHD-neeÿ dveer	

I want a quiet room.
Я хочу тихий номер.
ya KHO-choo TIH-khihÿ NO-mehr

How much is the room ...?
Скільки коштує номер ...?
SKEEL'-kih kosh-TOO-yeh NO-mehr

per night	за ніч	zah neech
per week	за тиждень	zah TIHẐH-dehn'
with breakfast	зі сніданком	zee snee-DAHN-kom
with full board	із повним харчуванням	
	eez POV-nihm khahr-choo-VAHN-nyam	

This is too expensive.
Це задорого.
tseh zah-DO-ro-ho

Do you have something less expensive?
Чи ви маєте щось дешевше?
chih vih MAH-yeh-teh shchos' deh-SHEHV-sheh

Does the room have ...?
   Чи є в номері ...?
   chih yeh v NO-meh-ree

a private bathroom	туалет	too-ah-LEHT
air conditioning	кондиціонер	kon-dih-tsee-o-NEHR
heat	отоплення	o-TOP-lehn-nya
radio	радіо	RAH-dee-o
a TV set	телевізор	teh-leh-VEE-zor

Can you set up an extra bed for a child?
   Чи ви можете поставити додаткове ліжко для дитини?
   chih vih MO-zheh-teh pos-TAH-vih-tih do-daht-KO-veh
   LEEZH-ko dlya DIH-tih-nih

Do you have special rates for children?
   Чи ви маєте знижку на дітей?
   chih vih MAH-yeh-teh ZNIHZH-koo nah dee-TEHЎ

May I see a room?
   Чи можна мені подивитись номер?
   chih MOZH-nah meh-NEE po-dih-VIH-tihs' NO-mehr

I'll take this room.
   Я візьму цей номер.
   ya veez'-MOO tsehў NO-mehr

I (don't) like the room.
   Мені (не) подобається номер.
   meh-NEE (neh) po-DO-bah-yeht'-sya NO-mehr

Do you have something else?
   Чи ви маєте інший номер?
   chih vih MAH-yeh-teh EEN-shihў NO-mehr

What's the phone number in my room?
   Який телефон в моєму номері?
   ya-KIHЎ teh-leh-FON v mo-YEH-moo NO-meh-ree

Where can I park my car?
   Де я можу поставити машину?
   deh ya MO-zhoo pos-TAH-vih-tih mah-SHIH-noo

Do you have a safe?
   Чи ви маєти сейф?
   chih vih mah-YEH-teh sehўf

Where can I leave my valuables?
Де я можу залишити мої цінності?
deh ya MO-zhoo zah-LIH-shih-tih mo-YEE TSEEN-nos-tee

May I have ...?
Чи можу я мати в номер ...?
chih MO-zhoo ya mah-tih v NO-mehr

another blanket	другу ковдру	DROO-hoo KOV-droo
another glass	другу склянку	DROO-hoo SKLYAN-koo
another key	другий ключ	DROO-hihў klyuch
a few hangers	декілька вішаків	DEH-keel'-kah VEE-shah-keev
an iron	залізко для прасування	zah-LIZ-ko dlya prah-SOO-vahn-nya
a sewing kit	набір для зашивання	nah-BEER dlya zah-shih-VAHN-nya
another towel	другий рушник	DROO-hihў roosh-NIHK
a TV	телевізор	teh-leh-VEE-sor

Is there ...
in the hotel?   Чи є в готелі ..?   chih yeh v ho-TEH-lee

an elevator	ліфт	leeft
laundry service	пральня	PRAHL'-nya
a restaurant	ресторан	rehs-to-RAHN
a bar	бар	bahr
a post office	пошта	POSH-tah
a service bureau	сервісне бюро	SEHR-vees-neh byu-RO
a snack bar	буфет	boo-FEHT
room service	їжа в номері	YEE-zhah v NO-meh-ree

Can I change money in the hotel?
Чи я можу обміняти валюту в готелі?
chih ya MO-zhoo ob-mee-NYA-tih vah-LYU-too v ho-TEH-lee

Where is the currency exchange office?
Де можна обміняти валюту?
deh MOZH-nah ob-mee-NYA-tih vah-LYU-too

May I have (breakfast) (dinner) in my room?
Чи я можу замовити (сніданок) (обід) у мій номер?
chih ya MO-zhoo zah-MO-vih-tih (snee-DAH-nok) (o-BEED) oo meeў NO-mehr

May I eat in the restaurant without a reservation?
Чи можу я поїсти в ресторані без попереднього замовлення?
chih MO-zhoo ya po-YEES-tih v rehs-to-RAH-nee behz
po-peh-REHD-n'o-ho zah-MOV-lehn-nya

Please wake me at ... o'clock.
Прошу розбудити мене в ... годині.
PRO-shoo roz-boo-DIH-tih meh-NEH v ... ho-DIH-nee

PROBLEMS AND COMPLAINTS

Problems and Complaints	Проблеми та Скарги	pro-BLEH-mih tah SKAHR-hih

I don't have my hotel card.
Я не маю з собою перепустки.
ya neh MAH-yu z so-BO-yu peh-reh-POOST-kih

My room isn't clean.
Мій номер не прибранний.
meeў NO-mehr neh PRIHB-rahn-nihў

There is no ... in the room.
В номері нема ....
v NO-meh-ree neh-MAH

blanket	ковдри	KOVD-rih
cold water	холодної води	kho-LOD-no-yee vo-DIH
drinking glass	склянки	SKLYAN-kih
hot water	гарячої води	hah-RYA-cho-yee vo-DIH
light	світла	SVEET-lah
pillows	подушок	po-DOO-shok
soap	мила	MIH-lah
toilet paper	туалетного паперу	too-ah-LEHT-no-ho pah-PEH-roo

The ... in my room isn't working.
В моєму номері не працює ....
v mo-YEH-moo NO-meh-ree neh prah-TSYU-yeh

air conditioning	кондиціонер	kon-dih-tsee-o-NEHR
electrical outlet	електрична розетка	eh-lehk-TRIHCH-nah ro-ZEHT-kah
fan	вентилятор	vehn-tih-LYA-tor

heat	отоплення	o-TOP-lehn-nya
light	світло	SVEET-lo
lock	замок	zah-MOK
shower	душ	doosh
toilet	туалет	too-ah-LEHT
TV	телевізор	teh-leh-VEE-zor
radio	радіо	RAH-dee-o

The washbasin is clogged.
Раковина забита.
RAH-ko-vih-nah zah-BIH-tah

The bathtub won't drain.
Вода з ванни не випускається.
vo-DAH z BAHN-nih neh vih-poo-SKAH-yeht'-sya

The curtains are stuck.
Завіса не затуляються.
ZAH-vee-sah neh zah-too-LYA-yut'-sya

The door (window) won't (open) (close).
Двері (вікно) не (відчиняється) (зачиняється).
DVEH-ree (veek-NO) neh (veed-chih-NYA-yeht'-sya)
(zah-chih-NYA-yeht'-sya)

Can you get it repaired?
Чи ви можете це відремонтувати?
chih vih MO-zheh-teh tseh veed-reh-MON-too-VAH-tih

CHECKING OUT

Be sure to leave a small tip for the maid and pick up your passport and
any valuables you may have left in the safe.

When is check-out time?
Коли час розрахунку?
ko-LIH chas roz-rah-KHOON-koo

I'm leaving tomorrow ....
Я від'їзжаю завтра ....
ya veed'-yeez-ZHAH-yu ZAHVT-rah

morning	вранці	VRAHN-tsee
noon	в обід	v o-BEED
afternoon	після обіду	PEES-lya o-BEE-doo

I need an itemized bill.
Мені треба подробний рахунок.
MEH-nee TREH-bah pod-ROB-nihў rah-KHOO-nok

Do you charge for domestic phone calls?
Чи треба платити додатково за місцеві телефонні розмови?
chih TREH-bah plah-TIH-tih do-daht-KO-vo zah mees-TSEH-vee
teh-leh-FON-nee roz-MO-vih

What additional charges are included in the bill?
Які додаткові плати включені в рахунок?
ya-KEE do-daht-KO-vee PLAH-tih BKLYU-cheh-nee v
rah-KHOO-nok

Do you accept this credit card?
Чи ви приймаєте цю кредитну карту? [showing card]
chih vih prihў-MAH-yeh-teh tsyu kreh-DIHT-noo KAHR-too

Can I pay with traveler's checks?
Чи я можу заплатити дорожніми чеками?
chih ya MO-zhoo zah-plah-TIH-tih do-ROZH-nee-mih
CHEH-kah-mih

Do you accept personal checks?
Чи ви приймаєте персональні чеки?
chih vih prihў-MAH-yeh-teh pehr-son-NAHL'-nee CHEH-kih

I'd like my passport back, please.
Поверніть мій паспорт, будь ласка.
po-vehr-NEET' meeў PAHS-port bood' LAHS-kah

I think you made a mistake.
Я думаю, що ви зробили помилку.
ya DOO-mah-yu shcho vih zro-BIH-lih-lih po-MIHL-koo

Can you order a taxi for (me) (us)?
Чи ви можете замовити таксі для (мене) (нас)?
chih vih MO-zheh-teh zah-MO-vih-tih tahk-SEE dlya
(MEH-neh) (nahs)

Would you have that luggage taken to the taxi?
Чи ви можете попросити принести цей багаж до таксі?
chih vih MO-zheh-teh po-pro-SIH-tih prih-NEHS-tih tsehў
bah-HAHZH do tahk-SEE

Please forward my mail to this address.
Прошу перешліть мою пошту на цю адресу.
PRO-shoo peh-rehsh-LEET' mo-YU POSH-too nah tsyu
ahd-REH-soo

Thank you, everything was fine.
Дякую, все було добре.
DYA-koo-yu vseh BOO-lo DOB-reh

THE SERVICE BUREAU

Service Bureau   Сервісне Бюро   SEHR-vees-neh byu-RO

The hotel service bureau is the place to go for information and help with
your various traveler's needs. Check there first for theater tickets, special
excursions, and help with transportation. Keep in mind that a service
bureau accepts only hard currency for the services it provides and adds
a surcharge, so you will always pay top price for what it provides.
Efficiency and friendliness varies from one hotel to another.

Is this the service bureau?
Чи це сервісне бюро?
chih tseh SEHR-vees-neh byu-RO

Do you have a map of the city?
Чи ви маєте карту міста?
chih vih MAH-yeh-teh KAHR-too MEES-tah

May I have it?
Чи можна взяти її?
chih MOZH-nah VZYA-tih yee-YEE

What do you suggest I visit?
Що ви порадити мені подивитись?
shcho vih po-RAH-dih-tih meh-NEE po-dih-VIH-tihs'

How can I get to ...?
Як можна добратись до ...?
yak MOZH-nah do-BRAH-tihs' do

the downtown area	центру	TSEHNT-roo
the opera theater	оперного театру	O-peh-no-ho teh-AHT-roo
the nearest park	найближчого	nahў-BLIHZH-cho-ho
	парку	PAHR-koo

the river	річки	REECH-kih
... Church	церкви...	TSEHRK-vih
... Street	вулиці ...	VOO-lih-tsee
... Square	площі ...	PLOSH-chee

| Can you ...? | Чи ви можете...? | chih vih MO-z͡heh-teh |

recommend a good restaurant
порадити добрий ресторан
po-RAH-dih-tih DOB-rihy̆ rehs-to-RAHN

order theater tickets for me
замовити квитки в театр для мене
zah-MO-vih-tih kviht-KIH v teh-AHTR dlya MEH-neh

find me a taxi
знайти для мене таксі
znahy̆-TIH dlya MEH-neh tahk-SEE

arrange a city tour for me
влаштувати для мене екскурсію по місту
vlahsh-too-VAH-tih dlya MEH-neh ehks-KOOR-see-yu po MEES-too

I'd like to hire a guide-translator.
    Я хочу найняти гіда-перекладача.
    ya KHO-choo nahy̆-NYA-tih *GEE-dah peh-reh-klan-dah-CHA

Where can I rent a car?
    Де можна найняти машину?
    deh MOZ͡H-nah nahy̆-NYA-tih mah-SHIH-noo

I need a car with a (driver) (guide) for (a day) (several days).
    Мені потрібна машина з (водієм) (гідом) на (один день) (декілька днів).
    meh-NEE po-TREEB-nah MAH-shih-nah z (vo-dee-YEHM) (*GEE-dom) nah (o-DIHN dehn') (DEH-keel'-kah dneev)

* GEE as in *geek*, not as in *gee-whiz*

THE TIP

Tip	Чаєві	chah-yeh-VEE

The term for "tip" in Ukrainian comes from the word for tea, perhaps because when the custom originated a gratuity was supposed to buy the recipient no more than a cup of tea. Tipping is more optional in Ukraine than in North America. A traveler need not feel obligated to reward service, particularly if it's less than satisfactory. Under the soviet system, the practice of giving a monetary tip was not encouraged, and travelers would reward Inturyst employees with small gifts. Lipstick or a pair of pantyhose are still a nice parting gift for the maid. Giving a small monetary tip to a maid, porter, taxi driver, guide, and interpreter for a job well done is entirely appropriate, and more and more, is expected.

Where's the ...?	Де знаходиться ...?	deh znah-KHO-diht'-sya
hall/floor monitor	коридорний	ko-rih-DOR-nihy̆
doorman, porter	портьєр	por-T'YEHR
maid	горнічна	HOR-neech-nah
bellboy	носильник	no-SIHL'-nihk
manager	менеджер	MEH-nehd-zhehr
receptionist	адміністратор	ahd-mee-nees-TRAH-tor
waitperson	офіціант	o-fee-tsee-AHNT

Thank you. Keep that for yourself.
Дякую, лишіть це собі.
DYA-koo-yu lih-SHEET' tseh so-BEE

LAUNDRY AND CLEANING

Laundry and Cleaning	Прання та Чистка	prahn-NYA tah CHIHST-kah

Usually the floor lady will do the laundry for you.

These clothes need to be ...
Ці речі потрібно ....
tsee REH-chee po-TREEB-no

dry-cleaned	почистити в хімчистці	po-CHIHS-tih-tih v kheem-CHIHST-tsee
ironed	попрасувати	po-prah-soo-VAH-tih
washed	випрати	VIHP-rah-tih

Can you get this stain out?
Чи ви можете вибавити цю пляму?
chih vih MO-zheh-teh VIH-bah-vih-tih tsyu PLYA-too

Can you mend this rip?
Чи ви можете зашите цю дірку?
chih vih MO-zheh-teh zah-SHIH-tih tsyu DIHR-koo

I need it ....   Мені треба це....   meh-NEE TREH-bah tse

today	сьогодні	s'o-HOD-nee
tonight	сьогодні ввечері	s'o-HOD-nee VVEH-cheh-ree
tomorrow morning	завтра вранці	ZAHV-trah VRAHN-tsee

Is my laundry ready? Чи мої речі готові?
chih mo-YEE REH-chee ho-TO-vee

This isn't mine.   Ця річ не моя.   tsya reech neh mo-YA

I'm missing   Тут не вистарчає деяких речей.
something.   toot neh vihs-tahr-CHAH-yeh DEH-ya-kihkh reh-CHEHY

Nice job.   Гарна робота.   HAHR-nah ro-BO-tah

How much do I owe you?
Скільки я повинен заплатити?
SKEEL'-kih ya po-VIH-nehn zah-plah-TIH-tih

HAIRDRESSER - BARBER

Hairdresser-barber   Перукар   peh-roo-KAHR

Where do I find the nearest (hairdresser) (barber)?
Де знаходиться найближча (жіноча перукарня) (чоловіча перукарня)?
deh znah-KHO-diht'-sya nahy-BLIHZH-chah (zhee-NO-chah peh-roo-KAHR-nya) (cho-lo-VEE-chah peh-roo-KAHR-nya)

I'd like to make an appointment for ...
Я хочу записатись на ....
ya KHO-choo zah-pih-SAH-tis' nah

| I'd like a haircut. | Я хочу підстригтись. |
| | ya KHO-choo peed-STRIHH-tihs' |

| I want it short. | Я хочу коротко. ya KHO-choo KO-rot-ko |

| Not very short, please. | Прошу не дуже коротко. |
| | pro-SHOO neh DOO-zheh KO-rot-ko |

Can you leave it long?	Чи ви можете лишите волосся довге?
	chih vih MO-zheh-teh lih-SHIH-tih
	vo-LOS-sya DOV-heh

| Just a trim, please. | Тільки підрівняти прошу. |
| | TEEL'-kih peed-reev-NYA-tih PRO-shoo |

| A little off .... | Зніміть трошки більше .... |
| | ZNEE-miht' TROSH-kih BEEL'-sheh |

the back	на потилиці	nah po-TIH-lih-tsee
the neck	на шиї	nah shih-YEE
the sides	по боках	po bo-KAHKH
the top	зверху	ZVEHR-khoo

| Would you trim ...? | Поправте будь ласка ...? |
| | po-PRAHV-teh bood' LAHS-kah |

my mustache	мої вуса	mo-YEE VOO-sah
my sideburns	мої бакенбарди	mo-YEE
		bah-kehn-BAHR-dih
my beard	мою бороду	mo-YU BO-ro-doo

| I want a shave. | Я хочу поголитись. |
| | ya KHO-choo po-ho-LIH-tihs' |

| I want a set. | Я хочу укладку. |
| | ya KHO-choo oo-KLAHD-koo |

| Shampoo and set please. | Помити і укласти, прошу. |
| | po-MIH-tih ee ook-LAHS-tih PRO-shoo |

| I don't want hair spray. | Я не хочу лаку. |
| | ya neh KHO-choo LAH-koo |

| I want a manicure. | Я хочу манікюр. |
| | ya KHO-choo mah-nee-KYUR |

BED-AND-BREAKFASTS AND HOMESTAYS

For a cozy and personal alternative to the hotels, two kinds of home lodging are available. In a bed and breakfast arrangement, a private family provides your lodging and breakfast and possibly dinner. During the day you go your own way. Many travel agencies that specialize in Ukraine can arrange this type of accommodation.

In a homestay arrangement, you stay with a private family for a week or more and that host family takes an active role in providing your touring and entertainment. You're expected to spend time with them. Homestays are usually sponsored by organizations devoted to fostering people-to-people contact with residents of the former Soviet Union.

When staying in a home, you'll be sharing a bath. Expect the rates to range from about $50 to $100 per day depending on the number of additional services offered. Basic service includes airport transfer and lodging with one or two meals. Other services your host family might include are guided sightseeing, providing tickets for cultural events, and arranging inter-city transportation. Agencies may be able to match you with families according to professional and personal interests or habits, such as smoking preference. Families usually speak English, but if you'd like to practice your Ukrainian, you can request a home in which only Ukrainian is spoken. It's customary to bring small gifts for the host families.

RENTALS

For a long term stay in one spot, renting a furnished apartment may be an option. An apartment will give more space and be cheaper than a hotel. However, it will require a certain amount of housework, shopping for food, and cooking.

Begin to look for a rental at least six months in advance of your trip. Points to consider are how far it is from your work or school, shopping, and public transportation. Find out what comes with the apartment. A phone is an absolute necessity and a lease might even include cleaning services.

Contact travel agencies that specialize in Ukrainian travel.

CHAPTER 10. COMMUNICATIONS

Ukrainian Proverb:
Моя хата скраю, нічого не знаю.
mo-YA KHA-tah SKRAH-yu, nee-CHO-ho neh ZNAH-yu
My house is on the edge, I don't know anything.

Modern technology has made the villager's lament about lack of communication seem quaint indeed. Thanks to UTEL, a joint venture of the Ukrainian Ministry of Telecommunications, AT&T, PTT Telekom of the Netherlands, and DBP Telekom of Germany, Ukraine's antiquated electro-mechanical telecommunications system is being replaced by a state-of-the-art digital system. Visitors to most oblasts of Ukraine can now call home by direct-dialing rather than by ordering a long-distance call from an operator and waiting hours for it to go through. Connections are very good.

TELEPHONING

Information. There are no phone books, but you can get local telephone numbers to private homes by dialing 09. You'll need to know the person's full name, including patronymic and the address. There is no long distance information service. Information kiosks prominently located throughout the larger cities or at the railroad station in the smaller cities can also provide you with telephone numbers and address of local businesses, cultural facilities, and public offices.

What is the phone number for ...?
Який номер телефону для ...?
ya-KIHУ no-MEHR teh-leh-FO-noo dlya ...

You gave me the wrong number.
Ви дали мені неправельний номер.
vih dah-LIH meh-NEE neh-PRAH-vehl'-nihỹ NO-mehr

Local Calls. The red and yellow phone booths on the street are for local calls. Local pay telephones are designed to make the connection before taking your coin. The cost of a local call used to be 15 kopecks, but became free because of the scarcity of coins in circulation. If you get quick short beeps, the line is busy.

Where is the nearest phone?
Де знаходиться найближчий телефон?
deh znah-KHO-diht′-sya naĥŷ-BLIHZ̃H-chihŷ teh-leh-FON

What coins must I drop into the phone?
Які монети мені треба опустити в телефон?
ya-KEE mo-NEH-tih meh-NEE TREH-bah o-poos-TIH-tih v
teh-leh-FON

Intercity Phones. To make a long-distance call to other cities in
Ukraine or to one of the newly-independent countries, use an inter-city
pay phone. In Ukraine these are commonly referred to by the Russian
word for intercity, міжгородній (meez̃h-ho-ROD-neeŷ) rather than the
Ukrainian word, міжміський (meezh-mees′-KIHY). At each inter-city
phone, there's a list of city codes. There should also be posted
instructions and a clerk nearby to help. These phones take tokens to
allow for a continual adjustment to inflation. Dial 017 to start your
intercity call. When you hear a dial tone, dial the city code and the local
telephone number. Telephone calls to towns without a city dialing code
should be made through an operator.

I need to call another city.
Мені треба подзвонити в інше місто.
meh-NEE TREH-bah pod-zvo-NIH-tih v EEN-sheh MEES-to

Where can I get telephone tokens?
Де я можу придбати жетони для телефону?
deh ya MO-zĥoo prihd-BAH-tih z̃heh-TO-nih dlya
teh-leh-FON-noo

Where is an inter-city phone?
Де знаходиться міжміський [міжгородній] телефон?
deh znah-KHO-diht′-sya meezh-mees′-KIHY
[meez̃h-ho-ROD-neeŷ] teh-leh-FON

How can I call to ...?
Як можна подзвонити до ...?
yak MOZ̃H-nah podz-vo-NIH-tih do

What time of day will a call to ... be the cheapest?
В який час дня тепефонні переговори з ... є найдешевші?
v ya-KIHŶ chahs dnya teh-leh-FON-nee peh-reh-ho-VOH-rih
z ... yeh naĥŷ-deh-SHEHV-shee

What's the cost of a minute call to ... ?
Скільки коштує хвилина розмови з ...?
SKEEL'-kih kosh-TOO-yeh khvih-LIH-nah roz- z

I want to talk ... minutes.
Я хочу говорити ... хвилин.
ya KHO-choo ho-vo-RIH-tih ... khvih-LIHN

Can you help me?
Чи ви можете мені допомогти?
chih vih MO-zheh-teh meh-NEE do-po-MOH-tih

Please help me use this phone.
Прошу допомогти мені подзвонити з цього телефону.
PRO-shoo do-po-moh-TIH meh-NEE pod-zvo-NIH-tih z ts'o-ho
teh-leh-FO-noo

International Calls. If you should be in an area without the direct-dial service, you can book your international call at the telephone office of the main post office or through your hotel communications center. To arrange your own call, contact the International Directory Service a day in advance and state the country and city you wish to call, the phone number, and the time when you wish to place your call. To get an English-speaking operator, dial 8-192.

Remember that all of Ukraine is on Kyiv Standard Time, which is seven hours ahead of New York and Toronto, and ten hours ahead of California. Calls to the U.S. cost approximately $2.50 USD per minute or possibly more if the hotel service bureau is involved. Collect calls are not permitted.

I need the international operator.
Мені потрібно міжнародного оператора.
meh-NEE po-TREEB-no meezh-nah-ROD-no-ho o-peh-RAH-to-rah

I need to call a foreign country.
Мені потрібно подзвонити закордон.
meh-NEE po-TREEB-no pod-zvo-NIH-tih zah-kor-DON

I want to order an international phone call to ... at ... o'clock.
Я хочу замовити міжнародну телефонну розмову з ... на ..
годину.
ya KHO-choo zah-MO-vih-tih meezh-nah-ROD-noo
teh-leh-FON-noo roz-MO-voo z ... nah ... ho-DIH-noo

How long must I wait?
Як довго мені треба чекати?
yak DOV-ho meh-NEE TREH-bah cheh-KAH-tih

Direct Dialing. To make an international call from your hotel, inquire at the reception desk. Hotels are sometimes reluctant to put them through because they've been cheated by guests who slip out without paying the phone bill. To direct dial an international call, dial 8, wait for a dial tone, dial 10 (the international service index), and then the country code, the area or city code, and the subscriber telephone number.

Phone Cards. In Kyiv you can charge your calls to your calling card number through your regular phone company, or buy a UTEL card which allows you to make long distance calls from a number of select phones in the city or at the airport.

I'd like to make an international call to ... now.
Мені треба подзвоннити закордон до ... тепер.
meh-NEE TREH-bah pod-zvon-NIH-tih zah-kor-DON do ... teh-PEHR

Can I dial to ... direct?
Чи можна набрати прямо до ... з автомату?
chih MOZ͡H-nah nahb-RAH-tih PRYAH-mo do ... z ahv-to-MAH-too

Can you dial this number for me?
Чи ви можете набрати цей номер для мене?
chih vih MO-z͡heh-teh nah-BRAH-tih tsehў NO-mehr dlya MEH-neh

Making a Call

May I use your phone?
Чи я можу подзвонити з вашого телефону?
chih ya MO-z͡hoo pod-zvo-NIH-tih z VAH-sho-ho teh-leh-FO-noo

Hello. Is this number ... ?
Ало. Чи це номер ...?
ah-LO chih tseh NO-mehr

I'd like extension ... please.
Прошу додатковий ...
PRO-shoo do-daht-KO-vihў

May I speak with ...   Чи можу я говорити з ...
                     chih MO-zhoo ya ho-vo-RIH-tih z

I'll call again later.   Я буду дзвонити пізніше.
                     ya BOO-doo dzvo-NIH-tih
                     peez-NEE-sheh

at ... o'clock.   в ... годині.
                     v ... ho-DIH-nee

Please ask (him) (her) to call me back.
Прошу попросити (його) (її) передзвонити мені.
PRO-shoo po-pro-SIH-tih (ўo-HO) (yee-YEE)
peh-rehd-zvo-NIH-tih meh-NEE

My number is ...   Мій номер є ...
                     meeў NO-mehr yeh

I don't understand Я не розумію вас.
  you.   ya neh ro-zoo-MEE-yu vahs

I don't understand Ukrainian.
Я не розумію по-українськи.
ya neh ro-zoo-MEE-yu po-oo-krah-YEEN-s'kih

Do you speak English?
Чи ви говорите по-англійськи?
chih vih ho-VO-rih-teh po-ahn-HLEEЎ-s'kih

I can't hear you.   Я не чую вас.
                     ya neh CHOO-yu vahs

Please talk louder. Прошу говорити голосніше.
                     PRO-shoo ho-vo-RIH-tih ho-los-NEE-sheh

Please speak more   Прошу говорите повільніше.
  slowly.   PRO-shoo ho-vo-RIH-tih po-veel'-NEE-sheh

Sorry, I must have the wrong number.
Пробачте, я (помилився, *m.*) (помилилась, *f.*) номером.
pro-BAHCH-teh ya (po-mih-LIHV-sya, *m.*) (po-mih-LIH-lahs', *f.*)
NO-meh-rom

I can't get through.	Я не можу додзвонитись.
	ya neh MO-zhoo dod-zvo-NIH-tihs'
We were interrupted.	Нас перервали.
	nahs peh-rehr-VAH-lih

TELEGRAMS

A telegram is a quicker way to send an international message than express mail and a lot cheaper than phoning. Most post offices and hotels can help you send a telegram within the country. To send one abroad, go to the window with the sign "Телеграми" in the main post office or the central telegraph office. Incoming telegrams, addressed to you at your hotel with your date of arrival, work very well.

In Kyiv, you can send a telegram on credit to all points in Ukraine and the newly-independent states simply by dialing 066 from a residential phone. This service is available 24 hours, seven days a week including holidays.

May I send a telegram from here?	Чи я можу відіслати телеграму звідси?
	chih ya MO-zhoo vee-dee-SLAH-tih teh-leh-HRA-moo ZVEED-sih
I want to send	Мені потрібно відіслати ....
	meh-NEE po-TREEB-no vee-dee-SLAH-tih
a domestic telegram	телеграму teh-leh-HRAH-moo
an international telegram	міжнародну телеграму
	meezh-nah-ROD-noo teh-leh-HRAH-moo
Do you have an international telegram form?	Чи ви маєте бланк міжнародної телеграми?
	chih vih MAH-yeh-teh blahnk meezh-nah-ROD-no-yee teh-leh-HRAH-mih
What is the cost per word...?	Яка ціна за слово ...?
	ya-KAH tsee-NAH zah SLO-vo

to Canada	до Канади	do kah-NAH-dih
to the United States	до Сполучених Штатів	
	do spo-LOO-cheh-nihkh SHTA-teev	
for a domestic	по країни	
telegram	po krah-YEE-nih	

TELEX (телекс), **FAX** (факс) **and E-MAIL** (електронна пошта)

Electronic communications technology is making telegramming obsolete except for contacting the smallest towns and villages. Telex is a common means of communication in Ukraine and many businesses use fax machine. To send an international telex or fax, go to the main post office or telegraphic office or check at your hotel. Some privately-run communications companies will telex or fax and may even provide e-mail services.

I need a fax machine. Мені треба факс машина.
    meh-NEE TREH-bah fahks mah-SHIH-nah

Do you have access to Internet or another e-mail system?
    Чи ви маєте вихід на Інтернет або на іншу систему?
    chih vih MAH-yeh-teh VIH-kheed nah EEN-tehr-neht AH-bo nah EEN-shoo sihs-TEH-moo
Note: It is common in Ukraine to use the English phrase "e-mail." Generally, you will be understood.

POSTAL SERVICES

Hours for post offices vary according to their size. The communications centers of large tourist hotels also provide postal services: they sell postcards, stamps, and envelopes, and can send express mail. At the hotel, however, you'll be charged in hard currency while at the post office you'll pay with Ukrainian money.

Express mail, the most reliable and expensive way of mailing, is available in larger post offices. You're allowed to ship internationally up to 10 kg. (22 lbs.) and 3 kg. (6.6 lbs.) of books by express mail. If you want to mail a package out of Ukraine, bring it to a post office unwrapped. It will be weighed, wrapped, and stamped for you.

When posting a note home, you may write the address as you usually do, using English, but be sure to write the name of the country of destination prominently at the top of the address. Postal employees can usually read English, but are in the habit of looking first to the top of the envelope for the country, since Ukrainians address envelopes in a reverse order from us. If writing to Ukraine or to one of the other countries of the NIS, write the country name and six-digits index number on the top line, the oblast on the second line, the city next, under that the street name and number and apartment number, and on the bottom line, the name of the recipient.

Mail originating in Ukraine is inconsistent. Most letters take no more than ten days to reach the U.S., others take a month or two, while a small number never arrive.

Mail boxes on the street are a dark blue color.

Where is the nearest mail box?
Де знаходиться найближча поштова скринька?
deh znah-KHO-diht'-sya nahў-BLIHZH-chah posh-TO-vah SKRIHN'-kah

Where's the nearest post office?
Де знаходиться найближча пошта?
deh znah-KHO-diht'-sya nahў-BLIHZH-chah POSH-tah

Will the post office be open now?
Чи пошта відкрита тепер?
chih POSH-tah veed-KRIH-tah teh-PEHR

What are the hours for the post office?
Коли працює пошта?
ko-LIH prah-TSYU-yeh POSH-tah

Can I buy here ...?   Чи можу я тут купити ...?
                          chih MO-zhoo yah toot koo-PIH-tih

an envelope	конверт	kon-VEHRT
stamps	марки	MAHR-kih
a post card	поштову картку	posh-TO-voo KAHRT-koo

I want to send	Я хочу відіслати	
	ya KHO-choo vee-dees-LAH-tih	
a letter	лист	lihst
a post card	поштову картку	posh-TO-voo KAHRT-koo
money to	гроші до	hro-SHEE do
a parcel	пакунок	pah-KOO-nok
a registered letter	рекомендований лист	
	reh-ko-mehn-DO-vah-nihỹ lihst	
a recorded delivery	лист з повідомленням про доставку	
	lihst z po-vee-DOM-lehn-nyam pro	
	dos-TAHV-koo	

I want to send this by express mail.
Я хочу відіслати це терміновою поштою.
ya KHO-choo vee-dee-SLAH-tih tseh tehr-mee-NO-vo-yu
POSH-to-yu

How long will it take to get there?
Як довго це буде іти?
yak DOV-ho tseh BOO-deh ee-TIH

How many stamps do I need to mail this?
Скільки марок треба тут наклеїти?
SKEEL'-kih MAH-rok TREH-bah toot nah-KLEH-yee-tih

Can you do it for me?
Чи ви можете це зробити для мене?
chih vih MO-zhch-teh tseh zro-BIH-tih dlya MEH-neh

Can you help me ...?
Чи ви можете допомогти мені ...?
chih vih MO-zheh-teh do-po-mo-HTIH meh-NEE

write this address	написати адресу	
	nah-pih-SAH-tih ahd-REH-soo	
wrap this	загорнути це	
	zah-hor-NOO-tih tseh	

Can you wrap it so it won't break?
Чи ви можете це загорнути так, щоб воно не розбилось?
chih vih MO-zheh-teh tseh zah-hor-NOO-tih tahk shchob
vo-NO neh roz-BIH-los'

How much do I owe you?
  Скільки я повинен заплатити?
  SKEEL'-kih ya po-VIH-nehn zah-plah-TIH-tih

I'd like a receipt.
  Мені потрібен чек.
  meh-NEE po-TREE-behn chehk

To claim mail forwarded to you at the post office, go to the general delivery counter. Look for a sign that says "for the asking:"

ДО ЗАПИТАННЯ

Where can I find the general delivery counter?
  Де знаходиться відділ до запитання?
  deh znah-KHO-diht'-sya VEED-deel do zah-PIH-tahn-nya

Here is my I. D.
  Ось моє посвідчення.
  os' MO-yeh pos-VEED-chehn-nya

CHAPTER 11. PUBLIC TRANSPORTATION

Ukrainian Proverb: В тісночі та не в обиді.
v tees-no-TEE tah neh v o-BIH-dee
There's no offense in crowding.

Public transportation is adequate, cheap, and reliable in Ukrainian cities. Generally, all cities and villages are served by bus, the larger cities have streetcars and trolleys as well, and the two largest, Kyiv and Kharkiv, have subway systems. Despite sardine-like conditions, a general attitude of good humor and friendliness pervades the public transportation in Ukraine. It's customary for riders to give up their seats to the elderly and infirm and pregnant women.

TAXIS

Taxis   Таксі   tahk-SEE

The phone number for taxi service is 058, but's easy to locate a taxi in Ukraine today; everyone who owns a car is a taxi driver. Simply point to the road with your finger. When a car stops, state your destination and ask:

How much?   Скільки?   SKEEL'kih

Once you're identified as a Westerner, the cost of the ride is likely to go up. Some seasoned travelers have found that engaging a cab works best if a Ukrainian contact, particularly a young woman, secures the ride and negotiates the fee while they wait behind the scenes. For a more conventional approach, you can get a taxi from a hotel by notifying the manager, service bureau, or doorman. There may be a small charge for this service.

If you're going to the airport or train station, you should reserve a taxi in advance. Expect rates to be higher during evening hours and for popular destinations. From Boryspil Airport to Kyiv center should cost about $20 USD. Word has it that the mafia controls the Boryspil taxis and they may cost as much as $75. To avoid a scam, bypass the taxis nearest the airport and railroad stations, walk a distance, and then hail one. A final caution: avoid taxis with two or more people in them.

Where can I get a taxi?
Де я можу знайти таксі?
deh yah MO-zhoo znahў-TIH tahk-SEE

Where is the taxi stop?
Де знаходиться зупинка таксі?
deh znah-KHO-diht'-sya zoo-PIHN-kah tahk-SEE

I need to go to	Мені треба їхати	meh-NEE TREH-bah YEE-khah-tih
Hotel...	до готелю ...	do ho-TEH-lyu
the airport	до аеропорту	do ah-eh-ro-POR-too
the train station	на вокзал	nah vok-ZAHL
downtown	до центру	do TSEHN-troo
this address	по цій адресі	po tseeў AHD-reh-see

How long will the ride take?
Як довго треба їхати?
yak DOV-ho TREH-bah YEE-khah-tih

| I'm in a hurry. | Я поспішаю. | ya po-spee-SHAH-yu |

Turn (left) (right) at the next corner.
Прошу повернути (наліво) (направо) на наступному повороті.
PRO-shoo po-vehr-NOO-tih (nah-LEE-vo) (nah-PRAH-vo) nah nah-STOOP-no-moo po-vo-RO-tee

| Go straight ahead. | Прямо. | PRYA-mo |

| Please stop here. | Прошу зупинитись тут. |
| | PRO-shoo zoo-pih-NIH-tihs' toot |

Please wait for me.
Прошу зачекати мене.
PRO-shoo zah-cheh-KAH-tih meh-NEH

I'll be back in ... minutes.
Я повернусь через ... хвилин.
yah po-vehr-NOOS' CHEH-rehz ... khvih-LIHN

Payment. Unless you have a Ukrainian associate arrange for the taxi, you'll be expected to pay in hard currency. Be sure you have a prior agreement on the fare. Tipping is optional. If you'd like to leave one, 10 to 15 percent is appropriate.

What is the fare to ...?

Скільки буде коштувати до ...?

SKEEL'-kih BOO-deh kosh-too-VAH-tih do

Thank you. Keep the change.

Дякую. Візьміть здачу собі.

DYA-koo-yu veez'-MEET' ZDAH-choo so-BEE

CITY TRANSPORTATION

Signs at the stops give the name of the stop and list the type of transportation that serves it. Stops are marked "A" for bus, "Tp" for tram, "T" for trolley, and "M" for metro or subway. Signs also tell the number of the route, the name of the terminal stop, and the frequency of the transportation.

The difference between a streetcar (or tram) and a trolley is that a street car runs on rails and is attached to an overhead electric wire while a trolley has wheels like a bus and is attached to two overhead wires. Usually these operate from 6 a.m. until 12 p.m.

bus	автобус "A"	ahv-TO-boos
streetcar or tram	трамвай "Тp"	trahm-VAHЎ
trolley	тролейбус "T"	tro-LEHЎ-boos
subway	метро "M"	meh-TRO

Where's the nearest stop for the (bus) (streetcar) (trolley) (metro)?

Де знаходиться найближча зупинка (автобуса) (трамваю) (тролейбуса) (метро)?

deh znah-KHO-diht'sya nahў-BLIHZH-chah zoo-PIHN-kah (ahv-TO-boo-sah) (tro-LEHЎ-boo-sah) (trahm-VAH-yu) (meh-TRO)

RIDING THE BUSES, STREETCARS, AND TROLLEYS

Tickets for city buses, trams, and trolleys are interchangeable. They come in books of 5, 10, or more called *talony* and are available at kiosks. The honor system is in effect. The rider tears one off and cancels it by running it through a box on the vehicle that punches it. Those not within reach of the validation box can pass their tickets along to the person nearest the machine who punches it and passes it back.

Vehicles in service carry a tremendous number of passengers. Those at the end of the queue may not be able to board; on board it may be impossible to get near the validation box — and sometimes, to even pass the tickets down. The crush of people may also make it impossible for the conductor to make spot checks for punched tickets. Hence, despite good intentions, you may wind up riding for free. Be alert when your stop is approaching as you'll have to push aggressively to get off.

Please, I want a book of ten tickets.
  Прошу дати мені десять талонів.
  PRO-shoo DAH-tih meh-NEE DEHS-yaht′ tah-LO-neev

When's the next (bus) (streetcar) (trolley)?
  Коли прийде наступний (автобус) (трамвай) (тролейбус)?
  ko-LIH prihў-DEH nahs-TOOP-nihў (avh-TO-boos)
  (trahm-VAHЎ) (tro-LEHЎ-boos)

Does this bus go to ...?
  Чи цей автобус їде до ...?
  chih tsehў ahv-TO-boos yee-DEH do

I want to go to ...
  Мені треба до ...
  meh-NEE TREH-bah do

Please tell me when to get off.
  Скажить будь ласка коли мені виходити.
  skah-ŽHIHT′ bood′ laska ko-LIH meh-NEE vih-KHO-dih-tih

What is this stop? Яка це зупинка?
        ya-KAH tseh zoo-PIHN-kah

I need to get off at the next stop.
  Мені треба вийти на наступній зупинці.
  meh-NEE TREH-bah VIHЎ-tih nah nahs-TOOP-neeў
  zoo-PIHN-tsee

Excuse me, I'm getting off.
  Перепрошую, я вихожу.
  peh-reh-PRO-shoo-yu ya vih-KHO-zhoo

May I get through, please?
  Чи можна мені пройти?
  chih MOŽH-nah meh-NEE proў-TIH

I missed my stop.
Я (пропустив, *m.*) (пропустила, *f.*) мою зупинку.
ya (pro-poos-TIHV) (pro-poos-TIH-lah) mo-YU zoo-PIHN-koo

WAIT!   ПОЧЕКАЙТЕ!   po-cheh-KAHY̆-teh
OUCH!   ОЙ!   oy

SUBWAYS

Subway   Метро   MEH-tro "M"

Kyiv's subway, one of the deepest in the world, consists of three lines
that intersect near the city center, covering most of the city. The subway
runs from 6 a.m. until 1 a.m. It's efficient, clean, and safe, even at night.
Travelers are impressed with the friendly atmosphere on the subway cars
in which passengers are likely to engage in polite and friendly chit-chat.
Pay by buying a token and dropping it in the turnstile slot. Due to
inflation, prices for tokens have been periodically increased and the
number sold at a time restricted to prevent hoarding. If you see a short
line for tokens, don't hesitate to buy your limit.

What does a token cost?
    Скільки коштує жетон на метро?
    SKEEL'-kih kosh-TOO-yeh zheh-TON nah meht-RO

I'd like two subway tokens.
    Мені треба два жетони на метро.
    meh-NEE TREH-bah dvah zheh-TO-nih nah meht-RO

Here are some signs you may see in the metro station:

EXIT TO CITY   ВИХІД ДО МІСТА
TRANSFER TO STATION -   ПЕРЕХІД НА СТАНЦІЮ -
TRANSFER TO LINE -   ПЕРЕХІД НА ЛІНІЮ -

LONG DISTANCE TRAVEL

A network of trains and buses link cities and villages. If the trains are
full, buses are an adventuresome way to get from place to place. These
are crowded; you may end up standing in the aisle or sharing a seat with

someone who also holds a ticket for it, or carrying a child on your lap. Luggage that won't fit under the bus is stacked in the stairwell. Nevertheless, the ride is cheap, reliable, and friendly.

Where can I get a schedule for the (bus) (train) (plane)?
Де можна знайти розклад на (автобуси) (поїзди) (літаки)?
deh MOẐH-nah znahỹ-TIH ROZ-klahd nah (ahv-TO-boo-sih) (po-yeez-DIH) (lee-tah-KIH)

Where is the nearest (train) (air) ticket office?
Де знаходяться найближчі квиткові каси на (поїзди) (літаки)?
deh znah-KHO-dyat'sya nahỹ-BLIHẐH-chee kviht-KO-vee KAH-sih nah (PO-yeezd) (lee-tah-KEE)

I need to go to the...
Мені потрібно їхати ...
meh-NEE po-TREE-no YEE-khah-tih

airport...	до аеропорт...	do ah-eh-ro-PORT
bus station...	на автовокзал...	nah AHV-to-vok-ZAHL
train station...	на вокзал...	nah vok-ZAHL
right now	тепер	teh-PEHR
today at noon	сьогодні в обід	s'o-HOD-nee v O-beed
this evening	сьогодні ввечорі	s'o-HOD-nee VVEH-cho-ree
tomorrow at ...	завтра в ...	ZAHV-trah v
tomorrow morning	завтра зранку	ZAHVT-rah ZRAHN-koo

GOING BY RAIL

Train travel is the major means of transportation, with service to virtually all towns. While long distance trains are clean and comfortable, the condition of the local trains serving the villages leave something to be desired. The longer distance routes usually involve overnight travel, which will save you the cost of lodging. The day journeys are an ideal way to see the countryside. In either case, trains in Ukraine are a good way to meet people.

On the whole, the trains are running on time, although for some popular destinations the travel time takes longer than it once did. The biggest problem with train travel is the difficulty in getting a ticket: when domestic plane service is cut, the demand for train tickets increases; seats on some routes are set aside for certain industries; others may be snapped up by budding entrepreneurs who resell them. First class tickets must be bought in advance. For a long trip, particularly on the most popular routes, try to get a ticket well ahead of your planned travel date.

There's a special window at the station that sells first class advance tickets, but ask first at your hotel. Even better, see if your travel agent at home can reserve a ticket before your trip. Tickets sold to foreigners, in dollars, will cost considerably more than those Ukrainian citizens can buy for coupons. Still, they're a bargain by our price standards.

How can I get to the railroad station?
Як можна добратись до вокзалу?
yak MOZH-nah do-BRAH-tihs' do vok-ZAH-loo

I'm taking the ... o'clock train.
Мій поїзд в ... годині.
meeў PO-yeezd v ... ho-DIH-nee.

Railroad stations tend to be dark and crowded and frequented by money changers and shady characters. With the numerous windows, it may be difficult to find the right place to buy a ticket.

Where is the ticket window?
Де знаходиться квиткова каса?
deh znah-KHO-diht'-sya kviht-KO-vah KAH-sah

Where is the advance reservation window?
Де каса попереднього продажу?
deh KAH-sah po-peh-REHD-n'o-ho PRO-dah-zhoo

I'd like to buy a ticket for ... [date].
Я хочу купити квиток на ...
ya KHO-choo koo-PIH-tih kvih-TOK nah

I need a ticket to ...
Мені треба квиток до ...
meh-NEE TREH-bah kvih-TOK do

I want to go on Friday at ... o'clock.
Я хочу їхати в п'ятницю в ... годині.
ya KHO-choo YEE-khah-tih v P'YAT-nih-tsyu v ... ho-DIH-nee

I need a return ticket on Saturday ...
Мені потрібен зворотній квиток на суботу ...
meh-NEE po-TREE-behn zvo-ROT-neeў kvih-TOK nah soo-BO-too

at ... o'clock.　　на ... годину.　　nah ... ho-DIH-noo

anytime during the day.
в любий час напротязі дня.
v lyu-BIHЎ chahs nah-PRO-tya-zee dnya

in the morning.	на ранок	nah RAH-nok
in the afternoon	на після обіду	nah PEES-lya o-BEE-doo
in the evening	на вечір	nah VEH-cheer

What does it cost?
Скільки це коштує?
SKEEL'-kih tseh kosh-TOO-yeh

At the station, there will be an information booth where you can get information about scheduled trains. Most stations will also have a large board that lists trains by number and destination, giving the arrival and departure time, track number, and whether the train is on schedule or running late.

Where is the information booth?
Де знаходиться інформаційне бюро?
deh znah-KHO-diht'-sya een-for-mah-TSEEY-neh byu-RO

Where is the information board?
Де знаходиться розклад?
deh znah-KHO-diht'-sya ROZ-klahd

Terms you'll find on the information board:

НОМЕР	NUMBER
ПРИБУТТЯ	ARRIVAL
ВІДПРАВЛЕННЯ	DEPARTURE
ПЕРОН	TRACK
ПЛАТФОРМА	PLATFORM
ПО РОЗКЛАДУ	ON SCHEDULE
ЗАПІЗНЮЄТЬСЯ	AMOUNT OF TIME BEHIND SCHEDULE

When does train number ... leave (arrive)?
Коли поїзд номер ... відправляється (прибуває)?
ko-LIH PO-yeezd NO-mehr ...veed-prah-VLYA-yeht'-sya
(prih-boo-VAH-yeh)

Is train number ... on schedule?

Чи поїзд номер ... їде по-розкладу?

chih PO-yeezd no-MEHR ... yee-DEH po ROZ-klah-doo

From which platform does train number ... leave?

З якої платформи відправляється поїзд номер ...?

z ya-KO-yee plaht-FOR-mih veed-prah-VLYA-yeht'-sya PO-yeezd
NO-mehr

From which end of the train does the numbering start?

З якого кінця поїзду починається нумерація вагонів?

z ya-KO-ho keen-TSYA PO-yeez-doo po-chih-NAH-yeht'-sya
noo-meh-RAH-tsee-ya vah-HO-neev

On the Train   На Поїзд   nah PO-yeezd

Long distance trains lack some of the amenities they used to offer. Dining cars are in service, for example, but the supply of food is not always reliable. On overnight trips, you should expect to have tea served in your sleeping cars for a small fee. Travelers are advised to bring enough bottled water and food to last the journey, as well as a supply of toilet paper and moist towelettes. It's a good idea also to wear layered clothing as the comfort level of the atmosphere varies with the season.

When you buy a ticket, you're either assigned a seat or, on overnight trains, sleeping accommodations. Sleeping compartments are on the "soft car," or м'ягкий вагон (m'yah-KIHY vah-HON) and may be first or second class, depending on the number of berths they contain. There are also compartments which contain four seats which convert to beds. These are always second class. Shortly after leaving the depot, an attendant will bring bedding to your compartment. You pay her a very small sum and make your own bed. She'll also collect your ticket and return it to you in the morning before you arrive at your station.

The best sleeping car in Ukraine may well be the "Grand Tour," which runs between Lviv and Kyiv. The two-bed compartments are well-maintained and comfortable - equipped with lavatories with running water - and provide attentive porter service. The car is managed by the Grand Hotel in Lviv, a Ukrainian-American joint venture luxury hotel. To book a compartment on the "Grand Tour," contact a travel agent who specializes in Ukraine.

Where's (my seat) (my compartment) (my berth)?
Де знаходиться (моє місце) (моє купе) (моя полиця)?
deh znah-KHO-diht'-sya mo-YEH MEES-tseh (mo-YEH
koo-PEH) (mo-YA po-LIH-tsya)

Permit me to pass.
Дозвольте пройти.
doz-VOL'-teh proў-TIH

Is this seat taken?
Чи це місце зайняте?
chih tseh MEES-tseh ZAHЎ-nya-teh

What station is this?
Яка це станція?
ya-KAH tseh STAHN-tsee-ya

How long does the train stop here?
Як довго стоїть тут поїзд?
yak DOV-ho sto-YEET' toot PO-yeezd

What is the next station?
Яка наступна станція?
ya-KAH nahs-TOOP-nah STAHN-tsee-ya

When does the train arrive in ...?
Коли поїзд прибуває до ...?
KO-lih PO-yeezd prih-boo-VAH-yeh do

How long does it take to get to ...?
Як довго до ...?
yak DOV-ho do

Does this train have a dining car?
Чи є в цьому поїзді вагон-ресторан?
chih yeh v TSO-moo PO-yeez-dee vah-HON rehs-to-RAHN

I need bedding for (two) (three) persons.
Мені треба білизна для (двох) (трьох) чоловік.
meh-NEE TREH-bah bee-LIHZ-nah dlya (dvokh) (tr'okh)
cho-lo-VEEK

I need an extra blanket.
Мені потрібна додаткова ковдра.
meh-NEE po-TREEB-nah do-daht-KO-vah KOVD-rah

I don't have ...	Я не маю ...	ya neh MAH-yu ...
a mattress	матрацу	mah-TRAH-tsoo
a pillow	подушки	po-DOOSH-kih
a blanket	ковдри	KOVD-rih
bed linens	білизни	bee-LIHZ-nih

When do you serve tea?
Коли буде чай?
ko-LIH BOO-deh chahỹ

What do you serve with tea?
Що ви маєте до чаю?
shcho vih MAH-yeh-teh do CHAH-yu

GOING BY PLANE

Boryspil Airport in Kyiv is a major international airport served by airlines from all over the world. Central Airport in Odesa is served by Austrian Airlines and Lufthansa and the airport in Lviv is served by Polish Airlines as well as Air Ukraine. The airport at Ivano-Frankivsk, which has a better runway than that at Lviv, is handling international passengers headed for the western part of the country.

In addition to these major tourist destinations, the following cities have runways for domestic travel: Cherkasy, Chernivtsi, Dnipropetrovsk, Donetsk, Kharkiv, Kherson, Khmelnytskyy, Kirovohrad, Kryvyy Rih, Luhansk, Mariupol, Mykolayiv, Poltava, Rivne, Sieverodonetsk, Simferopol, Uzhhorod, Vinnytsya. Zaporizhzhya, Zhytomyr. After an almost complete halt to domestic flights as an energy conservation measure, Air Ukraine is now running a number of intercity flights. The most frequent are likely to be those serving Kyiv, Kharkiv, Lviv, Chernivtsi, Uzhhorod, and Odesa. The price of a ticket on these is approximately three times as much for a foreign visitor as for a Ukrainian citizen. Be advised that the comfort and safety level of domestic flights is not up to Western standards.

For international flights, plan to be at the airport at least 90 minutes before departure to allow time for passport checks and, if necessary, the weighing of baggage. Be sure to have your passport ready at the initial point of departure even though you are not actually boarding your international flight, since airline personnel will check your passport and visas to make sure there will be no problem in making connections.

How can I get to the airport?
Як можна добратись до аеропорту?
yak MOZ̑H-nah do-BRAH-tihs′ do ah-eh-ro-POR-too

Where is the information booth?
Де знаходиться бюро інформації?
deh znah-KHO-diht′sya byu-RO een-for-MAH-tsee-yee

Are domestic planes flying?
Чи місцеві літаки літають?
chih mees-TSEH-vee lee-tah-KIH lee-TAH-yut′

Where can I buy a plane ticket?
Де я можу купити квиток на літак?
deh ya MO-z̑hoo koo-PIH-tih kvih-TOK nah lee-TAHK

Round trip tickets are not sold in Ukraine. You might be able to purchase at a single window a ticket to your destination plus a return ticket, but for the most part, tickets are sold only in the city where the flight originates.

I need a ticket to ... on ...
Мені потрібен квиток до ... на ...
meh-NEE po-TREE-behn kvih-TOK do ... nah

I need a return ticket for ....
Мені треба зворотній квиток на ....
meh-NEE TREH-bah zvo-ROT-neey̆ kvih-TOK nah...

Can you help me schedule a flight to ...?
Чи можете ви допомогти мені вибрати рейс до ...?
chih MO-z̑heh-teh vih do-po-mo-HTIH meh-NEE VIH-brah-tih rehy̆s do

I need a ticket to Kyiv on ..., then a ticket from Kyiv to Odesa on ... and then a return ticket to Lviv on ....
Мені треба квиток до Києва на .., потім квиток від Києва до Одеси на ..., а потім зворотній квиток до Львова на ....
meh-NEE TREH-bah kvih-TOK do KIH-yeh-vah nah ...,
po-TEEM kvih-TOK veed KIH-yeh-vah do o-DEH-sih nah ..., ah
po-TEEM zvo-ROT-neey̆ kvih-TOK do L′VO-vah nah ...

How long before the flight should I check in?
Як задовго до відльоту мені трсба зареєструватися?
yak zah-DOV-ho do veed-L'O-too meh-NEE TREH-bah
zah-reh-heest-roo-VAH-tih-sya

When (Where) should I confirm a ticket?
Де (Коли) мені треба підтвердити квиток?
deh (ko-LIH) meh-NEE TREH-bah peed-tvehr-DIH-tih kvih-TO

When is the next flight with an available seat?
Коли наступний рейс на який є місце?
ko-LIH nas-TOOP-nihў rehўs nah ya-KIHЎ yeh mees-TSEH

I want to return a ticket.
Я хочу здати квиток.
ya KHO-choo ZDAH-tih kvih-TOK

Where can I change a ticket?
Де я можу поміняти квиток?
deh ya MO-zhoo po-mee-NYA-tih kvih-TOK

Where is flight number ..?
Де знаходиться рейс ..?
deh znah-KHO-diht'-sya rehўs

From what gate does the plane leave?
З якого сектора відлітає літак?
z ya-KO-ho SEHK-to-rah veed-lee-TAH-yeh lee-TAHK

Where can I find a (porter) (luggage cart)?
Де я можу знайти (носильника) (візок для багажу)?
deh ya MO-zhoo znahў-TIH (no-SIHL'-nih-kah)
(vee-ZOK dlya bah-hah-ZHOO)

What time do we (leave) (arrive)?
Коли ми (відлітаємо) (прилітаємо)?
ko-LIH mih (veed-lee-TAH-yeh-mo) (prih-lee-TAH-yeh-mo)

How long will our flight be delayed?
Як на довго затримується наш рейс?
yak nah DOV-ho zah-TRIH-moo-yeht-sya nahsh rehўs

There are two information boards at the airport, one for arrivals and another for departures:

ПРИЛІТ	ARRIVAL
ВІДЛІТ	DEPARTURE

boarding gate	сектор	SEHK-tor
boarding pass	посадочний талон	po-SAH-doch-nihў tah-LON
pilot	пілот	pee-LOT
stewardess	стюардеса	styu-ahr-DEH-sah

"Fasten seat belt."   Застебніть прив'язні ремені
zahs-tehb-NEET' prih-V'YAZ-nee REH-meh-nee

CHAPTER 12. WORK AND STUDY

Ukrainian Proverb:
Робота не вовк, в ліс не втече.
ro-BO-tah neh vovk v lees neh vteh-CHEH
Work isn't a wolf; it won't run away into the forest.

Even though Ukrainians might joke about working, they have a reputation of being among the most industrious and diligent people of Europe. The labor force consists of about 25 million workers, nearly half of the population. About 28 percent are employed in industry or mining, and another 25 percent are in agriculture. Other large sectors of the work force are construction, eight percent, and transportation and communication, seven percent. Economic restructuring following independence has led to deteriorating labor conditions, a rising rate of unemployment, and a decline in production.

Note: In phrases containing the pronoun you, the familiar, singular form is first, followed by the polite or plural form.

Where do you work?
Де (ти працюєш, *s.*) (ви працюєте, *pl.*)?
deh (tih prah-TSYU-yehsh) (vih prah-TSYU-yeh-teh)

Do you like your job?
(Ти любиш, *s.*) (ви любите, *pl.*) свою роботу?
(tih LYU-bihsh) (vih LYU-bih-teh) svo-YU ro-BO-too

How much do you earn per month?
Скільки (ти заробляєш, *s.*) (ви заробляєте, *pl.*) в місяць?
SKEEL'-kih (tih zah-ro-BLYA-yehsh) (vih zah-ro-BLYA-yeh-teh)
v MEE-syats'

OCCUPATIONS

What is your occupation?
Яка (твоя, *s.*) (ваша, *pl.*) професія?
ya-KA (tvo-YA) (VAH-shah) pro-FE-see-ya

I'm an	Я	ya
actor	актор	ahk-TOR
agronomist	агроном	ah-hro-NOM
artist	митець	mih-TEHTS′
auto mechanic	автомеханік	AHV-to-meh-KHA-neek
baker	пекар	PEH-kahr
bank teller	банківський працівник	
	BAHN-keev-s′kihỹ prah-tseev-NIHK	
beekeeper	бджільник	bdzheel′-NIHK
bookkeeper	бухгалтер	bookh-HAHL-tehr
bricklayer	каменяр	kah-meh-NYAR
bus driver	водій автобуса	vo-DEEỸ av-TO-boo-sah
businessman	бізнесмен (m. or f.)	beez-nehs-MEHN
childcare worker	вихователь	vih-kho-VAH-tehl′
carpenter	тесляр	tehs-LYAR
construction worker	робітник-будівельник	
	ro-beet-NIHK-boo-dee-VEHL′-nihk	
cook	кухар	KOO-khahr
computer operator	оператор комп′ютера	
	o-peh-RAH-tor kom-P′YU-teh-rah	
dentist	зубний лікар	zoob-NIHỸ LEE-kahr
doctor	лікар	LEE-kahr
economist	економіст	eh-ko-no-MEEST
electrician	електрик	eh-LEHKT-rihk
engineer	інженер	een-zheh-NEHR
factory worker	робітник на заводі	
	ro-beet-NIHK nah zah-VO-dee	
farmer	фермер	FEHR-mehr
firefighter	пожежник	po-ZHEHZH-nihk
journalist	журналіст	zhoor-nah-LEEST
lawyer	адвокат	ahd-vo-KAHT
librarian	бібліотекер	beeb-lee-o-TEH-kahr
mailman	поштар	posh-TAHR
manager	менеджер	MEH-neh-zhehr
mechanic	механік	meh-KHAH-neek
merchant	продавець	pro-dah-VEHTS′
miner	шахтар	shahkh-TAHR
musician	музикант	moo-zih-KAHNT
nurse	медсестра	med-sehst-RAH
office worker	службовець	sloozh-BO-vehts′
pharmacist	фармецевт	fahr-mah-TSEHVT

plumber	сантехнік	sahn-TEHKH-neek
police officer	міліціонер	mee-lee-tsee-o-NEHR
postal worker	поштар	posh-TAHR
professor	професор	pro-FEH-sor
programmer	програміст	pro-hrah-MEEST
retiree	пенсіонер	pehn-see-oh-NEHR
salesclerk	продавець	pro-dah-VEHTS'
scientist	вчений	VCHEH-nihў
student	студент	stoo-DEHNT
tailor	кравець	krah-VEHTS'
teacher	вчитель	VCHIH-tehl'
technician	технік	TEHKH-neek
truck driver	шофер	sho-FEHR
waitperson	офіціант	o-fee-tsee-AHNT
writer	письменник	pihs'-MEHN-nihk

DOING BUSINESS IN UKRAINE

In a country where until recently capitalism was synonymous with evil, Ukrainians are just learning the business ethic and the ethics of doing business. Aspects of free market economy that we might take for granted — the need to risk money, to commit time and talent on long-term projects that may bring little return, to enter associations requiring trust and cooperation with virtual strangers — are new to a labor force that's not accustomed to a climate of free enterprise.

There are now more than 1,200 active joint ventures in Ukraine. Western firms are attracted by low cost of production, a labor market that's skilled and highly educated, and new markets for their product. A market exists in Ukraine, for example, for such consumer goods as soaps and cleansers, footwear, processed foods, and furniture.

Investment experts, however, warn companies not to expect to make a quick profit but regard a venture as a long-term enterprise. They point to the obstacles of setting up a business in Ukraine: an economy that is still largely centrally controlled by a government that shows little enthusiasm for a market economy; constantly changing tax laws and government decrees; governmental corruption and organized crime; and wild and uncontrolled inflation. And of course, it's only natural, given their history, that Ukrainians might be fearful of exploitation and wary of foreigners who want to come in and profit from their labor and their resources.   Experts advise investors to be prepared to risk capital, be flexible in their way of doing things, and be prepared for a long term relationship.   Give the venture at least five years.

Be careful with whom you get involved, they advise.   Few who want to be associated have the experience or know-how to provide meaningful help.   Especially avoid government bureaucrats in your dealings: at best they are ignorant of the requirements of a successful enterprise; but more likely, they're out to get a piece of the profits.   On the other hand, however, it's difficult to set up a business without an insider who's thoroughly familiar with the bureaucratic maze.

There are, of course, many competent and reliable potential business partners in Ukraine.   Don't make the mistake of underestimating Ukrainian business acumen.   Ukrainians are sharp traders and can sense a good opportunity.   Expect to solidify the business relationship over a lavish dinner with ceremonial undertones, during which many toasts are made to a successful partnership.

| My name is .... | Моє ім'я .... | mo-YEH EEM'-ya |
| I'm here on business. | Я тут по бізнесу. | ya toot po BEEZ-neh-soo |

I represent ... company.
    Я представляю кампанію ....
    ya prehd-stahv-LYA-yu kahm-PAH-nee-yu

I have my own business.
    Я маю свій бізнес.
    ya MAH-yu sveeў BEES-nehs

Here's my card.
    Ось моя візитка.
    os' mo-YA vee-ZIHT-kah

May I introduce ....
    Я хочу представити ....
    ya KHO-choo prehd-STAH-vih-tih

We are looking for partners in Ukraine.
    Ми шукаємо партнерів на Україні.
    mih shoo-KAH-yeh-mo pahrt-NEH-reev nah oo-krah-YEE-nee

What's the current rate of inflation?

Яка тепер інфляція?

ya-KAH teh-PEHR een-FLYA-tsee-ya

Can you estimate the cost?

Чи ви можете оцінити вартість?

chih vih MO-zheh-teh o-tsee-NIH-tih VAHR-teest'

I hope we can do business together.

Я надіюсь, що ми можемо співробітнічати.

ya nah-DEE-yus' shcho mih MO-zheh-mo
speev-ro-BEET-nee-chah-tih

Business Terminology

account	рахунок	rah-KHOO-nok
accountant	бухгалтер	bookh-HAHL-tehr
to advertise	рекламувати	rehk-lah-moo-VAH-tih
advertisement	реклама	rehk-LAH-mah
agribusiness	агробізнес	ah-hro-BEEZ-nehs
agriculture	сільське господарство	
	seel'-S'KEH hos-po-DAHRST-vo	
bankruptcy	банкрутство	bahnk-ROOTST-vo
to bargain	торгу-ватись	tor-hoo-VAH-tihs'
to bid	виступати з пропозицією	
	vihs-too-PAH-tih z pro-po-ZIH-tsee-yeh-yu	
bill	рахунок	rah-KHOO-nok
black market	чорний ринок	CHOR-nihў RIH-nok
board of directors	рада директорів	RAH-dah
		dih-rehk-to-REEV
broker	брокер	BRO-kehr
businessman	бізнесмен	beez-nehs-MEHN
buyer	покупець	po-koo-PEHTS'
capital	капітал	kah-pee-TAHL'
cash	наявні гроші	nah-YAV-nee HRO-shee
cash payment	плата готівкою	PLAH-tah ho-TEEV-ko-yu
collective farm	колективне господарство	
	ko-lehk-TIHV-neh hos-po-DAHRST-vo	
commission	комісійні	ko-mee-SEEЎ-nee
commodity market	товарна біржа	to-VAHR-nah BEER-zhah
cooperative enterprise	кооперативне підприємцтво	
	ko-o-peh-rah-TIHV-neh peed-prih-YEHMST-vo	

contract	контракт	kon-TRAHKT
to accept a contract	прийняти контракт	prihў-NYA-tih kon-TRAHKT
to break a contract	прервати контракт	prehr-VAH-tih kon-TRAHKT
consumer	споживач	spo-zhih-VAHCH
cost	вартість	VAHR-teest′
credit	кредит	kreh-DIHT
customer	клієнт	klee-YEHNT
debt	борг	borh
deposit	внесок	VNEH-sok
discount	скидка	SKIHD-kah
down payment	аванс	ah-VAHNS
economy	економіка	eh-ko-NO-mee-kah
employer	наймач	nahў-MAHCH
employees	працівники	prah-tseev-nih-KIH
enterprise	підприємство	peed-prih-YEHMST-vo
expenses	витрати	VIHT-rah-tih
exports	експорт	EHKS-port
income	дохід	do-KHEED
import	імпорт	EEM-port
insurance	страхування	strah-khoo-VAHN-nya
insurance company	страхова компанія	strah-kho-VAH kom-PAH-nee-ya
interest	проценти	pro-TSEHN-tih
investment	інвестування	een-vehs-too-VAHN-nya
joint venture	сумісне підприємство	soo-MEES-neh peed-prih-YEHMST-vo
loss	втрати	VTRAH-tih
management	управління	oop-rahv-LEEN-nya
manager	менеджер	MEH-nehd-zhehr
market	ринок	RIH-nok
domestic market	внутрішній ринок	vnoot-REESH-neeў RIH-nok
market economy	риночна економіка	RIH-noch-nah eh-ko-NO-mee-kah
free market	вільний ринок	VEEL′-nihў RIH-nok
ownership	власність	VLAHS-neest′
land ownership	земляна власність	zehm-lya-NAH VLAHS-neest′
payment	оплата	o-PLAH-tah

price	ціна	tsee-NAH
private ownership	приватна власність	prih-VAHT-nah VLAHS-neest′
privatization	приватизація	prih-vah-tih-ZAH-tsee-ya
production	виробництво	vih-rob-NIHTST-vo
profits	прибутки	prih-BOOT-kih
rent	оренда	o-REHN-dah
revenue	дохід	do-KHEED
risk	ризик	RIH-zihk
salary	зарплата	zahr-PLAH-tah
stock market	біржа	BEER-zhah
tax	податок	po-DAH-tok
income tax	подохідний податок po-do-KHEED-nihy̆ po-DAH-tok	
property tax	податок на нерухомість po-DAH-tok nah neh-roo-KHO-meest′	

AT THE OFFICE

At the office	В Офісі	v O-fee-see

I have an appointment with ... at ... o'clock.
У мене ділова зустріч з ... в ... годині.
oo MEH-neh dee-lo-VAH ZOOST-reech z ... v ... ho-DIH-ee.

Where can I ...
Де я можу ...
deh ya MO-zhoo

send a fax?	відіслати факс	vee-dee-SLAH-tih fahks
make a photocopy?	зробити копію	ZROBIH-tih KO-pee-yu

Can I receive a fax here?
Чи я можу тут отримати факс?
chih ya MO-zhoo toot ot-RIH-MAH-tih fahks

Can you help me e-mail a message?
Чи ви можете мені допомогти послати електронну пошту?
chih vih MO-zheh-teh MEH-nee do-po-moh-TIH po-SLAH-tih
eh-lehk-TRON-noo POSH-too

Do you have access to Internet?

Чи ви маєте вихід на Інтернет?

chih vih MAH-yeh-teh VIH-kheed nah een-tehr-NEHT

agenda	розпорядок	roz-po-RYA-dok
answering machine	автовідповідальна машина	
	ahv-to-veed-po-vee-DAHL'-nah mah-SHIH-nah	
conference	конференція	kon-feh-REHN-tsee-ya
calculator	калькулятор	kahl'-koo-LYA-tor
computer	комп'ютер	kom-P'YU-tehr
computer software	програмне забезпечення	
	pro-HRAHM-neh zah-behz-PEH-chehn-nya	
copy machine	копірувальна машина	
	ko-pee-roo-VAHL'-nah mah-SHIH-nah	

e-mail (It's customary to use the English term "e-mail," but you can also
use the Ukrainian phrase for "electronic mail" or for "computer mail.")

electronic mail	електронна пошта	
	eh-lehk-TRON-nah POSH-tah	
computer mail	комп'ютерна пошта	
	kom-P'YU-tehr-nah POSH-tah	
fax machine	факс машина	fahks mah-SHIH-nah
message	повідомлення	po-vee-DOM-lehn-nya
meeting	збори	ZBO-rih
office supplies	канцелярія	kahn-tseh-LYA-ree-ya
telephone	телефон	teh-leh-FON
typewriter	друкарська машинка	
	droo-KAHRS'-kah mah-SHIHN-kah	

EDUCATION

The educational system in Ukraine is organized somewhat differently
than in the United States. There are eight years of universal compulsory
education, starting with first grade when the students are six or seven.
The first four grades are called elementary school (початкові класи,
po-chah-KO-vee KLAH-sih). After 8th grade, students may choose to
go to work or to enter a 2-year trade school, but most attend 11 grades.

Those completing 11th grade have three options for higher education:

1. They can enter a technical college, which is lower level than a
university.

2. They can enroll in a special institute which is on the same level as a university, but provides specialized education in some discipline, for example, medical, polytechnical, and agricultural institutes and music conservatories.

3. Students may enter a university (університет, oo-nee-vehr-sih-TEHT).

Under the soviet system, higher education was free for qualified students. While scientific and technological education has been among the finest in the world, the social sciences suffered from lack of the method of free inquiry. This defect is being remedied with the opening of private institutions of higher education.

In 1992 Ukraine revived a revered tradition with the reopening of its first non-state-run university, the Kyiv Mohyla Academy. This oldest Eastern European university was established at the beginning of the 17th century, but closed more than 175 years ago by Tsar Alexander III who found its humanistic teachings threatening.

The Kyiv Mohyla Academy is modeled after the American liberal arts system. Its four departments include Culturological (philosophy, theology, anthropology, history, literature, foreign languages, and arts); Social Science (economics, law, political science); and Natural Science (ecology with an emphasis on radiology and biology). Masters and doctoral degree programs are in the offing. Official languages of instruction are Ukrainian and English. Several U.S. and Canadian universities have agreed to exchange students, faculty, and administrators.

Also recently established is the first Jewish institution of higher learning in the entire thousand-year history of Jewry in Ukraine. The Solomon International University in Kyiv is also a liberal arts institute whose purpose is to revive Jewish culture and education in Ukraine. Admission is open to all faiths.

Institutes of Higher Learning

Here are some of the major types of institutes in the Ukrainian educational system:

agricultural institute   сільсько-господарський інститут
                           SEEL'-s'-ko hos-po-DAHRS'-kihў eens-tih-TOOT

conservatory	консерваторія	kon-sehr-vah-TO-ree-ya
construction engineering institute	інжинерно-будівельний інститут een-zhih-NEHR-no boo-deev-VEHL'-nihў eens-tih-TOOT	
fine arts institute	інститут прикладного мистецтва eens-tih-TOOT prih-klahd-NO-ho mihs-TEHTS-tvah	
forestry institute	лісо-технічний інститут lee-so-tehkh-NEECH-nihў eens-tih-TOOT	
history institute	історичний інститут ees-to-RIHCH-nihў eens-tih-TOOT	
medical institute	медичний інститут meh-DIHCH-nihў eens-tih-TOOT	
pedagogical institute	педагогічний інститут peh-dah-ho-HEECH-nihў eens-tih-TOOT	
polygraphic (printing) institute	поліграфічний інститут po-lee-hrah-FEECH-nihў eens-tih-TOOT	
polytechnical institute	політехнічний інститут po-lee-tehk-NEECH-nihў eens-tih-TOOT	
veterinary institute	зоо-ветеринарний інститут ZO-O-veh-teh-rih-NAHR-nihў eens-tih-TOOT	

Universities perform both teaching and research although approximately 70 to 80 percent of research is concentrated in special research institutes which are under the academies of science. There are three academies of science: Academy of Science, Academy of Medical Science, and Academy of Pedagogical Science.

The head of a university is a *rector* (ректор, REHK-tor). The *rector* heads four to five pro-rectors, the equivalent of vice-presidents. The university contains departments or *fakultety* (Факультети, fah-kool'-TEH-tih) ranging from a few hundred to a few thousand students. The head of a *fakultet* is a *dekan* (декан, deh-KAHN) and his office is called the *dekanat* (деканат, deh-kah-NAHT). Each *fakultet* is divided into several divisions or branches called *kafedry* (кафедри, kah-FEHD-rih), headed by research professors and containing labs. These are not under the jurisdiction of the *dekan*.

Here are only some of the major departments or *fakultety* in Ukrainian educational institutions. As the educational system is highly specialized, these concentrations are offered only at their specific institutions.

applied math	прикладної математики	
	prih-klahd-NO-yee	mah-teh-MAH-tih-kih
architecture	архітектурний	ahr-khee-teh-TOOR-nihy̆
biology	біологічний	bee-o-lo-HEECH-nihy̆
building construction	будівельний	boo-dee-VEHL'-nihy̆
chemistry	хімічний	khee-MEECH-nihy̆
dentistry	стоматологічний	sto-mah-to-lo-HEECH-nihy̆
electronics	електроніки	eh-lehk-TRON-nee-kih
foreign language	іноземних мов	ee-no-ZEHM-nikh mov
history	історичний	ees-to-RIHCH-nihy̆
geophysics	геофізичний	heh-o-fee-ZIHCH-nihy̆
instrumental music	інструментальної музики	
	eens-troo-mehn-TAHL'-no-yee	MOO-zih-kih
folk art	народного мистецтва	
	nah-ROD-no-ho	mihs-TEHTST-vah
literature	літературний	lee-tehr-rah-TOOR-nihy̆
machinery	машинобудування	
construction	mah-shih-no-boo-doo-VAHN-nya	
mathematics	математичний	mah-teh-mah-TIHCH-nihy̆
painting	живопису	zhih-VO-pih-soo
pediatrics	педіатричний	peh-dee-ah-TRIHCH-nihy̆
physics	фізичний	fee-ZIHCH-nihy̆
sculpture	скульптури	skool'p-TOO-rih
surgery	хірургічний	khee-roor-HEECH-nihy̆
technology	технологічний	tekh-no-lo-HEECH-nihy̆
vocal music	вокальний	vo-KAHL'-nihy̆

UNIVERSITY STUDY

The five-to-six-year period of university study has no formally defined gradation between the undergraduate and graduate level, and there's no equivalent to the B.A. in the Ukrainian university system. Each *fakultet* has a set curricula. After three years of study, a student is assigned to certain *kafedra* which defines his or her speciality. After completion of the courses, a student undertakes an individual project and writes and defends his or her "diploma work" (дипломна робота, dee-PLOM-nah ro-BO-tah) to receive a degree that is comparable to an M.S. degree. At this stage, the student has earned an occupational title, such as engineer or medical doctor, and enjoys full status in his or her chosen profession.

A student who wants to go on to perform scientific research, becomes an *aspirant* (аспірант, ahs-pee-RAHNT), that is an applicant to a rigorous competition for admission to a 3-year period of study and research that leads to a Ph.D. Upon successful completion of this program, the student receives the equivalent of a Ph.D. degree and is called a candidate of science (кандидат наук, kahn-dih-DAHT nah-OOK). Candidates may apply for the position of *docent* (доцент, do-TSEHNT) which allows them to teach at the university level. There is a much higher degree, Doctor of Science, which requires a Ph.D. plus an additional dissertation of much higher scientific value. A Doctor of Science who teaches at a university is called a Professor.

The student-faculty relationship in Ukraine follows the European pattern in which the student does not question the authority of the professor. The idea of filling out an evaluation form rating a professor would be appalling to Ukrainians. The proper way to address a teacher is by the first name and patronymic, for example, "Good Morning, Iryna Ivanivna."

Where are you studying?
Де ви вчитесь?
deh vih vchih-TEHS'

I'm a student of ... University.
Я є (студент, *m.*) (студентка, *f.*)) ... Університету.
ya yeh (stoo-DEHNT) (stoo-DEHNT-kah) ...
oo-nee-vehr-sih-TEH-too

In which department are you?
На якому ви факультеті?
nah ya-KO-moo vih fah-kool'-TEH-tee

I'm in the physics department.
Я на фізичному факультеті.
ya nah fee-ZIHCH-no-moo fah-kool'-TEH-tee

In which division are you?
На якій ви кафедрі?
nah ya-KEEY̆ vih KAH-fehd-ree

I'm in ... division.
Я на кафедрі....
ya nah KAH-fehd-ree

My field is ....
 Моя область ....
 mo-YA OB-lahst' ....

What will your major be?
 Яка буде ваша спеціальність?
 ya-KAH BOO-deh VAH-shah speh-tsee-AHL'-neest'

I'm majoring in ....
 Я спеціалізуюсь в області....
 ya speh-tsee-ah-lee-ZOO-yus' v O-blahs-tee ....

What year are you?
 На якому ви курсі?
 nah ya-KO-moo vih KOOR-see

I'm a [number] year student.
 Я (студент, *m.*) (студентка, *f.*) третього ... курсу.
 ya (stoo-DEHNT) (stoo-DEHNT-kah) TREHT'-o-ho ... KOOR-soo

I'm here on an exchange program.
 Я тут по-обміну.
 ya toot po-OB-mee-noo

The program is between [name institutes].
 Ця програма між ....
 tsya pro-HRAH-mah meezh

I'll be here ... (weeks) (months) (years).
 Я буду тут ... (тижднів) (місяців) (років).
 ya BOO-doo toot ... (TIHZHD-neev) (MEES-ya-tseev)
 (RO-keev).

I'll be teaching	Я буду викладати ....
	ya BOO-doo vih-klah-DAH-tih

agribusiness	агробізнес	ah-hro-BEEZ-nehs
business	бізнес	BEEZ-nehs
economics	економіку	eh-ko-NO-mee-koo
English	англійську мову	ahn-HLEEYS'-koo MO-voo

I live in the dorm.
 Я живу в гуртожитку.
 ya zhih-VOO v hoor-TO-zhiht-koo

Education Vocabulary

courses of study	предмети	prehd-MEH-tih
education	освіта	os-VEE-tah
exams	екзамени	ehk-ZAH-meh-nih
humanities	гуманітарні науки	
	hoo-mah-nee-TAHR-nee nah-OO-kih	
Ph.D. thesis	кандидатська диссертація	
	kahn-dih-DAHTS'-kah dihs-sehr-TAH-tsee-ya	
prelim exams	кандидатський мінімум	
	kahn-dih-DAHTS'-kihy̆ MEE-nee-moom	
professor	професор	pro-FEHS-sor
science	наука	nah-OO-kah
scientist	науковець	nah-oo-KO-vehts'
semester	семестр	seh-MEHSTR
student	студент	stoo-DEHNT
undergraduate student	студент початкових курсів	
	stoo-DEHNT po-chaht-KO-vihkh KOOR-seev	

THE CAMPUS

The original campus is likely to be in the center of town. Newer additions such as sports facilities may be on the outskirts of the city. The dormitories offer less comfort and fewer amenities than American students are accustomed to. Typically only special category students, such as athletes and those on special diets, choose to eat in the cafeteria; most prefer to cook their own meals in the kitchens on each floor. Foreign exchange students are usually housed in the more comfortable married student dorms, which have cooking facilities in individual rooms. They usually buy their provisions at the open markets. Smoking is not permitted anywhere on university property — buildings nor campus.

Where is the ...?	Де знаходиться ...?	deh znah-KHO-diht'-ts'ya

administration building	головний корпус	ho-lov-NIHY̆ KOR-poos
cafeteria	їдальня, кафе	yee-DAHL'-nya, kah-FEH
gymnasium	спортивний корпус	por-TIHV-nihy̆ KOR-poos
lecture hall	аудиторія	ahoo-DIH-to-ree-ya
married students dorm	гуртожиток для сімейних	
	hoor-TO-zhih-tok dlya see-MEY̆-nihkh	
swimming pool	басейн	bah-SEHY̆N

CHAPTER 13. CHURCH IN UKRAINE

Ukrainian Proverb:
Як тривога, то до Бога.
yak trih-VO-hah to do BO-hah
In times of anxiety, one turns to God.

Two great events characterized religious life in Ukraine in recent years. In 1988 Ukraine celebrated the millennium of its Christianity, commemorating the conversion of ancient Kyiv to Byzantium Christianity under its ruler Volodymyr the Great.

No less noteworthy was the return, since Ukrainian independence, of the churches to their historic Ukrainian hierarchies which had been outlawed under communism and replaced by the Russian Orthodox Church. The re-emergence of the traditional religions saw the construction of new churches, refurbishing of decrepit ones, and reopening of monasteries and seminaries. Other forms of religious expression, such as catechism classes for children and adults, were revived.

With more than 35 million Ukrainians professing the Orthodox faith, the Ukrainian Orthodox Church (UOC) is the largest denomination in the country. It suffered some rebirth pains, splitting into several jurisdictions or patriarchates, according to their relationship to the Russian Orthodox Church. Many of the faithful either are not aware of or don't concern themselves with procedural differences, while the hierarchs hope for the eventual resolution of these differences and a union of all Ukrainian Orthodox. The Russian Orthodox Church is still a major confession in parts of the country that border Russia.

The Ukrainian Greek-Catholic Church emerged from the underground where it had survived since it was outlawed in 1946. Also commonly known as the Ukrainian Catholic Church, this church has allegiance to the Vatican but uses the Byzantine rite and architecture. It has more than five million faithful, primarily in the western oblasts of Ternopilska, Ivano-Frankivska, and Lvivska. Its ranking hierarch, the Patriarch, resides in Lviv in the complex of the Cathedral of St. George. An uninformed Westerner may not be able to distinguish — either architecturally or liturgically — among the various Byzantine rite churches in Ukraine.

With an estimated Jewish population of over 500,000, there are more than 50 Jewish communities throughout the country, and synagogues are being restored. There are also some 200 Roman Catholic parishes, mostly in the western region, whose members are primarily Poles and Hungarians. In the Crimea, there are Muslim mosques and Islamic schools. There are even Buddhists and animists in Ukraine, although they have no organized expression. In fact, there are more than 60 different faiths and over 14,000 religious communities in Ukraine.

The number of existing churches is not adequate to satisfy the claims for them. Sadly, there have been struggles — some physical — among the traditional denominations for the possession of church property. Evangelicizing Christians, including Baptist, Lutheran, Seventh Day Adventists, and Mormons, who can function without elaborate church buildings, are making great inroads. Many who find the rituals of the traditional churches incomprehensible are flocking to these churches that preach the Bible and emphasize a more personal relationship with God. The Ukrainian government has not discouraged proselytizing, and has allowed all religious groups to operate openly and freely.

CHURCH ARCHITECTURE

As early as the 9th century, Christian churches existed in the Kyivan-Rus territories. Constructed of wood, often covered with shingles, these first churches were small in size and built according to a tripartite plan, with the nave (нава, NAH-vah) or the central part or assembly flanked on the west by a vestibule (притвор, PRIHT-vor) and to the east by the sanctuary (святилище, svya-tih-LEE-shcheh). Often the central nave area stood taller than the adjoining sections. The segments were capped with domed cupolas.

As church architecture became more sophisticated, five-frame, seven-frame, and even nine-frame churches were built. The layout was always in the form of a cross, with the central nave surrounded by side chapels. There are many wooden churches in Ukraine; the oldest preserved churches, dating from the 16th and 17th centuries, are in the Carpathians. Stone churches date back to the beginning of the 11th century, especially in Kyiv and Chernihiv to the north. Their style followed the Byzantine cross structure. The practice of building freestanding bell towers carried over from wooden church construction.

Eventually, a national style of church architecture developed in Ukraine. Churches built or rebuilt between approximately 1650 and 1750 were designed in the style known as Ukrainian Baroque, a fusion of the Byzantine-cross church with the Western European baroque basilica. According to the Ukrainian Baroque style, the cupola evolved from a bud to a pear shape and the inner space expanded upward from the floor to the cupola. The facades were embellished with colorful glazed ceramic rosettes and inserts while the window and door lintels were embellished with fanciful stucco moldings incorporating vegetable and floral motifs.

Ukrainian church interiors are splendidly decorated with mosaics, murals, and icons. The highlight of interior design is the icon stand or iconostasis (іконостас, ee-ko-no-STAHS), a large screen or partition that separates the sanctuary from the body or nave of the church. It contains several doors that serve as the entrance and exit for the priest. The iconostasis may be composed of as many as six tiers of icons whose purpose is to instruct the faithful in the tenets of their faith by depicting Christ, the Virgin, John the Baptist, and other saints and prophets.

Where is the cathedral?
Де знаходиться собор?
deh znah-KHO-diht'-sya so-BOR

What's the name of this church?
Як називається ця церква?
yak nah-zih-VAH-yeht'-sya tsya TSEHRK-vah

What denomination is it?
До якої церкви він належить?
do ya-KO-yee TSEHRK-vih veen nah-LEH-zhiht'

When was it built? Коли він був побудован?
ko-LIH veen boov po-boo-DO-vahn

Is it all right to look inside?
Чи можна зайти в середину?
chih MOZH-nah zahỹ-TIH v seh-reh-DIH-noo

Is it all right to take a picture?
Чи можна тут фотографувати?
chih MOZH-nah toot fo-to-hrah-foo-VAH-tih

Monasteries. A monastery (монастир, mo-nahs-TIHR) is a community of monks or nuns that includes an ensemble of buildings — churches, seminary, dormitories, refectory. Historically the monasteries were important centers of religious, educational, scholarly, cultural and artistic life. A *lavra* (лавра, LAHV-rah) is a large and important monastery under the direct jurisdiction of the patriarch. Two Orthodox monasteries in Ukraine have *lavra* status, the Pecherska Lavra in Kyiv and the Pochayivska Lavra in the Ternopil region.

May I see the (monastery) (lavra)?
Чи я можу подивитись (монастирь) (лавру)?
chih ya MO-zhoo po-dih-VIH-tihs' (mo-nahs-TIH-r'yu) (LAHV-roo)

How old is this monastery?
Скільки цьому монастирю років?
SKEEL'-kih TS'O-moo mo-nahs-tih-RYU RO-keev

ATTENDING A SERVICE

Visitors are not only welcome at church services, it's common for the worshippers to step aside and urge a foreigner to the front, no matter how crowded the church. Orthodox and Greek-Catholic liturgies can be of marathon length by western religious standards. Some worshippers attend only part of the service, so you needn't feel uncomfortable about arriving late or leaving before the conclusion.

Participants stand throughout the service as there are no benches for sitting or kneeling. Chairs provided for the elderly or infirm may ring the sides of the church. The lack of seating allows the worshippers mobility. Rather than appearing tied to the every move of the priest, many move about during the liturgy to visit icons. Don't be fooled by this apparently casual behavior: worshippers are attentive and deeply respectful, even the hundreds who may have to stand outside and listen to the service over the loudspeakers.

Instrumental music is never used, but Ukraine has a rich tradition of choral liturgical music. Ukrainian is the language of the service, but the choir sings in Old Slavonic since liturgical sheet music is not widely available in Ukrainian. It's customary for women to wear skirts and cover their heads in church, but only in the *lavra* churches are dresses mandatory. In these churches men should not wear shorts. While discreetly taking photographs during a service is acceptable, it would be bad manners to distract the priest or worshippers with a flash.

Where is the nearest ...?
Де знаходиться найближча ...?
deh znah-KHO-diht′-sya nahў-BLIHZH-chah

Ukrainian Orthodox church
Українська Православна церква
oo-krah-YEENS′-kah prah-vo-SLAHV-nah TSEHRK-vah

Ukrainian Greek-Catholic church
Українська Греко-католицька церква
oo-krah-YEENS′-kah HREH-ko kah-to-LIHTS′-kah TSERHK-vah

Russian Orthodox church
Російська Православна церква
ro-SEEЎS′-kah prah-vo-SLAHV-nah TSERHK-vah

Roman Catholic church
Римо-католицька церва
RIH-mo kah-to-LIHTS′-kah TSEHRK-vah
In western Ukraine, Костьол (kos-T′OL) is the term for a Roman
Catholic church.

Protestant church	Протестантська церква	
	pro-tehs-TAHNTS′-kah TSEHRK-vah	
synagogue	синагога	sih-nah-HO-hah
mosque	мечеть	meh-CHEHT′

When is the next service?
Коли наступна служба?
ko-LIH nahs-TOOP-nah SLOOZH-bah

Will the choir be singing?
Чи буде співати хор?
chih BOO-deh spee-VAH-tih khor

How long will the service last?
Як довго буде служба?
yak DOV-ho BOO-deh SLOOZH-bah

I'd like to meet the (priest) (rabbi).
Я би (хотів, *m.*) (хотіла, *f.*) побачити (священника) (равина).
ya bih (kho-TEEV) (kho-TEE-lah) po-BAH-chi-tih
(svya-SHCHEHN-nih-kah) (rah-VIH-nah)

Vocabulary

baptism	хрещення	KREH-shchehn-nya
Bible	Біблія	BEEB-lee-ya
Buddhist	Будист	boo-DIHST
Christian (*noun*)	Християнин	khrihs-tih-YA-nihn
Christian (*adj.*)	християнський, (-а)	
		khrihs-tih-YANS'-(kihỹ)(-kah)
convent	жіночий монастир	
		z͡heen-NO-chihỹ mo-nahs-TIHR
to convert	залучити	zah-loo-CHIH-tih
cross	хрест	khrehst
Divine Liturgy (Orthodox and Greek-Catholic)		
	Служба Божа	SLOOZH-bah BO-z͡hah
funeral (burial)	похорон	PO-kho-ron
funeral church service	відспівивання	veed-SPEE-vih-vahn-nya
God	Бог	boh
hymn	гімн	heemn
holy	святий, свята	svya-TIHỸ, svya-TAH
holy day	свято	SVYA-to
icons	ікони	ee-KO-nih
Jesus	Ісус	ee-SOOS
Jew	Єврей, *m.*	yehv-REHỸ
	Єврейка, *f.*	yehv-REHỸ-kah
Jewish	Єврейский, *m.*	yehv-REHỸ-skihỹ
	Єврейска, *f.*	yehv-REHỸ-skah
Mass (RC)	Месса	MEHS-sah
missionary	міссіонер	mees-see-o-NEHR
Moslem	Мусульманен	moo-sool'- MAH-nehn
Mother of God	Мати Божа	MAH-tih BO-z͡hah
offering	підносіння	peed-nos-SEEN-nya
prayer book	молитвенник	mo-LIHT-vehn-nihk
prayers	молитви	mo-LIHT-vih
preacher	проповідник	pro-po-VEED-nihk
relics, saints' bones	мощі	MO-shchee
requiem, memorial		
service	панахида	pah-nah-KHIH-dah
saint	святий, *m.* свята, *f.*	svya-TIHỸ, svya-TAH
wedding	весілля	veh-SEEL-lya

CHAPTER 14. UKRAINIAN CUISINE

Ukrainian Proverb:
Борщ та каша - їжа наша.
borshch tah KAH-shah yee-ZHAH NAH-shah
Borshch and kasha - that's our food.

Ukrainian cuisine is a lot more varied than the *borshch* and *varenyky* often associated with it. The wealth of plants and animals raised in this fertile land account for a rich and varied diet; in addition, the cuisine was enriched from historical contacts with Europe and Asia. Despite the foreign influences, there is something original and distinctive about the way Ukrainians transform food into cuisine.

Like Italian cuisine, Ukrainian dishes show a sophisticated simplicity based on the goodness of the ingredients themselves and their natural flavors. Dishes are neither highly spiced nor bland, but subtle and pleasing, seasoned to perfection.

Bread, of course, is the mainstay of the Ukrainian diet and it is marvelous. Ukraine's reputation as the "breadbasket of Europe" is well-deserved. The French writer Honore de Balzac, who lived in Ukraine from 1847 through 1850, counted 77 ways of preparing bread. Bread is so important a part of life that Ukrainians have a custom of greeting honored guests with a loaf of bread topped with a mound of salt. Ukrainian groups still use this custom today in welcoming ceremonies for dignitaries and important persons.

The most important vegetables are beets, cabbage, cucumbers, potatoes, tomatoes, onions, and beans. These simple ingredients are transformed into sophisticated combinations of flavor and texture when spiced with the holy trinity of Ukrainian cuisine — garlic, vinegar, and dill.

Food is seasonal, therefore, preserved and pickled to last through the winter; pickled cucumbers, cabbage, tomatoes, mushrooms, peppers, and even apples lend flavor and tartness to many dishes. Salads are very common, not the lettuce-based kind Americans eat, but combinations of fresh, cooked and occasionally preserved vegetables, often mixed with meats and cheeses in creative yet subtle blendings of flavors.

UKRAINIAN SPECIALTIES

Borshch (борщ), the mildly tart beet-vegetable soup, is truly the national dish of Ukraine. A staple in all restaurants and served frequently in homes, *borshch* is not only the most popular dish in all Ukraine, it is uniquely Ukrainian. Although other Slavic cultures have adopted *borshch*, Ukraine is where it originated, and even as recently as 40 years ago *borshch* could not be found in restaurants in other soviet republics.

The many versions of *borshch* served throughout the country reflect the individuality of Ukrainians as well as their ingenuity. Generally all *borshch* contains many different ingredients, as many as 20, but the combinations and proportions vary according to region and season, as well as from personal preference. In the western regions, beets predominate, while in the central areas, more cabbage is used. *Borshch* may be meatless or it may be prepared from a base of a rich meat stock and contain either beef or fresh or smoked pork. It may be served either hot or cold.

Varenyky (вареники) are dumplings made from a soft rolled dough that are usually filled with either cottage cheese, potatoes, or cabbage and sauerkraut. Sour cherries are very popular in dessert *varenyky*. *Varenyky* are prepared by boiling. Many Ukrainians in North America are accustomed to calling *varenyky "pyrohy"* (пироги, pih-ro-HIH). Those with roots in western Ukraine especially use the terms synonymously, perhaps because in nearby Poland the boiled dumplings are called "pierogi," which is the Polish equivalent of the word *pyrohy*. In Ukraine, however, *pyrohy* are made from a yeast-risen dough and are baked rather than boiled.

Borshch and *varenyky*, served together, make a nourishing and tasty meal. Both are accompanied by sour cream. Here are some other quintessential Ukrainian dishes:

Cabbage rolls stuffed with meat and rice or buckwheat are *holubtsi* (голубці, HO-loob-tsee). The word *holubtsi* literally means "little pigeons." A meatless version of *holubtsi* is a traditional Christmas Eve dish.

Several pastries start with the word "pyr," which means "banquet," perhaps indicating that these originated as banquet foods. Made from yeast-raised dough or a short puff pastry, they're distinguished from one another primarily by their size:

A *pyrih* (пиріг, pih-REEH) is a large pie filled with meat or vegetables and usually covered with a yeast dough.

When these pastries are made smaller, a single serving will consist of several, and they're called *pyrohy* (пироги, pih-ro-HIH).

Made even smaller, as appetizers, they're *pyrizhky* (пиріжки, pih-reezh-KIH).

Either the boiled *varenyky* or the baked *pyrohy* can be filled

with cherries	з вишнями	z VIHSH-nya-mih
with cabbage	з капустою	z kah-POOS-to-yu
with cabbage and egg	з капустою і яйцем	z kah-POOS-to-yu ee yaў-TSEHM
with cheese	з сиром	z SIH-rom
with fish	з рибою	z RIH-bo-yu
with jam	з повидлом	z po-VIHD-lom
with meat	з м'ясом	z M'YA-som
with mushrooms	з грибами	z hrih-BAH-mih
with potato	з картоплею	z kahr-TOP-leh-yu
with raisins	з родзинками	z rod-ZIHN-kah-mih

BREAD

Bread	Хліб	khleeb

Bread is truly the staff of life for Ukrainians, the most important item in the diet. It's made fresh daily and sold unwrapped. Each region has its own specialty, based on shape and ingredients, so there are literally hundreds of different kinds of Ukrainian bread. Generally, the bread is tangy and chewy. When you're choosing bread, decide if you want "white" or "dark." The dark comes from the rye content and other ingredients such as molasses.

white bread	білий хліб	BEE-lihў khleeb
dark bread	чорний хліб	CHOR-nihў khleeb

Rolls are *bulochky* (булочки, BOO-loch-kih). These can be dark or light, plain or sweet.

Special occasions call for particular sweet breads:

Babka (бабка, BAHB-kah) is an egg-rich dessert bread, baked in a cylindrical-shaped mold and served especially at Easter.

Kalach (калач, kah-LACH) or *kolach* (колач, ko-LACH) is a sweet bread that's braided and ring-shaped. *Kalach* is traditional at weddings and on Christmas Eve.

Paska (паска, PAHS-kah) is the traditional Easter bread. The loaf is round-shaped and decorated with dough ornamentation in the shape of a cross.

CEREALS

Cereals	Каши	KAH-shih

Grains and starchy foods are more important in the Ukrainian diet than meats. *Kasha* (каша), breakfast gruel, is traditionally made from buckwheat, a very favored grain in Ukraine, but is a generic term for porridge. *Kasha* can also be served as a side dish with meat or poultry.

hot cereal	каша	KAH-shah
buckwheat	гречана	hreh-CHAH-nah
wheat	манна	MAHN-nah
millet	пшоняна	psho-NYA-nah
rice	рисова	RIH-so-vah
oatmeal	вівсяна	veev-SYA-nah
macaroni, pasta	макарони	mah-kah-RO-nih

CHEESES AND DAIRY PRODUCTS

Cheeses and Dairy Products	Сири та Молочні Продукти	SIH-rih tah mo-LOCH-nee pro-DOOK-tih

Much of Ukrainian cuisine is based on dairy products. There are numerous kinds of hard cheeses for eating uncooked. Farmer's cheese, a soft, cottage-like cheese, is used in many luncheon or dessert dishes. Cream sauces enrich meat and vegetable dishes and sour cream is used very liberally to add flavor to soups and sauces.

cheese	сир	sihr
milk	молоко	mo-lo-KO
butter	масло	MAHS-lo
cream	вершки	ver-SHKIH
sour cream	сметана	smeh-TAH-nah
cream cheese	м'ягий сир	m'ya-HIHY̆ sihr
farmer's (cottage) cheese	сир	sihr
kefir (a yogurt-like drink)	кефір	keh-FEER
sour milk	простокваша	pros-to-KVAH-sha
yogurt	йогурт	Y̆O-hoort
brynza is a semi-soft cheese from goat's milk:		
	бринза	BRIHN-zah
hard cheese	твердий сир	tvehr-DIHY̆ sihr

FISH

Fish	Риба	RIH-bah

Many kinds of fish are found in Ukraine, from the ubiquitous carp and salted herring to the Carpathian delicacy, trout. In the markets, fish is available in many forms — frozen, canned, smoked, salted, and fresh.

carp	короп	KO-rop
catfish	сом	som
crayfish	рак	rahk
flounder	камбала	KAHM-bah-lah
halibut, turbot	палтус	PAHL-toos
herring (salted)	оселедець	o-seh-LEH-dehts'

lobster	лобстер	LOB-stehr
mackerel	скумбрія, мокрель	
	SKOOM-bree-ya, mok-REHL'	
perch	судак	soo-DAHK
pike	щука	SHCHOO-kah
salmon	лосось	los-OS'
shrimp	креветки	kreh-VEHT-kih
sturgeon	осетр	o-SEHTR
trout	форель	fo-REHL'

MEAT AND POULTRY

| Meat and Poultry | М'ясо та Птиця | M'YA-so tah PTIH-tsya |

Traditionally, meat is a central part of the Ukrainian diet:

beef	яловичина	YA-lo-vih-chih-nah
lamb	баранина	bah-RAH-nih-nah
pork	свинина	svih-NIH-nah
poultry	птиця	PTIH-tsya
chicken	курка	KOOR-kah
duck	качка	KACH-kah
goose	гуска	HOOS-kah
turkey	індик	EEN-dihk
game	дичина	dih-chih-NAH
boar	кабан	kah-BAHN
hare	заєць	ZAH-yehts'
rabbit	кролик	KRO-lihk

Ukrainian Meat Dishes. The most basic Ukrainian meat is sausage, *kovbasa* (ковбаса). Often it contains pork and garlic but there are many different types of sausage and prepared meats. Here are a few:

headcheese	холодець	kho-lo-DEHTS'
liver or blood sausage	кров'янка	kro-V'YAN-kah
ham	шинка	SHIHN-kah
hot dogs	сосиски	so-SIHS-kih

Chicken Kiev (котлети по-київськи, kot-LEH-tih po KIH-yeev-s'kih) is boneless, skinless chicken breasts, pounded flat, stuffed with butter, rolled in seasoned flour, and deep fried. Chicken Kiev is a popular item in establishments that cater to tourists. Here are some other very popular meat dishes:

shish-ka-bob	шашлик	shash-LIHK
meat varenyky	вареники з м'ясом	
	vah-REH-nih-kih z M'YA-som	
veal cutlet	телячя котлета	teh-LYA-chya kot-LEH-tah

Siberian dumplings (пельмені, pehl'-MEH-nee), are stuffed with beef, pork and onions.

roasted pieces of meat in a sauce		
	піджарка	peed-$\widehat{ZH}$AHR-kah
steak	біфштекс	beef-SHTEHKS
hare in sour cream	заєць в сметані	
	ZAH-yets' v smeh-TAH-nee	
roast beef	ростбіф	ROST-beef
duck stuffed with apples	качка з яблуками	KACH-kah z YAB-loo-kah-mih
goulash	гуляш	hoo-LYASH

Organ meats are less popular, but far more common than in the United States.

tongue	язик	ya-ZIHK
liver	печінка	peh-CHEEN-kah
heart	серце	SEHR-tseh
kidneys	нирки	NIHR-kih
brains (fried)	мозок	MO-zok
tripe (boiled)	флячки	FLYACH-kih

VEGETABLES AND SEASONINGS

Vegetables	Овочі	O-vo-chee

Ukrainians rely largely on fresh, seasonal produce. A sure sign of spring — and a great delicacy — is the green, leek-like shoots of fresh garlic, which pop up before the weather is warm and the bulbs develop. Also in spring, the tender young roots of horseradish make a pungent Easter ritual food. In summer, you'll find an array of vegetables at central markets or sold by women on street corners who come in from the countryside.

beans	фасоля	fah-SOL-ya
beets	буряки	boo-rya-KIH
brussels sprouts	брюсельська капуста	
	bryu-SEHL's'kah kah-POOS-tah	
green cabbage	зелена капуста	
	zeh-LEH-nah kah-POOS-tah	
red cabbage	червона капуста	
	chehr-VO-nah kah-POOS-tah	
cauliflower	цвітна капуста	tsveet-NAH kah-POOS-tah
carrots	морква	MORK-vah
cucumber	огірки	o-heer-KIH
dill	кріп	kreep
eggplant	баклажани	bahk-lah-ZHAH-nih
garlic	часник	chahs-NIHK
horseradish	хрін	khreen
mushrooms	гриби	hrih-BIH
onion	цибуля	tsih-BOO-lya
onion, green	зелена цибуля	zeh-LEH-nah tsih-BOO-lya
parsley	петрушка	peh-TROOSH-kah
peas	горох	ho-ROKH
pepper	перець	PEH-rehts'
black pepper (spice)	чорний перець	CHOR-nihў PEH-rehts'
red pepper (hot)	червоний перець	cheh-VO-nihў PEH-rets'
sweet (Bulgarian)	солодкий (Болгарський) перець	
pepper	so-LOD-kihў (bol-HAHRS'-kihў) PEH-rehts'	
pumpkin	гарбуз	hahr-BOOZ
potatoes	картопля	kahr-TOP-lya
radishes	редька	REHD'-kah
squash	кабачки	kah-bahch-KIH
tomatoes	помідори	po-mee-DO-rih
turnip	ріпка	REEP-kah

FRUITS AND NUTS

Fruits and Nuts   Фрукти і Горіхи
                         FROOK-tih ee ho-REE-khih

Open markets are well-stocked with seasonal fruits and some that are
shipped in from warmer climates. In some regions of Ukraine, fresh
fruits are available all year round.

apples	яблука	YAB-loo-kah
almonds	мигдаль	mih-HDAHL′
apricots	абрикоси	ahb-rih-KO-sih
bananas	банани	bah-NAH-nih
blackberries	ожина	o-ZHIH-nah
cherries	вишні	VIHSH-nee
cherries, sweet	черешні	cheh-REHSH-nee
currants, black	смородина	smo-ROH-dih-nah
currants, red	порічки	po-REECH-kih
cranberries	клюква	KLYUK-vah
filberts	лісові горіхи	lee-so-VEE ho-REE-kih
gooseberries	агрус	AHH-roos
grapefruit	грейпфрути	hrehўp-FROO-tih
grapes	виноград	vih-no-HRAHD
lemons	лимони	lih-MO-nih
melon	диня	DIH-nya
oranges	апельсини	ah-pehl′-SIH-nih
peaches	персики	PEHR-sih-kih
pineapple	ананас	ah-nah-NAHS
plum	алича	a-LIH-chah
plums (purple prune)	сливи	SLIH-vih
peanuts	земляні горіхи	
	zehm-lya-NEE ho-REE-khih	
pomegranate	гранат	HRAH-naht
raisins	ізюм	ee-ZYUM
raspberries	малина	mah-LIH-nah
strawberries	суниці (East Ukr.)	soo-NIH-tsee
	трускавки (W. Ukr.)	TROOS-kahv-kih
tangerines	мандарини	mahn-dah-RIH-nih
walnuts	грецькі горіхи	
	HREHTS′-kee ho-REE-khih	
watermelon	кавун	kah-VOON
wild strawberries	полуниці	po-loo-NIH-tsee

DESSERTS

Desserts   Десерти   deh-SEHR-tih

Desserts are more of a special occasion treat than an everyday indulgence, but not because Ukrainians are calorie-conscious. Bakeries sell beautifully decorated, luscious, rich cakes, that are not very sweet. These are packed in colorful round cardboard boxes, each type of cake in its characteristic box. Each establishment has its own speciality and each family recipe collection has its own version of the popular pastries.

Most pastries are made from several basic kinds of dough:

puff pastry	слойоне тісто	slo-ŶHO-neh TEES-to
short cake	пісочне тісто	pee-SOCH-neh TEES-to
sponge cake	бісквітне тісто	bees-KVEET-neh TEES-to
yeast	дріжджове тісто	dreezhd-zho-VEH TEES-to

Cakes, or tortes (торти, tor-TIH), are elaborate affairs, with rich fillings of fruit, nuts, or pastry cream spread between sponge layers. Here are just a few of the many, many different kinds of cakes:

cheesecake	сирник	SIHR-nihk
chocolate cake	шоколадний торт	sho-ko-LAHD-nihў tort
honey cake	медовий торт	meh-DO-vihў tort
lemon cake	лемонний торт	leh-MON-nihў tort
nut cake	торт з горіхами	tort z ho-REE-khah-mih

Kyiv is known for its tortes. The most noted is its namesake, Kyiv cake (торт Київський, tort KIH-yeev-s′kihy), a rich hazelnut and cream-filled cake with a chocolate glaze embellished with a chestnut leaf design. Prague cake (торт Прага, tort PRAH-hah) is a rich cake containing chocolate, coffee, and nuts.

Tistechko (тістечко, TEES-tehch-ko) are single-serving-sized pastries, called *pyrozhne* (пирожне, pih-ROZH-neh) in Russian. There are many kinds of small pastries:

almond *tistechko*	миндальне тістечко
	mihn-DAHL′-neh TEES-tehch-ko

nut *tistechko*   горіхове тістечко
                         ho-REE-kho-veh TEES-tehch-ko

A "potato," (картопля, kahr-TOP-lya) is a pastry made from bread
crumbs, cocoa, butter, and sugar, that's shaped to resemble a potato.

Napoleon   Наполеон   nah-po-leh-ON
eclair   еклер   ehk-LEHR

Other popular desserts:

apples in pastry   яблуко в тісті   YAB-loo-ko v TEES-tee
baba au rhum   ромова бабка   RO-mo-vah BAHB-kah
baked cheese   сирник   SIHR-nihk
biscuits   коржики   KOR-zhih-kih
cookies   печиво   PEH-chih-vo
honey cake   медівник   meh-deev-NIHK
honey cookies   медівнички   meh-deev-NIHCH-kih
ice cream   морозиво   mo-RO-zih-vo

Khrusty (хрусти, KHROOS-tih) are strips of egg-rich batter that are
deep-fried.

Makivnyk (маківник, mah-KEEV-nihk), a poppyseed roll, is a
Christmastime treat.

Pampushky (пампушки, pahm-POOSH-kih), literally "puffs," come
in several versions. In western Ukraine they're deep-fried doughnuts with
a thick filling of either jam, farmer's cheese, or peas. In Kyiv and eastern
Ukraine, *pampushky* are not fritters but small yeast-raised rolls served
with tea. In eastern Ukraine, *pampushky* can also be delicious yeast rolls
topped with garlic sauce that accompany borshch.

CHAPTER 15. DINING OUT

Ukrainian Proverb:
Апетит надходит під час їди.
ah-peh-TIHT nahd-KHO-diht peed chahs yee-DIH
The appetite comes during the meal.

TYPES OF EATING ESTABLISHMENTS

Whether you're looking for a quick meal in an informal setting or a multi-course meal with music and dancing, you'll be able to find something to suit your taste in Ukraine. The old soviet anecdote that the only answer to the waiter's question, "What do you want?" is "What do you have?" is no longer reality now that cooperative (private) restaurants are competing for the patronage of numerous Western visitors.

A restaurant (ресторан, rehs-tor-AHN), whether an elegant white-tablecloth establishment or an informal place, provides multi-course meals and table service. Ukrainians don't patronize restaurants regularly but go when they're celebrating special occasions or looking for an evening's entertainment as well as dining. Dinner may be followed by cognac and champagne with a round of toasts, then singing or dancing.

There are a number of cafes which are named after the particular dish they feature. Perhaps the most common, for example, is the *pyrizhkova* (пиріжкова), which specializes in ready-made *pyrizhky*, pastries filled with either fruit, vegetable, or meat. The *varenychna* (варенична) specializes in dumplings and the *shashlychna* (шашлична) serves shish kebob. These cafes also have tea, coffee, milk, or juice. You pay at the cashier and may stand at a counter rather than sit down.

The cafeteria (їдальня, yee-DAHL'-nya) is a self-service dining room where you can get anything from a snack to a whole meal in an informal setting. Also called *stolova* (столова), the cafeteria is found primarily in public institutions. A *kulynariya* (кулинарія) is a shop that sells ready-cooked dishes.

The *bufet* (буфет) is a simple snack bar found in public places such as the theater or station where you can get a light meal. In the larger cities and at the open markets, you might find food sold in the street. This is an easy and quick way to eat, but much of this kind of food is too greasy for western palates and stomachs.

RESERVATIONS

Restaurants don't show a rapid turnover of tables, so it's a good idea to make reservations, either through Inturyst or another travel service agency, or stop in the restaurant earlier in the day.

Can you recommend a good restaurant nearby?
Чи ви можете порекомендувати гарний ресторан поблизу?
chih vih MO-zheh-teh po-reh-ko-mehn-doo-VAH-tih HAHR-nihў rehs-to-RAHN po-BLIH-zoo

I'd like to reserve a table for four people ...
Я хочу замовити столик на чотирьох персон....
ya KHO-choo zah-MO-vih-tih STO-lik nah cho-tih-R'OKH pehr-SON

for 6 o'clock	на шосту годину	nah SHOS-too ho-DIH-noo
for 6:30	на пів сьомої	nah peev S'O-mo-yee
for 7 o'clock	на сьому годину.	nah S'O-moo ho-DIH-noo

We need to finish dinner by ... o'clock.
Нам треба закінчити обід до ... години.
nahm TREH-bah zah-KEEN-chih-tih o-BEED do ... ho-DIH-nih

AT THE RESTAURANT

| At the Restaurant | В Ресторані | v rehs-to-RAH-nee |

Restaurants that begin serving at noon generally are open until 11 p.m. Some may close for several hours, typically between 4 and 7 p.m. Restaurants are usually smoke-free, with the exception of those that provide evening entertainment. In those where smoking is allowed, don't expect to find a special section for non-smokers. A few restaurants display their menus outside, but posting menus is not typical in Ukraine. When choosing a place to eat, you might want to go inside and check the menu and prices. Opposite the prices are a series of numbers that tell the amount of grams per serving of meat, starch, and vegetables, respectively, in a given dish.

When you arrive at the restaurant, wait to be seated.

We've reserved a table for .... [name of party]
    Ми замовляли столик на прізвище ...
    mih zah-MO-vlya-lih STO-lihk nah PREEZ-vih-shcheh

May we sit over there?
    Чи можемо ми сісти ось там?
    chih MO-zheh-mo mih SEES-tih os' tahm

Is this table free?
    Чи цей столик вільний?
    chih tsehy̆ STO-lihk VEEL'-nihy̆

Would you set another place?
    Чи ви можете зробити ще одне місце?
    chih vih MO-zheh-teh zro-BIH-tih shcheh od-NEH MEES-tseh

Is smoking allowed here?
    Чи можна тут курити?
    chih MOZH-nah toot koo-RIH-tih

Please bring a menu.
    Прошу принести меню.
    PRO-shoo prih-NEHS-tih meh-NYU

Waiter! [To summon the waiter.]
    Офіціант!
    o-fee-tsee-ANHT

What do you recommend?
    Що ви порадити?
    shcho vih po-RAH-dih-tih

Which local specialties do you serve?
    Які місцеві делікатеси ви сервіруєте?
    ya-KEE mees-TSEH-vee deh-lee-kah-TEH-see vih
    sehr-vee-ROO-yeh-teh

"What drinks are you having on the table"
    Які напої ви маєте до столу?
    ya-KEE nah-PO-yee vih MAH-yeh-teh do STO-loo

Do you have ...?   Чи ви маєте ...?
                   chih vih MAH-yeh-teh

Would you first bring ...?
Чи ви можете принести спочатку ...?
chih vih MO-zheh-teh prih-NEHS-tih spo-CHAHT-koo

Then later I'd like ...
Потім пізніше я хочу ...
PO-teem peez-NEE-sheh ya KHO-choo

I'd like to order this. [pointing]
Я хочу це замовити.
ya KHO-choo tseh zah-MO-vih-tih

Would you please bring more (bread) (water)?
Прошу принести більше (хліба) (води)?
PRO-shoo prih-NEHS-tih beel'-sheh (KHLEE-bah) (vo-DIH)

Please bring an extra plate.
Прошу принести додаткову тарілку.
PRO-shoo prih-NEHS-tih do-daht-KO-voo tah-REEL-ko

Please pass the salt.
Передайте мені, будь ласка, сіль.
peh-reh-DAHY̆-teh meh-NEE bood' LAHS-kah seel'

Nothing more, thanks.
Ні, дякую.
nee DYA-koo-yu

Where's the restroom?
Де є туалет?
deh yeh too-ah-LEHT

Please give (me) (us) the check.
Прошу розрахувати (мене) (нас).
PRO-shoo roz-rah-khoo-VAH-tih (meh-NEH) (nahs)

Thank you, everything (tasted good) (was fine).
Дякую, все було (смачно) (добре).
DYA-koo-yu vseh boo-LO (SMAHCH-no) (DOB-reh)

BREAKFAST

Breakfast	Снiданок	snee-DAH-nok

Since city restaurants generally open at lunchtime, hotel dining rooms are the place to go for breakfast. For those staying at hotels, breakfast usually is included in the cost of the room. Have your hotel card handy to show the waiter.

Kasha (каша) or cooked cereal may be available, with a choice of buckwheat or other grain. Cheese, sausage, and eggs may also be on the menu, and there will be excellent rolls, butter, jam and a pot of steaming tea.

When is breakfast served?
    Коли є снiданок?
    ko-LIH yeh snee-DAH-nok

I'd like	Чи можу я мати	
	chih MO-zhoo ya MAH-tih	
fruit juice	фруктовий сiк	frook-TO-vihў seek
boiled egg	варене яйце	vah-REH-neh yaў-TSEH
fried egg	яєшню	ya-YEHSH-nyu
bacon	бекон	beh-KON
ham	шинку	SHIHN-koo
jam	повидло	po-VIHD-lo
sausage	ковбасу	kov-bah-SOO
toast	грiнки	HREEN-kih
some bread	хлiб	khleeb
some butter	масло	MAHS-loh
sour cream	сметану	smeh-TAH-noo
hard cheese	твердий сир	tvehr-DIHЎ sihr
cottage cheese	сир	sihr
yogurt	йогурт	ЎO-hoort
buckwheat cereal	гречану кашу	hreh-CHAH-noo KAH-shoo
cream of wheat	манну кашу	MAHN-noo KAH-shoo
millet cereal	пшоняну кашу	pshon-YA-noo KAH-shoo
rice cereal	рисову кашу	RIH-so-voo KAH-shoo
oatmeal	вiвсяну кашу	veev-SYA-noo KAH-shoo
a cup of tea	чашку чаю	CHASH-koo CHAH-yu
coffee	каву	KAH-voo

milk	молоко	mo-lo-KO
hot chocolate	гарячий шоколад	
	hah-RYAH-chihў sho-ko-LAHD	
sugar	цукор	TSOO-kor

DINNER

| Dinner | Обід | o-BEED |

Dinner in a restaurant consists of several courses. As eating plays an important part in Ukrainian social life, you can expect to spend hours at the table and eat and drink more than you had anticipated.

Appetizers   Закуски   zah-KOOS-kih

The word for appetizer, *zakuska* (закуска), means "the little bite," but with the numerous possibilities, the appetizer course can be a meal in itself. Most appetizers are cold — for example, smoked or jellied meats, jellied or pickled fish, pickled vegetables, and aged cheese. For hot appetizers, try *pyrizhky* with savory fillings.

For the first course I want ....
      На закуску я хочу ....
      nah zah-KOO-skoo ya KHO-choo

mixed appetizers	асорті	as-sor-TEE
black caviar	чорну ікру	CHOR-noo eek-ROO
red caviar	червону ікру	cher-VO-noo eek-ROO
cheese	сир	sihr
eggs under	яйце під майонезом	
mayonnaise	YAЎ-tseh peed mah-ўo-NEH-zom	
herring	оселедець	o-seh-LEH-dets'
pate	паштет	pash-TEHT
pickled ...	мариновані ...	mah-rih-NO-vah-nee
cucumber	огірки	o-heer-KIH
mushrooms	гриби	hrih-BIH
tomatoes	помідори	po-mee-DO-rih
sausage	ковбасу	kov-bah-SOO
smoked cured pork	копчену шинку	KOP-cheh-noo SHIHN-koo
smoked salt pork	копчене сало	KOP-cheh-neh SAH-lo

Soup   Суп   soop

No Ukrainian meal is complete without soup served with a dollop of sour cream. Soups aren't considered strictly cold weather food; you'll find them at eating establishments all year round. Borshch (борщ), the quintessential Ukrainian soup, is the most common. Here are some other favorites.

I'd like ....
  Я би (хотів, *m.*) (хотіла, *f.*)
  ya bih (kho-TEEV) (kho-TEE-lah)

barley soup	крупник	KROOP-nihk
buckwheat soup	гречаний суп	greh-CHAH-nihў soop
bouillon	бульйон	bool'-ŸON
chicken noodle soup	суп з куки та лапші	
	soop z KOOR-kih tah lahp-SHEE	
pickled cucumber		
soup	розсільнік	roz-SEEL'-nihk
fish soup	юшку	YUSH-koo
fruit soup	фруктовий суп	frook-TO-vihў soop
green borshch (nettles or other wild greens soup)		
	борщ зелений	borshch zeh-LEH-nihў
mushroom soup	грибний суп	hrihb-NIHŸ soop
oatmeal soup	вівсяний суп	veev-SYA-nihў soop
pea soup	гороховий суп	ho-RO-kho-vihў soop
potato soup	картопляний суп	kahr-top-LYA-nihў soop
rice soup	рисовий суп	rih-SO-vihў soop
sauerkraut soup	капусняк	kah-poos-NYAK
vegetable soup	овочевий суп	o-vo-CHEH-vihў soop

The Main Course   Друге   DROO-heh

For the entree I'd like this. [pointing]
  На друге я хочу це.
  nah DROO-heh ya KHO-choo tseh

What kind of meat do you have?
  Яке м'ясо ви маюте?
  ya-keh M'YA-so vih MAH-yeh-teh

I'd like fish, please.
   Я би (хотів, *m.*) (хотіла, *f.*) рибу.
   ya bih (kho-TEEV) (kho-TEE-lah) RIH-boo

May I have it...?
   Чи я можу мати це...?
   chih ya MO-zhoo MAH-tih tseh

baked	печене	PEH-cheh-neh
boiled	варене	VAH-reh-neh
fried	жарене	ZHAH-rehn-neh
grilled	смажене	SMAH-zheh-neh
marinated	мариноване	mah-rih-NO-vah-neh
smoked	копчене	KOP-cheh-neh
steamed	парене	PAH-reh-neh

I'd like a vegetarian meal.
   Я хочу вегетеріанську їжу.
   ya KHO-choo veh-heh-teh-ree-AHNS'-koo YEE-zhoo

Which vegetables do you have?
   Які овочі ви маєте?
   a-KEE O-vo-chee vih MAH-yeh-teh

Do you have ... potatoes?
   Чи ви маєте ... картоплю?
   chih vih MAH-yeh-teh ... kahr-TOP-lyu

baked	печену	PEH-cheh-noo
boiled	варену	VAH-reh-noo
fried	смажену	SMAH-zheh-noo
mashed	пюре	pyu-REH

DESSERT

Dessert	Десерт	deh-SEHRT

What do you have for dessert?
   Що ви маєте на десерт?
   shcho vih MAH-yeh-teh nah deh-SEHRT

Something light please.
   Щось легке будь ласка.
   shchos' LEH-keh bood' LAHS-kah

Please bring me....
Будь ласка, принесіть мені ....
bood' LAHS-kah prih-neh-SEET' meh-NEE

baked cheese	сирник	SIHR-nihk
chocolate ice cream	шоколадне морозиво	sho-ko-LAHD-neh mo-RO-zih-vo
fruit ice cream	фруктове морозиво	frook-TO-veh mo-RO-zih-vo
vanilla ice cream	ванільне морозиво	vah-NEEL'-neh mo-RO-zih-vo
ice cream with fruit topping	морозиво з варенням	mo-RO-zih-vo z vah-REHN-nyam
a piece of cake	кусок торту	koo-SOK TOR-too
a slice of ... pie	кусок пирога ...	koo-SOK pih-ro-HAH
apple	з яблуками	z YAB-loo-kah-mih
cherry	з вишнями	z VIHSH-nya-mih
plum	зі сливами	zee SLIH-vah-mih
a small pastry	тістечко	TEES-tehch-ko

Nothing more, thank you.
Дякую, нічого більше.
DYA-koo-yu nee-CHO-ho BEEL'-sheh

DRINKS

Drinks   Напої   nah-PO-yee

The most popular alcoholic beverages in Ukraine are vodka, beer, cognac, champagne, and wine. Ukrainians don't generally drink mixed drinks. Vodka, called *horilka* (горілка), is always drunk very cold; the bartender may ask you if you want your beer cold or warm ("холодне або тепле," kho-LO-neh AH-bo TEHP-leh).

"What'll you be drinking?"
Що ви будете пити?
shcho vih BOO-deh-teh PIH-tih

I'd like ...
Я би (хотів, *m.*) (хотіла, *f.*) ...
ya bih (kho-TEEV) (kho-TEE-lah)

a bottle of beer	пляшку пива	PLYAHSH-koo PIH-vah
a cold beer, on tap	холодне бочкове пиво	
	kho-LOD-neh boch-KO-veh PIH-vo	
cognac	кон'як	kon'-YAK
cherry liqueur	вишневий лікер	vihsh-NEH-vihў lee-KEHR
chocolate liqueur	шоколадний лікер	
	sho-ko-LAHD-nihў lee-KEHR	
citrus liqueur	цитрусовий лікер	
	TSIHT-roo-so-vihў lee-KEHR	
coffee liqueur	кавовий лікер	kah-VO-vihў lee-KEHR
vodka	горілку	ho-REEL-koo

Vodka comes in various flavors, from black currant to the berries of the *kalyna* or viburnum. By far, the most popular is the spicy hot pepper vodka. The name of the leading brand literally means "Ukrainian with pepper." The proper way to enjoy it is very cold.

I want a shot of ...
    Чи можу я мати келішок ...
    chih MO-zhoo ya MAH-tih KEH-lee-shok

Ukrainian Pepper Vodka
    Української з перцем
    oo-krah-YEENS'-koo z PEHR-tsehm

lemon vodka
    лимонної горілки
    lih-MOHN-no-yee ho-REEL-kih

honey brandy   медовуха   meh-do-VOO-kha

Please bring a (glass) (bottle) ...
    Прошу принести (склянку) (пляшку) ...
    PRO-shoo prih-NEHS-tih (SKLYAN-koo) (PLYASH-koo)

of white wine	білого вина	BEE-lo-ho vih-NAH
of red wine	червоного вина	chehr-VO-no-ho vih-NAH
of dry wine	сухого вина	soo-KHO-ho vih-NAH
of sweet wine	солодкого вина	so-LOD-ko-ho vih-NAH
of fruit wine	фруктового вина	frook-TO-vo-ho vih-nah

I want a bottle of your best champagne.
    Я хочу пляшку вашого найкращого шампанського.
    ya KHO-choo PLYASH-koo VAH-sho-ho nahў-KRAH-shcho-ho
    shahm-PAHNS'-ko-ho

I want ... champagne.
Я хочу ... шампанське.
ya KHO-choo ... shahm-PAHNS'-keh

sweet	солодке	so-LOD-keh
half sweet	напівсолодке	nah-PEEV-so-lod-keh
dry	сухе	soo-KHEH
half dry	е	nah-PEEV-soo-kheh
very dry	брют	bryut

Please bring another...
Прошу принести ще ...
PRO-shoo prih-NEHS-tih shcheh

beer	пива	PIH-vah
cocktail	один коктель	o-DIHN KOK-tehl'
vodka	горілку	ho-REEL-koo
wine	вина	vih-NAH

PROBLEMS

Problems	Проблеми	pro-BLEH-mih

Can you seat us at a different table?
Чи можна нам сісти за інший столик?
chih MOZH-nah nahm SEES-tih zah EEN-shihў STO-lihk

Over there.	Ось там.	os'-tahm

I'm sorry, we're in a hurry.
Перепрошую, ми спішимо.
peh-reh-PRO-shoo-yu mih spee-shih-MO

How quickly can you serve us?
Як швидко ви можете нас обслугувати?
yak SHVID-ko vih MO-zheh-teh nahs ob-SLOO-hoo-vah-tih

I don't have a ...	Я не маю ...	ya neh MAH-yu
fork	виделки	vih-DEHL-kih
knife	ножа	no-ZHAH
spoon	ложки	LOZH-kih
glass	келіха	KEH-lee-khah

plate	тарілки	tah-REEL-kih
napkin	серветки	sehr-VEHT-kih
ashtray	попільнички	po-peel'-NIHCH-kih
This isn't clean.	Це не чисте.	tseh neh CHIHS-teh

I (we) didn't order that.
Я (ми) це не (замовляв, *m.*) (замовляла, *f.*) (замовляли, *pl.*).
ya (mih) tseh neh (zah-mov-LYAV) (zah-mov-LYA-lah)
(zah-mov-LYA-lih)

I (we) asked for ...
Я (ми) (просив, *m.*) (просила, *f.*) (просили, *pl.*)
ya (mih) (pro-SIHV) (pro-SIH-lah) (pro-SIH-lih)

I'd like to change that.
Я хочу поміняти це.
ya KHO-choo po-mee-NYA-tih tseh

I (we) ordered a small portion.
Я (Ми) (замовляв, *m.*) (замовляла, *f.*) (замовляли, *pl.*) малу
порцію.
ya (mih) (zah-mov-LYAV) (za-mov-LYA-lah) (zah-mov-LYA-lih)
mah-LOO POR-tsee-yu.

I don't like it.	Мені це не подобається.	
	meh-NEE tseh neh po-DO-bah-yeht'-sya	
It isn't fresh.	Це не свіже.	tseh neh SVEE-zheh
This isn't warm	Це не достатньо тепле.	
enough.	tseh neh dos-TAHT-n'o TEHP-leh	
This is too salty.	Це засолене.	tseh zah-so-LEH-neh
It's bitter.	Це гірке.	tseh heer-KEH

The meat is (tough) (too greasy).
М'ясо (тверде) (зажирне).
M'YA-so (tvehr-DEH) (zah-ZHIHR-neh)

I want to talk with the manager.
Я хочу говорити з менеджером.
ya KHO-choo ho-vo-RIH-tih z MEH-nehd-zheh-rom

PAYING THE BILL

Joint venture restaurants — which very likely don't serve the local cuisine — may cost even more than a comparable meal at a restaurant in the partner country. These accept only hard currency. Locally run restaurants are considerably cheaper; they're supposed to accept Ukrainian currency but many prefer to be paid in hard currency; sometimes they'll accept a combination of both currencies. Hotel restaurants may accept either type of hard currency or credit cards. A service charge is usually included. If you wish to reward good service, a 10 to 15 percent tip is appropriate, but don't put it on your credit card because the waiter probably won't receive it. It's possible that your waitperson won't have the correct change and you'll end up tipping the difference.

[To summon the waiter] Waiter!
   Офіціант!
   o-fee-tsee-AHNT

We'd like the check please.
   Прошу розрахувати нас.
   PRO-shoo roz-rah-khoo-VAH-tih nahs

We'd like a single check please.
   Прошу один рахунок на всіх.
   PRO-shoo o-DIHN rah-KHOO-nok nah vseekh

We'd like separate checks please.
   Прошу рахунок для кожного окремо.
   PRO-shoo rah-KHOO-nok dlya KOZH-no-ho o-KREH-mo

Is a service charge included?
   Чи сервіс вкнодить в рахунок?
   chih SEHR-vees VKHO-diht' v rah-KHOO-nok

Is the tip included?
   Чи чайові вкнодять в рахунок?
   chih chah-ўo-VEE VKHO-dyat' v rah-KHOO-nok

May we pay in (hryvni) (coupons)?
   Чи можна заплатити в (гривнях) (купонах)?
   chih MOZH-nah zah-plah-TIH-tih v (HRIHV-nyakh)
   (koo-PO-nahkh)

Do you accept ...?
　Чи ви приймаєте ...?
　chih　vih　prihy̆-MAH-yeh-teh

American (Canadian) (Australian) dollars
　американські (канадські) (австралійські) долари
　ah-meh-rih-KAHNS′-kee (kah-NAHDS′-kee)
　(ahv-strah-LEEY̆S′-kee) do-LAH-rih

English pounds
　англійські фунти
　ahnh-LEEY̆S′-kee　FOON-tih

Do you accept this credit card? [showing card]
　Чи ви приймаєте цю кредитну карту?
　chih　vih　prihy̆-MAH-yeh-teh　tsyu　creh-DIHT-noo　KAHR-too

Do you accept travelers′ checks?
　Чи ви приймаєте дорожні чеки?
　chih　vih　prihy̆-MAH-yeh-teh　do-ROZH-nee　CHEH-kih

I think you made a mistake.
　Я думаю що ви зробили помилку.
　ya　DOO-mah-yu　shcho　vih　zro-BIH-lih　po-MIHL-koo

I need a receipt.
　Мені треба чек.
　meh-NEE　TREH-bah　chehk

Thank you. Keep that for yourself.
　Дякую, залиште це собі.
　DYA-koo-yu　zah-LIHSH-teh　tseh　so-BEE

CHAPTER 16. SHOPPING FOR NECESSITIES

Ukrainian Proverb
Скупий два рази платить.
skoo-PIHY̆ dvah RAH-zih PLAH-tiht'
The miser pays twice.

SHOPPING

Shopping   Робити Покупки   ro-BIH-tih po-KOOP-kih

Large department stores are typically open from 8 a.m. until 9:30 p.m. Food stores open at 9 a.m. and close at 8 p.m. or 9 p.m. Smaller shops, such as those selling books or souvenirs, may open later in the morning. Stores are usually closed on Sunday, except for those selling groceries. Locating a particular item can be a challenge; merchandise is organized differently than in western stores and many stores carry a unique assortment of items. Be sure to bring a shopping bag.

While *mahazyn* (магазин) is a general word for store, the word *kramnytsya* (крамиця, krahm-NIH-tsya), meaning "shop" is found on many small stores in Ukraine.

Where is the nearest ...?
    Де знаходиться найближчий ...?
    deh znah-KHO-diht'-sya nahy̆-BLIHZ͡H-chihy̆

antique shop	антикварний магазин	
	ahn-tihk-VAHR-nihy̆ mah-hah-ZIHN	
art store	художній салон	khoo-DOZ͡H-neey̆ sah-LON
bookstore	книжковий магазин	
	knihzh-KO-vihy̆ mah-hah-ZIHN	
camera shop	фотомагазин	FO-to-mah-hah-ZIHN
children's store	дитячий магазин	
	dih-TYA-chihy̆ mah-hah-ZIHN	
clothing store	магазин одягу	mah-hah-ZIHN O-dya-hoo
department store	універмаг	oo-nee-vehr-MAHH
fabric store	магазин тканин	mah-hah-ZIHN tkah-NIHN
florist	магазин квітів	mah-hah-ZIHN KVEE-teev
gift shop	магазин подарунків	
	mah-hah-ZIHN po-dah-ROON-keev	

grocery	продуктовий магазин	
	pro-dook-TO-vihў mah-hah-ZIHN	
open market	базар	bah-ZAHR
shoestore	магазин взуття	mah-hah-ZIHN vzoot-TYA
souvenir shop	сувеніри	soo-veh-NEE-rih
tobacconist	магазин тютюна	
	mah-hah-ZIHN tyu-TYU-nah	
toy store	магазин іграшки	
	mah-hah-ZIHN EEH-rahsh-kih	

THE KIOSK

The Kiosk	Кіоск	kee-OSK

The kiosk is a little booth on a busy thoroughfare or near a bus station that functions much like our convenience store. It's the place to go for every necessity — newspapers and magazines, cigarettes, drinks, snacks, local bus tickets, stamps and stationery. Some kiosks specialize in a single item such as newspapers or souvenirs. More and more, kiosks are stocking all sorts of Western luxuries such as Snickers bars, Adidas running suits, and Christian Dior perfumes.

Where is the nearest (newspaper) (cigarette) kiosk?
Де знаходиться найближчий (газетний) (сигаретний) кіоск?
deh znah-KHO-diht'sya nahў-BLIHZ͡H-chihў (hah-ZEHT-nihў) (sih-hah-REHT-nihў) kee-OSK

Do you have American (newspapers) (magazines)?
Чи ви маєте американські (газети) (журнали)?
chih vih MAH-yeh-teh ah-meh-rih-KAHNS'-kee (hah-ZEH-tih) (z͡hoor-NAH-lih)

Do you have American cigarettes?
Чи ви маєте американські сигарети?
chih vih MAH-yeh-teh ah-meh-rih-KAHNS'-kee sih-hah-REH-tih

What kind of cigarettes do you recommend?
Які сигарети ви порадите мені?
ya-KEE sih-hah-REH-tih vih po-RAH-dih-teh meh-NEE

I need	Мені треба	meh-NEE TREH-bah
a lighter	запальничка	zah-pahl'-NIHCH-kah
matches	сірники	seer-nih-KIH
pipe tobacco	тютюн	tyu-TYUN

Do you have ...?	Чи ви маєте ...?	chih vih MAH-yeh-teh
a city map	карту міста	KAHR-too MEES-tah
postage stamps (for	поштові марки (закордон)	
overseas mail)	posh-TO-vee MAHR-kih (zah-kor-DON)	
postcards	поштові картки	posh-TO-vee KAHRT-kih
souvenirs	сувеніри	soo-veh-NEE-rih
subway tokens	жетони на метро	z͡heh-TO-nih nah meht-RO
tickets for ...	талони на ...	tah-LO-nih nah
the city bus	автобус	ahv-TO-boos
the trolley	тролейбус	tro-LEHY̆-boos
the streetcar	трамвай	trahm-VAHY̆

A kiosk may have soft drinks and mineral water in half liter bottles. You can also purchase fruit juices (фруктовий сік, FROOK-to-vihy̆ seek) in individual glasses in many different flavors.

I'd like	Я хочу	ya KHO-choo
a soft drink	лемонад	leh-mon-NAHD
mineral water	мінеральну воду	
	mee-neh-RAHL'-noo VO-doo	
a glass of fruit juice	склянку фруктового соку	
	SKLYAN-koo frook-TO-vo-ho SO-koo	
apple juice	яблучний сік	YAB-looch-nihy̆ seek
grape juice	виноградний сік	vih-no-HRAHD-nihy̆ seek
grapefruit juice	грейпфруктовий сік	
	grehyp-frook-TO-vihy̆ seek	
orange juice	апельсиновий сік	ah-pehl'-SIH-no-vihy̆ seek
plum juice	сливовий сік	slih-VO-vihy̆ seek
raspberry juice	малиновий сік	mah-LIH-no-vihy̆ seek
tomato juice	томатний сік	to-MAHT-nihy̆ seek

I need a bottle opener.
  Мені потрібен ключ для відкривання пляшок.
  meh-NEE po-TREE-behn klyuch dlya veed-krih-VAHN-nya
  plya-SHOK

SHOPPING FOR GROCERIES

In larger cities you may find an *universam* (універсам, oo-nee-vehr-SAHM), a self-service supermarket which carries household items as well as food. A *hastronom* (гастроном, hahs-tro-NOM) or *produkty* (продукти, pro-DOOK-tih) is a grocery with counter service which carry meats, cheeses, fish, and canned items. The most enjoyable way to shop for food is at the *bazar* (базар, bah-ZAHR) or farmer's market. At one of these open markets (which may actually be in a covered building), you can find fruits and vegetables, as well as meats, cheeses, and prepared foods. The individual stalls are run by independent merchants who set prices according to supply and demand. Browsing in an open market is a great way to experience the daily life of a city and mingle with its people. There are also a number of food specialty shops:

bakery	хлібний магазин
	KHLEEB-nihỹ mah-hah-ZIHN
butcher shop	м'ясний магазин
	M'YAS-nihỹ mah-hah-ZIHN
candy store	кондитерський магазин
	kon-DIHT-tehrs'-kihỹ mah-hah-ZIHN
cheese store	магазин сир mah-hah-ZIHN sihr
dairy store	молочний магазин
	mo-LOCH-nihỹ mah-hah-ZIHN
deli	кулінарія koo-lee-nah-REE-ya
fish market	рибний магазин RIHB-nihỹ mah-hah-ZIHN
ice cream shop	кафе морозиво
	kah-FEH ih-vo mo-RO-zih-vo
liquor store	винний магазин VIHN-nihỹ mah-hah-ZIHN
pastry shop	кондитерський магазин
	kon-DIH-tehrs'-kihỹ mah-hah-ZIHN
produce market	магазин овочі-фрукти
	mah-hah-ZIHN O-vo-chee FROOK-tih
sausage shop	магазин ковбаси
	mah-hah-ZIHN kov-BAH-sih

Metric Measures. Food is commonly sold by mass, according to the metric system. Here are a few equivalents:
- There are approximately 28 grams (грами, HRAH-mih) in an ounce.
- 1 kilogram (кілограм, kee-lo-HRAHM) equals 2.2 pounds.
- 1 liter (літр, LEE-tr) is slightly more than 1 quart.
- There are 3.8 liters (літри, LEE-trih) in a gallon.

When making a selection, Ukrainians ask for a specific weight rather than a number. If you want to buy something by the piece, ask for so many *shtuky* (штуки, SHTOO-kih). The concept "dozen" is unfamiliar in countries using the metric system, although there is a Ukrainian word for it, *dyuzhyna* (дюжина, DYU-zhih-nah).

I want	Я хочу....	ya KHO-choo
some of these	трошки цих	TROSH-kih tsihkh
that one on the shelf	ось те на полиці	os' teh nah po-LIH-tsee
a loaf of bread	буханку хліба	boo-KHAHN-koo KHLEE-bah
a roll	булку	BOOL-koo
a cake	торт	tort
half a kilogram of cookies	пів кілограму печива	peev kee-lo-HRAH-moo PEH-chih-vah
a (box) (bag) of candy	(коробку) (кульок) цукерок	(ko-ROB-koo) (koo-L'OK) tsoo-KEH-rok
a chocolate bar	шоколадку	sho-ko-LAHD-koo
a small package of tea	пачку чаю	PAHCH-koo CHAH-yu
a small can of fish	банку рибних консервів	BAHN-koo RIHB-nihkh kon-SEHR-veev
200 grams of sausage	двісті грам ковбаси	DVEES-tee hrahm kov-bah-SIH
a (bottle) (carton) of milk	(пляшку) (пакет) молока	(PLYASH-koo) (pah-KEHT) mo-lo-KAH
cream	вершки	vehrsh-KIH
hard cheese	твердий сир	tvehr-DIHY̆ sihr
cottage cheese	сир	sihr
ice cream	морозиво	mo-RO-zih-vo
kefir, a yogurt drink	кефір	KEH-feer
some apples	декілька яблук	DEH-keel'-kah YAB-look
some grapes	трошки винограду	TROSH-kih vih-no-HRAH-doo
some oranges	делкілька апельсин	DEH-keel'-kah ah-pehl'-SIH
some pears	декілька груш	DEH-keel'-kah hroosh
some plums	трошки сливок	TROSH-kih slih-VOK
some tangerines	декілька мандарин	DEH-keel'-kah mahn-dah-RIHN
Is it fresh?	Це свіже?	tseh SVEE-zheh

SELECTING AND PAYING FOR MERCHANDISE

In small stores, some hard currency stores, and in the open markets, you simply pay the salesperson. In the larger stores, purchasing may be a little more complicated. When you decide upon the item you want, take note of the price. Then go to the cash desk and pay for it. You'll receive a receipt (чек, chehk), which you must take to another counter to pick up your purchase.

Would you please show me ...? [pointing]
Чи ви можете мені показати ...?
chih vih MO-zheh-teh meh-NEE po-kah-ZAH-tih

this one	це	tseh
something like that	щось таке як це	shchos' tah-KEH yak tseh
that one in the window	то в вікні	to v veek-NEE

This isn't quite what I want.
Це не зовсім, що я хочу.
tseh neh ZOV-seem shcho ya KHO-choo

I would like better quality.
Я би (хотів, *m.*) (хотіла, *f.*) ліпшої якості.
ya bih (kho-TEEV) (kho-TEE-lah) LEEP-sho-yee YA-kos-tee

I'll take this one.	Я візьму це.	ya veez'-MOO tseh
What does it cost?	Скільки це коштує?	SKEEL'-kih tseh kosh-TOO-yeh
Where do I pay?	Де мені заплатити?	deh meh-NEE zahp-lah-TIH-tih

Do you accept this credit card? [showing card]
Чи ви приймаєте цю кредитну карту?
chih vih prihy-MAH-yeh-teh tsyu kreh-DIHT-noo KAHR-too

Can I take this out of the country?
Чи можна це вивозити закордон?
chih MOZH-nah tseh vih-VO-zih-tih zah-kor-DOHN

I'll need a receipt.
Мені потрібен чек.
meh-NEE po-TREE-behn chehk

Would you please wrap it for me?
Чи ви це можете загорнути?
chih vih tseh MO-zheh-teh zah-hor-NOO-tih

Can this be exchanged?
Чи можна це замінити?
chih MOZH-nah tseh zah-mee-NIH-tih

I want to return this.	Я хочу це повернути.
	ya KHO-choo tseh po-vehr-NOO-tih
I'd like a refund.	Я хочу гроші назад.
	ya KHO-choo HRO-shee nah-ZAHD
Here's the receipt.	Ось тут чек. os' toot chehk

IN THE DRUGSTORE

In the Drugstore	В Аптеці	v ahp-TEH-tsee

The *apteka* (аптека, ahp-TEH-kah) carries prescription drugs and other medicines (including some antibiotics) that can be purchased without a prescription. The word for medicine is ліки (LEE-kih). In the *apteka* there's also a *hemiopatychnyy* (геміопатичний, heh-mee-o-pah-TIHCH-nihy) department which stocks a fascinating array of herbal remedies and homeopathic cures. Because Ukrainians are very reluctant to take drugs and prefer more natural methods of healing, traditional homeopathy is popular among all segments of the population including urban, well-educated people.

Where's the nearest pharmacy?
Де знаходиться найближча аптека?
deh znah-KHO-diht'-sya nahȳ-BLIHZH-chah ahp-TEH-kah

I want something for....
Я хочу щось від ....
ya KHO-choo shchos' veed

allergy	аллергії	ahl-LEHR-hee-yee
bee sting	укусу бджоли	oo-KOO-soo BDZHO-lih
a cold	простуди	pros-TOO-dih
a cough	кашлю	KAHSH-lyu
a headache	головної болі	ho-lov-NO-yee BO-lee

insect bite	укусів комах	oo-KOO-seev ko-MAHKH
nausea	тошноти	tosh-no-TIH
sunburn	сонячного опіку	SO-nyach-no-ho O-pee-koo
travel sickness	морської хороби	mors'-KO-yee kho-RO-bih

Can I get it without a prescription?
    Чи можна це отримати без рецепту?
    chih MOZ͡H-nah tseh ot-RIH-mah-tih behz reh-TSEHP-too

Can you prepare this prescription for me?
    Чи ви можете виписати цей рецепт для мене?
    chih vih MO-z͡heh-teh VIH-pih-sah-tih tsehy͡ reh-TSEHPT
    dlya MEH-neh

May I wait?
    Можна мені чекати?
    MOZ͡H-nah meh-NEE cheh-KAH-tih

When do I need to come back?
    Коли мені треба прийти знову?
    ko-LIH meh-NEE TREH-bah prihy͡-TIH ZNO-voo

Do you have ...?	Чи є у вас...?	chih yeh oo vahs
adhesive bandages	пластер	PLAHS-tehr
antibiotics	антибіотики	ahn-tih-bee-O-tih-kih
aspirin	аспірин	ahs-pee-RIHN
antiseptic cream	антисептичний крем	
	ahn-tih-sehp-TIHCH-nihy͡ krehm	
bandage	бинт	bihnt
calcium supplement	кальцій глюканат	
	KAHL'-tseey͡ hlyu-kah-NAHT	
contraceptives	контрасептиви	kon-trah-sehp-TIH-vih
cotton wool	вата	VAH-tah
ear drops	в ушні каплі	v oosh-NIH KAHP-lee
eye drops	очні каплі	och-NEE KAHP-lee
gauze	марля	MAHR-lya
iodine	йод	y͡od
iron supplement	гематоген	heh-mah-to-HEHN
sanitary napkins	марлеві серветки	
	mahr-LEH-vee sehr-VEHT-kih	
sleeping pills	снотворні таблетки	
	snot-VOHR-nee tah-BLEHT-kih	

throat lozenges	таблетки для горла	
	tah-BLEHT-kih dlya HOR-lah	
vitamin pills	вітаміни	vee-tah-MEE-nih
Do you have ...	Чи є у вас ...?	chih yeh oo vahs
baby food	дитяче харчування	
	dih-TYA-cheh khahr-choo-VAHN-nya	
diapers	пелюшки	peh-LYUSH-kih
baby oil	дитяче масло	dih-TYA-cheh MAHS-lo
baby powder	дитяча пудра	dih-TYA-chah POO-drah

TOILETRIES AND COSMETICS

Toiletries and Cosmetics
Туалетні та Косметичні Принадлежності
too-ah-LEHT-nee tah kos-meh-TIHCH-nee
prih-nahd-LEHZ̑H-nos-tee

For toiletries and cosmetics, look for a *parfyumeriya* (парфюмерія, pahr-fyu-MEH-ree-ya). However, it's a good idea to bring from home everything you'll need throughout your stay.

Do you have ...?	Чи є у вас ...?	chih yeh oo vahs
after shave lotion	одеколон після гоління	
	o-deh-ko-LON PEES-lya ho-LEEN-nya	
bath salts	екстракт для ванни	
	EHKS-trahkt dlya VAHN-nih	
blush	рум'яна	room'-YA-nah
cologne	трійний одеколон	
	TREEY̆-nihy̆ o-deh-ko-LON	
comb	гребінець	hreh-bee-NEHTS'
cosmetics	косметика	kos-MEH-tih-kah
cleansing cream	крем для зняття косметики	
	krehm dlya znyat-TYA kos-MEH-tih-kih	
deodorant	дезодорант	deh-zo-do-RAHNT
eyebrow pencil	олівець для бровів	
	o-lee-VEHTS' dlya bro-VEEV	
eyeliner	олівець для вік	o-lee-VEHTS' dlya veek
eyeshadow	тіні для вік	TEE-nee dlya veek
face cream	крем для лиця	khrehm dlya lih-TSYA

face powder	пудра	POOD-rah
hand cream	крем для рук	krehm dlya rook
hairbrush	щітка для волосся	
	SHCHEET-kah dlya vo-LOS-sya	
hair coloring	фарба для волосся	
	FAHR-bah dlya vo-LOS-sya	
lip balm	гігієнічна помада	
	hee-hee-yeh-NEECH-nah po-MAH-dah	
lipstick	губна помада	hoob-NAH po-MAH-dah
make-up	косметика	kos-MEH-tih-kah
make-up remover	лосьон для зняття косметики	
	los'-ON dlya znyat-TYA kos-MEH-tih-kih	
mascara	туш для вій	toosh dlya veeў
nailbrush	щітка для ногтей	
	SHCHEET-kah dlya noh-TEHЎ	
nail file	пилка для нігтів	PIHL-kah dlya nih-TIV
nail polish	лак для нігтів	lahk dlya nih-TIV
nail polish remover	ацетон	ah-tseh-TON
nail scissors	ножиці для нігтів	
	NO-zhih-tsee dlya nih-TIV	
perfume	парфюми	pahr-FYU-mih
razor	бритва	BRIHT-vah
razor blades	леза для бритви	LEH-zah dlya BRIHT-vih
safety pins	англійські булавки	
	ahn-HLEEЎ'S-kee boo-LAHV-kih	
shampoo	шампунь	shahm-POON'
shaving brush	помазок	po-mah-ZOK
shaving cream	крем для гоління	krehm dlya ho-LEEN-nya
soap	мило	MIH-lo
sponge	губка	HOOB-kah
suntan cream	крем для загару	krehm dlya zah-HAH-roo
sunscreen	масло від загару	
	MAHS-lo veed zah-HAH-roo	
talcum powder	тальк	tahl'k
toilet paper	туалетний папір	
	too-ah-LEHT-nihў pah-PEER	
toilet water	одеколон	o-deh-ko-LON
toothbrush	зубна щітка	zoob-NAH SHCHEET-kah
toothpaste	зубна паста	zoob-NAH PAHS-tah
towel	рушник	roosh-NIHK
tweezers	пінцет	peen-TSEHT

St. Sophia Cathedral in Kyiv is on everyone's list of masterpieces of world architecture. Established by Yaroslav the Wise in 1037, it was named after Hagia Sophia (Holy Wisdom) Cathedral in Istanbul, but was the Kyivan interpretation of the Byzantine style. The basic structure of the interior and several interior mosaics are original, but the outward appearance reflects the additions during the Ukrainian Baroque period of the late 17th and early 18th century.

Lviv Theater of Opera and Ballet. In Ukraine's largest cities, opera and ballet companies share a magnificent theater building. The Lviv Theater of Opera and Ballet, built in 1900, reflects the city's Austro-Hungarian past. It seats 1100 and was recently restored.

At right is an interior view of the (T. Schevchenko) Theater of Opera and Ballet in Kyiv.

A Ukrainian Catholic church in Kalush, in the Ivano-Frankivska region in western Ukraine, overflows with parishioners at services. Ukrainian Catholic churches are found primarily in the three western oblasts: Ivano-Frankivska, Lvivska, and Ternopilska.

Garlic seller in Kalush market. Ukrainians value garlic for its health benefits as well as its tangy addition to their cuisine.

On street corners in big cities you can find villagers who ride the bus in to sell produce. This woman in Lviv is selling medicinal herbs, basil and St. John's-wort blossoms, that she gathered in the country side.

Ukrainian farmers in horse-drawn carts are a common sight in the country.

This retired collective farm worker in western Ukraine supplies her city grandchildren with many dairy products.

Folk art museums throughout Ukraine display collections of traditional dress and other intricately embroidered fabrics.

This little girl in the village Chertizh in the Lvivska oblast is dressed in her Sunday best, a blouse embroidered by her grandmother.

Bread is truly the staff of life in Ukraine. Bakeries have marvelous selections, like this one in Lviv ... but home bakers also are skilled breadmakers.

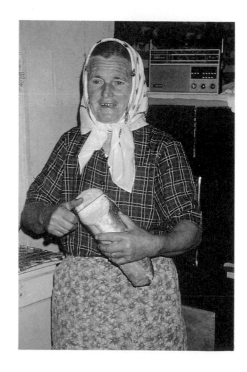

Pastry shop tortes are special occasion desserts. Under the pretty icing are layers of sponge cake with pastry cream, nuts, or fruit jam. In this shop in Kalush the cakes are packed in pretty boxes that say "tort."

Rural homes in Ukraine are colorful and well-kept and ornamented with flowers. This one is in the Carpathian Mountains.

Nesting storks are a common sight in villages in western Ukraine.

Facing page: *The tragic allegory "Kateryna," the story of a Ukrainian country girl who is seduced by a Russian soldier, is a recurrent theme in the works of Taras Shevchenko. His oil painting "Kateryna" is on display at the Shevchenko Literary-memorial Museum at Kaniv.*

Ukraine's greatest hero, Taras Shevchenko, is memorialized in many ways. This large portrait of Shevchenko in plants was a long-time familiar landmark in Lviv, but recently was replaced by a concrete monument to another famous Ukrainian, Mykhaylo Hrushevsky.

A village woman in western Ukraine embroidered a portrait of Shevchenko using a pattern she found in a magazine.

CHAPTER 17. SIGHTSEEING

Ukrainian Proverb:

Краще один раз побачити ніж сто раз почути.
KRAH-shch o-DIHN rahz po-BAH-chi-tih neezh sto rahz
po-CHOO-tih
It's better to see something once than hear about it a hundred times.

Reading Street Names. In expressing street names, the type of thoroughfare — "street," "avenue," "lane," etc. — precedes the proper name and is not capitalized. Thus Taras Shevchenko Boulevard is бульвар Тараса Шевченка (boulevard of Taras Shevchenko) and Freedom Avenue is проспект Свободи (avenue of Freedom). Note that street names in the Ukrainian language are in the possessive case, thus accounting for the many names on street signs that end in the letters -a, -и, -ого, or -их. Here are some useful words and their abbreviations:

алея (а.)	ah-LEH-ya	alley
бульвар (бул.)	bool'-VAHR	boulevard
вулиця (вул.)	VOO-lih-tsya	street
дорога (д.)	do-RO-HAH	road
набережна (наб.)	NAH-beh-rehzh-nah	embankment
площа (пл.)	PLO-shchah	square
провулок (пр.)	pro-VOO-lok	side street
проїзд (п.)	pro-YEEZD	passage
проспект (просп.)	pros-PEHKT	prospect, avenue
спуск (сп.)	spoosk	descent
узвіз (уз.)	ooz-VEEZ	ascent
шосе (ш.)	sho-SEH	highway

ARRANGING A TOUR

Your hotel service bureau can arrange for you to see the main points of interest in the city. It may also be able to arrange special excursions outside of the city, such as a visit to a collective farm or a craft fair. If you're not staying at an Inturyst hotel, there's a local office in town as well as many other travel agencies. Some travelers believe that Inturyst still offers the widest range of services while others find that the competition is more flexible.

Where is the service bureau?
Де знаходиться сервісне бюро?
deh znah-KHO-diht′-sya SEHR-vees-neh byu-RO

Where is the (travel agency) (Inturyst office)?
Де знаходиться (транспортне аґентсво) (бюро Інтуриста)?
deh znah-KHO-diht′-sya (TRAHNS-port-neh ah-HEHNS-vo)
(byu-RO een-too-RIHS-tah)

Where can I find a guide-translator?
Де я можу знайти ґіда-перекладача?
deh ya MO-zhoo znahў-TIH GEE-dah-peh-reh-klah-dah-CHAH
(Note: The "GEE" sound in ґіда is pronounced as in the word "geek" rather than the "gee" sound in "gee-whiz.")

How much do you charge per (day) (week)?
Скільки це буде коштувати за (день) (тиждень)?
SKEEL′-kih tseh BOO-deh kosh-too-VAH-tih zah (dehn′)
(TIHZH-den′)?

I'm (we're) here for (a day) (three days) (one week).
Я (ми) тут на (один день) (три дні) (один тиждень).
ya (mih) toot nah (o-DIHN dehn′) (trih dnee) (O-dihn
TIHZH-dehn′).

What do you recommend I see?
Що ви порадити мені подивитись?
shcho vih po-RAH-dih-tih meh-NEE po-dih-VIH-tihs′

Do you have any special excursions?
Чи ви маєте планові екскурсії?
chih vih MAH-yeh-teh PLAH-no-vee ehks-KOOR-see-yee

How much does the tour cost?
Скільки коштує екскурсія?
SKEEL′-kih kosh-TOO-yeh ehks-KOOR-see-ya

What time does the tour start?
Коли починається екскурсія?
ko-LIH po-chih-NAH-yeht′-sya ehks-KOOR-see-ya

Where does the tour start?
Де починається екскурсія?
deh po-chih-NAH-yeht′-sya ehks-KOOR-see-ya

What time will we return?

Коли ми повертаємось назад?

ko-LIH mih po-vehr-TAH-yeh-mos′ nah-ZAHD

Does the cost include lunch?

Чи обід входить в плату?

chih o-BEED VKHO-diht′ v PLAH-too

Will we have to walk a lot?

Чи ми будемо багато ходити?

chih mih BOO-deh-mo bah-HAH-to kho-DIH-tih

Should we take our coats?

Чи треба нам взяти теплу одежу?

chih TREH-bah nahm VZYA-tih TEHP-loo o-DEH-z͡hoo

SEEING THE HIGHLIGHTS

It pays to check in advance whether the attraction you want to see is open. Museums tend to change their schedules frequently, and smaller ones don't always follow their stated schedules. Most museums and tourist attractions charge a small admission fee. If you're given a small receipt, you may later be asked to produce it by an attendant.

Is the museum open (today) (tomorrow)?

Чи музей відкритий (сьогодні) (завтра)?

chih moo-ZEHY̆ VEED-krih-tihy̆ (s′o-HOD-nee) (ZAHV-trah)

Let's go to the (museum) (fine arts gallery).

Давайте підем в (музей) (художню галерею).

dah-VAHY̆-teh pee-DEHM v (moo-ZEHY̆) (khoo-DOZ͡H-nyu hah-leh-REH-yu)

When does this (open) (close)?

Коли це (відкривається) (закривається)?

ko-LIH tseh (veed-krih-VAH-yeht′-sya) (zah-krih-VAH-yeht′sya)

What's the admission fee?

Яка вхідна плата?

ya-KAH vkheed-NAH PLAH-tah

Two adults, please.

Два дорослих, будь ласка.

dvah do-ROS-lihkh bood′ LAHS-kah

Is there an English-speaking guide?
Чи там є гід, який говорить по-англійськи?
chih tahm yeh geed yah-KIHȲ ho-VO-riht′ po ahnh-LEEȲS′-kih

Where is the (cloakroom) (restroom)?
Де знаходиться (гардероб) (туалет)?
deh znah-KHO-diht′-sya (hahr-deh-ROB) (too-ah-LEHT)

May I take a photo?
Чи можна тут фотографувати?
chih MOẐH-nah toot fo-to-hrah-foo-VAH-tih

What's the highlight of this museum?
Що видатного в цьому музеї?
shcho vih-daht-NO-ho v TS′O-moo moo-ZEH-yee

Which collections are in this museum?
Які колекції представлені в цьому музеї?
ya-KEE ko-lehk-TSEE-yee prehd-STAHV-leh-nee v t′so-MOO
moo-ZEH-yee

How many artists are represented here?
Скільки художників представлено тут?
SKEEL′-kih khoo-DOẐH-nih-keev prehd-STAHV-leh-no toot

Who's the (artist) (sculptor)?
Хто є (художник) (скульптор)?
kho yeh (khoo-DOẐH-nihk) (SKOOLP′-tor)

I want to see the folk art museum.
Я хочу подивитись музей народного мистецтва.
ya KHO-choo po-dih-VIH-tihs′ moo-ZEHȲ nah-ROD-NO-ho
mihs-TEHTST-vah

From what (region) (period) are these crafts?
З якого (району) (періоду) ці вироби?
z ya-KO-ho (rah-ȲO-noo) (peh-REE-o-doo) tsee VIH-ro-bih

Where can I buy...?
Де я можу купити ...?
deh ya MO-zĥoo koo-PIH-tih

postcards	поштові картки	posh-TO-vee KAHRT-kih
books	книжки	KNIHẐH-kih
souvenirs	сувеніри	soo-veh-NEE-rih

Let's go downtown.
Давайте підем в центр міста.
dah-VAHỸ-teh pee-DEHM v tsehntr MEES-tah

What important historical sites are here?
Які історично-важливі місця знаходяться тут?
ya-KEE ees-to-RIHCH-no vazh-LIH-vee mees-TSYA
znah-KHO-dyat'-sya toot

What's that (building) (monument)?
Що це за (будинок) (монумент)?
shcho tseh zah (boo-DIH-nok) (mo-noo-MEHT)

Can we take a look inside?
Чи можна зайти і подивитись в середину?
chih MOZH-nah zahỹ-TIH ee po-dih-VIH-tihs' v
seh-reh-DIH-noo

I'd like to see the opera house.
Я хочу подивитись оперний театр.
ya KHO-choo po-dih-VIH-tihs' O-pehr-nihỹ teh-AHTR

Who is the architect?   Хто архітектор?
khto ar-khee-TEHK-tor

Couldn't we go to the central library?
Чи ми би могли піти в центральну бібліотеку?
chih mih bih moh-LIH pee-TIH v tsehnt-RAHL'noo
beeb-lee-o-TEH-koo

How many books are here?
Скільки книжок знаходиться тут?
SKEEL'-kih knih-ZHOK znah-KHO-diht'sya toot

Where is the Taras Shevchenko monument?
Де знаходиться монумент Тараса Шевченка?
deh znah-KHO-diht'-sya mo-noo-MEHNT tah-RAH-sah
shehv-CHEHN-kah

Which other monuments are worth seeing?
Які інші монументи варто подивитись?
ya-KEE EEN-shee mo-noo-MEHN-tih VAHR-to po-dih-VIH-tihs'

I want to see the castle.
Я хочу подивитись замок.
ya KHO-choo po-dih-VIH-tihs' ZAH-mok

How difficult is it to climb there?
Як важко піднятись туда?
yak VAZH-ko peed-NYA-tihs too-DAH

How old is it?   Скільки йому років?
                     SKEEL'-kih ўo-MOO RO-keev

Has it been restored? Чи він був реставрований?
                     chih veen boov rehs-tahv-RO-vah-nihў

Let's go to the botanical garden.
Давайте підем в ботанічний сад.
dah-VAHУ-teh pee-DEHM v bo-tahn-NEECH-nihў sahd

How big is it?   Який він великий?
                     yah-KIHУ veen veh-LIH-kihў

When was it   Коли він заснован?
  established?   ko-LIH veen zahs-NO-vahn

How many varieties of plants are here?
Скільки різноманітних рослин представлено тут?
SKEEL'-kih REEZ-no-mah-NEET-nihkh ros-LIHN
prehd-STAHV-leh-no toot?

Can we go to the   Чи ми можемо піти в парк?
  park?   chih mih MO-zheh-mo pee-TIH v pahrk

I want to go to the zoo.
Я хочу піти в зоопарк.
ya KHO-choo pee-TIH v zo-o-PAHRK

What kind of animals are most numerous here?
Які тварини представленні тут?
ya-KEE tvah-RIH-nih prehd-STAHV-lehn-nee toot

I want to go to the open market.
Я хочу піти на базар.
ya KHO-choo pee-TIH nah bah-ZAHR

How much does this cost?
Скільки це коштує?
SKEEL'-kih tseh kosh-TOO-yeh

Where was this grown?
Де це вирощується?
deh tseh vih-RO-shchoo-yeht'-sya

I want to see the cemetery.

Я хочу подивитись кладовище.

ya KHO-choo po-dih-VIH-tihs′ klah-DO-vih-shcheh

Are any famous people buried here?

Хто з відомих людей похован тут?

khto z vee-DO-mihkh lyu-DEHŸ po-KHO-vahn toot

Is it still in use?   Чи воно в дії?

chih vo-NO v dee-YEE

How can I get to the stadium?

Як добратись до стадіону?

yak do-BRAH-tihs′ do stah-dee-O-noo

TAKING PHOTOS

There are no longer security restrictions on photographing government or military installations. However, museums and churches may forbid use of flashbulbs or ban cameras entirely. When photographing scenes that include people, it's a good idea to exercise common courtesy. To some, being photographed without consent is an invasion of privacy. Unless you can be entirely unobtrusive, ask permission first.

You may, however, encounter people who would appreciate a nice color photo of their children, since many Ukrainians don't own cameras, and for those who do, black and white film has been the standard for the home market. If photography as a means of making friends is a priority, a Polaroid camera is a great ice-breaker. It's especially suited for color portraits and solves the problem of having to send prints over when you return home.

May I photograph (you) (it)?

Чи можна (вас) (це) фотографувати?

chih MOZH-nah (vahs) (tseh) fo-to-hrah-foo-VAH-tih

Would you take a photo of us, please?

Чи можна вас попросити сфотографувати нас?

chih MOZH-nah vahs po-pro-SIH-tih sfo-to-hrah-foo-VAH-tih nahs

For any of your photography needs, look for the word "фото." You'll see it where cameras or photographic equipment are being sold or where film is processed.

Camera Supply Shop   Фотомагазин   fo-to-mah-hah-ZIHN

It's smart planning to pack more film than you think you'll need along with the necessary accessories such as batteries and flash cubes. Western and Japanese film is available in outlets in the larger cities. Some of the big tourist hotels now have Kodak franchise outlets that sell 110-size and 35-mm print film and Ektachrome slide film. These are sold for hard currency. If you're buying from a kiosk or another newly-private entrepreneur, check the expiration date as it's possible that out-dated film is being sold.

Where is the nearest camera shop?
Де знаходиться найближчий фофомагазин?
deh znah-KHO-diht'-sya nahў-BLIHZH-chihў fo-to-mah-ha-ZIHN

I'd like for this camera [showing the camera] ...
Я хочу для цого фотоапарату ...
ya KHO-choo dlya TS'O-ho fo-to-ahp-ah-RAH-too

black and white film	чорно-білу плівку
	CHOR-no BEE-loo PLEEV-koo
color print film	негативну кольорову плівку
	neh-hah-TIHV-noo ko-l'o-RO-voo PLEEV-koo
color slide film	кольорову плівку для слайдів
	ko-l'o-RO-voo PLEEV-koo dlya SLAHŸ-deev
(24) (36) exposures	(двадцять чотири) (тридцать шість) кадрів.
	DVAHD-tsyat' cho-TIH-rih (TRIHD-tsyat'
	sheest') KAH-dreev

I need ... rolls.
Мені треба ... плівок.
meh-NEE TREH-bah ... PLEE-vok

What speed is this film?
Яка чутливість цієї плівки?
ya-KAH choot-LIH-veest' tsee-YEH-yee PLEEV-kee

The sensitivity of Ukrainian film is measured in DOST (ДОСТ) units. It comes in speeds of 32, 64, 135, 250, etc. Here is its approximate equivalent to the International/American (ISO/ASA) and the German (DIN) film speeds:

ISO (ASA)	DIN	DOST
(36)		32
(71)		64
100	21	(90)
(150)		135
200	24	(180)
(280)		250
400	27	360

What is the expiration date?
Який срок гідності?
ya-KIHY̆ srok HEED-nos-tee

I need for this camera...
Мені треба для цієї камери...
meh-NEE TREH-bah dlya tsee-YEH-yee KAH-meh-rih

a battery	батарейка	bah-tah-REHY̆-kah
flashcubes	фотоспалах	fo-to-SPAH-lahkh
a UV filter	ультрафіолетовий фільтр	ool-trah-fee-o-LEH-to-vihY̆ feel'tr

Photo Developing Shop Фотомайстерня fo-to-mahy̆s-TEHR-nya

The *fotomaysternya* is where you take your film to be developed. If you've bought film manufactured in a former Soviet republic, you may want to have it processed in Ukraine as it requires a different process than western film. If you know that your film is transparency film that requires the E6 process or color negative film requiring the C-41 process, it's better to bring it home to be processed, unless you locate a Kodak franchise.

(Where can I) (Can you) develop this film?
(Де я можу) (Чи ви можете) проявити цю плівку?
(deh ya MO-zhoo) (chih vih MO-zheh-teh) pro-yah-VIH-tih tsyu PLEEV-koo

How much do you charge for processing?
Скільки коштує проявка?
SKEEL'-kih kosh-TOO-yeh pro-YAV-kah

When will the film be ready?
Коли будуть готові плівки?
ko-LIH BOO-doot′ ho-TO-vee PLEEV-kih

Can you mail them to this address?
Чи ви можете надіслати їх на цю адресу?
chih vih MO-zheh-teh nah-dees-LAH-tih yeekh nah tsyu
ahd-REH-soo

Camera Repair Shop   Фотомайстерня   fo-to-mahӱs-TEHR-nya

Where can I get this camera repaired?
Де я можу відремонтувати цей фотоапарат?
deh yah MO-zhoo veed-reh-mon-too-VAH-tih tsehӱ
FO-to-ah-pah-RAHT

Can you fix this camera?
Чи ви можете відремонтувати цей фотоапарат?
chih vih MO-zheh-teh veed-reh-mon-too-VAH-tih tsehӱ
FO-to-ah-pah-RAHT

The shutter is stuck.   Затвір не працює.
                        zaht-VEER neh prah-TSYU-yeh

The film is jammed.   Плівка не перемотується.
                      PLEEV-kah neh peh-reh-MO-too-yeht′-sya

The meter doesn't   Експонометр не працює.
work.   ehks-po-NO-mehtr neh prah-TSYU-yeh

Can you repair a camcorder?
Чи ви можете відремонтувати відеокамеру?
chih vih MO-zheh-teh veed-reh-mon-too-VAH-tih
VEE-deh-o-KAH-meh-roo

I need a video tape.   Мені потрібна плівка.
                       meh-NEE pot-REEB-nah PLEEV-kah

I need an adapter to 110 volts.
Мені потрібен адаптор на сто десять вольт.
meh-NEE pot-REE-behn ah-DAHP-tor nah sto DEHS-yat′ vol′t.

CHAPTER 18. AMUSEMENTS

Ukrainian Proverb:
Зробив діло гуляй сміло.
zro-BIHV DEE-lo hoo-LYAĬ SMEE-lo
When the work is finished, go ahead and have a good time.

Ukraine has a strong tradition of performing arts that is growing even richer with the greater freedoms that have come with independence. Now there are even more artistic groups, new festivals with greater exploration of traditional Ukrainian themes, and an increased number of performances in the Ukrainian language. Unfortunately, however, the state cannot afford to subsidize the arts to extent to which they're accustomed, and some of the more expensive Ukrainian arts, such as the cinema, have curtailed production. Tickets to the performing arts are still inexpensive, but may not be so easy to obtain as formerly. Evening performances of most plays and concerts usually begin at 7 p.m. (19:00).

BUYING TICKETS

To buy theater and concert tickets, try the service bureaus in hotels or the Inturyst office. If you really want a bargain, purchase your tickets in Ukrainian currency directly at the box office. You might start by asking:

"Where are tickets sold for concerts?"
Де продаються квитки на концерти?
deh pro-dah-YUT-sya kviht-KIH nah kon-TSEHR-tih

(The word *kontsert* (концерт) is a very general term that includes all sorts of entertainment from plays to musical performances.)

Are there any tickets for (today's) (tonight's) ...
Чи є квитки на (сьогодні) (вечір) ...
chih yeh kviht-KIH nah (s'o-HOD-nee) (VEH-cheer)

I need two tickets for (today's) (tonight's) ....
Мені потрібно два квитки на (сьогодні) (вечер) ...
meh-NEE po-TREEB-no dvah kviht-KIH nah s'o-HOD-nee

ballet	на балет	nah bah-LEHT
circus	до цирку	do TSIHR-koo

concert	на концерт	nah kohn-SEHRT
folk dance	на концерт народних танців	
	nah KOHN-tsert nah-ROD-nihkh TAHN-tseev	
opera	на оперу	nah O-peh-roo
play	на виставу	nah vihs-TAH-voo
symphony	на симфонічний концерт	
	nah sihm-fo-NEECH-nihў kohn-SEHRT	

For when do you have tickets?
На який день ви маєте квитки?
nah ya-KIHЎ dehn′ vih MAH-yeh-teh kviht-KIH

I'd like to reserve two tickets....
Я хочу зарезервувати два квитки ....
ya KHO-choo zah-reh-zehr-voo-VAH-tih dvah kviht-KIH

for the Wednesday matinee
на денну виставу на середу
nah DEHN-noo vihs-TAH-voo nah SEH-reh-doo

for Friday evening
на п′ятницю вечір
nah P′YAT-nih-tsyu VEH-cheer

I want to sit ....　Я хочу сидіти ....　ya KHO-choo sih-DEE-tih

in the orchestra stalls	в партері	v pahr-TEH-ree
in the center	в центрі	v TSEHT-ree
on the right side	зправа	ZPRAH-vah
on the left side	зліва	ZLEE-vah
in the balcony	на балконі	nah bahl-KO-nee
in a box	в лоджі	v LOD-zhee

If you can't find a ticket at an official tourist outlet, go down to the theater early and see if tickets are still available. Payment will be in Ukrainian currency and a real bargain. If no tickets are left, it's a very common practice to try to buy a spare ticket from someone outside the theater. Simply ask:

Excuse me, do you have any spare tickets?
Перепрошую, чи ви не маєте зайвого квитка?
peh-reh-PRO-shoo-yu chih vih neh MAH-yeh-teh ZAHЎ-vo-ho
KVIHT-kah

IN THE THEATER

In the Theater   В Театрі   v teh-AH-tree

Where can I get a program?
Де я можу взяти програму?
deh ya MO-zhoo VZYA-tih pro-HRAH-moo

Allow me to pass, please.
Дозвольте пройти.
doz-VOL'-teh proў-TIH

That's my seat, please.
Перепрошую, це моє місце.
peh-reh-PRO-shoo-yu tseh mo-YEH MEES-tseh

How long will the intermission last?
Як довго буде перерва?
yak DOV-ho BOO-deh peh-REHR-vah

Where is the ...?
Де знаходиться ...?
deh znah-KHO-diht'-sya

cloak room	роздягалка	roz-DYA-hahl-kah
designated smoking area	місце для куріння	MEES-tseh dlya KOO-reen-nya
entrance to the auditorium	вхід до залу	vkheed do ZAH-loo
exit	вихід	VIH-kheed
phone	телефон	teh-leh-FON
rest room	туалет	too-a-LEHT
snack bar	буфет	boo-FEHT

What a wonderful performance!
Яка чудова вистава!
ya-KAH choo-DO-vah vihs-TAH-vah

Opera and Ballet Theaters

In Ukraine's largest cities, opera and ballet companies share a single theater whose season's repertoire includes ballet and operatic works. These theaters are not only splendid architectural gems, they also have superior acoustics for the orchestral accompaniment of the works.

Ballet repertoires in Ukraine include both classical Western and Russian ballet as well as Ukrainian ballet which developed largely in the last 40 years from a synthesis of classical ballet and national folk dance.

Which company is performing?
Яка трупа виступає?
ya-KAH   TROO-pah   vihs-too-PAH-yeh

Who's dancing the lead?
Хто танцює головну партію?
khto   tahn-TSYU-yeh   ho-lov-NOO   PAHR-tee-yu

Opera is usually performed in the original language of the composer. In addition to Italian and an occasional German opera, companies usually include some Ukrainian opera in their repertoire.   A few of the best-known are the comic opera "The Kozak Beyond the Danube," by Semen Hulak-Artemovsky; "Taras Bulba," by Mykola Lysenko, who was the founder of Ukrainian classical music; and "Kupalo," by western Ukrainian composer Anatol Vakhnianyn.

What's the name of the opera?
Як називається опера?
yak   nah-zih-VAH-yeht'-sya   O-peh-rah

Is it a Ukrainian opera?
Чи це українска опера?
chih   tseh   oo-krah-YEENS'kah   O-peh-rah

Who's singing the lead?
Хто співає головну партію?
khto   spee-VAH-yeh   ho-lov-NOO   PAHR-tee-yu

Folk Dance

Folk dancing dates back to prehistoric times in Ukraine when ritual dancing was a means of communicating with nature and divinity.   In ancient times, dancers often formed a circle to represent the sun.   The circle formation persisted into the Christian era when the agricultural significance of the dance was replaced by religious meaning.   Folk dances also became a way of commemorating life's major events.   With its colorful folk costumes and melodic musical accompaniment, either choral or instrumental, folk dancing reflects regional differences in Ukraine.

Almost all Ukrainian dance ensembles — both professional and amateur — culminate their repertoire with the *hopak* (гопак), an energetic dance movement of improvised squats, stretches, and leaps. The *hopak* originated in the 16th century as a solo male acrobatic feat of the Zaporozhzhian Kozaks. Gradually it was incorporated into group dances and spread throughout the country. Modern Ukrainian dance ensembles usually blend traditional *hopak* movements with new choreographic improvisations.

I'd like to go to a folk dance performance.
    Я хочу піти на концерт народних танців.
    ya KHO-choo pee-TIH nah kon-TSEHRT nah-ROD-nih TAHN-tseev

What can you suggest?
    Що ви можете порадити?
    shcho vih MO-zheh-teh po-RAH-dih-tih

Choral Music

Ukraine is noted for its choral performers.. The Verovka State Chorus of Kyiv is a mixed chorus, dance troupe, and folk orchestra whose repertoire includes traditional and recent Ukrainian folk songs. The Ukrainian State Choir Dumka, founded in 1919, has been an enduring repository of Ukrainian choral music, incorporating into its repertory the choral works of all the noted Ukrainian composers. The Bukovyna Choir sings folk songs of the Chernivtsi region. The Tchaikovsky Conservatory Choir from Kyiv is made up of students majoring in choral conducting. Children's choirs are more popular in Europe than in America, and Kyiv has the world-class Shchedryk Children's Choir, which took first place in a recent International Children's Choir Festival.

Which choir is singing?
    Який хор виступає?
    yah-KIHY khor vih-stoo-PAH-yeh

Instrumental Music

Musical ensembles have been part of Ukrainian tradition for at least a thousand years. Today Ukraine has nine symphony orchestras, seven chamber orchestras, two pop orchestras, and numerous theater orchestras, army bands, and semiprofessional ensembles.

Which (orchestra) (ensemble) is playing?
(Який оркестр) (яка група) виступає?
(ya-KIHÝ or-KEHSTR) (ya-KAH HROO-pah) vihs-too-PAH-yeh

Who's the (conductor) (soloist)?
Хто (диригент) (соліст)?
khto (dih-rih-HEHNT) (so-LEEST)

Folk Instruments

There are a number of traditional Ukrainian stringed, wind, and percussion instruments. Occasionally they show up in classical orchestras.

The *kobza* (кобза) is an oval or round-bodied lute with a long, fretted neck and three or four strings.   The *kobza* is predecessor of the Ukrainian national instrument, the *bandura* (бандура), and the terms *"kobza"* and *"bandura"* are often used interchangeably. The *bandura* is distinguished by its asymmetrical shape and its numerous single-note strings, as many as 60, which are plucked with the tips of the fingers or with the nails.   The *bandura* has many treble strings or *prystrunky* (приструнки) on which the melody is played.

By the seventeenth century, the *bandura* became the national instrument of Ukraine but later fell into oblivion. In the nineteenth century, the art was kept alive by blind, semi-professional *bandurysts* who traveled the countryside performing. In modern times, *bandura* playing is enjoying a revival and there are festivals and competitions on both amateur an professional levels.

Among wind instruments, the most known is the *trembita* (трембіта), a straight, slightly tapered wooden tube about ten feet long from the Hutsul region. Made from a single piece of wood that's cut and hollowed out and wrapped with birch bark, the *trembita* produces a sad, muffled sound. In traditional use, the *trembita* is played by a lone mountaineer on a high pasture, or by a group of musicians at funerals and folk festivals.

In ensemble, the most frequently heard folk instrumental combo is the triple music combination (троїста музика, tro-YEES-tah moo-ZIH-kah) in which, typically, the violin plays the melody; the bass viola, drum, or tambourine provides the rhythm; and dulcimers, a second violin or clarinet provides the accompaniment. Folk instrumental ensemble music is used exclusively for dancing or as an introduction to dances.

Among the folk instrument performing groups, the most prestigious is the State Banduryst Kapelle; there are also numerous groups which combine folk instrumental and choral music with dance, such as the Verovka State Chorus.

STAGE AND SCREEN

Ukraine has many drama companies as well as a strong tradition of musical comedy. Spoken drama has historically suffered, however, because of government restrictions on the Ukrainian language.

Starting back in the days of silent film, studios in Kyiv, Kharkiv, and Odesa produced movies with Ukrainian themes, and despite a history of government suppression of "nationalistic" elements, the Ukrainian film industry managed to flourish with many artistic successes. The major motion-picture studio in Ukraine is the Kyiv Film Studio, which produced the internationally awarded film "Shadows of Forgotten Ancestors" (Тіні Забутих Предків, TEE-nee zah-BOO-tihk PREHD-keev), by lauded director Serhei Paradzhanov.

Ukrainians are avid movie-goers. You'll find many cinemas and a wide choice of international films, including many of questionable merit. Dubbing rather than subtitles is the preferred method of presenting foreign films. Films acquired from western countries are dubbed into the Ukrainian language while those coming by way of Russia have been dubbed into Russian. Foreign film festivals are popular in Ukraine; for festivals of newly-released, yet undubbed films, an interpreter stands at a microphone in front of the theater and translates the dialogue, as it's spoken, from its foreign language into Ukrainian.

Buy your movie ticket directly from the box office; you will have an assigned seat. It's not considered polite to enter a movie theater once the film has started, refreshments are not allowed in the theater, and chattering to your companion during the screening is definitely a no-no.

To check what's playing in town, look for a printed circular showing a listing of the current movies. Check the domestic newspapers as well.

Where can I get a program of the movies in town?
Де можна знайти програму кіно?
deh MOZH-nah ZNAHЎ-tih proh-RAH-moo kee-NO

What's playing at the movies tonight?
Яке кіно демонструється сьогодні ввечері?
yah-KEH kee-NO deh-mon-STROO-yeht'-sya s'o-HOD-nee
v-VEH-cho-ree

What language is it in?
На якій мові це кіно?
nah yah-KEEЎ MO-vee tseh kee-NO

Who's the director?
Хто режисер?
khto reh-zhih-SEHR

Who's in the leading role?
Хто в головних ролях?
khto v ho-lov-NIHKH ro-LYAKH

I like...	Я люблю...	ya lyub-LYU
action film	бойовик	vo-ўo-VIHK
comedy	комедію	ko-MEH-dee-yu
documentary	документальний фільм	do-koo-mehn-TAHL'-nihў feel'm
drama	драму	DRAH-moo

There are special separate theaters for documentary films. Children's films, which also have their own theaters, consist mostly of cartoon features.

documentary film theater
кінотеатр документального фільму
kee-no-teh-AHTR do-koo-mehn-TAHL'-no-ho FEEL'-moo

children's theater
кінотеатер для дітей
kee-no-teh-AHTR dlya dee-TEHЎ

OTHER AMUSEMENTS

Circus. The Ukrainian love for the circus (цирк, tsihrk) is reflected in the many professional troupes throughout the country. A circus performer might spend years at the Kyiv Circus School perfecting an acrobatic routine and then join a circus company. Each city with greater than 500,000 population has a resident circus housed in a handsome permanent building. Every year the circus presents an all-new program with a new theme. Popular acts involve bareback riding, gymnastic feats, juggling, clowns, and lots of animals, all accompanied by live music. During the summer, you might be able to catch a troupe on tour in one of the smaller towns.

Is the circus in town now?
Чи цирк в місті тепер?
chih tsihrk v MEES-tee teh-PEHR

Where is the circus?
Де знаходиться цирк?
deh znah-KHO-diht'-sya tsihrk

What's the program called?
Як називається програма?
yak nah-zih-VAH-yehts'-sya pro-HRAH-mah

acrobats	акробати	ahk-ro-BAH-tih
animal trainer	дресирувальник	dreh-sih-roo-VAHL'-nihk
clowns	клоуни	KLO-oo-nih
jugglers	жонглери	ZHONH-leh-rih
strongmen	атлети	aht-LEH-tih

Puppet Shows. Puppetry (ляльковий театр, lyal'-KO-vihy̆ teh-AH-tehr) is a popular art throughout Europe. In Ukraine every sizable city has a puppet theater whose actors use hand puppets — and less frequently marionettes — to act out classic fairy tales, such as Pinocchio. Ukrainian folklore is also a source of themes. The most promising companies participate in international festivals, which sometimes are held in Ukraine. Ukrainian puppet companies differ from those in western Europe in employing a much larger staff — typically two dozen professional actors — and relying less on mechanical equipment.

Ballet on Ice. Ballet on Ice is classical ballet performed on ice. You should be able to find performances in Kyiv and Odesa.

Is there a ballet on ice in this city?
Чи в місті є балет на льоді?
chih v MEES-tee yeh bah-LEHT nah L'O-dee

SPORTS EVENTS

The most popular spectator sport in Ukraine is soccer. The team *Dynamo* Kyiv is a repeated national champion. Other popular sports with organized competitions are ice and field hockey, volleyball, tennis, table tennis, wrestling, and motorcycle racing. Most team sports, from basketball to water polo, have both men's and women's teams.

While inter-city competitions draw avid crowds, keep in mind that many sporting events are international, which now, of course, includes Russia and other newly-independent countries. Changing economic factors have resulted in a restructuring in popularity of certain sports. For example, kickboxing, a combination of boxing and traditional Eastern martial arts, is replacing boxing as a popular sport because its practitioners have found that it offers greater earning power.

From their Olympic and World Championship success, Ukraine has athletes of international fame. Olexandra Tymoshenko in callisthenics, Tetyana Hutsul and Hryhory Misyutin in gymnastics, Serhiy Bubka in track and field and figure skaters Oksana Baiul and Viktor Petrenko are known to sports fans around the world.

Which sporting events are going on now in the city?
Які спортивні міроприємства проходять тепер в місті?
ya-KEE spor-TIHV-nee mee-ro-prih-YEHM-strah pro-KHO-dyat' teh-PEHR v MEES-tee

Is it an international competition?
Чи це міжнародні змагання?
chih tseh meezh-nah-ROD-nee zmah-HAHN-nya

Who's playing?
Хто грає?
kho HRAH-yeh

Where can I get a ticket?
Де я можу придбати квиток?
deh ya MO-zhoo prihd-BAH-tih kvih-TOK

When does it start?
Коли це починається?
ko-LIH tseh po-chih-NAH-yeht'-sya

Where is it being played?
Де це проходить?
deh tseh pro-KHO-diht'

How can I get there?
Як можна туди добратись?
yak MOZH-nah too-DAH do-BRAH-tihs'

Who's winning?
Хто виграє?
kho vih-hrah-YEH

What's the score?
Який рахунок?
ya-IHY rah-KHOO-nok

That was a good game.
Це була добра гра.
tseh boo-LAH DO-brah hrah

Sports Vocabulary

ball	м'яч	m'yach
basketball	баскетбол	bahs-keht-BOL
basketball court	баскетбольна площадка	
		bahs-keht-BOL'-nah plo-SHCHAHD-kah
bicycle racing	гонки на велосипедах	
		HON-kih nah veh-lo-sih-PEH-dahkh
boxing	бокс	bohks
figure skating	фігурне катання	
		fee-HOOR-neh kah-TAHN-nya
gymnastics	гімнастика	heem-NAHS-tih-kah
handball	гандбол	hahnd-BOL
horse racing	скачки	SKAHCH-kih
kickboxing	кікбоксінг	keek-BOK-sihnh

net	сітка	SEET-kah
pole vaulting	стпбки з шестом	strihb-KIH z shes-TOM
skates	ковзани	kov-zah-NIH
skis	лижі	LIH-zhee
sled	санки	SAHN-kih
soccer	футбол	foot-BOL
soccer field	футбольне поле	foot-BOL'-neh PO-leh
speed skating	біг на ковзанах	
	beeh nah kov-zah-NAHKH	
racquet	рокетка	ro-KEHT-kah
swimming	плавання	PLAH-vahn-nya
swimming pool	басейн	bah-SEHY̌N
table tennis	настільний теніс (пінг-понг)	
(ping pong)	nahs-TEEL'-nihy̌ TEH-nees (peenh-ponh)	
tennis	теніс	TEH-nees
tennis court	тенісні корти	TEH-nees-nee KOR-tih
volleyball	волейбол	vo-lehy̌-BOL
volleyball court	волейбольна площадка	
	vo-lehy̌-BOL'-nah plo-SHCHAHD-kah	
water polo	водне поло	VOD-neh PO-lo
weightlifting	важка атлетика	
	vahzh-KAH aht-LEH-tih-kah	
wrestling	боротьба	bo-rot'-BAH

CHAPTER 19. SHOPPING FOR FUN

Ukrainian Proverb:
Очі бачили що руки брали.
O-chee BAH-chih-lih shcho ROO-kih BRAH-lih
The eyes saw what the hands were taking.

The conventional wisdom of resisting impulse buying doesn't apply when you're picking up souvenirs of your trip to Ukraine. If you find something you like, buy it. You won't find a better one or a cheaper one near the end of your trip.

UKRAINIAN CRAFTS AND SOUVENIRS

Ukraine has very well-developed, sophisticated forms of folk art, some of which date back to antiquity. During prehistoric times, religious beliefs and natural events determined symbols, motifs and colors. Over time, designs were influenced by contacts with foreign cultures and civilizations. Byzantium and the Far East left their mark on indigenous art forms as well as Western styles such as Gothic, Renaissance, and Baroque.

There is a similarity of basic patterns among the different media, whether *pysanky* or tapestry. Intricate geometric patterns were the earliest to develop and are still the most common today. Plant and animal motifs developed later out of the geometric forms. Colors and patterns differ according to region. For example, in eastern Ukraine black and red are the predominant colors, but blue and white are also common. Green is favored in certain western areas.

Ukraine has always valued its folk art. Throughout the country, numerous ethnological museums display folk art collections of breathtaking beauty. Craftsmakers attend *tekhnikums* of folk handicrafts, and designers go to schools of applied art.

Handcrafted items are sold everywhere — art salons, gift and souvenir shops, department stores, museum shops, kiosks, and on city sidewalks. You'll also find plenty of the usual touristy plastic knick-knacks and tee shirts for sale. These are the major Ukrainian folk arts:

Embroidery (вишивка, VIH-shiv-kah), the most popular Ukrainian folk art, with a variety and complexity of stitches, wealth of colors, and intricacy of designs. In traditional culture all household linens and items of folk dress, both female and male, were elaborately embroidered. There were special patterns for special occasions. Today virtually every family has an expert embroiderer. The most common embroidered items are towels, blouses and shirts. The towels are used for accenting furniture or — stitched with religious motifs — as the cover for the ritual basket of food taken to church for the Easter blessing. The sign of skilled embroidery is a reverse side as neat and finished as the front.

Weaving (ткацтво, TKAHTS-tvo) had developed into a cottage industry by the 14th century. Weavers produced various articles of folk dress, towels, tablecloths, *kylyms,* and bed coverings from flax, hemp, or woolen thread.

Especially important is the *kylym* (килим), an ornamental woven floor or wall covering. Folk carpet-making dates back to antiquity, but the opening of large mills in the 18th century made *kylym* production widespread. The basic designs of geometric and plant motifs show some oriental and southern European influence; over time individual weavers developed their own styles, composition, and harmonized coloration. In homes throughout Ukraine, walls are frequently covered with *kylyms,* but rarely are they used as floor coverings.

Rushnyky (Рушники) are towels, about 3 to 8 inches wide and 3 to 12 feet long, with geometric or floral patterns primarily near the ends. Traditionally, the *rushnyk* was used in various folk rituals and religious celebrations. It played a role in every milestone of human life, from birth to death. You can find *rushnyky* hanging on walls in many homes, particularly in rural areas, where they're draped over icons or favorite paintings. Highly embroidered ones are used in wedding ceremonies.

Factories throughout Ukraine produce both *kylyms* and *rushnyky.*

Pottery (кераміки, keh-RAHM-ee-kih) production is widespread in Ukraine because of the large deposits of various clays, particularly kaolin (china clay). The ceramic arts date back to prehistoric times. The elegant forms and polychrome designs of the clay artifacts of the Trypilian culture (5,000 To 4,000 B.C.) indicate a high level of sophistication in the process of clay preparation, firing, and decoration. Later ceramics showed complicated geometric designs and were formed in the figures of birds and animals. The introduction of the potter's wheel after the Mongol period changed the craft. With the development of the stove in the 18th century, all ceramic-producing centers in Ukraine began to produce enameled tiles. Today ceramic centers turn out much functional ceramic ware — pitchers, plates, candle holders, and tiles, and also some ornamental sculpture and toys.

Pysanky (писанки, PIH-sahn-kih), Easter eggs colored with intricate traditional symbolic designs, are perhaps the most widely known items of Ukrainian culture. The name *pysanky* comes from the verb *pysaty*, meaning "to write," because the designs are written on the shell of a whole raw egg with melted beeswax. A batik technique is used: the egg is dipped in a series of dye baths, ranging from the lightest color to the darkest, with wax designs applied by means of a fine pointed stylus following each bath. After hours of work, the wax is removed from the completed egg.

Pysanky date back to prehistoric times. Then, the eggs had a ritual significance. The yolk represented the sun, a pagan god. The eggs were believed to possess magic power to protect against evil, thunder, or fire. In Christian times, the eggs also became objects of good fortune that could bring luck, wealth, health, fertility, good harvest, and protection from harm. As soon as the cock crowed on Ash Wednesday, women and girls rushed to the barns to collect the eggs. They then spent the 40 days of Lent creating the designs. On Easter morning they brought the *pysanky* to the church, along with some ritual food, for the blessing, but these special eggs were not for eating. The best became gifts and often served as a not-so-subtle invitation to courtship.

Authentic *pysanky* use traditional symbols which have evolved over millennia. Earliest designs were sun motifs. The meander or endless line representing eternity comes from the Neolithic era. It represents eternity. With Christianity came crosses and miniature churches combined with decorative geometrical designs. Animal motifs originated much later. Colors also have meaning. Each region, even village, had its own designs and pigments.

The symbols, designs, and colors used in *pysanky* are repeated in other forms of Ukrainian art. In gift shops you'll find a variety of wood-crafted *pysanky* — lacquered, carved, or inlaid — and with luck you may even find some real ones.

Woodcarving (художне різьблення, khoo-DOZH-neh RIHZ-blehn-nya). Ukrainian wood sculpture developed along with church architecture, resulting in elaborate iconostases, lecterns, and columns.

At the same time, the common people began decorating the interior and exterior of their home with carved and ornamented details. The Hutsul region in western Ukraine, with its forest resources, is the major woodcarving center in Ukraine. Hutsul work is characterized by geometric designs ornamented with inlays of colored wood, bone, mother-of-pearl, beads and metal work. Carved boxes — both rectangular and circular — and plates are the most popular examples. Candle-holders, spoon racks, pipes, and the *bulava*, or hetman's mace, are also typical Hutsul woodcrafts. When pricing inlaid woodcrafts, notice how much of the ornamentation is actually inlaid compared to what is merely painted on the wood. Lemkos, an ethnic group along the Polish border, are noted for their woodcarvings of animal figures. North of Kyiv, in the Chernihiv area, wooden folk music instruments such as the *bandura*, are produced.

In addition to traditional crafts, signed artwork is widely available. Landscape and still life paintings and pottery and ceramic works are the most numerous. When buying directly from the artisan, bargaining is possible, but don't expect greater than a twenty percent reduction of the original asking price.

Would you please show me this? [pointing]
    Прошу мені показати це?
    PRO-shoo meh-NEE po-kah-ZAH-tih tseh

Would you please show me ...?
    Прошу мені показати ...?
    PRO-shoo meh-NEE po-kah-ZAH-tih

that bandura	ту бандуру	too bahn-DOO-roo
that blouse	ту блузку	too BLOOZ-koo
that embroidery	ту вишивку	too VIH-shihv-koo
that picture	ту картину	too kahr-TIH-noo
that plate	ту тарілку	too tah-REEL-koo
that scarf	той шарф	toў shahrf
that sculpture	ту скульптуру	too skool'p-TOO-roo
that shirt	ту сорочку	too so-ROCH-koo
that sweater	той светер	toў SVEH-tehr
that T-shirt	ту футболку	too foot-BOL-koo

Can you show me those ...?
    Прошу мені показати ті ...?
    PRO-shoo meh-NEE po-kah-ZAH-tih tee

painted eggs	писанки	PIH-sahn-kih
dolls	ляльки	LYAL'-kih
glassware	шкляні вироби	shklya-NEE VIH-ro-bih
jewelry	ювелірні вироби	
		yu-veh-LEER-nee VIH-ro-bih

Do you have any ...?	Чи ви маєте...?	chih vih MAH-yeh-teh

amber	бурштин	boorsch-TIHN
chess sets	шахи	SHAH-khih
icons	ікони	ee-KO-nih
musical instruments	музичні інструменти	
		moo-ZIHCH-nee eens-stroo-MEHN-tih
pottery	кераміку	keh-RAH-mee-koo
samovars	самовари	sah-mo-VAH-rih
wooden boxes	дерев'яні скринькі	
		deh-reh-V'YA-nee SKRIHN'-kee
wood crafts	різьбу по дереву	
		REEZ'-boo po DEH-reh-voo

Is it (wooden) (plastic) (metal)?
Чи це (дерев'яне) (пластмасове) (залізне)?
chih tseh (deh-rehv'-YA-neh) (plast-MAH-so-veh)
(zah-LEEZ-neh)

BOOKS AND STATIONERY

Books and Stationery Книжки та Канцелярія
KNIHZH-kih tah kahn-tseh-LYA-ree-ya

Among the best tourist buys are the wonderfully inexpensive books,
postcards, and posters of Ukrainian history, art, and culture.

I want a book about ....
Я хочу книжку про ....
ya KHO-choo KNIHZH-koo pro

Kyiv	Київ	KIH-yeev
this city	це місто	tseh MEES-to
Ukraine	Україну	oo-krah-YEE-noo
Ukrainian art	українське мистецтво	
		oo-krah-YEENS'-keh mihs-TEHTST-vo

Ukrainian folklore	Український фолкльор	
	oo-krah-YEENS'-kihў folk-L'OR	
Ukrainian history	Історію України	
	ees-TO-ree-yu oo-krah-YEE-nih	

I want	Я хочу	ya KHO-choo
a calendar	календар	kah-lehn-DAHR
playing cards	гральні карти	HRAHL'-nee KAHR-tih
stationery	канцелярія	kahn-tseh-LYA-ree-ya
that poster	той плакат	toў plah-KAHT

Where are the ...?	Де знаходяться ...?	deh znah-KHO-dyat'-sya
dictionaries	словники	slov-NIH-kih
maps	географічні карти	
	he-ho-hrah-FEECH-nee KAHR-tih	
postcards	поштові картки	posh-TO-vee KAHRT-kih

RECORDS

| Records | Пластинки | PLAHS-tihn-kih |

I'm looking for (cassettes) (records) of ...
    Я шукаю (записи) (пластинки) ....
    ya shoo-KAH-yu (ZAH-pih-sih) (plahs-TIHN-kih)

classical music	класичної музики	
	klah-SIHCH-no-yee MOO-zih-kih	
folk music	народної музики	
	nah-ROD-no-yee MOO-zih-kih	
jazz	джазу	DZHAH-zoo
pop music	поп-музики	pop MOO-zih-kih

May I listen to this record?
    Чи я можу прослухати цей запис?
    chih ya MO-zhoo pro-SLOO-kha-tih tsehў ZAH-pihs

Do you have any videos about ...
    Чи ви маєте відео про ....
    chih vih MAH-yeh-teh VEE-deh-o pro

CLOTHING

Clothing	Одяг	od-YAH
I need a	Мені треба	meh-NEE TREH-bah
swim suit (women's)	купальник	koo-PAHL'-nihk
swim trunks (men's)	плавки	PLAHV-kih
bathrobe	халат	khah-LAHT
blouse	блузка	BLOOZ-kah
bra	бюстгальтер	byust-HAHL'-tehr
cap	шапка	SHAHP-kah
coat (summer)	плащ	plashch
coat (winter)	пальто	pahl'-TO
dress	сукня	SOOK-nya
fur coat	шуба	SHOO-bah
fur hat	хутрова шапка	khoot-RO-vah SHAHP-kah
gloves	рукавиці	roo-kah-VIHT-see
jacket	куртка	KOORT-kah
jeans	джінси	DZHEEN-sih
nylons	панчохи	pahn-CHO-khih
pantyhose	колготи	kol-HO-tih
pajamas	піжама	pee-ZHAH-mah
raincoat	плащ від дощу	
	plahshch veed do-SHCHOO shahrf	
shirt	сорочка	so-ROCH-kah
skirt	спідниця	speed-NIH-tsya
socks	шкарпетки	skhahr-PEHT-kih
suit	костюм	kos-TYUM
sweater	светер	SVEH-tehr
sweatshirt	футболка	foot-BOL-kah
sweatsuit	спортивниий костюм	
	spor-TIHV-nihў kos-TYUM	
t-shirt	футболка	foot-BOL-kah
undershirt	майка	MAHЎ-kah
underwear	нижня білизна	NIHZH-nya bee-LIHZ-nah
vest	желет	zheh-LEHT
... for women	для жінок	dlya ZHEE-nok
... for men	для чоловіків	dlya cho-lo-vee-KEEV
... for girls	для дівчат	dlya deev-CHANT
... for boys	для хлопців	dlya KHLOP-tseev
... for children	для дитини	dlya dih-TIH-nih

May I try this on?
Чи можу я це приміpити?
chih MO-zhoo ya tseh prih-MEE-rih-tih

Where's a mirror?
Де знаходиться дзеркало?
deh znah-KHO-diht'-sya DZEHR-kah-lo

It (fits) (doesn't fit) me.
Це (підходить) (не підходить) мені.
tseh (peed-KHO-diht') (neh peed-KHO-diht') meh-NEE

Do you have this in another color?
Чи ви маєте інший колір?
chih vih MAH-yeh-teh EEN-shihў ko-LEER

Is it washable?   Чи це можна прати?
                         chih tseh MOZH-nah PRAH-tih

Is it machine washable?
Чи це можна прати в машині?
chih tseh MOZH-nah PRAH-tih v mah-SHIH-nee

I'll take this one.   Я візьму це.   ya veez'-MOO tseh

FOOTWEAR

Footwear	Взуття	vzoot-TYA
I'd like ...	Я би (хотів, *m.*) (хотіла, *f.*) ... ya bih (kho-TEEV) (kho-TEE-lah)	
boots	чоботи	CHO-bo-tih
sandals	сандалі	sahn-DAH-lee
flat shoes	мешти	MEHSH-tih
high-heeled shoes	черевики	cheh-reh-VIH-kih
slippers	домашнє взуття do-MAHSH-neh vzoot-TYA	
tennis shoes	кросовки	kro-SOV-kih
These are too	Вони є	vo-NIH yeh
narrow/wide	завузькі / заширокі zah-vooz'-KEE / zah-shih-RO-kee	
small/large	замалі / завеликі zah-mah-LEE / zah-veh-LIH-kee	

Do you have a (larger) (smaller) size?
Чи ви маєте (більший) (менший) розмір?
chih vih MAH-yeh-teh (BEEL'-shihў) (MEN-shihў) ROZ-meer

Is this genuine leather?
Чи це натуральна шкіра?
chih tseh nah-too-RAHL'-nah SHKEE-rah

I need some (shoelaces) (shoe polish).
Мені треба (шнурки) (крем для взуття).
meh-NEE TREH-bah (shnoor-KIH) (krehm dlya vzoot-TYA)

Can you repair these shoes?
Чи ви можете відремонтувати це взуття?
chih vih MO-zheh-teh veed-reh-mohn-too-VAH-tih tseh
vzoot-TYA

I need new soles and heels.
Мені треба нові підметки і набійки.
meh-NEE TREH-bah NO-vee peed-MEHT-kih ee nah-BEEЎ-kih

When will they be ready?
Коли вони будуть готові?
ko-LIH vo-NIH BOO-doot' ho-TO-vee

ACCESSORIES/JEWELRY

Accessories/Jewlery	Галантерея/Біжутерія	hah-lahn-tch-REH ya / bee-zhoo-TEH-ree-ya
belt (men's)	ремінь	reh-MEEN'
belt (women's)	ремінець	reh-mee-NEHTS'
bookbag	сумка	SOOM-kah
bracelet	браслет	brahs-LEHT
briefcase	портфель, дипломат	port-FEHL', dihp-lo-MAHT
collar	комір	KO-meer
duffle bag	спортивна сумка	spor-TIHV-nah SOOM-kah
earrings	кульчики	KOOL'-chih-kih
handbag, purse	сумка	SOOM-kah
handkerchief, hanky	хустка, хустинка	KHOOST-kah, khoos-TIHN-kah
jewelry (costume)	біжутерія	bee-zhoo-TEH-ree-ya

jewelry (real)	ювелірні вироби	
	yu-veh-LEER-nee	VIH-ro-bih
key ring	брелок	breh-LOK
luggage	багаж	bah-HAHZH
necklace	намисто	nah-MIHS-to
pocket knife	ніж	neezh
ring	кільце	keel'-TSEH
scarf	шарф	shahrf
suitcase	сумка	SOOM-kah
sun glasses	окуляри від сонца	
	o-koo-LYA-rih veed	SON-tsya
suspenders	підтяжки	peed-TYAZH-kih
tie	краватка	krah-VAHT-kah
trunk	чемодан	cheh-mo-DAHN
umbrella	парасоля	pah-rah-SOL-ya
wallet	гаманець	hah-mah-NETS'
watch	годинник	ho-DIHN-nihk

SIZES

| Sizes | Розміри | ROZ-mee-rih |

Clothing sizes are according to the metric system, and all clothing — whether women's, men's, or children's — are based on a single scale. Like American clothing, standardization of sizing in ready-made garments is not perfect. In any particular size, you'll find some variation of fit, so the chart on the next page should serve only as a point of reference.

I don't know my size.
    Я не знаю мій розмір.
    ya neh ZNAH-yu meeў ROZ-meer

It's too (big) (small).
    Це (завелике) (замале).
    tseh (zah-veh-LIH-keh) (zah-mah-LEH)

It's too (long) (short).
    Це (задовге) (закоротке).
    tseh (zah-DOV-heh) (zah-ko-ROT-keh)

Conversion Chart for Clothing

Women's Sizes Жіночні розміри
Clothes (dresses, blouses, skirts)

Ukrainian	44	46	48	50	52	54
American	6	8	10	12	14	16

Shoes

Ukrainian	35	36	37	38	39	40
American	5	6	7	8	9	10

Men's Sizes Чоловічі розміри
Suits and Coats

Ukrainian	46	48	50	52	54	56
American	36	38	40	42	44	46

Shirts

Ukrainian	38	40	41	42	43	44
American	15	15 1/2	16	16 1/2	17	17 1/2

Do you have a (bigger) (smaller) size?
   Чи ви маєте (більший) (менший) розмір?
   chih vih MAH-yeh-teh (BEEL'-shihў) (MEHN-shihў) ROZ-meer

FABRICS AND NOTIONS

Fabrics and Notions Тканини та Галантерея
   tkah-NIH-nih tah hah-lahn-teh-REH-ya

What is this fabric?
   Яка це тканина?
   ya-KAH tseh tkah-NIH-nah

batiste	батист	bah-TIHST
cotton	бавовна	bah-VOV-nah
corduroy	вельвет	vehl'-VEHT
denim	джінсова тканина	
	DZHEEN-so-vah tkah-NIH-nah	
felt	фетр	fehtr
flannel	фланель	flah-NEHL'
lace	круживо	KROO-zhih-vo
leather	шкіра	SHKEE-rah
linen	льон	l'on

nylon	нейлон	nehỹ-LON
rayon	район	rah-ӲON
rubber	гума	HOO-mah
satin	сатин	sah-TIHN
silk	шовк	shovk
suede	замша	ZAHM-shah
velvet	оксамит	ok-sah-MIHT
vinyl	штучна шкіра	
	SHTOOCH-nah SHKEE-rah	
wool	вовна, шерсть	VOV-nah, sherst'

What's the width of this fabric?
   Яка ширина цієї ткануни?
   ya-KAH shih-rih-NAH tsee-YEH-yee tkah-NIH-nih

What's the price per meter?
(A meter is a little more than a yard, about 39 inches.)
   Яка ціна за метер?
   ya-KAH tsee-NAH zah MEH-tehr

I want two meters.   Я хочу два метри.
   ya KHO-choo dvah MEH-trih

I need ...   Мені потрібно ...   meh-NEE po-TREEB-no

a button   гудзик   HOOD-zihk

embroidery thread   нитки для вишивання
   NIHT-kih dlya vih-shih-VAHN-nya

a needle and thread   голка і нитки   HOH-kah ee NIHT-kih

a safety pin   англійська шпилька
   ahn-HLEEӲ-s'kah SHPIHL'-kah

scissors   ножиці   NO-zhih-tsee

a straight pin   шпилька   SHPIHL'-kah

a tape measure   сантеметр   sahn-tih-MEHTR

a thimble   наперсток   nah-PEHRS-tok

a zipper   замок   zah-MOK

CHAPTER 20. LEISURE

Ukrainian Proverb:
В здоровому тілі, здоровий дух.
v zdo-RO-vo-moo TEE-lee zdo-RO-vihў dookh
In a healthy body, a healthy mind.

If you want to participate in sports, Ukraine offers plenty of opportunities
and numerous facilities for swimming, bathing, tennis, skiing, hunting
and a wealth of other outdoor and indoor activities for fun and fitness.

At the end of your work-out, you might say to your companion:

That was good exercise.
Було дуже добре позайматись.
BOO-lo DOO-zheh DOB-reh po-zahў-MAH-tihs'.

That was fun!　　　　Було дуже гарно!
　　　　　　　　　　BOO-lo DOO-zheh HAHR-no

SUMMER SPORTS

Summer Sports	Літні Види Спорту LEET-nee VIH-dih SPOR-too	
I'd like to play	Я хочу пограти в.... ya KHO-choo po-hrah-tih v	
badminton	бадмінтон	bahd-meen-TON
basketball	баскетбол	bahs-keht-BOL
tennis	теніс	TEH-nees
volleyball	волейбол	vo-lehў-BOL
I'd like to	Я хочу	ya KHO-choo
go bicycling	покататись на велосипеді po-kah-TAH-tihs' nah veh-lo-sih-PEH-dee	
go hiking	піти в похід	pee-TIH v po-KHEED
go rock climbing	піти на скали	pee-TIH nah SKAH-lih
go rowing	поплавати на човні з веслами po-PLAH-vah-tih nah chov-NEE z VEHS-lah-mih	

go swimming	піти в басейн	pee-TIH v bah-SEHЎN
go water skiing	кататись на водних лижах	
	kah-TAH-tihs' nah VOD-nihkh LIH-zhahkh	

WINTER SPORTS

| Winter Sports | Зимові Види Спорту | |
| | zih-MO-vee VIH-dih SPOR-too | |

I want to go	Я хочу	ya KHO-choo
cross country skiing	кататись на бігових лижах	
	kah-TAH-tihs' nah bee-ho-VIHKH LIH-zhahkh	
downhill skiing	покататись на горних лижах	
	po-kah-TAH-tihs' nah HOR-nihkh LIH-zhahkh	
skating	покататись на ковзанах	
	po-kah-TAH-tihs' nah kov-zah-NAHKH	
sledding	покататись на санах	
	po-kah-TAH-tihs' nah SAH-nahkh	

| I'd like to rent.... | Я хочу взяти на прокат .... | |
| | ya KHO-choo VZYA-tih nah pro-KAHT | |

skates	ковзани	kov-zah-NIH
skis	лижі	LIH-zhee
a sled	сани	SAH-nih

THE SAUNA

| The Sauna | Сауна | SAH-oo-nah |

In ancient Kyivan Rus, each home had a log cabin that the whole family used for bathing. Today rural homes may still have their own bathhouses, but the practice has been institutionalized in the public saunas that are found in resorts as well as in cities of any size. Their purpose is not for washing the body, but for fun and health. At a sauna you lounge around in a steam-filled room, beat your naked body with a bundle of birch branches, then plunge into cold water, all in the pursuit of invigoration, relaxation, and good health. If this doesn't sound like fun and you don't think the health benefits are worth the bodily punishment, you'd best not try a sauna.

Ukrainians have two kinds of saunas. In the Finnish sauna (сауна, SAH-oo-nah) the participant sits in a room of dry steam, that is, one in which the temperature remains so hot (hovering above 212° F.) that the water vapor does not condense. In the Russian wet bath or *banya* (баня, BAHN-ya), the temperature is kept just below boiling so that the steam that fills the room condenses on the bather. In either one, the session in the wood-lined steam room is capped off by jumping into a pool of cold water. In winter the pool may be located outdoors with a hole cut through the ice.

I'd like to go to the baths.
Я би (хотів, *m.*) (хотіла, *f.*) піти в баню.
ya bih (kho-TEEV) (kho-TEE-lah) pee-TIH v BAH-nyu

Where is the entrance ... ?	Де знаходиться вхід ...? deh znah-KHO-diht'-sya vkheed	
for men	для чоловіків	dlya cho-lo-vee-KEEV
for women	для жінок	dlya zhee-NOK

Where's the pool? Де знаходиться басейн?
deh znah-KHO-diht'-sya bah-SEHY̆N

Where are the lockers?
Де знаходиться роздягалка?
deh znah-KHO-diht'-sya roz-dya-HAHL-kah

AT THE BEACH

At the Beach   На Пляжі   nah PLYA-zhee

Sandy and rocky seaside beaches stretch north and south of Odesa, with the more picturesque, less crowded beaches to the south. In the Crimea, many beaches are reserved for use by health resorts or hotels, but there are also some public beaches. You may also find some wild beaches. The cleanliness of the water varies.

Is the beach sandy or stony?
На пляжі пісок чи каміння?
nah PLYA-zhee pee-SOK chih kah-MEEN-nya

Is the water cold?   Чи вода холодна?
chih vo-DAH kho-LOD-nah

Is it deep here?   Чи тут глибоко?
chih toot hlih-BO-ko

Is it safe to swim here?
Чи безпечно тут плавати?
chih behz-PEHCH-no toot PLAH-vah-tih

Is there a lifeguard on duty?
Чи тут є рятувальна служба?
chih toot yeh rya-too-VAHL'-nah SLOOZH-bah

I prefer a swimming pool.
Я люблю більш басейн.
ya lyu-BLYU BEEL'SH bah-SEHЎN

IN THE FOREST AND MOUNTAINS

In the Forest and Mountains
В Лісі та в Горах
v LEES-see tah v ho-RAHKH

Ukraine has two beautiful mountainous areas. In the southwestern corner
are the Carpathians, a relatively low eastward continuation of the Alps.
The tallest mountain is Mt. Hoverla at 6679 feet. Coniferous forests,
alpine meadows, and charming villages nestled among the rolling hills
make this part of the country worth a visit. The Crimean Mountains
along the southern part of the Crimean peninsula are a chain of low,
rocky mountains whose narrow foothills taper into a seacoast.

Let's go hiking in a forest.
Давайти підем до лісу.
dah-VAHЎ-teh PEE-dehm do LEE-soo

I'd like to go mushroom hunting.
Я хочу піти за грибами.
ya KHO-choo pee-TIH zah hrih-BAH-mih

Can we hike over there?
Чи можемо ми піти туда?
chih MO-zheh-mo mih pee-TIH too-DAH

Can we rest for a while?
Чи можемо ми трохи відпочити?
chih MO-zheh-mo mih TRO-khih veed-po-CHIH-tih

I don't want to go any farther.
Перепрошую, я не хочу іти далі.
peh-reh-PRO-shoo-yu ya neh KHO-choo ee-TIH DAH-lee

What's the name of that (plant) (tree)?
Як називається (ця рослина) (це дерево)?
yak nah-zih-VAH-yeht'-sya (tsya ros-LIH-nah) (tseh DEH-reh-vo)

Can we go to the mountains?
Чи ми можете піти в гори?
chih mih MO-zheh-teh pee-TIH v HO-rih

I want to go mountain climbing.
Я хочу піднятись в гори.
ya KHO-choo peed-NYA-tihs' v HO-rih

I'm a mountain climber.
Я альпініст.
ya ahl'-pee-NEEST.

I want to climb that mountain.
Я хочу піднятись на ту гору.
ya KHO-choo peed-NYA-tihs' nah too HO-roo

HUNTING AND FISHING

Hunting and Fishing   Полювання та Рибалка
po-lyu-VAHN-nya tah rih-BAHL-kah

You'll need a license for fishing or hunting in Ukraine; the licensing of hunting is especially strictly enforced. For information on how to acquire one or where to find the nearest hunting ground or fishing hole, ask at a fishing-hunting club (клуб риболова-мисливця, kloob rih-bo-LO-vah mihs-LIHV-tsya).

Where is the nearest fishing-hunting club?
Де знаходиться найближчий клуб риболова-мисливця?
deh znah-KHO-diht'-sya nahÿ-BLIHZ͡H-chihÿ kloob
rih-bo-LO-vah mihs-LIHV-tsya

I want to go (fishing) (hunting).
Я хочу піти на (рибалку) (полювання).
ya KHO-choo pee-TIH nah (rih-BAHL-koo) (po-lyu-VAHN-nya)

Is the fishing good here?
   Чи тут добра рибалка?
   chih toot DOB-rah rih-BAL-kah

Is the hunting good here?
   Чи тут добре полювання?
   chih toot DOB-reh pol-yu-VAHN-nya

bait	наживка	nah-Z͡HIHV-kah
fish	ріба, *s.*, риби, *pl.*	RIH-bah, RIH-bih
to fish	рибачити	rih-BAH-chih-tih
fisherman	рибалка, риболов	rih-BAHL-kah, rih-bo-LOV
fishing pole	вудка	VOOD-kah
fishing pole, small	вудочка	VOO-doch-kah
hook	гачок	ha-CHOK
line	жилка	Z͡HIHL-kah
hunter	мисливець	mihs-LIH-vehts′
game	дичина	dih-chih-NAH
rifle	рушниця	roosh-NIH-tsya

CAMPING

Camping	Кемпінг	KEHM-peenh

Developed campsites are rare in Ukraine, but Inturyst runs some camps outside of major cities that offer an alternative to hotels. The best might have cabins with private toilets.

Where is the nearest campground?
   Де знаходиться найближчий кемпінг?
   deh znah-KHO-diht′-sya nahy̆-BLIHZ͡H-chihy̆ KEHM-peenh?

Does this camp- ground have ... ?	Чи є на кемпінгу ...? chih yeh nah KEHM-peen-hoo	
electricity	електроенергія eh-LEHK-tro-eh-NEHR-hee-ya	
hot water	гаряча вода	hah-RYA-chah vo-DAH
a grocery	продуктовий магазин pro-dook-TO-vihy̆ mah-hah-ZIHN	
a shower	душ	doosh
swimming pool	басейн	bah-SEHY̆N
a restaurant	ресторан	rehs-to-RAHN

Where can I ...?	Де можна ...?	deh MOZ͡H-nah
park a car	поставити машину	
	pos-TAH-vih-tih mah-SHIH-noo	
light a fire	палити вогнище	
	pah-LIH-tih VOH-nih-shcheh	
pitch a tent	поставити намет	
	pos-TAH-vih-tih nah-MEHT	

Where can I buy camping equipment?
Де я можу придбати обладнання для туризму?
deh ya MO-z͡hoo prihd-BAH-tih ob-lahd-NAHN-nya dlya too-RIHZ-moo

I need	Мені треба	meh-NEE TREH-bah
a backpack	рюкзак	RYUK-zahk
a small portable		
camping stove	примус	PRIH-moos
a can opener	консервний ніж	kon-SEHRV-nih͡y neez͡h
a compass	компас	KOM-pahs
dishes	посуда	po-SOO-dah
first aid kit	аптечка	ahp-TEHCH-kah
a flashlight	ліхтар	leekh-TAHR
a lighter	запальничка	zah-pahl'-NIHCH-kah
matches	сірники	sihr-nih-KIH
a mattress	матрас	maht-RAHS
a sleeping bag	спальний мішок	SPAHL'-nih͡y mee-SHOK
a tent	намет	nah-MEHT

May we camp here?
Чи тут можна влаштувати стоянку?
chih toot MOZ͡H-nah vlahsh-too-VAH-tih sto-YAHN-ko

May we pitch a tent here?
Чи тут можна поставити намет?
chih toot MOZ͡H-nah pos-TAH-vih-tih nah-MEHT

May we build a fire here?
Чи тут можна палити вогнище?
chih toot MOZ͡H-nah pah-LIH-tih VOH-nih-shcheh

We'll be using a gas stove.
Ми будемо користувати примус.
mih BOO-deh-mo ko-rihs-too-VAH-tih PRIH-moos

BOAT CRUISES

Ukrainian River Fleet (Укррічфлот, *Ukrrichflot*), now privatized, handles all aspects of river transportation in Ukraine, from ship building to moving cargo to pleasure trips. During the April through October Dnipro cruising season, the company offers rides on several different types of vessels. The northern port city is Kyiv. Boats dock also in Cherkasy, Dnipropetrovsk, Zaporozhzhya, Nova Kakhovka, Kherson, and Odesa.

The hydrofoil is the speediest way to get from one port to another, but the view from its airplane-like cabin is somewhat restricted. An especially popular excursion goes from Kyiv to the Taras Shevchenko gravesite and museum at Kaniv. Purchase tickets one to five days in advance at the ticket office at the ferry station at *ploshcha Poshtova* (площа Поштова) near the metro station.

For a longer trip in grand style, Ukrrichflot operates 12 comfortable first-class 300-passenger vessels. The star of the fleet is the 400-foot by 50-foot *M/S Akademik Viktor Glushkov*, which was completely rebuilt in 1990 to meet the highest international standards. Cuisine is Ukrainian and Russian. From May through October, the *Glushkov* makes 14-day round trips between Kyiv and Odesa. To book a tour, contact Odesa America Cruise Company, 170 Old Country Rd., Suite 608, Mineola, New York 11501.

Dnipro River Shipping Company also operates luxury cruises on the Dnipro on two new German-built vessels, the *Taras Shevchenko* and the *General Lavrinenko*. Dnipro River Shipping is a Russian company run by a Swiss management team. The cuisine is Swiss. Contact River Cruises International, 104 S. Michigan Ave., Suite 802, Chicago, Ill. 60603. (312)782-1882.

From Odesa, you can also catch a hydrofoil, a passenger or vehicle ferry, or a ship to Yalta and other Black Sea port cities.

Where is the river transport station?
Де знаходиться річковий транспорт вокзал?
deh znah-KHO-diht'-sya reech-ko-VIHЎ TRAHNS-port vok-ZAHL

I want to go on the excursion to Kaniv.
Я хочу поїхати на екскурсію до Канева.
ya KHO-choo po-YEE-khah-tih nah ehks-KOOR-see-yu do
KAH-neh-vah

When is the tour   Коли екскурсія до ...?
to ... ?   ko-LIH ehks-KOOR-see-ya do

I'd like a ticket for tomorrow's cruise to ....
Мені треба квиток на завтрішній круїз до . ...
meh-NEE TREH-bah kvih-TOK nah ZAHV-treesh-neeў
kroo-YEEZ do

What time does the ship leave?
Коли відпливає корабель?
ko-LIH veed-plih-VAH-yeh ko-rah-BEHL'

How long does the trip last?
Як довго триває поїздка?
yak DOV-ho trih-VAH-yeh po-YEEZD-kah

What stops does the (ship) (boat) make?
Де зупиняється (корабель) (пароплав)?
deh zoo-pih-NYA-yeht'-SYA (ko-rah-BEHL') (pah-ro-PLAHV)

How long will we have in ... ?
Як довго ми будемо в ... ?
yak DOV-ho mih BOO-deh-mo v

boat (small, either motorized or with oars)
                        човен   cho-VEHN
boat (medium-sized)   катер   KAH-tehr
boat (larger, steamer) пароплав   pah-ro-PLAHV
boat (large ship or ocean liner)
                        корабель   ko-rah-BEHL'
Black Sea   Чорне Море   CHOR-neh MO-reh
dock   причал   prih-CHAHL
Dnipro River   Дніпро   dneep-RO
Dnister River   Дністер   DNEES-tehr
ferry   пором   po-ROM
hydrofoil   човен на підводних крилах
                        cho-VEHN nah peed-VOD nihkh KRIH-lahkh
life boat   рятувальний човен
                        rya-too-VAHL'-nihў CHO-vehn

life jacket	спасальний жилет	
	spah-SAHL'-nihў z͡hih-LEHT	
port	порт	port

Life vest under seat
Рятувальний жилет під сидінням
rya-too-VAHL'-nihў zhih-LEHT peed sih-DEEN-nyam

INDOOR GAMES

Chess and checkers are very popular in Ukraine, as well as a variety of card games and casino games. Casinos — strictly hard currency, of course — have opened up in major tourist hotels in large cities.

casino	казино	kah-zih-NO
cards	карти	KAHR-tih
blackjack	очко	och-KO
bridge	брідж	breed͡zh
poker	покер	PO-kehr
preference (A form of whist, preference is a game of skill with complicated rules. A single game can last many hours.)		
	преферанс	preh-feh-RANHS
checkers	шашки	SHASH-kih
chess	шахи	shah-KHIH
pool, billiards	біліярд	bee-lee-YARD
roulette	рулетка	roo-LEHT-kah

NIGHTLIFE

The older Ukrainian nightclubs and discos, usually found in tourist hotels, are pretty much the same as everywhere else — crowded, noisy, and lacking atmosphere other than that of a bar. New establishments, with names like Bar Manhattan, Miami Blues, Club Flamingo, and Hollywood Night Club, cater to Kyiv's youthful movers and shakers. The ambience is American, with lots of neon lights and exotic drinks. Besides the gaming tables, dance floors, and western-style floor shows, some of these clubs feature fine dining, European style. They're open to 4 or 6 a.m. and accept hard currency only.

I want to go dancing.
Я хочу піти потанцювати.
ya KHO-choo pee-TIH po-tahn-tsyu-VAH-tih

Where can we go dancing?
Куди ми можемо піти на танці?
koo-DIH mih MO-zheh-mo pee-TIH nah TAHN-tsee

Can you recommend a good (nightclub) (disco)?
Чи ви можете порадити гарний (нічний клуб) (диско)?
chih vih MO-zheh-teh po-RAH-dih-tih HAHR-nihỹ
(neech-NIHỸ kloob) (DIHS-ko)

[Inside] We have (haven't) a reservation.
Ми (не) замовляли попередньо.
mih (neh) zah-MO-vlya-lih po-peh-REHD'no

Ukrainians are fond of dancing, and it's not uncommon for a man to ask a stranger to be his partner. If someone who wants to try out the latest western dance craze approaches you, he may ask:

"May I have this dance?"
Чи можна вас запросити?
chih MOZH-nah vahs zah-pro-SIH-tih

If you don't care to dance, simply say:

No, thank you.	Ні, дякую.	nee DYA-koo-yu

or you may feel that

This dance is too fast for me.
Ця музика зашвидка для мене.
tsya MOO-zih-kah zah-SHVIHD-kah dlya MEH-neh

CHAPTER 21. MOTORING

Ukrainian Proverb:
Хто має висіти, той не утоне.
khto MAH-yeh vih-SEE-tih toў neh oo-TO-neh
Who is going to be hanged will not drown.

For every journey, there's a low point. For those who go to Ukraine and have anything to do with a car, the worst moment is likely to involve that car. The limited number of gas stations and getting replacement parts makes a car more of a liability than an advantage. Many thefts involve cars or parts for them. Traffic is less regulated than in North America and drivers take more chances. With these words of caution, we provide the vocabulary to help you, if you choose to travel by car.

The speed limit in Ukraine is 90 km per hour on the highway. On some sections of highway, speed up to 110 km per hour is permitted, but these limits are usually not posted. In the cities, 60 km per hour is allowed.

CAR RENTAL

Most visitors to Ukraine who want the convenience of a car and driver when going off the beaten track rely on their Ukrainian connections. For the truly adventurous, self-drive rental cars are available from service bureaus of some larger tourist hotel or at the border. Major international car rental companies have not yet discovered Ukraine.

To drive in Ukraine, you'll need a valid driving license from your home state. It's also a good idea to carry with it an International Driving Permit (IDP), which basically is a translation of your license. The IDP can be obtained from the American Automobile Association (AAA).

You are not required to be insured, but generally rental cars include insurance.

Where can I rent a car?
Де я можу взяти машину напрокат?
deh ya MO-zhoo VZYA-tih mah-SHIH-noo nah-pro-KAHT

I need a car for ... days.
Мені треба машина на ... днів.
meh-NEE TREH-bah mah-SHIH-nah nah ... dneev

Can I leave the car ...?
Чи можу я лишити машину ...?
chih MO-zhoo ya lih-SHIH-tih mah-SHIH-noo

at the airport   в аеропорту   v ah-ehro-por-TOO
in the hotel   в готелі   v ho-TEH-lee
somewhere in [name of city]
                       десь в ...   dehs' v

What is the charge per (day) (week)?
Скільки це коштує за (день) (тиждень)?
SKEEL'-kih tseh kosh-TOO-yeh zah (dehn') (TIHZH-den')

Do you charge by the day or by mileage?
Ви берете плату за дні чи за кілометри?
vih beh-REH-teh PLAH-too zah dnee chih zah
kee-lo-MEHT-rih

Can I buy gas coupons?
Чи я можу купити талони на бензин?
chih ya MO-zhoo koo-PIH-tih tah-LO-nih nah behn-ZIHN

PARKING

Where can I leave my car?
Де я можу поставити мою машину?
deh ya MO-zhoo pos-TAH-vih-tih mo-YU mah-SHIH-noo

May I leave my car here?
Чи я можу тут поставити машину?
chih ya MO-zhoo toot po-STAH-vih-tih mah-SHIH-noo

For how long?   Як довго?   yak DOV-ho

How much will it cost ...?
Скільки це коштує ...?
SKEEL'-kih tseh kosh-TOO-yeh

per hour   за годину   zah ho-DIH-noo
per day   за день   zah dehn'

Is it safe to leave a car here?
Чи безпечно лишити тут машину?
chih behz-PEHCH-no lih-SHIH-tih toot mah-SHIH-noo

Is this parking lot guarded?
Чи ця стоянка охороняється?
chih tsya sto-YAN-kah o-kho-ro-NYA-yeht'-sya

ROAD SERVICE

Road Service   Дорожній Сервіс   do-ROZH-nihў SEHR-vees

The network of roads and highways in Ukraine is not dense. Main two-lane highways link the major cities, single-lane roads link the intermediate cities, and travel in rural areas is on unpaved roads. M - 17 is the main east-west route. Roads names are so numbered, but informally, they're identified by the direction in which one is heading, for example, the Poltava - Hadyach road.

Scattered throughout the country on the main roads are service areas (автосервіс, ahv-to-SEHR-vees) consisting of a filling station and a repair station. These are often located just outside of cities. Don't count on them being able to supply you with gas or needed parts, however. If you see people selling it along the side of the road, be advised that they didn't come by their supply honestly.

Where can I find some gasoline?
Де я можу знайти бензин?
deh ya MO-zhoo znahў-TIH behn-ZIHN

Where is the nearest gas station?
Де знаходиться найближча бензозаправочна станція?
deh znah-KHO-diht'-sya nahў-BLIHZH-chah
behn-zo-zahp-RAH-voch-nah STAHN-tsee-ya

Can you sell me some gas?
Чи ви можете продати мені бензин?
chih vih MO-zheh-teh pro-DAH-tih meh-NEE behn-ZIHN

I need 20 litres of 91 octane gas. [One gallon of gas = 3.8 litres.]
Мені треба двадцять літрів дев'яносто першого бензину.
meh-NEE TREH-bah DVAHD-tsyat' lee-TREEV
deh-VYA-NOS-to PEHR-sho-ho behn-ZIHN-noo

Do you have diesel?
Чи ви маєте дізельне паливо?
chih vih MAH-yeh-teh DEE-zehl'-neh PAHL-lih-vo

Full tank, please.	Прошу, повний бак.	
	PRO-shoo POV-nihў bahk	
Please check the ...	Прочу провірити	
	PRO-shoo pro-VEE-riht-tih	

oil	масло	MAHS-lo
water	воду	VO-doo
brake fluid	тормозну рідину	tor-moz-NOO ree-dih-NOO
battery	аккумулятор	ahk-koo-moo-LYA-tor
tire pressure	тиск в шинах	tihsk v SHIH-nahkh

Would you wash the car windows?
    Чи ви можете помити вікна в машині?
    chih vih MO-zheh-teh po-MIH-tih veek-NAH v mah-SHIH-nee

Can you fix this flat tire?
    Чи ви можете залатати дірку в колесі?
    chih vih MO-zheh-teh zah-lah-TAH-tih DEER-koo v ko-leh-SEE

Please pump up the spare tire.
    Прошу накачати запасну шину.
    PRO-shoo nah-kah-CHAH-tih zah-pahs-NOO SHIH-noo

| I need to change | Мені треба замінити .... | |
| the ... | meh-NEE TREH-bah zah-mih-NIH-tih ... | |

tire	шину	SHIH-noo
spark plugs	свічки	SVEECH-kih
wipers	щітки	SHCHEET-kih
fan belt	ремінь	reh-MEEN'

I need a windshield wiper.
    Мені треба двірники.
    meh-NEE TREH-bah dveer-nih-KIH

How much do I owe you?
    Скільки я повинен заплатити?
    SKEEL'-kih ya po-VIH-nehn zah-PLAH-tih-tih

CAR BREAKDOWN

| Car Breakdown | Поломка Машини | |
| | po-LOM-kah mah-SHIH-nih | |

Where is the nearest service station?
Де знаходиться найближчий автосервіс?
deh znah-KHO-diht'-sya nahỹ-BLIHZH-chihỹ ahv-to-SEHR-vees

My car has broken down.
Моя машина зламалась.
mo-YA mah-SHIH-nah zlah-MAH-lahs'

I can't start my car.
Я не можу завезти машину.
ya neh MO-zhoo zah-VEHZ-tih mah-SHIH-noo

I ran out of gasoline.
У мене закінчився бензин.
oo MEH-neh zah-KEEN-chihv-sya behn-ZIHN

The battery is dead.   Аккуммулятор сів.
ahk-koom-moo-LYA-tor seev

My brakes won't work.
У мене не працюють тормоза.
oo MEH-neh neh prah-TSYU-yut' tor-mo-ZAH

My lights won't work.   Не працюють фари.
neh prah-TSYU-yut' FAH-rih

I have a flat tire.   У мене проколота шина.
oo MEH-neh pro-KO-lo-tah SHIH-nah

I can't shift gears.
Я не можу переключити швидкість.
ya neh MO-zhoo peh-reh-klyu-CHIH-tih SHVIHD-keest'

My steering wheel doesn't work.
У мене не працює кермо.
oo MEH-neh neh prah-TSYU-yeh kehr-MO

I don't have oil.
Я не маю масла в двигуні.
ya neh MAH-yu MAHS-lah v dvih-hoo-NEE

I don't have any coolant.
Я не маю води в радіаторі.
ya neh MAH-yu VO-dih v rah-dee-AH-to-ree

I need gasoline.
Мені треба бензин.
meh-NEE TREH-bah behn-ZIHN

ROAD EMERGENCY

Road Emergency   Допомога на Дорозі
                        do-po-MO-hah nah do-RO-zee

If you're traveling at night, you may find roadblocks of militiamen at the outskirts of the bigger cities recording license plate numbers and drivers' registrations. Presumably this is for your safety. Otherwise, you're not likely to find much official help on the road. If you have access to a telephone, you can dial 02 to summon the police and 03 for an ambulance.

Please help me!   Прошу помогти мені!
                         PRO-shoo po-moh-TIH meh-NEE

Please call the police! Прошу, подзвонити в міліцію!
                         PRO-shoo podz-VO-nih-tih v mee-LEE-tsee-yu

Where can I call ...?   Де я можу подзвонити ...?
                         deh ya MO-zhoo podz-VO-nih-tih

the police   в міліцію   v mee-LEE-tsee-yu

an ambulance   в швидку   v shvihd-KOO
                         допомогу   do-po-MO-hoo

"What happened?"   Що трапилось?   shcho TRAH-pih-los'

An accident.   Аварія.   ah-VAH-ree-ya

A breakdown.   Поломка.   po-LOM-kah

A person in the car is (sick) (injured) and needs help.
        Людина в машині (хвора) (ранена) і потребує допомоги.
        lyu-DIH-nah v mah-SHIH-nee (KHVO-rah) (RAH-neh-nah) ee
        po-treh-BOO-yeh do-po-MOH-hih

Please take (her) (him) (them) to the hospital.
        Прошу, завезти (її) (його) (їх) до лікарні.
        PRO-shoo ZAH-vehz-tih (yee-YEE) (ŬHO-ho) (yeekh) do
        LEE-kahr-nee

Nobody is injured.   Ніхто не постраждав.
                         nee-KHTO neh pos-trahzh-DAHV

CHAPTER 22. GETTING HELP

Ukrainian Proverb:
Лякана ворона і куща боїться.
LYA-kah-nah VO-ro-nah ee koo-SHCHAH bo-YEET'-sya
A scared crow is even afraid of the bushes.

Problems that might seem trivial at home can be overwhelming when one is away. In troubling circumstances, it's natural to long for the comfort of a familiar setting and the accustomed ways of doing things. Receiving help in strange surroundings delivered in a strange language does not put one at ease, and when that help is different from the way it's done at home, all the more we might question its value.

VARIOUS PROBLEMS

Various Problems	Різні Проблеми	REEZ-nee pro-BLEH-mih

I'm lost. Я заблудився. ya zah-bloo-DIHV-sya

I missed my (plane) (train) (bus).
Я (пропустив, *m.*) (пропустил а, *f.*) мій (літак) (поїзд) (автобус).
yah (pro-poos-TIHV) (pro-poos-TIH-lah) meey (LEE-tahk) (PO-yeezd) (ahv-TO-boos)

I forgot my (money) (keys).
Я (забув, *m.*) (забула, *f.*) (гроші) (ключі).
ya (zah-BOOV) (zah-BOO-lah) (HRO-shee) (klyu-CHEE)

I've been robbed. Мене ограбували.
MEH-neh oh-rah-boo-VAH-lih

They stole my .... У мене вкрали ....
oo MEH-neh VKRAH-lih

I lost my.... Я (загубив, *m.*) (загубила, *f.*) ....
ya (zah-hoo-BIHV) (zah-hoo-BIH-lah)

camera	фотоапарат	fo-to-ah-pah-RAHT
car	машину	mah-SHIH-noo
documents	документи	do-koo-MEHN-tih
keys	ключі	kloo-CHEE

luggage	багаж	bah-HAHƵH
money	гроші	HRO-shee
passport	паспорт	PAHS-port
purse/suitcase	сумку	SOOM-koo
wallet	гаманець	hah-mah-NEHTS′

(He's) (they're) bothering me.
　(Він переслідує) (вони переслідують) мене.
　(veen peh-reh-SLEE-doo-yeh) (vo-NIH peh-reh-SLEE-doo-yut′)
　meh-NEH

Go away.　　　　　Відійдіть від мене.
　　　　　　　　　vee-deeў-DEET′ veed MEH-neh
Get help quickly.　Покличте допомогу.
　　　　　　　　　po-KLIHCH-teh do-po-MO-hoo

Lost Objects: If you lose your passport, go to your embassy or consulate; if you lose your visa, go to the local visa office. The replacement process is easier if you pack in your luggage a photocopy of the identification page of your passport, your visa number and two passport-sized photos. In Ukraine, there's a "finders-keepers" attitude toward found personal objects. Nevertheless, railroads, bus stations, and airports do have a place called the "room of forgotten things" for storage of lost and found items.

Where's the lost and　Де камера забутих речей?
　found room?　　　deh KAH-meh-rah zah-BOO-tihkh reh-CHEHŬ

ASKING DIRECTIONS

If it's you that's lost, these phrases might be helpful:

Excuse me, would you please help me?
　Прошу, допомогти мені.
　PRO-shoo do-po-MOH-tih meh-NEE

I can't find my hotel.　Я не можу знайти мій готель.
　　　　　　　　　　ya neh MO-ȥhoo znahў-TIH meeў HO-tel′

Can you show me on the map where I am?
　Прошу, показати мені на карті де я знаходжусь?
　PRO-shoo po-kah-ZAH-tih meh-NEE nah KAHR-tee deh ya
　znah-KHOD-zhoos′

Is this the road to the airport?
Чи це дорога до аеропорту?
chih tseh do-RO-hah do ah-eh-ro-POR-too

How far is it from here to the center?
Як далеко звідси до центру?
yak DAH-leh-ko ZVEED-sih do tsehn-TROO

Please tell me where to find....
Прошу сказати мені де знаходиться ....
PRO-shoo skah-ZAH-tih meh-NEE deh znah-KHO-diht'sya

... Street	вулиця	VOO-lih-tsya
Hotel...	Готель ...	ho-TEHL'
this address	ця адреса	tsya ahd-REH-sah
a hospital	лікарня	lee-KAHR-nya
a pharmacy	аптека	ahp-TEH-kah
the police	міліція	mee-LEE-tsee-ya

the (American) (Canadian) Embassy
(Американське) (Канадське) Посольство
(ah-meh-rih-KAHNS'-keh) (kah-NAHD-s'keh) po-SOL'ST-vo

the (American) (Canadian) Consulate
(Американське) (Канадське) Консульство
(ah-meh-rih-KAHNS'-keh) (kah-NAHD-s'keh) KON-sool'st-vo

north	північ	PEEV-neech
to the north	на північ	nah PEEV-neech
south	південь	PEEV-dehn'
to the south	на південь	nah PEEV-dehn'
west	захід	ZAH-kheed
to the west	на захід	nah ZAH-kheed
east	схід	skheed
to the east	на схід	nah skheed

SOURCES OF HELP

Consulates: Your country's consulate is there for problems. Go to your consulate in case your passport is lost or stolen and in emergency situations, such as severe illness. Americans residing permanently or on a long-term basis in Ukraine should register at the consular section of the U.S. Embassy.

U.S. Embassy, Consular Division
10 Yuri Kotsyubynsky Street (вулица Юря Коцюбинского)
Kyiv 53. Tel. 044-244-7354.

The Embassy has a 24-hour emergency phone answered only in English after working hours: 044-244-7345.

Canadian Embassy
31 Yaroslaviv val (Ярославів вал) Street
Kyiv. Tel. 044-212-2235.

Emergency Phone Numbers. Three universal phone numbers for specific emergencies are engraved in every public phone booth and displayed on phones in private homes. They are universal throughout Ukraine:

01	Fire Department	Пожежної Служби
		po-ẐHEHẐH-no-yee SLOOẐH-bih
02	Police	Міліція
		meel-ee-TSEE-ya
03	Ambulance	Швидкої Допомоги
		shvihd-KO-yee do-po-MO-hih

In addition, the universal phone number for a gas emergency is 04.

Police. There are two types of police in Ukraine. Under the jurisdiction of the local governments are traffic police, Державна Авто Інспекція, (dehr-ẐHAHV-nah AVH-to eens-PEHK-tsee-ya). Commonly called *DAI,* (ДАІ, dah-EE), the traffic police are responsible for traffic control and violations. They may stop a driver and ask to see the driver's license as well as inspect the car upon suspicion of criminal activity. The regular police force, under the jurisdiction of the Minister of Internal Affairs, investigates all crime that does not involve motor vehicles. Citizens are not required to show their driver's license to them.

If you are involved in a traffic accident or a crime that occurs on the highways, notify the state traffic inspection. Call the regular police for all other needs.

Call the police.	Викличте міліцію.
	VIH-klihch-teh mee-LEE-tsee-yu

I NEED A DOCTOR

I Need a Doctor   Мені Потрібен Лікар
meh-NEE po-TREE-behn LEE-kahr

In Ukraine, medical treatment is dispensed on a walk-in basis at a polyclinic (поліклініка, po-lee-KLEE-nee-kah) or in a hospital (лікарня, lee-KAHR-nya). The public clinics are free of charge and there are now private clinics where you pay, and, in the opinion of some travelers, receive better care. If you're in need of a doctor, your host may take you to a free clinic. If you're staying in a hotel, notify the manager or receptionist.

There is a shortage of basic medical supplies in Ukraine, including disposable needles and gloves, antibiotics, and anesthetics. Nevertheless, Ukrainian medical personnel will do their best to help you. Check with your embassy for the name of a doctor or clinic that's best equipped — there are usually some western doctors in Kyiv helping with Chornobyl problems, for example. Although the embassies are not supposed to provide medical or ambulance services for private visitors to Ukraine, they have been known to do so in emergency situations.

Where can I get medical care?
    Де я можу отримати медичну допомогу?
    deh ya MO-zhoo o-TRIH-mah-tih meh-DIHCH-noo
    do-po-MO-hoo

I want a private clinic.
    Я хочу приватну клініку.
    ya KHO-choo prih-VAHT-noo KLEE-nee-koo

Where's the nearest hospital?
    Де знаходиться найближча лікарня?
    deh znah-KHO-diht'-sya nahỹ-BLIHZH-chah lee-KAHR-nya

I want to see ....   Я хочу бачити ....
    ya KHO-choo BAH-chih-tih

a cardiologist	кардіолога	kahr-dee-O-lo-hah
a general practitioner	терапевта	teh-rah-PEHV-tah
a gynecologist	гінеколога	hee-neh-KO-loh-hah
an ophthalmologist	окуліста	o-koo-LEES-tah

a pediatrician	педіатора	peh-dee-AH-to-rah
a neurologist	неврапатолога	neh-vrah-pah-TO-lo-hah
a surgeon	хірурга	khee-ROOR-hah

How long must I wait for the doctor?
Як довго чекати на лікаря?
yak DOV-ho cheh-KAH-tih nah LEE-kahr-ya

I feel sick.
Я почуваю себе (хворим, *m.*) (хворою, *f.*).
ya po-choo-VAH-yu seh-BEH (KHVO-rihm) (KHVO-ro-yu)

| I feel nauseous. | Мене нудить. | meh-NEH NOO-diht′ |
| I've been vomiting. | Мене рве. | MEH-neh rveh |

I feel dizzy.
Я відчуваю голово-кружіння.
a veed-choo-VAH-yu ho-lo-vo-kroo-Z͡HEEN-nya
I feel weak.
Я почуваю себе слабим.
ya po-choo-VAH-yu seh-BEH slah-BIHM
I ache all over.
У мене все болить.
oo MEH-neh vseh bo-LIHT′
I have an earache.
У мене болить вухо.
oo MEH-neh bo-LIHT′ VOO-kho
I have a headache.
У мене болить голова.
oo MEH-neh bo-LIHT′ ho-lo-VAH
I have a sore throat.
У мене болить горло.
oo MEH-neh bo-LIHT′ HOR-lo
It hurts here. [pointing]
У мене болить тут.
oo MEH-neh bo-LIHT′ toot
I have a fever.
У мене гарячка.
oo MEH-neh hah-RYACH-kah

According to the centigrade system used in Ukraine, anything over 37°C
is considered an elevated temperature. 38°C degrees is equivalent to
100.4° F.

I have a runny nose.	У мене насморк.	oo MEH-neh NAHS-mork

I have a bloody nose. У мене тече кров з носа.
oo MEH-neh teh-CHEH krov z NO-sah

I have a cough.	Я кашляю.	ya KAHSH-lya-yu

I'm taking this Я приймаю ці ліки.
medication ya-prihỹ-MAH-yu tsee LEE-kih

I'm	Я є	ya yeh

allergic	аллергик	ahl-LEHR-hihk
asthmatic	астматик	ahst-MAH-tihk
diabetic	діабетик	dee-ah-BEH-tihk
pregnant	вагітна	vah-HEET-nah

I'm constipated.	У мене запір.	oo MEH-neh zah-PEER

I've got diarrhea.	У мене понос.	oo MEH-neh po-NOS

I have a pain in my chest.
Я почуваю біль в грудах.
ya po-choo-VAH-yu beel' v HROO-dahkh

I have a heart condition.
У мене слабе сердце.
oo MEH-neh slah-BEH SEHRD-tseh

I have (high) (low) blood pressure.
У мене (високий) (низький) кров'яний тиск.
oo MEH-neh (vih-SO-kihỹ) (nihz'-KIHỸ) krov'-ya-NIHỸ tihsk

Please check my blood pressure.
Прошу поміряти мій тиск.
PRO-shoo po-MEE-rya-tih meeỹ tihsk

What's wrong with me?	Що зі мною?	shcho zee MNO-yu

Is it a virus?	Чи це вірус?	chih tseh VEE-roos

Is it ...?	Чи це ..?	chih tseh

serious	серйозно	sehr-ỸOZ-no
contagious	заразне	zah-RAHZ-neh
bleeding	кровотеча	kro-vo-TEH-chah
infected	інфекція	een-FEHK-tsee-ya
healing	загоюється	zah-HO-yu-yeht'-sya

Is there a complication?
Чи є ускаднення?
chih yeh oos-KLAHD-nehn-nya

When will I feel better?
Коли я поправлюсь?
ko-LIH ya po-PRAHV-lyus'

Do I need medicine?
Чи треба мені приймати ліки?
chih TREH-bah meh-NEE prihў-MAH-tih LEE-kih

For how long?   Як довго?   yak DOV-ho

I'm allergic to penicillin.
Я аллергик до пеніциліну.
ya ahl-LEHR-hihk do peh-nee-tsih-LEE-noo

The Doctor Says ... Лікар Каже ...   LEE-kahr KAH-zheh

"Open your mouth, please."
Прошу відкрити рот.
PRO-shoo veed-KRIH-tih rot

"Take a deep breath."
Прошу вдихнути глибоко.
PRO-shoo vdihkh-NOO-tih hlih-BO-ko

"Does this hurt?"   Тут болить?   toot bo-LIHT'?

"Take this ..."   Приймайте це...   prihў-MAHЎ-teh tseh ...

once a day	один раз на день	o-DIHN rahz nah dehn'
two times a day	два раза на день	dvah RAH-zah nah dehn'
three times per day	три раза на день	trih RAH-zah nah dehn'
every six hours	кожних шість годин	
	KOZH-nihkh sheest' ho-DIHN	
for ... days	напротязі ... днів	nah-PRO-tya-zee ... dneev
before meals	перед їдою	PEH-rehd yee-DO-yu
after meals	після їди	PEES-lya yee-DIH
with meals	з їдою	z yee-DO-yu
before bedtime	перед сном	PEH-rehd snom

"Rest, remain quiet." Дотримуйтесь спокою.
dot-RIH-mooў-tehs′ SPO-ko-yu

"Stay in bed for ... days."
Бути в ліжку ... днів.
BOO-tih v LEEZH-koo ... dneev

"Go to the hospital."
Вам треба в лікарню.
vahm TREH-bah v lee-KAHR-nyu

"It's nothing serious."
Нічого серйозного.
nee-CHO-ho sehr-ŸOZ-no-ho

"Come back and see me in ... days (a week)."
Прийдіть до мене через ... днів (тиждень).
prihў-DEET′ do MEH-neh CHEH-rehz ... dneev (TIHZH-dehn′).

AFFLICTIONS/DISEASES

Afflictions/diseases	Хвороби	khvo-RO-bih
AIDS	СНІД	sneed
appendicitis	апендицит	ah-pehn-dih-TSIHT
bronchitis	бронхіт	bron-KHEET
cancer	рак	rahk
chicken pox	вітряна віспа	veet-rya-NAH VEES-pah
cold	простуда	pros-TOO-dah
coronary	інфаркт	een-FAHRKT
diphtheria	дифтерит	dihf-teh-RIHT
flu	грип	hrihp
hemorrhage	крововилив	kro-vo-VIH-lihv
hepatitis	гепатит	heh-pah-TIHT
infection	інфекція	een-FEHK-tsee-ya
jaundice	жовтуха	zhov-TOO-khah
measles	кір	keer
migraine	мігрень	mee-HREHN′
mumps	свинка	SVIHN-kah
pneumonia	пневмонія	pnehv-mo-NEE-ya
smallpox	віспа	VEES-pah
stroke	інсульт	een-SOOL′T

tetanus	стовбняк	stovb-NYAK
tuberculosis	туберкульоз	too-behr-koo-L'OZ
ulcer	виразка	VIH-rahz-kah

PARTS OF THE BODY

| Parts of the Body | Частини Тіла | chah-STIH-nih TEE-lah |

My ... hurts.	У мене болить....	oo MEH-neh bo-LIHT
ankle	кісточка	KEES-toch-kah
arm	рука	roo-KAH
bone(s)	кістка, кістки	KEEST-kah, KEEST-kih
back	спина	spih-NAH
blood	кров	krov
breast, chest	груди	HROO-dih
elbow	лікоть	LEE-kot'
ear(s)	вухо, вуха	VOO-kho, VOO-khah
eye(s)	око, очі	O-ko, O-chee
face	обличчя	ob-LIHCH-chya
finger(s)	палець, пальці	PAH-lehts', PAHL'-tsee
foot, feet	стопа, стопи	sto-PAH, STO-pih
gum(s)	десна, десни	dehs-NAH, dehs-NIH
hair	волосся	vo-LOS-sya
head	голова	ho-lo-VAH
heart	сердце	SEHRD-tseh
heel	п'ятка	P'YAT-kah
kidneys	нирки	NIHR-kih
leg(s)	нога, ноги	no-HAH, NO-hih
liver	печінка	peh-CHEEN-kah
lungs	легені	leh-HEH-nee
muscles	м'язи	M'YA-zih
mouth	рот	rot
nails	нігті	NEEH-tee
nerve(s)	нерв, нерви	nehrv, NEHR-vih
knee(s)	коліно, коліна	ko-LEE-no, ko-LEE-nah
neck	шия	SHIH-ya
nose	ніс	nees
rib(s)	ребро, ребра	rehb-RO, REHB-rah
shoulder(s)	плече, плечі	pleh-CHEH, PLEH-chee
spine	позвонок	poz-vo-NOK

stomach	живіт	z͡hih-VEET
tooth, teeth	зуб, зуби	zoob, ZOO-bih
thumb	великий палець	veh-LIH-kih͝y PAH-lehts′
throat	горло	HOR-lo
toes	пальці на нозі	PAHL′-tsee nah no-ZEE
tongue	язик	ya-ZIHK
tonsils	гланди	HLAHN-dih
wrist	кисть	kihst′

A VISIT TO THE DENTIST

A Visit to the Dentist   Візит до Зубного Лікаря
vee-ZIHT do zoob-NO-ho LEE-kah-rya

Please recommend a good dentist.
Прошу порекомендувати доброго зубного лікаря.
pro-SHOO po-reh-ko-mehn-doo-VAH-tih DO-bro-ho zoob-NO-ho
LEE-kah-rya

I'd like to make an appointment.
Я хочу записатись на прийом.
ya KHO-choo zah-pih-SAH-tihs′ nah prih-Y͝OM.

It's urgent!   Це терміново.   tseh tehr-mee-NO-vo

How long will I have to wait?
Скільки мені треба чекати?
SKEEL′kih meh-NEE TREH-bah cheh-KAH-tih

My gums are very sore.
Мої десна дуже чутливі.
mo-YEE DEHS-nah DOO-z͡heh choot-LIH-vee

My gums are bleeding.
Мої десна кровоточать.
mo-YEE DEHS-nah kro-vo-TO-chat′

I have a toothache.   У мене болить зуб.
oo MEH-neh bo-LIHT′ zoob

It hurts up here.   Болить тут вверху.
bo-LIHT′ toot vvehr-KHOO

It hurts down here.   Болить тут внизу.
                         bo-LIHT' toot vnih-ZOO

I've lost a filling.   У мене випала пломба.
                         oo MEH-neh VIH-pah-lah PLOM-bah

I have a broken tooth.   У мене поламався зуб.
                         oo MEH-neh po-lah-MAHV-sya zoob

Can you repair it?   Прошу вилікувати це?
                         pro-SHOO VIH-lee-koo-vah-tih tseh

I don't want it pulled. Я не хочу його рвати.
                         ya neh KHO-choo yo-HO RVAH-tih

What kind of anethestic do you use?
      Яку анестезію ви приміняєте?
      ya-KOO ah-nehs-teh-ZEE-yu vih prih-mee-nya-YEH-teh

AT THE OPTICIAN'S

At the Optician's   У Оптика   oo OP-tih-kah

Please fix these glasses.
      Прошу відремонтувати ці окуляри.
      PRO-shoo veed-reh-mon-too-VAH-tih tsee o-koo-LYA-rih

I lost a contact lens.
      Я (загубив, *m.*) (загубила, *f.*) контактну лінзу.
      ya zah-hoo-BIHV (zah-hoo-BIH-lah) kon-TAHKT-noo
      LEENS-zoo

I'm near-sighted.   Я (близорукий, *m.*) (близорука, *f.*).
                       ya (blih-zo-ROO-kihў) (blih-zo-ROO-kah)

I'm far-sighted.   Я (дальнозоркий, *m.*) (дальнозорка, *f.*).
                       ya (dahl'-no-ZOR-kihў) (dahl'-no-ZOR-kah)

I'd like to have my eyesight tested.
      Я хочу перевірити мій зір.
      ya KHO-choo peh-reh-VEE-rih-tih meeў zeer

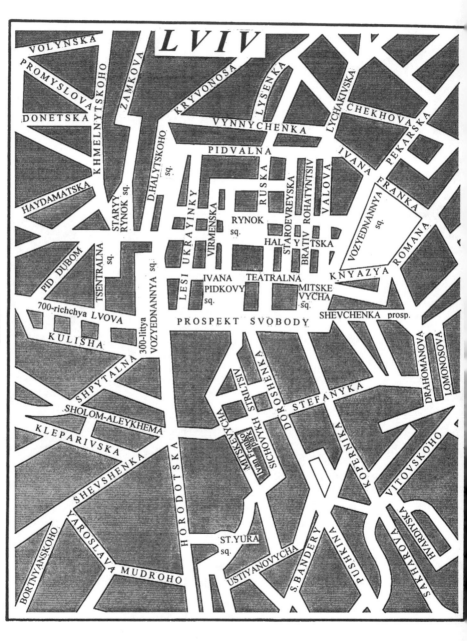

CHAPTER 23.
LVIV: "CAPITAL" OF WESTERN UKRAINE
Львів l'veev

Imagine a couple who were born in Austria, married and raised their children in Poland, lived in Germany, died in the Soviet Union, and are buried in Ukraine. Yet during their entire lifetime, they lived in the same house and never moved. That could have happened in the fascinating city of Lviv.

Name: Lviv is an example of a city that has changed hands many times throughout its long history. Just in this century alone, it's also been known as Lemberg, Lwow, and L'vov. The word *Lviv* is the possessive adjective form of the Ukrainian name Lev (Leo), the person for whom it was named. Note that in the transliteration of Lviv adopted by the United States Board on Geographical Names, no symbol is used to represent the Ukrainian soft sign (ь).

Location: Situated in west central Ukraine, Lviv is close to the Polish border, only some 85 km (53 miles) away. It's about 250 km (155 miles) from Chop, an access point from Slovakia and Hungary on the southwestern border. Lviv is the hub of main roads that extend to major Ukrainian cities. From Lviv to Kyiv are 545 km (340 miles); to Ivano-Frankivsk are 135 km (85 miles); to Uzhhorod, 275 km (170 miles); to Chernivtsi, 275 km (170 miles); to Lutsk, 150 km (95 miles).

Population: There are about 800,000 people in Lviv. About 80 percent are Ukrainian, 15 percent are Russian, 2 percent Jewish, and 1 percent Polish. This represents a radical change from the ethnic composition before World War II, when Poles made up 50 percent of the city, Jews constituted over 30 percent, Ukrainians less than 20 percent, and there were no Russians. Throughout the history of this cosmopolitan city, the various ethnic groups that have made up its population have, for the most part, lived together harmoniously. And, despite a succession of foreign rule and shifting populations, Lviv has maintained a Ukrainian consciousness. As the traditional economic, cultural, and political center of western Ukraine, it's sometimes referred to as the "most Ukrainian" of Ukrainian cities.

Climate: The climate is moderate continental. The average daily temperature is -4° C (24.6° F) in January and 18° C (64.9° F) in June. While temperatures are never extreme in winter or summer, there is usually some humidity that may cause slight discomfort. The annual rainfall is about 26 inches. July is the rainiest month with four inches and January is the driest month with about one inch. Lviv averages 66 cloudy days per year; December is the cloudiest month and August the clearest.

Business and Industry: With ten institutions of higher education, Lviv has the ambience of a college town. It has many publishing houses, and its manufacture includes buses, radios and televisions, machinery, and food products. The Svitoch candy factory, a brewery that makes "Lvivsky Pivo" brand beer, and a joint distillery enterprise, the Canadian-Ukrainian Seagram's, are located in Lviv.

Public Transportation: Lviv is served by a number of streetcar, trolleybus lines. Public transportation to other Ukrainian cities and to European cities is readily available.

Bus: The long-distance bus station is at 271 Stryyska (Стрийська) Street. Buses link Lviv to various cities of western Ukraine and Poland. Take Trolleybus No. 5 or Bus No. 18. Schedules change frequently; for information telephone 63-24-73.

Rail: Lviv is a hub of eastern European rail travel. There are daily trips to major international cities, among them, Budapest, Prague, Belgrade, Sofia, Riga, and Moscow. There is also good service to cities all throughout Ukraine, including several trips a day to Kyiv. Buying tickets several weeks in advance is recommended; it's easiest, though more expensive, to go through a hotel service bureau. The railroad station at *ploshcha Dvirtseva* at the end of Chernivetska (Чернівецька) Street, is undergoing some refurbishing and promises to be attractive. Bottled water, soft drinks, and fruit is sold inside the terminal. Call 005 for information on arrivals and departures.

Air: Lviv's airport is due for some upgrading and it doesn't handle much international traffic. At this writing, Lot Polish Airline is the only foreign carrier that flies into Lviv. Ukrainian International runs flights between Lviv and London, Manchester, Amsterdam, and Frankfurt; winter schedule is reduced. Its domestic branch, Air Ukraine, links Lviv to cities throughout Ukraine. Foreigners pay several times more than Ukrainian citizens for intercity flights. The Air Ukraine office is at *ploshcha Peremoha, 5.* Trolleybus No. 9 goes to the airport at *vulytsya Lybinska.*

Tourism: Lviv is a city of great charm. Its central part, designated a national architectural preserve in the mid-1970's, is small enough to cover on foot. Following independence, a huge number of streets and squares were renamed, and you may find some inconsistency of usage. Tourist hotels will accept credit cards, and banks in the central area are reported to cash personal checks for a small percentage. Lviv has a history of water pressure problems. In some of the residential neighborhoods, water use may be restricted to certain hours of the day. The situation is likely to be better in the downtown, tourist area. For conservation, electricity may be shut off for several hours each day in some parts of town.

HISTORY

Lviv was founded in 1256 by Danylo Halytsky, prince of Galicia-Volynia, a western principality of Kyivan Rus. Danylo named the city for his son Prince Lev (Leo). Its strategic position as a stopping point on east-west trade routes and Carpathian passes made it vulnerable to siege.

The onslaught of invaders started in the early part of the 14th century when the nobleman ruler Dmytro Detko and his forces successfully repulsed the troops of Polish King Casimir. Soon, however, Lviv did fall under Polish domination which brought to it a European influence. A major adaptation was the establishment in 1596 of the Uniate Church, also known as the Ukrainian Greek Catholic Church. This church was a compromise between Polish Roman Catholicism and Ukrainian Orthodoxy: The Ukrainian Greek Catholic Church acknowledged the supremacy of the Rome while maintaining the Orthodox form of worship.

In 1772, the First Partition of Poland brought Galicia under the jurisdiction of the Austro-Hungarian Empire. Lviv then became the administrative center of a newly-created province dominated by Poles. With the collapse of the Hapsburg Empire at the end of World War I, a newly formed Ukrainian national *rada* (council) proclaimed an independent government known variously as Ruthenia, West Ukraine, or East Galicia, with Lviv as the seat.

Polish troops, however, occupied Lviv and returned western Ukraine to Polish rule. The 1939 German-Soviet Nonaggression Agreement (Molotov-Ribbentrop Pact) transferred most of western Ukraine from Poland to the U.S.S.R. This transfer — against the will of its residents — marked the first time in its long history that Lviv was ruled by Moscow. The take-over of the Red Army put a stop to Ukrainian cultural and political activity and ushered in a climate of severe repression, including mass arrests and executions of Ukrainians. In 1941, Lviv was occupied by Germany and much of its Jewish population was wiped out.

After the Nazis' retreat in 1944, Lviv was regained by Soviet forces who reinstituted their campaign of repression against the nationally conscious Ukrainian people. Opposition to soviet totalitarianism festered in western Ukraine, particularly in Lviv, and grew into dissident movements that eventually were instrumental in winning independence for Ukraine.

SIGHTSEEING

Lviv's architectural monuments have been more fortunate than those in other Ukrainian cities. During World War II there was no fighting in its streets; the Soviets arrived later than in other parts of Ukraine and did not bother to raze landmarks and initiate monumental building projects such as those that had disfigured Kyiv and other eastern cities.

With its narrow cobblestone streets and its assortment of western architectural styles — Renaissance, Baroque, Rococo, and Neoclassical — that came with its various rulers, Lviv has a central European ambience. The city's 14th and 15th century Gothic architecture was destroyed by fire in 1527, but Lviv is the only city in Ukraine that still has some original Renaissance structures. The main street used to be named after Lenin, but now it's called *prospekt Svobody* (проспект Свободи), which means "Avenue of Freedom." This wide street runs some 600 meters (approximately one-third of a mile) from Mickiewicz Square (площа Міцкевича, *ploshcha Mitskevycha*) to the opera theater. A central parkade featuring a monument to Taras Shevchenko is a popular local gathering place; on Sunday afternoon the benches are full of men playing chess.

To the east of *prospekt Svobody* is **Market Square** (площа Ринок, *Ploshcha Rynok*), the heart of the old town area. This charming square was first mentioned in 1381 in the municipal acts of Lviv as the site of the first city hall. In the Middle Ages the nobility built their homes here. The area became the trading center of Lviv and remained the commercial hub through the 19th century. The present structures were built during the 16th century, and enlarged, restored, and rebuilt through the 18th century. The 44 buildings that ring the square, each with its own beauty and historical significance, reflect the evolving architectural fashions. Standing in the square's center is the city hall, last reconstructed in 1848. Surrounding it and making for a lively neighborhood is a blend of cafes, bars, and interesting shops, including a few joint ventures carrying the most sought-after western brand names. At No. 20 is a large, well-known restaurant "Under the Lion" (Під Левом, *Pid Levom*), which specializes in traditional Lviv cuisine served in medieval surroundings, often accompanied by live classical music.

Castle Hill (Замкова Гора, *Zamkova Hora*), northeast of Lviv, overlooks the city and offers a fine panorama. Reputed to be the site of the founding of Lviv, the 90-acre park was planted in 1853 with 45 species of trees and shrubs. On the apex are the ruins of **High Castle**, (Високий Замок, *Vysokyy Zamok*), a 14th century fortress barely visible from the lookout point below.

Lychakiv Cemetery (Личаківська Кладовище, *Lychakivska Kladovyshche*), considered one of the most beautiful cemeteries in Europe, was designated a historical landmark in 1991. A stroll along its lovely, winding tree-line walks is a passage through the history of Lviv. Among its 100 acres are some 3,600 monuments and sculptures by prominent artists and architects. Markers are in several different languages, reflecting the layers of cultures that have characterized Lviv. Many noted Ukrainians are buried here including poet Ivan Franko. Take Streetcar No. 7 to Mechnikova (Мечнікова) Street.

Churches: Lviv's multi-ethnic history is reflected in its churches and houses of worship which represent the art and architecture brought by diverse religious influences.

St. George's Cathedral (Собор Святого Юра, *Sobor Svyatoho Yura*) at Ploshcha Svyatoyurska (площа Святоюрська), was constructed on a hill between 1744 and 1770 as a replacement for a medieval church of the same name. The cathedral is a fine example of Ukrainian Baroque architecture, complete with a sculpture on a turret of St. George the dragon slayer. This cathedral was the traditional seat of the Ukrainian Greek-Catholic Church. In 1990 it reverted — with great pomp and ceremony — to the Ukrainian Catholic faithful from the jurisdiction of the Russian Orthodox Church which had taken it in 1946. The complex contains the Metropolitan's Palace and a courtyard belltower. In the lower church are crypts containing the remains of Metropolitan Andrey Sheptytsky, who was the highest ranking clergyman in all of Europe to publicly speak out against the Nazis, and his successor, Patriarch Yosyf Slipyj, who died in exile in Rome after spending 18 years in a Siberian prison.

Uspenska (Assumption) Church Complex, 9 Pidvalna (Підвальна) Street at the corner of Ruska (Руська) Street, is one of the finest examples of a harmonious blend of Renaissance architecture with traditional Ukrainian elements. Historically, the complex is the focal point of the Orthodox church in Lviv. It was built for the Dormition Brotherhood which was founded here in the mid-16th century.

The 180-foot Renaissance bell tower was the first structure to be built. Named the Kornyakt Tower after the Greek donor who financed it, the tower was erected between 1572 and 1578; it was restored after a siege in 1695 to its present four stories.

The three-domed Three Saints (Трьох Святителів, *Trokh Svyatyteliv*) Chapel adjoins the west face of the tower and is accessible through a small courtyard. The chapel's stone portal carved with grapevines and lion faces is especially worth noting. The chapel was constructed by Lviv master builder A. Pidlisny starting in 1578; in the mid-19th century it was integrated with the Uspenska Church which was completed in 1631 in the tri-part design of traditional Ukrainian wooden churches. The Chapel is a functioning Ukrainian Autocephalous Orthodox church.

Roman Catholic Cathedral, Kafedralna (Кафедрална) Square, was constructed from 1360 to 1479 after the Polish gained control of the city. Later reconstructions replaced some of the original Gothic features with Baroque architectural elements. Boyim Chapel was added to the southeast corner from 1609 to 1615. The chapel was built for Georgy Boyim whose portrait and that of his son are inside above the door. More imposing, however, are the sculptural reliefs, notably the "Pieta" sculptural grouping by J. Pfister. The exterior facade consists of stone carvings of Biblical themes, including Ss. Peter and Paul and the passion of Christ.

Kampiany Chapel was added to the north side of the church in 1619. Its interior is of black, white, and pink marble and its exterior is noted for its stone carvings depicting Biblical scenes.

Armenian Cathedral (Вірменський Собор, *Virmenskyy Sobor*), at 7-9 Virmenska (Вірменська) Street, shows the influence of the Armenian community in Lviv's history. The cathedral is part of a complex consisting of a monastery, an archbishop's residence, a printing press, and a cemetery. The cathedral was originally built from 1363 to 1370 in the Armenian style with three apses and a twelve-sided tent-shaped dome. A Renaissance gallery was added to the south side in 1437, and over the centuries there have been many enlargements and restorations, with the final, extensive renovations in the early part of this century. Of special interest is a 15th century sculptural grouping depicting St. Thomas with St. Sophia and her daughters.

Dominican Roman Catholic Church at Muzeyna (Музейна) Square, (formerly Stavropihiyska), was originally built from 1745 to 1764 and restored by the sculptor K. Fesinger from 1792 to 1798 following a fire. The interior contains alabaster and marble monuments and tombs. This Dominican monastery church is Lviv's most splendid rococo architecture.

On Khmelnytsky Boulevard (бульвар Богдана Хмельницькога, *bulvar Bohdana Khmelnytskoha*), in the Old Town, are three of Lviv's oldest churches:

St. Nicolas Church (Святого Миколая, *Svyatoho Mykolaya*), 28 Khmelnytsky, noted as the first church built in Lviv, was built by Prince Lev in the 13th century. The church burned down and was restored to its present appearance in the 17th and 18th centuries.

St. Onuphrius Church (Святого Онюфрія, *Svyatoho Onufriya*), 36 Khmelnytsky, also was established in the princely era and rebuilt or restored in each subsequent century. In 1574 Ivan Fedorov published the first book in Ukraine in the monastery here and the tomb of Federov is inside the church. The church is used by the Basilian Order of the Ukrainian Greek Catholic Church.

St. Parasceve-Pyatnytsya Church (Параскея-П'ятниця Церква, *Paraskeya-Pyatnytsya Tserkva*) is a Ukrainian Orthodox church at 63

Khmelnytsky, at the foot of Castle Hill. It was first built in the 15th century, financed by Moldavan prince Vasyl Lupul; several Moldavan rulers are buried in the church. Later reconstruction gave it a fortress-like look with its thick stone walls and small, high windows. A highly ornamented Renaissance iconostasis consisting of seventy icons arranged in five tiers enlivens the severe stone interior. A sixth tier, added in 1870, makes a total of 70 icons.

St. Peter and Paul Church (Святого Петра I Павла, *Svyatoho Petra I Pavla),* 82 Lychakivska (Личаківська) Street. This little jewel of a church was built in 1786 in the baroque style. It belongs to the Autocephalous Ukrainian Orthodox Church.

Museums and Culture: Museums in Lviv, while worthwhile, are not very large and provide a pleasant diversion during a sudden cloudburst.

Lviv Historical Museum is located in the picturesque Market Square. The main holdings are in the building *ploscha Rynok* (площа Ринок), 24, which has a facade with interesting stone heads. The museum has some 270,000 items, most showing the city's history beginning from the 13th century. There's also a large number of exhibits from western Ukraine from the 15th to 18th centuries.

Also part of the Historical Museum is the **Kornyakt Mansion,** *ploshcha Rynok,* 6. This palazzo, built for a wealthy Greek merchant in 1580, dominates the square. The hallway leads out a rear door to a courtyard with a three-tiered Italian Renaissance columned arcade that was restored in the 1930s. An Italian-style coffee shop is in the courtyard. To the left of the street entrance is "Gothic Hall," a shop of works by Lviv's top artisans. Part of the proceeds of the sale of the paintings, graphics, embroidery, ceramics, and dolls goes toward upkeep of the museum. The museum complex is open daily from 10 a.m. to 6 p.m.; closed on Wednesday.

The Museum of Furniture and China, *ploshcha Rynok,* 10, consists of three floors of furniture, tapestries, and porcelain from the 15 to the 20th centuries. Especially interesting are the 18th century Chinese furniture, Italian majolica, English Wedgewood, and 18th and 19th century Austrian and French china. Museum hours are 10 a.m. to 6 p.m. Wednesday through Saturday.

The National Museum (Національний Музей, *Natsionalnyy Musey*) has two branches. The older -- and of far greater interest -- branch is located at 42 Drahomanov (Драгоманов) Street. Founded by Metropolitan Andrey Sheptytsky in 1905, it's noted for its icon collection dating from the 14th through the 18th century. It also has landscapes, portraits, graphics, and sculpture by Ukrainian artists. Of special interest are the church antiquities, early manuscript books, maps, and engravings. The frontispiece of the first book published in Ukraine, Ivan Fedorov's *Book of the Apostles*, is on display. In the crafts section are examples of Ukrainian glasswork and ceramics, textiles and clothing, rugs, embroidery, woodcarving and metalwork. The museum is open 11 a.m. to 6 p.m. daily except on Thursday and Friday. Photography is permitted, but flash is not allowed.

Contemporary Ukrainian art is on display in the new branch of the National Museum at *prospekt Svobody*, 20, across from the Grand Hotel, housed in an imposing exhibition hall built in 1904.

Lviv Picture Gallery, 3 Stefanyka (Стефаника) Street, features European masterpieces of Italian, Polish, Russian, Flemish, and Austrian schools, including paintings by Rembrandt, Rubens, and Goya. Because only a small number of its 40,000 holdings can be shown, a new gallery is under construction. Normal hours are 10 a.m. to 6 p.m. daily except Monday.

Olesky Castle (Олеський Замок, *Oleskyy Zamok*) is a branch of the Lviv Picture Gallery located 72 km (about 45 miles) from Lviv on the Lviv-Kyiv Highway. Public transportation does not regularly go to the castle, but by car it's a pleasant drive through some pretty countryside.

First recorded mention of the castle was in 1387; in the 17th century it figured in the national liberation struggle against the Poles and Turks. The furniture, tapestries, icons, paintings, and other objects on display have been collected from all over and are displayed in groupings in the sequence of rooms to suggest a walk though a functioning manor. The view of the surrounding countryside is lovely. Admission is free and the castle is open from 10 a.m. to 5 p.m. daily, with the exception of one day per week, which may vary. Flash cameras are permitted.

Museum of Regional Ethnology and Handicrafts, *prospekt Svobody* (проспект Свободи) 15, is in an imposing renaissance-baroque-style building that was built in 1891 as the Galicia Savings Bank. The first floor has farm implements from the 19th and 20th centuries and costumes from various parts of Ukraine. Upstairs are ceramics, embroidery, and glass. Highlights are its decorated eggs or *pysanky* (писанки) and a large collection of *rushnyky* (рушники), or embroidered ceremonial towels. Open 10 a.m. to 7 p.m. daily except Monday and Tuesday.

Arsenal Weapons Museum, 5 Pidvalna (Підвальна) Street, dates back to 1554. The arsenal is a rectangular structure with eight-foot-thick walls that are stone on the outside and brick inside. Originally built as a fortified structure, the arsenal was destroyed by Swedish forces in 1704 but soon rebuilt. It displays weapons from more than 30 countries from the 11 to 20th century. The museum is open from 10 a.m. to 5:45 p.m. every day except Wednesday.

Museum of Folk Architecture and Folkways, commonly called *Shevchenkivsky Hai,* is in Shevchenko Park, 1½ miles northeast of the city center at *Chernecha Hora* (Чернеча Гора). This open-air museum consists of approximately 100 old wooden buildings spread out over 165 acres. The museum is divided into miniature villages representing historical-ethnographic areas of western Ukraine — Lviv, Hutsul, Lemko, Podilya, Polisya, Bukovyna, and Volhynya. Each village features 15 to 20 buildings — churches, school, windmill, cottages, and farm buildings. Household utensils, farm implements, tools, and articles of clothing are also on display. The centerpiece of the collection is the 1763 St. Mykola Church from Kryvka in the Boiko region. The museum is open daily except on Monday from 9 a.m. to 6 p.m..

Lviv Theater of Opera and Ballet, at the head of *prospekt Svobody* (проспект Свободи), was built in 1900 as the Lviv Municipal Theater. The architect was Z. Gorgolevsky. Topped by sculptures representing Victory, Glory, and Love, the ornate architecture is typical of the period's Austro-Hungarian Empire. The interior is resplendent with its balcony tiers under a gilded ceiling. It seats 1100. The theater was restored a few years ago and has permanent opera and ballet companies.

Heading out 700-Richchya Lvova Street behind the opera, about a mile past the city center, is an impressive monument, constructed since independence, that commemorates the Jewish victims of Lviv's Nazi invasion. It consists of a large statue of the prophet Ezekiel with a tablet inscribed with a verse from the Book of Ezekiel in Ukrainian and Hebrew, and a large granite menorah.

FAMOUS NAMES IN LVIV

As you sightsee in Lviv, you'll come across certain streets, squares, parks, buildings, and monuments that are named after historical and literary figures. Some who left their mark on Lviv are:

Ivan Fedorov, a 16th century Russian, was forced to flee Moscow after he enraged the Muscovite clergy by printing a religious book. Federov established the first permanent printing shop on Ukrainian territory in Lviv in 1573, and in 1574 he printed the first book printed in Ukraine, *Book of the Apostles*. Fedorov died in Lviv in 1583 and is buried in St. Onuphrius Church. A monument to him was erected in 1977 on Pidvalna (Підвальна) Street.

Ivan Franko (1856-1916), scholar of western Ukraine, is most noted for his poetry but also wrote fiction, plays, literary criticism and translated literary masterpieces from 14 languages into Ukrainian. A monument to Franko was erected in 1964 in a 30-acre park named after him in the center of Lviv, opposite the State University. Ivan Franko Literary-Memorial Museum at 152 Ivan Franko Street (вулиця Івана Франка, *vulytsya Ivana Franka*), south of Striyskyy Park, is in the building where Franko spent his last 14 years and died. It contains manuscripts, photographs, correspondence, and first editions of his printed works.

Mykhaylo Hrushevsky (1866-1934), the most distinguished Ukrainian historian and a prominent scholar, is remembered as Ukraine's first president. He was elected President of the Ukrainian National Republic in 1918. In June 1994, Ukraine's first modern president, Leonid Kravchuk, unveiled a monument to Hrushevsky at Hrushevsky Square, at the foot of Drahomanova Street where it intersects with *prospekt Shevchenka*. This monument is at the site where a giant portrait of Taras Shevchenko in plants stood for many years.

Yahn Mateyko, born Nykyfor Dvorniak, was a folk artist and painter who died in 1968. His allegorical painting of the development of science lines the conference room of the main building of the Lviv Polytechnical Institute, 12 Bandera Street (вулиця С. Бандери, *vulytsya S. Bandery*). The street named for Mateyko (вулиця Матейка, *vulytsya Mateyka*) is a short distance east, heading toward the center of town.

Adam Mickiewicz (1798-1855) was the leading poet of Polish Romanticism and a lifelong advocate of Polish national freedom. His works had a marked influence on Ukrainian literature, particularly on Taras Shevchenko. Mickiewicz is not associated with Lviv, but a monument to him erected in 1905 dominates Mickiewicz Square, an area of hotels and shops that in Ukrainian is called *ploshch*a *Mitskevycha* (площа Міцкевича).

Ivan Pidkova (died 1578) was a Kozak otaman who led the Moldovan and Ukrainian struggle against Turkish domination. Pidkova was captured by the Polish (who were allied with Turkey) and executed in Market Square in Lviv. A monument to him was dedicated in 1981 in the square named after him in the center of town, to the northwest of Market Square.

Taras Shevchenko. After some debate on location, a large statue of Ukraine's greatest hero, financed by the Ukrainian diaspora in Argentina, was erected in 1992 in one of the island parkades of the city's center at *prospekt Svobody*. There are those who say that artistic merit was sacrificed in the rush to honor Shevchenko. There are also a street and an avenue named after him in separate parts of the central city, but neither adjoins the monument.

Vasyl Stefanyk (1871-1936) was a noted western Ukrainian writer of short stories and a political activist. The research library of the Academy of Sciences of Ukraine is named for him; a statue representing Stefanyk stands in front of the library on Stefanyka (Стефаника) Street.

Ivan Trush (1869-1941) was an impressionist artist from the Lviv region who became a master of Ukrainian landscape painting and portraiture. Major collections of his work are at the Ivan Trush Memorial Art Museum in his former residence at 28 Trush Street (вулиця Труша, *vulytsya Trusha*) as well as at the National Museum.

ACCOMMODATIONS

Most of the hotels in Lviv can benefit from refurbishing; some of them are definitely "no frills" and cater to travelers from former Soviet countries or western bargain hunters. Western tourists usually book into the following three:

The Grand Hotel, *prospekt Svobody* (проспект Свободи) 13, across from the Shevchenko Monument in the heart of Lviv's business district, is one of the finest hotels in Ukraine. Built in 1898, it's been restored to its Austro-Hungarian splendor by a joint partnership with an American travel agency. Restoration includes carved molded ceilings, murals, and lots of stained glass. The Grand Hotel's 62 guest rooms are modern and tasteful, but don't offer much elbow room. A double costs $110 per night, less in off-season. With a very professional and courteous western-trained staff that, for the most part, speak English, the hotel provides many guest and business services. The food in the restaurant is good, but service can be slow. Payment is in hard currency. Credit cards accepted. Tel. (0322) 76-90-60; Fax (0322) 72-76-65.

There are two other large tourist hotels that offer a good range of services but, in appearances, fall far short of the Grand Hotel. Few if any staff members are fluent in English. Prices for a double room are about $50 to $60-per night. The **Hotel Dnister** (Дністер) on Mateyko (Матейка) Street overlooks the 30-acre Ivan Franko Park near Lviv University on the west edge of the central area. It has a lively night bar with discotheque. **Hotel George** (Жеорж) is the new name for the Hotel Inturyst at Mickiewicz Square (площа Міцкевича, *ploshcha Mitskevycha*) in the city center. The George has larger rooms and, with its striking staircase, an atmosphere of faded grandeur. It contains the main Inturyst service center.

SHOPPING

Some pricey western brand names are showing up in joint venture shops in the central district, but bargain hunting in the city's authentic Ukrainian shops is more fun. Shops are centered around *prospekt Svobody*; another street for shopping is Horodotska (Городоцка).

Lviv is a great place to buy art. Ask Inuryst or other travel agencies to arrange a visit to a factory that produces woodcarvings, ceramics, or linens or to an artist's studio. Or visit the following shops for Ukrainian crafts and souvenirs:

The Art Salon or *Khudozhnyk* (Художник) at *ploshcha Mitskevycha,* 5 is an especially nice shop with a selection of handicrafts not found everywhere; a carved hardwood cane with wolf's head handle cost $8 USD. *Suveniry*, at 18 Market Square (площа Ринок, *ploshcha Rynok*) has some nice embroidered linens and decorated eggs, and the *Suveniry* at number 28 has Hutsul crafts and ceramics. *Ukrayinski Suveniry* is at 35 Horodotska (Городоцка) Street.

Every day there's a very nice large artists' market not far from the opera theater, in the square across from the *prospekt Svobody* branch of the National Museum and the Zankovetska Drama Theater on *boulevard Lesi Ukrayinky.* Woodcrafts and embroidered linens and blouses are sold, but the majority of the art consists of oil paintings and graphics. Flowers, scenes of Lviv, and landscapes are popular subjects.

A permanent art gallery for Lviv's artists is at 4 Slovatskoho (Словацького) Street. Hours for the *Fond Dukhovnoho Vidrodzhennya* are Monday through Friday from 10 a.m. until 6 p.m. Closed from 2 p.m. until 3 p.m.

There are many small shops, but if you'd like to check out the **TSUM** *(ЦУМ)* or Central Department Store (Централний Універмаг, *Tsentralny Univermah*), go to 1 Shpytalna (Шпитальна) Street. It has a branch at 35 Market Square (площа Ринок, *ploscha Rynok*).

Prospekt Svobody and the streets running off it are a good place to find pastries, bread, and excellent chocolates and other candies made by the Svitoch Candy Factory in Lviv. Good ice cream is available at several shops; foremost is the *Korona* at *prospekt Svobody,* 7, with a small choice of flavors, including a wonderful rum raisin.

For books, try **Druzhba** (Дружба) at *ploshcha Mitskevycha,* 10; **Molodist** (Молодіст) at *ploshcha Mitskevycha,* 5; or **Ukrayinska Knyharnya** (Українска Книгарня) at *prospekt Shevchenka,* 12.

Open markets are an authentic way to enjoy the color of the city and feel like a participant in the everyday life of its residents. At these you'll find a wide range of vegetables, fruits, flowers, meat and dairy products as well as some crafts, sold at fluctuating market prices. Lviv has seven open markets. The best are the *Halytskyy,* the *Krakivskyy,* and the *Pryvokzalnyy.*

USEFUL ADDRESSES

Main Post Office: 1 Slovatskoho (Словацького) Street, between Doroshenka and Kopernika. Tel. 065. Hours of operation are Monday through Friday from 8 a.m. to 8 p.m.; Saturday from 8 a.m. to 6 p.m.; and Sunday from 8 a.m. to 2 p.m. An international telegram office is located on the main floor of the post office building.

E-Mail: For information about gaining access to Internet or other e-mail services, phone LITech at 74-23-39 or HOST at 42-71-09. Those with access to Internet can subscribe to the Ukrainian Arts Monitor (UAM), a free e-publication about arts in the Lviv area. Subscribe by sending a message with the word "RFEED 25 ukrainet.eng.uam" in the body of a message to <news@litech.lviv.ua>.

Pharmacies: You can dial 067 to check availability of medications in Lviv pharmacies. In the central area are two very different pharmacies: Pharmacy No. 24 at 1 Kopernika (Коперніка) Street is an interesting old pharmacy stocked with a variety of medicinal herbs. Next door at 9 Kopernika is a Canadian-Ukrainian joint venture that sells western drugs for hard currency.

Travel Services: If you'd like to visit historic sites, castles, museums, and monuments outside of Lviv or make an excursion to the Carpathian mountains, local travel agencies — most state run — can help you: Inturyst is in the Hotel George (formerly Inturyst Hotel) at Mickiewicz Square; The Lviv branch of the Suputnyk International Youth Tourism Company is at 18 Oniyenko (Онієнко) Street; Lvivturyst Company is at 12 Stryyska (Стрийська) Street; Lviv Travel and Excursion Agency is at 18 Kostyushko (Костюшко) Street.

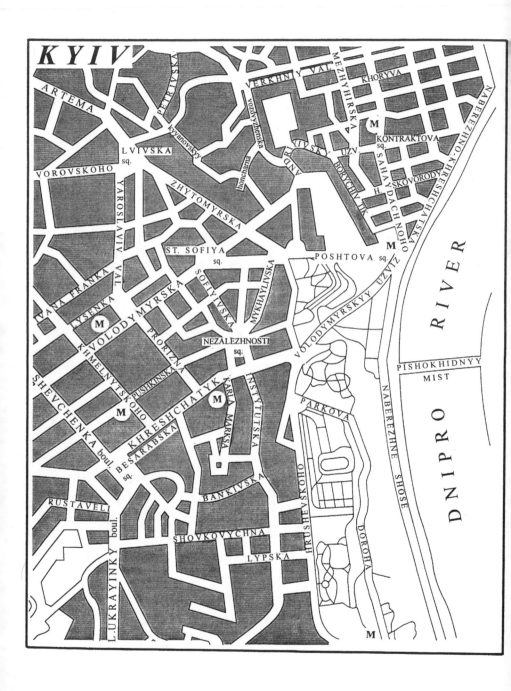

CHAPTER 24.
KYIV: UKRAINE'S CAPITAL CITY

КИЇВ   KIH-yeev

Kyiv is the historical, political, cultural, and scientific capital of Ukraine. Archeological discoveries around Kyiv date human habitation in the area to the Stone Age (40 to 10 B.C.). A settlement existed in some form as far back as the first century A.D.

Name: Legend has it that the city was founded by a prince of a Slavic tribe named Кyy (Кий) and his two younger brothers and sister. The name Київ (KIH-yeev) is the possessive adjective form of the word Кий — literally it means "of Kyy." For centuries, Kyiv has been called the golden-domed (золотоверхий, *zolotoverkhyy*) city because of the numerous church cupolas covered with gold leaf.

Population and Language: Kyiv is Ukraine's most populous city, with 3 million residents. Although Ukrainians constitute 72.5 percent of the population and Russians only 21 percent, 81 percent of the residents are fluent in Ukrainian while 92 percent can speak Russian. Ukrainian literacy is expected to increase as more and more educational institutions are beginning to conduct classes in Ukrainian.

Climate: Summers are moderately warm with the average July temperature 19.3° C (66.7° F). The average July high is 22.7° C (73° F). Winters are moderately cold with the average January temperature -6° C (21° F). There's usually a snow cover from mid-November until the end of March.

Business and Industry: As the administrative center of its oblast and the capital of Ukraine, Kyiv has a great number of government workers. It's the seat of the Ukrainian Academy of Sciences and has numerous research and educational institutions. It's rich with theater, opera, dance, and other cultural and entertainment opportunities.

The major economic activity is heavy industry, especially machine building and metal working and the manufacture of chemicals, and wood products. Electronics and printing are also important. Nevertheless, Kyiv is a very green city, with an official count of 300 parks and gardens.

Transportation: There's an old Ukrainian saying that all roads lead to Kyiv. Situated on the bank of the Dnipro River in north central Ukraine, the city is indeed a major road and rail junction and a port city. By highway, Kyiv is about 480 km (300 miles) from Odesa, 544 km (338 miles) from Lviv, and 487 km (302 miles) from Kharkiv.

Airports: Boryspil Airport (Бориспіл Аеропорт) is about 39 km (24 miles) southeast of the city center on a rare stretch of four-lane road, Kharkhiv Highway (Харківському Шосе, *Kharkivskomu Shose*). Major refurbishing and upgrading of technology, including a much-needed baggage carousel, has put Boryspil on par with other European airports. There's also an attractive and comfortable lounge, a duty-free shop, a coffee shop and bar, and modern clean restrooms. An express bus between the airport and Peremohy Avenue (проспект Перемоги, *prospekt Peremohy*) downtown, runs every twenty minutes or so. The ride takes one hour. It's advisable to allow several extra hours when checking in to the airport. The phone number of the airport is 216-67-30.

Zhulyany Airport (Жуляни Аеропорт), just 11 km (7 miles) southwest of the city serves domestic flights and flights to newly independent states of the former Soviet Union. Tickets are sold at the airport or at several downtown locations: 1 Menzhynsky Street (вулиця Менжинського, *vulytsya Menzhynskoho*) and *prospekt Peremohy* (проспект Перемоги), 4.

Rail. The railroad station is at 1 *ploshcha Vokzalna* (площа Вокзальна) near the western edge of the city center. Trains go daily all over Ukraine and direct to major cities of eastern Europe. The train to Moscow takes from 12 to 15 hours. Tickets for international train travel are sold on the second floor, around the clock, except during breaks from 2 a.m. to 3 a.m. and 7 a.m. to 8 a.m., and from 2 p.m. to 3 p.m. and 7 p.m. to 8 p.m. Take the Vokzalna Station Metro or Trolley No. 2, 8, or 17 to the station. For advance train tickets for domestic travel, go to 38/40 Taras Shevchenko Boulevard (бульвар Тараса Шевченка, *bulvar Tarasa Shevchenka*).

City Transportation: The efficient bus, streetcar, and trolley system makes public transportation a good way to see the city and, combined with a rapid subway, can get you around the city quickly. Trolleybuses, streetcars, and most buses run frequently and round the clock. Passengers form queues to board the bus; those near the end of the line may not be able to squeeze on board. Sightseers are well advised not to try for a bus during the rush hours. There are six subway lines which run either east-west or north-south through the city. The main transfer point is at the Kreshchchatyk station in the center of the city. The metro connects the center of the city to the new residential districts across the Dnipro River by means of a line that crosses the 800-meter-long (2600 feet) Metro Bridge. Even if you don't need to ride the subway, check out the attractive metro stations for their individual themes. Each stop is named after a prominent nearby site or building and decorated to carry out the theme. The metro runs from 6 a.m. to 1 a.m. daily.

Bus: The terminal for intercity bus travel is at *ploshcha Moskovska* (площа Московська), 3. Take trams No. 9 or 10 or trolleys 1, 11, or 12 to get to the long distance bus terminal. There are additional depots for shorter-distance trips throughout the city. For advance bus tickets to all destinations, go to 14 Lesya Ukrayinka Boulevard (бульвар Лесі Українки, *bulvar Lesi Ukrayinky*).

Boat: Ukraine's largest river, the Dnipro (Дніпро), is the third largest in Europe, after the Volga and the Danube. It flows southwardly through the center of Ukraine, linking forest and steppe regions and connecting them to the Black Sea. Within Kyiv, the Dnipro is 160 to 400 meters wide (525 to 1312 feet) and 2 to 9 meters (6 1/2 to 30 feet) deep. From April through October, the River Transport Agency (Річний Вокзал, *Richnyy Vokzal*) runs cruises around the city's environs and down the river to other port cities. The boat terminal and ticket office are at *ploshcha Poshtova* (площа Поштова), 3 near the metro stop.

HISTORY

Although there have been settlements at the site of modern-day Kyiv for over 15,000 years, historians date its founding to the late 5th century. The traditional date is 482 and the city celebrated its 1500th anniversary in 1982. According to an 11th century chronicle, when Prince Oleh ascended the throne, he asserted his dominion over all the Kyivan principalities by calling Kyiv the seat of great princes and saying "This will be the mother to all the Rus' cities." The word "Rus" is thought to be of Scandinavian origin and was an ancient term for Ukraine and actually a term for much of Eastern Europe.

Its site on the Dnipro River gave Kyiv access to the Black Sea. It developed into a regional trade center and a gateway for economic relations with countries of western Europe, the Baltics, Asia Minor and Byzantium. This crossroads of the East and West grew in wealth, power, and influence. By the time Volodymyr came to rule in 980, Kyiv-Rus was the leading power in Europe. It occupied the territory from the Baltics and the Carpathians to the Black Sea and the Volga. Volodymyr's search for a religion for his people and his choice of Byzantine Christianity is legendary.

Under the reign of his son Yaroslav the Wise (1017-1054), the city continued to flourish. It became a great cultural center, with development of a written language, literature and art. Magnificent structures were built, and by the 12th century the city had approximately 400 churches.

During the last half of 12th century, Kyiv's strength was weakened by internal conflicts among members of the ruling family. The final blow was the invasion of the Tatars (Mongols) in 1240. They held the city for 80 years, then it passed into Lithuanian and Polish rule. Kyiv experienced a revival in the early 17th century and became a great political, religious, and cultural center of Ukraine, but was ravaged by the Polish-Lithuanian army in 1651.

In order to free Kyiv and Ukraine from the Polish, the Kozak leader Bohdan Khmelnytsky turned to Tsar Aleksei of Russia (then Moscovy) for help. While it's not clear whether the 1654 agreement was a simple military alliance or a submission, this desperate act placed Kyiv under Moscow's control. Russia subverted the Kozak leaders and war between Russia and Poland devastated Ukrainian lands.

After the Second Partition of Poland in 1793, Poland retreated from Right-Bank Ukraine. All of Kyiv (as well as much Ukrainian territory to the east) passed to Russian rule. Kyiv grew in importance as the capitol of Ukrainian Russia, but tsarist policies suppressed Ukrainian culture and language and promoted Russification, including the encouragement of Russian settlement in Kyiv.

Reconstruction after a great fire in 1811 ushered in a policy of urban planning. The city grew rapidly in the second half of the 19th century. A new railroad line linked Kyiv to Odesa and Moscow, strengthening its role as a center of industry, commerce and administration.

Communication and transportation were modernized and the population grew. By the eve of the First World War, Kyiv's population was 626,000, almost ten times greater than it was before the railroad.

The Revolution of 1905 was followed by a period of liberalization. Kyiv became the focal point of Ukrainian cultural, scholarly, publishing, and political activity. After the tsarist empire was overthrown in 1917, forces promoting Ukrainian autonomy — always ready to surface — proclaimed an independent Ukrainian National Republic on January 22, 1918. It was a period of great chaos, however, and Ukrainians were not able to maintain firm control. The next few years saw a continual struggle between Ukrainian, White, and Red forces. Frequent battles for control of the city caused much destruction. In a single year the population dropped by almost 200,000 residents; many died, others fled because of hunger and terror.

Kyiv became part of the Ukrainian Soviet Socialist Republic in 1920, but because of its Ukrainian activists, the capital was temporarily moved to Kharkiv. In the twenties and thirties Kyiv intelligentsia were persecuted and Ukrainianization stamped out. In 1934, the capital was returned to Kyiv and the city was again built up; new machine tool, electrical, and chemical industries were established. The intensive industrialization was fueled by impoverished peasants who flocked to the city from the countryside.

The German invasion of 1941 and its two-year occupation brought severe suffering and devastation. Forty percent of Kyiv's buildings and three-quarters of its industrial enterprises were destroyed; hundreds of thousands lost their lives and 80 percent were homeless by the time the Red Army entered the city on November 6, 1943. The post-war period saw an industrial boom and growth of the suburbs. The Ukrainian Helsinki Monitoring Group was founded in Kyiv in 1976. In the late 1980's the democratic movement culminated in the establishment of Rukh, the Popular Movement in Ukraine for Restructuring. Independence was declared in Kyiv on August 24, 1991.

SIGHTSEEING

Kyiv's lovely historic architecture that accents its vast green areas, its spacious boulevards lined with chestnut, poplar, and linden trees, give it an ambience of peaceful elegance that doesn't suggest the turbulence, suffering, and death that took place here in the first half of this century. Bolsheviks, Nazis, Soviets, and Ukrainian leaders battled for control of the city. When the Soviet government returned Ukraine's capital to Kyiv in the 1930's, over two dozen ancient churches and historic landmarks in the old city were senselessly destroyed to make way for new government buildings. Especially singled out were those churches built in the Ukrainian style by hetman Ivan Mazepa, who fought against Russia in 1709. During this decade, the city was modernized and industrialized, with improvements in railway, public utilities, and transportation.

The most devastating period was the two and one-half years of German occupation from 1941 to 1943 when 40 percent of the city was destroyed. Much of the damage was caused by the retreating Soviets who destroyed buildings on Khreshchatyk and adjacent streets and also blew up the Dormition Cathedral of the Monastery of the Caves. Before the Red Army regained the city, hundreds of thousands of citizens and troops lost their lives.

The three decades following the war saw the construction of massive edifices that catered to popular culture. The Palace of Sports, Palace of Culture, and Central Stadium were built, as well as the large tourist hotels that dot the city. The victories and heroes of the war are commemorated in bronze, granite, and concrete throughout the city.

While there's a reverent attitude toward the monuments honoring brave soldiers, others have not been so well received. To many, the massive works of "socialist monumentalism" that tower over the city with their excess of concrete and steel undermine the delicate beauty of the golden domed-churches. Furthermore, many feel little enthusiasm for the events commemorated by these monuments. For example, the gigantic arch resembling a steel rainbow that rises from the park behind the Philharmonic Building is supposed to commemorate the "union" of Russia and Ukraine, but Ukrainians often referred to it as "The Yoke."

Following the Ukrainian declaration of independence in 1991, changes took place at a dizzying pace. Statues of communist heroes were toppled;

streets, squares, and avenues were renamed. Not only were street names posted in Ukrainian rather than Russian, the shuffling of names seemed like a cartographical version of the musical chairs game; the prominent square named for Bohdan Khmelnytsky was given its old name Sofiyivsky Square, while the name of Bohdan Khmelnytsky went to the street named Lenin. Local speculation has it that in the climate of change that's sweeping over the city, anything named for Bohdan Khmelnytsky is also destined for oblivion, since he's the hetman who signed the Pereyaslav Treaty of unification with Russia.

Rapid changes, particularly the economic instability, have created an almost palpable sense of anxiety in Kyiv, not felt in other Ukrainian cities. Nevertheless, it remains a city where culture, art, and history are important and temporary difficulties are met with acceptance and forbearance. Kyiv is a wonderful city to visit for its sightseeing and cultural opportunities. The people are friendly and the city is relatively crime-free; a visitor feels safe wandering around the city and riding the metro at night. Extreme caution is necessary, however, in crossing the street. Pedestrians are not given the right-of-way and drivers speed. Whenever possible, use the pedestrian underpasses.

A word about Chornobyl: The Chornobyl nuclear power station is only about 90 km (60 miles) north of Kyiv. While medical experts agree there is no danger to short-term visitors in the Kyiv area, a single note of caution is necessary. Enjoy the pretty sandy beaches and tree-lined parks of Trukhanov Island and on the east bank of the Dnipro, but don't swim in the river. The water itself no longer enjoys a reputation of being unpolluted, and even worse, the silt bottom is believed to be radioactive. While it's possible to clean the river channel, it's unfeasible since there's no good method for disposing of the contaminated particles.

Orientation to Kyiv

Kyiv straddles the Dnipro River, which divides it into two unequal parts. The western or right bank — as the river flows from north to south — is the larger of the two. On this side lies the modern city and the historical old town or upper town which was built on a hilly terrain. The eastern or left bank of the city is on an extensive flat plain characterized by a 10 km (6 miles) stretch of fine bathing beaches and a lovely recreational area that merges into drab industrialized suburbs.

The most efficient and convenient way to see the city is to take a sightseeing tour of the whole city when you first arrive in order to understand the layout. An individual guided motor tour of Kyiv that costs about $30 for three hours can be arranged through the service bureaus of hotels. You can then choose which attractions you want to see in depth, and walk to many of them or easily zip from one another on the metro system.

For sightseeing purposes, Kyiv can be divided into sections according to the separate settlement areas that historically grew around the city's hilly terrain. The main street and shopping area is **Khreshchatyk Street** (вулиця Хрещатик, *vulytsya Khreshchayk*). According to one account, its name comes from the word *khreshchennya* (хрещення) meaning "baptism," because it was the eastward route of Volodymyr's subjects to the Dnipro where they received the Christian faith.

The Old Town (Старий Город, *Staryy Horod*), also known as Upper Town (Верхний Город, *Verkhnyy Horod*) contains most of the city's surviving historical and architectural monuments. North of the Old Town, down below on the flat land along the Dnipro, is **Podil** (Поділ). This area contains the river port. To the south, on top of the riverbank, is **Pechersk** (Печерськ), the site of Ukraine's largest monastery.

The Modern City

After World War II, **Khreshchatyk Street** was totally built anew. Today the mile-long street runs from Bohdan Khmelnytsky Square (the former Lenin Komsomol Square) to Bessarabian Square. Khreshchatyk is 70 to 100 meters (230 to 328 feet) wide, and includes a tree-lined pedestrian boulevard. This is the street on which to stroll, window shop, and enjoy people watching. While it's not noted for restaurants, Khreshchatyk Street does have cafes where you can get ice cream, pastry, juice, and coffee.

Towards the east end of Khreshchatyk Street is **Independence Square** (площа Незалежності, *ploshcha Nezalezhnosti*, formerly October Revolution Square). The metro station beneath Khreshchatyk in front of the post office by Independence Square is a lively gathering place for musicians, poets, and activists. You can also buy tickets for some cultural events here.

Side streets along Khreshchatyk did not suffer much during the war and have preserved much of their turn-of-the-century appearance. About half way down, to the south, is **Luteranska Street**, with its late 19th-early-20th century mansions and luxurious apartment buildings, now apartments for the newly rich and government offices. The street joins **Bankivska Street**, characterized by Art Nouveau Style architecture with its floral and animal motifs. The outstanding building in this style is the **House with Chimeras**, at 10 Bankivska (Банківська) Street, just above Ivan Franko Square. Built by noted architect Vladyslav Horodetsky in 1902 to 1903 as an apartment for himself, the building is lavishly embellished with gigantic concrete fantasy creatures -- mermaids, elephants, fat bullfrogs on gigantic lilypads. The bizarre-looking residence was Horodetsky's homage to the new building material of his day, concrete. Today the building serves as a clinic for the Cabinet of Ministers.   Heading back toward Khreshchatyk, down **Karl Marx Street**, one notices more fine old apartments and offices as well as movie theaters and the city's poshest Western stores, such as Seagram's and Lancombe.

At the west end of Kheshchatyk Street is **Bessarabian Square** (площа Бессарабська, *ploshcha Bessarabska*). Here the first covered market in Ukraine was established in 1910. **Bessarabian Market** (Бессарабский Ринок, *Bessarabskyy Rynok)* is still the major farmers' market in Kyiv. Open daily, it's a great place to buy fresh seasonal produce as well as other foodstuff.

Intersecting Khreshchatyk Street and running northwest is **Taras Shevchenko Boulevard** (бульвар Тараса Шевченка, *bulvar Tarasa Shevchenka*).   A 5.8 meter (19 feet) tall bronze statue of the great poet-patriot set on a red granite pedestal stands in Shevchenko Park here.

On the east side of the park at 9 Tereshchenkivska (Терещенківська) Street is **The Museum of Russian Art** (Музей Російського Мистецтва, *Muzey Rosiyiskoho Mystetstva*). Among the largest art museums in Ukraine, it features Russian art from all periods.   The porcelain collection is the highlight of its large applied art collection.

Across Shevchenko Boulevard at number 12, the **Taras Shevchenko Museum** (Музей Т.Г. Шевченко) contains hundreds of paintings, drawings, and prints of the great poet. Hours are 10 a.m. to 5 p.m. every day except Monday.   The **Shevchenko Memorial Museum** at A

Shevchenko Lane is the house in which he lived and worked in 1846. Landscape paintings he completed while living here are on display and in the room upstairs are some of his personal belongings. Open 1 p.m. to 5:30 p.m. every day except Friday. There's an admission charge.

The red-painted Classic-style building on the west side of Shevchenko Park at 64 Volodymyrska (Володимирська) Street is the main building of Taras Shevchenko University, also known as **Kyiv State University.** Founded in 1834, it was destroyed during the Nazi occupation of Kyiv and rebuilt from 1946 to 1952. Today it's the most prestigious institute of higher education in Ukraine.

The **A. Fomin Kyiv State University Botanical Gardens** are behind the University's main building on Shevchenko Boulevard and extend to Komintern Street. (вулиця Комінтерна, *vulytsya Kominterna*). The 23 hectares (56 acres) of neatly arranged and well-kept plots contain some 10,000 plants, shrubs, and trees arranged by habitat.

Opposite the gardens on 20 Shevchenko Boulevard is the massive **St. Volodymyr Cathedral** (Володимирський Собор, *Volodymyrskyy Sobor*). The church was built in the late 19th century in the pseudo-Byzantine style to commemorate the 900th anniversary of Christianity in Kyiv. Especially noteworthy are the frescoes. This is the seat of the Ukrainian Orthodox Church -- Kyyivan Patriarchate. There's a morning and a 6 p.m. daily liturgy; Sunday services are at 9 a.m., 12 and 6 p.m., with the Patriarch presiding at the noon service. The choir singing is excellent.

Old Town   Старий Город   Staryy Horod

Volodymyr Street (вулиця Володимирска, *vulytsya Volodymyrska*), is the main street of the old town. At number 35, in front of the metro stop of the same name, stands Kyiv's oldest architecture, **The Golden Gate** (Золоті Ворота, *Zoloti Vorota*). This site was the center of ancient Kyiv during the reigns of princes Volodymyr the Great and Yaroslav the Wise. Constructed in 1037, The Golden Gate served as the main triumphal entrance to the city as well as a watch tower. The original structure was of brick and stone and consisted of a tower with a vaulted passageway topped by a platform for guards and a small Church of the Annunciation. The doors and cupola of the gate-church were covered with gilded copper sheets, giving the gate its name.

The arch was damaged in 1240 during the Tatar-Mongol raids, but continued to serve as the city's entrance until the 17th century. Eventually the arch fell into disuse and became buried under the earth. In 1837 the ruins — consisting of some brick and stone columns and portions of the arch — were excavated and reinforced. In 1982 the Golden Gate was restored according to scholarly research to commemorate the city's 1,500th birthday. Today it consists of a tower over the vaulted passageway with a small church and pavilion on top. Take the metro to Golden Gate Station, which, with its mosaic work and candelabra, is possibly the city's most beautiful subway stop.

St. Sophia Cathedral (Софійський Собор, *Sofiyskyy Sobor*) adjoins one of the city's major squares, St. Sophia's Square (площа Софійска, *ploshcha Sofiyska*). Formerly named after Bohdan Khmelnytsky, the square is the site of a 10.85 meter (36 foot-high) monument to the Kozak leader. The 10-ton bronze sculpture of Hetman Khmelnytsky stands on the spot where Kyivites gave him a triumphal welcome in 1648 after he defeated the Polish invaders.

With its beautiful mosaics and frescoes of religious and secular themes that blend harmoniously with mosaic floors and marble decorations, the cathedral is a masterpiece of world architecture. It was established by Yaroslav the Wise in 1037 to commemorate his victory on the site over the invading Pechenegs. St. Sophia's became the center of official state ceremonies and commemorations as well as a library and center of writing. The early Kyivan princes were entombed here but the only remaining tomb is that of Yaroslav the Wise who was buried in 1054 in a six-ton carved marble sarcophagus.

The cathedral and monastery complex was built over a period of nine centuries. The basic structure of the church is original. Its thousands of square feet of mosaics and frescoes in combination are a Kyivan interpretation of the Byzantine style. Especially noteworthy are the color gradations of the mosaic stones: 25 tons of gold and silver alone are used. Of the one-third of the original mosaics that survive, the most noted is that of the Christ Pantokrator in the central dome.

During its long history, the cathedral was repeatedly gutted by fire and rebuilt, so that the bulk of what there is to see comes from restorations and additions over the centuries. It grew from nine to 19 domes. The original Romanesque style was preserved until the 17th century when St. Sophia was enlarged and rebuilt in the Ukrainian Baroque style. The Ukrainian Orthodox Church uses the cathedral for major events only. It still functions as a museum with exhibits on the cathedral's history and on the architecture of Kyivan Rus. It's open 10 a.m. to 5 p.m. every day except Thursdays. An extra fee is required in order to photograph the cathedral interior.

The 76 meter (250-foot) **Bell Tower** is southeast of the cathedral. Built in the 18th century and rebuilt in the 19th, the tower's four stories reflect the evolution of Ukrainian architecture.

From St. Sophia, proceed about two hundred meters up Voloydymyr Street to another landmark, **St. Andrew Church** (Андріївска, *Andryivska*), at the top of Andriyivsky Hirka. With its white and turquoise facade and green domes all accented with ornate golden trim, St. Andrew's is another familiar postcard subject. This rococo church was built from 1747-1753 by Bartolomea Rastrelli, an Italian who founded the Russian Baroque style. The central dome flanked by four slender towers topped with small cupolas is a variation of the traditional Ukrainian five-domed church. The graceful interior is accented with an iconostasis that's decorated with carved gilded ornaments, sculptures, and icon paintings. The terrace surrounding the church is a vantage point for a great view of the river and the Podil district below.

St. Andrew Church is not far from the highest point of the city, **Volodymyr Hill.** The terraces and parks on the Hill were laid out in the 1830's and 1840's. In 1853 a 4.5-meter (15 feet), six-ton statue of the prince-saint was erected here. This solitary bronze figure — perhaps the quintessential image of the city — is dressed as an ancient warrior and, cross in hand, overlooks the flowing river in which he had his subjects baptized. Visible below is a pedestrian bridge which connects the west bank with the beaches.

You can get down to the lower town or Podil district by descending **Andriyivskyy Uzviz** (Андріївський Узвіз) Street from St. Andrew Church. On this long, steep, winding cobblestone street, artists sell their paintings and small cafes and shops flourish. Or take the funicular railroad at Kalinina Square down the steep slope of Volodymyr Hill to Post Office Square (площа Поштова, *ploshcha Poshtova*) in the Podil district below. The railroad, built in 1905, has all-metal cars and accommodates 80 passengers.

Podil   Поділ   po-DEEL

The Podil district begins at the foot of Volodymyr Hill and extends north along the river flats. While in olden times the upper city was the home of the nobility and ecclesiastics, Podil was settled by fishermen, merchants, and artisans, and it still has a small town ambience. Much of the architecture has undergone restoration in recent years. The focal point of Podil is **Contract Square** (площа Контрактова, *ploshcha Kontraktova*). The square is named after its most prominent landmark, the House of Contracts, which was built in 1817 in the Classic style as a hall for negotiating agreements between merchants and landowners. In the vicinity are Hospitable Court or **Hostynnyy Dvir** (Гостинний Двір), built as a mansion in 1809 and restored from 1983 to 1987 with shops and a restaurant; the **Kyivan Brotherhood** or *Bratsky* **Monastery** with the old **Kyivan Mohyla Academy**, now functioning again, and a monument to **Hryhoriy Skovoroda**, the 18th century philosopher known as the "Ukrainian Socrates." To visit these Podil landmarks, take the metro to Ploshcha Kontraktova Station.

The **Kyivan Brotherhood Monastery** (Києво-Братський монастир, *Kyivo-Bratskyy Monastyr*) 2 Skovoroda Street (вулиця Сковороди, *vulytsya Skovorody*), was founded in 1616. It was affiliated with the Kyiv Epiphany Brotherhood, an Orthodox order founded by wealthy burghers, nobles, clerics, and Kozaks to protect the Orthodox faith from the onslaught of Polish rule and Roman Catholicism. The complex includes a seminary, refectory, and Holy Spirit Church, in the Ukrainian Baroque style, dating from the 18th century. Nearby is the Kyivan Mohyla Academy, which was established in 1632 by the merging of the Epiphany Brotherhood School with the Kyivan Cave Monastery School.

St. Nicholas Naberezhna Church (Набережно-Микільська Церква, *Naberezhno-Mykilska Tserkva*), 12 Skovoroda Street, is a Ukrainian Baroque church from 1775. It has an elegant facade, highlighted by the ornamentation of the drum supporting the cupola; inside the Classic-style iconostasis is noteworthy. In 1863, a church with a belfry was added on to the earlier church.

St. Flor Convent (Флорівський Монастир, *Florivskyy Monastyr*), 5 Liever Street and 6/8 Florivska Street, dates back to the 15th century. It merged with the Ascension Convent in 1712 to become one of the country's largest; daughters of the most aristocratic Ukrainian and

Russian families took the veil here. It's functioning as a convent again today. Most of the architectural ensemble was constructed in the 18th and 19th centuries and includes the 1732 Church of the Ascension, the 1824 Resurrection Church , a belltower, and dormitories.

St. Cyril Church (Кирилівьска, *Kyrylivska*), 103 Frunze (Фрюнзе) Street, about 4.8 km (3 miles) northwest of the city center, is a valuable specimen of Kyivan-Rus architecture of the 12th century. Its original form and extensive mural paintings of the 12th, 17th, and 19th centuries have been preserved. The church was commissioned by the wife of the Prince of Chernivhiv around 1146 to serve as the cathedral of an ancestral monastery. The rectangular structure was built according to a cruciform construction with three naves and apses, six pillars, and a single dome. In the 12th and 13th century it was a royal burial place. In the mid-18th century, exterior reconstruction gave it a Ukrainian Baroque appearance. To get there take Trolleybus No. 18.

Pechersk   Печерськ   peh-CHEHR'SK

Pechersk gets its name from the **Pecherska Lavra** (Печерська Лавра) literally "the Cave Monastery", a complex of 40 structures representing eight centuries of art and architecture. This section of the city contains a large riverfront stretch of parkland that extends about 5 km (3 miles) from St. Andrew Church near Podil as far south as the Academy of Sciences Botanical Garden. The park is an enjoyable place to stroll and observe the residents of Kyiv in their leisure, to take in a concert, or stop for a snack. Monuments, restaurants, and a large amphitheater are in this area. This area also contains government buildings, notably the glass-domed Parliament and the ten-story block that houses the Council of Ministers.

Mariyinskyy Palace (Маріїнський Палац), 5 Hrushevsky   Street (вулиця Грушевського, *vulytsya Hrushevskoho*), is behind the Parliament building just over half a mile from the art museum. The blue and white palace was designed in the rococo style by Bartolomeo Rastrelli, the Italian architect who also designed many of St. Petersburg's great buildings. It was originally built from 1747 to 1755 as tsarist palace. Used sporadically, it was renovated in 1870 for the visit of Emperior Alexander II and Empress Maria, for whom it's named. Today it's used for official state functions. To get there take Trolleybus No. 20 or Bus No. 15 or 62.

Museum of Ukrainian Art (Музей Українського Облазотворчого Мистецтва, Musey Ykrayinskoho Oblazotborchoho Mystetstva) 6 Hrushevsky Street, is housed in a stately Greek neoclassical building erected from 1897 to 1900. It has the largest collection of Ukrainian icons, paintings, drawings, and sculpture from ancient times to the present. The museum contains sections on old art, 19th and early 20th-century art, and contemporary art. Take Trolleybus No. 20.

The Pecherska Lavra covers 28 hectares (70 acres) of the riverfront parkland between the Metro Bridge and the Paton Bridge. It originated in 1051 when two monks, Antoniy and Feodosiy (Theodosius), founded a monastery in natural caves and built a church above it. Supported by the Kyivan princes and boyars, the monastery prospered and grew into one of the largest religious and intellectual centers in the Orthodox world. Noted chroniclers, scholars, architects, painters, and physicians lived and worked at the monastery. From the 11th through the 20th century, 86 buildings were constructed. For centuries, hundreds of thousands of Orthodox faithful have come to visit the relics of Antoniy and Feodosiy, who were canonized in 1643, and of the later saints entombed in the caves.

In 1926 the complex was declared the Kyivan Cave Historical-Cultural Preserve. In recent years it was returned to the Ukrainian Orthodox Church, and today functions half as an active monastery and half as a museum. Several of the churches on the grounds hold services, others are just for viewing. Touring the caves and a couple other highlights can be done in three hours, but at least a day is necessary to do the complex justice. A cafeteria and gift shop are on the grounds. The Pecherska Lavra complex is open daily except on Tuesday from 9:30 a.m. to 6 p.m. The caves close at 4 p.m. The ticket office at 25 Sichnevoho Povstannya (Січневого Повстання) Street, outside the Trinity Gate Church, sells general admission tickets; inside, tickets are sold for a few of the individual attractions. Take Trollcybus No. 20 to the Pecherska Lavra.

The Caves (Печери, *Pechery*) are situated in the Lower Lavra, the hilly southern half of the complex. They consist of two underground labyrinths of tunnels ranging from 5 to 10 meters deep (16 to 33 feet) with corridors up to 1.5 meters (5 feet) wide and 2 meters (6 and one-half feet) deep. Excavated in these soft sandstone catacombs are small burial niches containing the remains of monks and saints that have been naturally mummified due to the chemical composition of the soil and the cool, constant temperature. The caves are divided into the Near and Far Caves.

The **Near, or St. Antoniy Caves**, are 228 meters (750 feet) long. They contain 75 burial niches, including those of Antoniy and of the monk Nestor, the first Ukrainian historian, who died in 1115. Interspersed among the crypts are frescoes and three churches: Church of the Presentation of the Temple (Введенська, *Vvedenska*); St. Antoniy Church (Антонівська, *Antonivska*); and St. Varlaam Church (Варлаамська, *Varlaamska*). Each of them has a gilded bronze iconostasis.

Just west of the entrance to the caves is the exquisitely decorated church of the **Elevation of the Holy Cross** (Хрестовоздвиженська, *Khrestovozdvyzhenska*), dating from 1700. The church has three apses and a Baroque-style wood-carved and gilded iconostasis built in 1769. The southern portal is richly decorated with stuccowork.

The **Far, or St. Theodosius Caves**, extend for 280 meters (920 feet). Their entrance is in the **Conception of St. Anne Church** (Аннозачатіївська, *Annozachatiyivska*). The church dates back to 1679. It features a tent-shaped cupola and a carved oak iconostasis. The cave beneath contains 45 burial niches and three churches: **Nativity** (Різдва, *Rizdva*); **St. Theodosius** (Феодосіївська, *Feodosiyivska*); and the **Annunciation Church** (Благовіщенська, *Blahovishchenska*).

The underground passages of the caves go deep into the ground, and are narrow, and in places, dimly lit and a bit slippery. Your admission fee gets you a candle from the attending monks, but a tiny flashlight is more dependable. Rubber-soled walking shoes are also recommended. Visitors to the caves are encouraged, but they are reminded that these are holy places for Orthodox believers and an attitude of reverence is maintained at all times. Women should wear skirts and men should wear long pants.

Upper Lavra. The majority of the architectural structures are situated on the flat plateau that constitutes the Upper Lavra. Over the centuries many of the buildings suffered from periodic looting or destruction by invaders or damage from fire. Reconstruction in the 17th and 18th centuries funded by Kozak hetmen and officers give the complex a Ukrainian Baroque feel. Later construction in the 19th and 20th centuries was in a Russian synodal style.

Here are some of the noteworthy structures in the Upper Lavra:

Holy Trinity Gate Church (Троїцька Надбрамна Церква, *Troyitska Nadbramna Tserkva*) is a narrow four-tiered, single-domed church located above the main entranceway to the complex. Originally built from 1106 to 1108, it's not been changed since its early 18th century reconstruction. It is a good example of Ukrainian Baroque art and architecture. The interior features an openwork gilded iconostasis made by Lavra woodcarvers, wonderful painted murals, and a floor of molded cast-iron slabs.

The **Great Belltower**, 96.5 meters (318 feet) high, was built by architect Johann Shädel from 1731 to 1745 in the classical style, and topped by a gilded cupola. Each of its four octagonal tiers are adorned with columns, pilasters, and cornices. There's a stairway to the top from which you can see the extent of the Lavra grounds and enjoy a magnificent windowed vista of every corner of the city. A small gift shop is at the top. There's a separate admission charge for the belltower.

Behind the Belltower to the east are the ruins of **Dormition Cathedral**. First constructed from 1073 to 1078, this was the first stone structure of the complex and the primary church. Over the years the cathedral was damaged, rebuilt, and enlarged several times, and finally destroyed in 1941 by mines laid by Soviet forces retreating from the Germans. In 1991 the Cabinet of Minister of Ukraine passed a resolution to reconstruct it and this work has begun.

The church of **All Saints** (Всік Святих, *Vseek Svyatykh*, 1695—1698), is located above the Economic Gate, the administrative and service office on the north edge of the complex. Often called the gem of Ukrainian Baroque architecture, this five-gilded-domed church was modeled after Ukrainian wooden 2-storied, cruciform churches. It contains a carved and gilded wooden iconostasis from the 18th century and brilliant interior murals painted in 1905 by students of the Lavra icon painting school. The exterior is delicately ornamented with pilasters, ledges, cornices, and moldings.

In the center of the complex is the **Refectory Church**, so-called because it's adjacent to the two-story refectory. Built in 1893-1895 in the official Russian synodal style, the church has a large central dome topped by a small cupola and surrounded by four gilded cupolas. The church is the head church of the Moscow Patriarchate of the Ukrainian Orthodox Church. Liturgy is performed daily at 9 a.m. and 4:30 p.m. and Saturdays at 4:30 p.m.

Several museums are in the Upper Lavra. Each requires a separate admission fee. Fees are two-tiered: Ukrainian citizens pay in local currency while Westerners must pay in hard currency, up to several USD per museum. Having a Ukrainian colleague purchase your ticket will not work; if you are noticed entering with the cheaper ticket, you'll have to pay the hard currency price. Museums are open daily at 10 and close in the later afternoon, except for Tuesdays when the Lavra is closed.

Historical Museum of Treasures (Історичний Музеи Коштовностей, *Istorychnyy Muzey Koshtovnostey*), in the former monastery bakery, is extremely popular and oriented to group tours. It features precious stones or metals found or made in Ukraine. The museum is organized according to historical era, and contains departments of pre-historic cultures, the Scythian period, Kyivan Rus era, 14th to 18th century Ukraine, and 19th and 20th century Ukraine. The highlight is the ornate Scythian jewelry collected from fourth-century burial mounds in the Dnipropetrovska and Zaporizhska regions. A numismatics section has a display of coins of ancient Greece, Rome, and Kyiv-Rus. Photography is not permitted.

Museum of Books and Bookprinting is in the building that originally housed the monastery's press. The museum is devoted to the history of printing in Ukraine. On display are some of the first books printed by Ivan Fedorov, the first printer in Russia and Ukraine.

Kyiv Museum of Ukrainian Decorative Folk Art, attached to the Refectory Church, is in the former residence of the Kyivan Metropolitan. The museum covers the historical development of each type of folk art from the 16th to the 20th century. On display are printed and woven textiles, dress, ceramics, glass, porcelain, woodcarving, embroidery, and fabrics from the past as well as from contemporary masters. There's an especially good collection of old carpets woven in different parts of Ukraine.

Near the Museum of Decorative Art is an offbeat but fascinating museum containing micro-miniature art of all sorts — paintings, carvings, and engravings — so small they can be seen only with a microscope. On display are the world's tiniest book, a copy of Shevchenko's *Kobzar* with a carved portrait of the poet, and various works of art on fruit and vegetable seeds. All the miniatures are the creation of contemporary artist Mykola Syadrysty from Kharkiv.

Kyiv Museum of Theater, Music, and Cinema Arts (Київский Музей Театрального, Музучного та Кіномистецтва, *Kyivskyy Muzey Teatralnoho, Muzychnoho ta Kinomystetstva*) displays costumes, stage decorations, posters, drama manuscripts, musical scores, folk instruments, and all sorts of memorabilia from outstanding Ukrainian actors, directors, filmmakers, playwrights, and composers dating back to the early part of the century.

In the Pechersk area

Directly north of the Lavra, is a rather plain-looking church remnant with considerable historical and architectural interest. **The Church of the Savior at Berestove** is generally believed to date to the second half of the 11th century with major rebuilding in the Ukrainian Baroque style in the 17th century. Frescoes and murals from the 12th to the 17th century have been uncovered, and excavations are still going on. Originally thought to be the burial place of the ruling family of ancient Kyiv, only the tomb of Yuri Dolgoruky, the founder of Moscow, remains.

At 29 Sichnevoho Povstannya (Січневого Повстання) Street, not far from the Lavra entrance, is the **Ivan Honchar Museum.** Established in 1993, the museum houses the folk art and traditional costumes collected from all over Ukraine by artist Ivan Honchar.

A short walk south of the Caves Monastery, up a hillside to 33 Sichnevoho Povstannya Street, is the **Great Patriotic War Museum.** The museum depicts the history of Soviet participation in World War II with a display of tanks on a plaza outside. Topping the museum is "The Motherland", a huge steel statue of a woman holding a sword and shield. In a city fueled by rumors, many of them concern this unpopular Soviet-style monument that has dominated the city's architecture since it was erected in 1981. Local lore has it that Kyivites objected to anything taller than the nearby Great Bell Tower of the Caves Monastery, so the sword was shortened. There is a dubious attitude toward official statistics that rank the combined pedestal and female statue some 5 to 10 meters taller than the bell tower. According to a current story -- merely wishful thinking, say some — the monument is slowly and unevenly sinking into the cave-like foundation beneath it, and some day it will topple over.

Just over a half mile south of this controversial monument is a pretty little complex, **St. Vydubytskyy Monastery** (Видубицький Монастир), that was originally established in the 11th century and restored through the 18th.   Its centerpiece is **St. George Cathedral** (Георгіївський Собор, *Heorhiyivskyy Sobor*, 1696—1701), built in a cruciform design with nine chambers.   The cathedral's tall, narrow towers are topped by five cupolas set on polygonal drums, giving it the vertical appearance typical of wooden churches of the Dnipro region. There is also a refectory, a belfry with a pretty top dotted with gold stars, and a remnant of the **St. Michael Cathedral** (Мигайлівський Собор, *Mykhaylivskyy Sobor,* 1070—1088), with some of its original frescoes.   Take Trolleybus No. 14 or 15 to 40 Vydubytska Street.

The Botanical Gardens of the Ukrainian Academy of Sciences are adjacent to the Vydubytskyy Monastery. The Academy uses the gardens for horticultural research. The collection of plants is from all continents; the lilac collection is particularly noteworthy. The song of the nightingale, the view of the river and the beautiful monastery below, make this garden a lovely walking tour. The Gardens are open from 10 a.m. until 9 p.m. every day except Monday.

Other Things To See

Babyn Yar (Бабин Яр), the memorial to Kyivites slaughtered by the Nazis during World War II is about 3.2 km (2 miles) northwest of the city center between Teliha (formerly Korotchenko), Melnykov, and Dorohozhytsky Streets in a tranquil city park lined with birch trees. Actually there are two monuments that commemorate the horrifying event. In 1976 a monument consisting of 11 bronze figures was erected in memory of "Soviet citizens" who were "victims of fascism." The central figure was a communist resistance fighter. The monument ignored the fact that Jews constituted the majority of the 150,000 victims; others were Soviet prisoners of war, partisans, Ukrainian nationalists, gypsies, and anyone considered a threat to German authority.   The monument was controversial also because the Soviet government had erected it some distance from the actual execution and burial site which it had leveled and upon which it had constructed a highway and housing complex. Following independence, the Ukrainian government invited the government of Israel to erect a new monument. Dedicated in 1991 to commemorate the 50th anniversary of the slaughter, the new monument consists of a large bronze menorah and was erected about three-quarters of a mile from the first one, closer to the actual site of execution. Take Trolleybus No. 16.

The Museum of Folk Architecture and Folkways is worth the 19-km (12-mile) trip south of the city to the village of Pyrohovo (Пирогово). The 81-hectare (200-acre) outdoor display recreates 18th to 20th-century village life in different regions of Ukraine. The restored cottages, wooden churches, and farmsteads are meticulously preserved and furnished with period furniture, utensils, and embroidered linens. Folk art demonstrations are sometimes featured and there's a cafe in one of the cottages. A fair amount of walking is required. Take Bus No. 24 from the Ukrainian Exhibition of Economic Achievement in Holosiyivskyy Park im. Maksyma Rylskoho (Голосіївський парк ім. Максима Рильського) at *prospekt 40-richchya Zhovtnya*. The museum is open from 10 a.m. to 6 p.m. daily except Wednesday. Between November and May the hours are shortened and some of the buildings are closed.

RECREATION AND ENTERTAINMENT

Kyiv has a lot more to offer than museums and architectural monuments. Whether your tastes runs to high culture or sports, there are plenty of opportunities.

T. Shevchenko Theater of Opera and Ballet (Театр Опери І Балету im. Т. Г. Шевченка), 50 Volodymyrska (Володимирська) Street, was built in 1901 by architect Victor Shreter. This fine company produces many classical and new Ukrainian and foreign operas.

The Philharmonic Building is at 2 Volodymyrskyy Uzviz. While this traditional home of the Symphony Orchestra of Ukraine is undergoing renovation, the orchestra performs at other locations. The Symphony has an extensive repertoire including world classics, 20th-century Ukrainian symphonic music, and works by early Ukrainian composers.

I. Franko Ukrainian Drama Theater at 3 Ivan Franko Square (площа Івана Франка, *ploshcha Ivana Franka)*, performs Ukrainian plays; the **Lesya Ukrayinka Russian Drama Theater** at 4 Khmelnytsky Street (вулиця Хмельницька, *vulytsya Khmelnytska*) features plays by Russian playwrights.

The Ukrainian Home (Українс'кий Дім, *Ukrayinskyy Dim*), 57 Volodymyr Street, is an exhibition hall for Ukrainian arts and a meeting hall for Ukrainian cultural events. This fine building of natural stone was formerly the Lenin Museum.

Dynamo Stadium, 3 Hrushevsky Street (вулиця Грушевського, *vulytsya Hrushevskoho*), is a complex of gymnasiums, fields, courts, and pools. You can use the indoor swimming pool and handball and tennis courts, but if you want to watch the city's championship soccer team, Dynamo, in action, you need to go to Ukraine's largest stadium, the 100,000-seat **Republican Stadium**, 55 Chervonoarmiyska (Червоно-армійська) Street.

The Palace of Sports at *ploshcha Sportyvna* (площа Спортивна) seats up to 12,000 and is used for national and international sports competitions, theatrical performances, concerts, and mass meetings. Built in 1960, the Sports Palace's arena converts into an auditorium while the stands are turned into a stage and orchestra pit.

The Kyiv Circus performs in a 2,000-seat amphitheater located at Victory Square (площа Перемоги, *ploshcha Peremohy*).

Hidropark is a beach on an island near the left bank. This popular summer place for boating and sunbathing is easily accessible by the subway to the Hidropark Station.

"Day of Kyiv," a celebration of the birthday of Kyiv, takes place the last weekend of May during the "Days of Spring," an annual carnival and art festival that attracts artists from the whole country. The festival originated in 1982 as a celebration of the 1500th anniversary of Kyiv. The chestnut trees lining city streets and lilacs in the parks are in full bloom, and the rainy weather that often occurs during the festival doesn't dampen the genuine attitude of merriment that pervades the city. Booths selling snacks and souvenirs, parades and performers are in the Khreshchatyk Street area, and a vast stretch in the vicinity of Andriyivsky Uzviz Street becomes a gigantic art market.

HOTELS

Although the accommodations are very good, the ambience and service in tourist hotels in Kyiv generally fall short of that in comparably-priced hotels in western countries. These all have restaurants, bars, shops, and various services for travelers:

Hotel Dnipro (Дніпро), 1/2 Khreshchatyk Street, recently renovated, is considered one of Kyiv's finest hotels. Its excellent central location, river view, good restaurant, and services for business travelers can't be beat. The **Kyivska** (Київська), formerly the Inturyst, at 12 Hospitalna Street, is a large, new hotel with a good travel service as well as a pool, sauna, and shops. Its sister hotel, the **Rus** (Рус'), nearby at 4 Hospitalna Street, is also very nice. The Kyivska Rus complex has an underground garage for guests. The hotels are situated on hilly terrain; their city views are magnificent but the walk from the business center is a bit arduous. The **Moskva** (Моськва) at 4 Bankivska (Банківська) Street, is less expensive than the Kyivska and is in a particularly good location within walking distance of downtown, tourist attractions, and near a metro stop. **Hotel Domus** (Домус) is a small, newly-opened hotel at 19 Yaroslavska Street in the Podil district. Italian managed and with an Italian chef, the Domus may well be Kyiv's most expensive hotel, charging about $185 USD for a night's lodging. **Hotel Bratyslava**, across the river at 1 Malyshko Street, is a pared-down, but clean and serviceable alternative. Its rooms cost about half the average price of hotels in the business district and the metro ride across the bridge is convenient and picturesque.

Prolisok Tourist Complex, 139 Prospekt Peremohy, is 19 km (12 miles) west of the city center. The campsite includes a large motel and cabins, some with their own toilets, as well as shops, bars and casino. Three restaurants are on the premises including **Kara's House** (Хата Карася, *Khata Karasya*), with lots of traditional ambience, and specializing in Ukrainian banquets with folk music. This enterprise caters to groups and offers a variety of reasonably-priced package tours around central Ukraine and Crimea as well as hunting excursions. Tel./Fax: (044) 444-0395.

RESTAURANTS AND NIGHTLIFE

The late night scene is expanding in Kyiv. Western-style nightclubs with fancy bars, casinos, and floor shows are springing up. Posh restaurants with doormen and other pretensions of grandeur (French generally means very expensive) are all over the central business district. Prices are very high, and visitors can expect to pay even more than they would for a comparable experience in their own country. Payment in these establishments are in hard currency only and major credit cards are accepted.

Pizza places and other medium-priced western-style restaurants designed to appeal to tourists are also opening up. These too are usually joint ventures and take hard currency. It's also possible to find some cafes and simpler restaurants serving authentic Ukrainian cuisine at very reasonable prices. These will accept payment in either Ukrainian or hard currency. For any of the restaurants in the Old Town district, you'll need to make reservations in advance.

Hotel restaurants are usually quite good. These keep longer hours than restaurants in town, can accommodate more diners, and may be less likely to require reservations. Prices in hotel restaurants may be no higher than those in town, and they may take payment in hard currency, Ukrainian currency, or credit cards.

Ukrainian-Style Restaurants: The Attic (Світлиця, *Svitlytsya),* is a traditional-Ukrainian theme cafe, with wooden picnic tables, a tile stove, and embroidery. It serves light lunches and beverages. *Svitlytsya* attracts an artsy crowd in its location at 13 Andriyvsky Uzviz.
Dnipro (Дніпро) **Restaurant,** in the hotel of the same name, is usually open from 8 a.m. until 11 p.m., except for late morning and late afternoon breaks. A nice view of the square below, good Ukrainian food and reasonable prices. Make reservations in person for the same day. Located at 1 Khreshchatyk Street.
Heritage (Спадщина, *Spadshchyna),* a homey two-room restaurant that specializes in *varenyky* and *borshch,* is at 8 Spaska Street near the Kyiv Mohyla Academy in the Podil district. Payment is in coupons. It's open daily except Monday from noon until 5 p.m. and 6 p.m. until 11 p.m.
Hospitable Court (Гостунний Двір, *Hostynnyy Dvir)* is an airy attractive restaurant with a courtyard. Specialties include mushrooms in a cream sauce and a variety of broiled or boiled fish. A musical ensemble entertains evenings with Ukrainian folk songs and international favorites. Prices are rather expensive, but food and service is good.

Payment is in hard currency. Open daily from noon until 5 p.m. and 7 to 11 p.m., except Monday when it's open for lunch only. Reservations are required. Go to Kontraktova Square in the Podil region.

Kyivskyy (Київский) is located in the hotel of the same name (formerly the Inturyst) near the Republican Stadium. Specialties include *borshch* and chicken Kiev. Open from 7:30 p.m. until midnight. 12 Hospitalna Street.

Maksym (Максим), one of the city's first private restaurants, serves fine Ukrainian cuisine cooked to order in a subdued, clubby atmosphere. Reservations are strongly advised and jacket and tie are necessary, nevertheless the prices, at noon at least, are very reasonable and payment is in coupons. The restaurant is at 21 Bohdan Khmelnytsky Street, near the opera theater. Open daily except Sunday from noon until midnight.

Hotel Natsionalnyy (Національний) on Lypky (formerly R. Luxemburg) Street near the Supreme Council building has three restaurants that share one kitchen. Open daily from 8 a.m. until 10 p.m. Reservations are advised.

The Stairs (Сходи, *Skhody*) was one of Ukraine's first private restaurants. Specialties in this basement restaurant include *varenyky* and beef stew with smoked plums served in ceramic pots. A piano and violin duet entertain. Open from noon until 4 p.m. and 7 to 11 p.m. every day except Sunday. Reservations are advised. Located downstairs in the House of Architects on Borys Hrinchenko Street (вулиця Бориса Грінченка, *vulytsya Borysa Hrinchenka*) off Independence Square.

Ukrayina (Україна) is located in the hotel of the same name. It specializes in Ukrainian cuisine and the chicken cutlets are worth a try. It's open daily from noon until 11 p.m. 5 Shevchenko Boulevard.

New Joint-Venture Restaurants that some recent visitors to Kyiv especially recommended:

Ristorante Italia, at 8 Prorizna Street, off Khreshchatyk, for pizza and all the trimmings.

Bon Bons for its desserts, in the Passage off 15 Khreshchatyk Street.

Apollo, also in the Passage, is a pricy elegant restaurant and bar. It serves continental cuisine and has a good selection of French and Italian wine and German draught beer.

Nika Cafe, and next door in the same building at 2 Shevchenko Boulevard, **Bitburgers**.

The Studio, 4 Muzeyniy Lane, near the Hotel Dnipro, has a Sunday all-you-can-eat-and-drink brunch for $25 USD.

These are western-style in decor and cuisine. Payment is in hard currency; some accept credit cards.

SHOPPING

Bright new shops filled with luxury foreign goods are popping up all over the city. Shops offering the most-sought-after western brand names, such as Seagram's and Benneton, can be found alongside Ukrainian department stores. The Khreshchatyk Street vicinity is the main shopping area. Running off Kreshchatyk is a narrow arched passage known as *Pasazh* (Пасаж) that has a number of cafes and specialty shops full of western high-tech goods. A popular destination here, on Shevchenko Boulevard, right around the corner from the west end of Khreshchatyk, is a joint venture, Nika, that sells all sorts of basic items, from the office supplies in the front shop to the groceries in the western-style self-service supermarket (with an adjoining pizza shop) in the rear.

For more traditional Ukrainian shopping, go to **Chervonoarmiyska Street**, which extends westward from Kheshchatyk. Here, in the local currency shops, you may find some bargains in crafts, books, or gifts.

The main department store is the *Tsentralnyy Univermah or TSUM* (Центральний Універмаг or ЦУМ) at 2 Khmelnytsky Street, just off Khreshchatyk. Across town at Ploshcha Peremohy at the beginning of Shevchenko Boulevard, *Univermah Ukrayina* (Універмаг Україна) has four floors, stocked with food products, felt and fur hats, linens, woodenware, and toys.

There are a number of gift shops scattered about the city: *Ukrayinski Suveniry* (Укрїнські Сувеніри), 23 Chervoarmiyska Street, just off Tolstoy Square (площа Льва Толстого, *ploshcha Lva Tolstoho*), has an especially nice selection of crafts and linens. Other gift shops are *Podarunky* (Подарунки), 15 Khreshchatyk Street and *Budynok Podarunkiv* (Будинок Подарунків) at 5 Lesya Ukrayinka Boulevard (бульвар Лесі Українки, *bulvar Lesi Ukrayinky*).

Farfor, (Фарфор) at 34 Khreshchatyk, has a nice selection of porcelain plates, tea services, and a few figurines, from various factories throughout Ukraine. A complete tea service for six costs about $30 USD. It's open 10 a.m. to 7 p.m. Monday through Friday and 10 a.m. to 6 p.m. on Saturday. Directly next door is a very nice *Ukrayinski Suveniry* shop. For signed art, go to the art shops and galleries centered around the **Andriyivskyy Uzviz** Street area. Historical sites are a good place to find souvenir books and postcards and even some fine art. Artists sell their prints at the *Pecherska Lavra*, for example, and there's a shop for icons there.

OTHER USEFUL ADDRESSES

Embassies: United States: 10 Yuri Kotsyubynsky Street (вулиця Юря Коцюбинского, *vulytsya Yurya Kotsyubynskoho*); Tel. 044-244-7354; Fax 044-244-7350.

Canada: 31 Yaroslaviv val (Ярославів вал) Street; Tel. 044-212-2235.

Great Britain: 9 Desyatynna (Десятинна) Street; Tel. 044-228-0504; 044-290-7317; Fax 044-228-3972.

Main Post Office: 22 Khreshchatyk Street; Tel. 065. Public fax and telex machines available.

Banking Services: Most banks are open from 9 a.m. to 1 p.m. Generally, the more central its location, the more services a bank will provide. A few will cash traveler's checks, for example, the Eximbank (Export-Import Bank of Ukraine) at 8 Khreshchatyk Street, A Western Union office at the Lybid Hotel at Victory Square (*ploscha Peremohy*) can supply you with hard currency charged against your Visa or MasterCard. Simply have someone at home contact a local Western Union or call 1-800-CALL-CASH, anytime day or night. The office in the Lybid is open from 9 a.m. until 7 p.m., Kyiv time.

Medical Services: The universal number for emergency ambulance service is 03. In Kyiv you can also call 294-7008 or 294-7009 for a private ambulance. Check with your embassy for the names of clinics or doctors prepared to treat foreigners. Here are several that are recommended by the U.S. Embassy:
*Polyclinic No. 1, 5 Verkhna (Верхна) Street, Room 335. Foreign patients phone 296-6668. The Kyiv Research Institute of Urology and Nephrology provides medical services for the Cabinet of Ministers. It also provides a variety of services for foreigners: surgery, X-ray and laboratory testing, dental care, and private ambulances ($150). Most staff members speak English. Payment is in hard currency.
*Polyclinic No. 14, 1/29 Mechnikova (Мечнікова) Street, Tel. 224-7364, offers a variety of services and apparently has agreements with western medical assistance organizations.

Pharmacy: Drugs and medical supplies are in not easily available in Kyiv. A few pharmacies will fill prescriptions for hard currency only. Among them are: Pharmacy No. 1, 51 Volodymyrska (Володимирска) Street, Tel. 225-3255; Pharmacy No. 24, 10 Chervonoarmiyska (Червоноармійска) Street, Tel. 225-4308; and Hard Currency Pharmacy, 30 Prorizna (Прорізна) Street, Tel. 228-2871.

Travel Agencies: The Inturyst main office is at 12 Hospitalna Street in the Kyivskyy Hotel. It's open 8 a.m. to 8 p.m. The Kyiv travel bureau Slavutych at 22 Sichnevoho Povystannya offers excursion guides and translators in the Kyiv region.

Church Services: Most of the churches that are again functioning as houses of worship belong to one of the branches of the Ukrainian Orthodox Church. Many other religious groups have scheduled services around the city; the larger of these have their own buildings.

The Ukrainian Greek-Catholic Church didn't have a foothold in Kyiv when the churches returned to their traditional congregations; its services were held at a belltower in the Podil district. Eventually this community, numbering 30,000, acquired a site at Velyka Zhytomirska Street near Lvivska Square for the construction of a cathedral.

Roman Catholic Masses are held at **St. Nicholas Polish Roman-Catholic Church**, 61 Chervonoarmiyska (Червоноармійська) Street. With its gingerbread Gothic spires, the church is quite striking in a city full of Ukrainian Baroque church architecture. Actually the church is a neo-Gothic recreation of a medieval cathedral. It was designed by architect V. Horodetsky and built in 1899-1909. Take Trolleybus No. 11 or 12.

Kyiv Jewish Religious Congregation is Kyiv's only synagogue that was not destroyed by Bolsheviks or Nazis. It's located at 29 Shchekavytska (Щекавицка) Street in the Podil neighborhood. Services are daily at 8 a.m. and 3:30 p.m.; Jewish holy days are observed.

German Evangelical-Lutheran Church of Ukraine is St. Kateryna at 22 Lyuteranska (Лютеранська) Street. Services on Sunday and holy days are at 10 a.m. and 7 p.m.

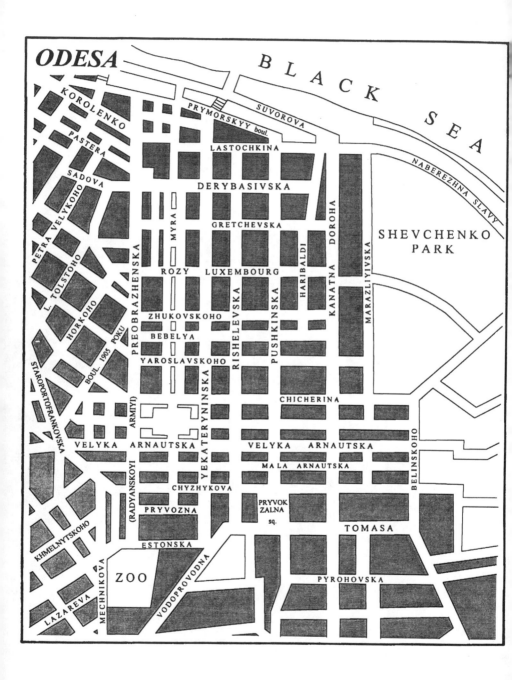

CHAPTER 25.
ODESA: PEARL OF THE BLACK SEA

Одеса   o-DEH-sah

Odesa has always shown more color, spunk, and irreverence than other cities of the former Soviet Union. There's an excitement, a verve, an anything-is-possible feeling in its streets.

Odesa is a city of contrasts. Its stately 19th century Classical architecture is set on orderly planned streets surrounded with green space, giving it an air of elegance. Strikingly ornate buildings of the late 19th and early 20th century are reminiscent of Right Bank Paris. It's also a seaport with bathing beaches and boardwalks, a resort city with health spas. With its balmy climate, seaside vistas and sandy beaches, and year-round lively street life, Odesa has an ambience more Mediterranean than Slavic.

Odesa is a city renowned for its scholarly, artistic, and cultural life.
At the same time, it's a bustling commercial port with its share of urban blight and pollution. Its dependence on its industrialized waterfront give it a large blue-collar population as well as a reputation as a place where you can buy anything.

Location: Odesa is on a high plateau overlooking a bay in the Black Sea-Azov Sea Basin, near the mouths of the Danube, Dnister, Boh, and Dnipro rivers. By road Odesa is 290 miles (480 km) south of Kyiv and 110 miles (180 km) southeast of the Moldovan capital, Chisinau.

Population and Language: The Odesa region has a rich multi-ethnic cultural legacy, with Ukrainians, Russians, Bulgarians, Moldovans, and Jews. The city's population of 1,100,000 is one of the most cosmopolitan in Ukraine. At the turn of the century, less than six percent were Ukrainian, while some 33 percent were Jewish and more than half were Russian. Odesa's Ukrainian population grew during the rebuilding period following both world wars when people from the countryside moved into the city, and Ukrainians predominated during the period after World War II to the mid-1970's. The newcomers usually tried to conform to the dominant Russian culture and many of them lost their ability to speak in their native tongue. Today there's no clear distinction between who is Russian and who is Ukrainian -- no one born in Odesa claims to be anything but Odesan. Issues of nationality and politics don't concern Odesans -- they are more interested in weightier matters, love and money.

Both Ukrainian and Russian are official languages in Odesa. Street signs and official forms in government offices are bilingual. Unofficially, the language is Russian with an Odesa-Ukrainian flavor, resulting in a unique dialect. The Ukrainian language is taught as a foreign language in the schools, but is not as popular a choice as the more advantageous English language. With one of Ukraine's largest and most cohesive Jewish communities, Odesa is also a center of modern Yiddish and Hebrew literature.

Climate: May to September are the best months, with average highs between 20° and 27° C (68° to 81° F). In July, the warmest month, the temperature averages 22.1° C (71.8° F). The January average is -2.8° C (27° F). Odesa is rather dry with an average annual precipitation of only 13.8 inches (351 mm).

Business and Industry: Odesa achieved renown as the Soviet Union's biggest Black Sea port city, but was relieved of some of its cargo handling when a new port was built in 1957 at Illichivsk 20 km (12 miles) to the southwest. Together they handle almost half the freight moving through Ukrainian ports.

Odesa became industrialized during the Soviet period. Metalworking and machine building account for more than a third of the industrial production. Chemical industry makes fertilizers, paints, dyes, and other materials. There's also an oil refinery, jute mill, and food-processing factories. Most factories lie to the north of the port along the waterfront.

Cultural Life: Odesa is an important scientific and cultural center with 14 higher educational institutes including the University, the Polytechnical Institute, the Conservatory, the Medical Institute, and the Institute of Naval Engineers. Odesa has a strong tradition of performing arts, with many theaters and a world class opera house. In the 1920's the city was the leading Ukrainian filmmaking center, and today there's an annual film festival at the end of summer. In 1995, Odesa hosted its first international festival of contemporary music.

Transportation: A comprehensive network of bus, tram, and trolleybus lines covers the city and go within walking distance of the beaches. In what the city government calls the "democratization of public transportation," trams and trolleybuses at this writing are free, with no tickets or tokens required. Besides the inevitable overcrowding, the city can no longer afford their upkeep, and the public vehicles are in a sorry state.

Bus: Avtovokzal (Автовокзал). The long distance bus station is at 58 Dzerzhynskyy (Дзержинский) Street.

Rail: The station is on Pryvokzalna Square (площа Привокзална, *ploshcha Pryvokzalna)* at the south end of Pushkin Street (вулиця Пушкінска, *vulytsya Pushinska)*. There's service to major cities daily. Of the several daily trains to Moscow, the Odesa Express is the fastest and should take less than 24 hours. It has sleeping cars. Daily trains from Kyiv take 11 hours. Train tickets are available for hard currency at 2 Shorsa (Шорса) Street or at the Intouryst office in Hotel Krasnaya on Pushkin Street.

Air: Central Airport is 12 km (7 miles) southwest of the city center off Ovidiopilska Road. Take bus No. 101 to and from Martynovskoho Square in the city center. Air Ukraine flies regularly between Odesa and Kyiv. Foreign airlines that serve Odesa are Aeroflot from Moscow, Austrian Airlines from Vienna, and Lufthansa from Frankfurt.

Boat: Morskyy Vokzal (Морський Вокзал), the Sea Passenger Terminal is on Suvorova (Суворова) Street. Inside the terminal you can get a timetable and tickets for several services. Passenger ferries and hydrofoils go from Morskyy Vokzal to the beaches from May through September from 8 a.m. to 8 p.m. The Black Sea Shipping Company has a booking office for trips at top of Potemkin steps at 7 Prymorskyy Boulevard. This company operates passenger and vehicle ferries to other port cities of Ukraine, to Russia, and all over the Mediterranean, making it theoretically possible to enter or leave Ukraine with a car by sea.

Taxi: There are cabstands in front of hotels and at major intersections throughout the city, but it's easy to find an unofficial cab. The best way to insure a reasonable fare is to have a Ukrainian friend engage the cab and negotiate the price beforehand. A taxi ride to the airport may be exorbitantly expensive reputedly because taxi drivers pay off bus drivers not to service the airport.

Rental Car: Check at your hotel service bureau or Inturyst office for a joint-venture car rental company. You can rent a car with or without a driver. Road service stations are at 27 Leningrad Highway (Ленінградське Шосе, *Leninhradske Shose*) and 20 Promyslova (Промислова) Street.

Tourism Concerns: Since Ukrainian independence, major streets have been renamed, but because many natives don't accept the new names, there's not a lot of consistency in their use. Opportunism is rampant in Odesa, corruption is said to permeate official circles, and bribery is an art form, but violent crime is not a problem. While murder and muggings are rare, thievery is not, and there's a real chance of losing your wallet when riding public transportation. Odesa practices water and power conservation. Hot water is rare, water shut off in the middle of the night, and in winter months electricity may be cut off for several hours each day, but these measures are not likely to affect the tourist hotels. Restaurants that are oriented toward special occasions and entertainment of businesspersons may initiate entertainment for your benefit and then add it to your bill.

HISTORY

Odesa observed its two hundredth birthday in 1994. The site of the present-day city had been settled by various peoples and tribes since prehistoric times. In 1415 the Ottoman Turks established a settlement called Khadzhibei. It was captured by the Russian army and a Ukrainian division of Kozaks during the Russo-Turkish War of 1787 to 1791. The Russians rebuilt it from 1792 to 1794 as a fortress and naval port and named it "Odessa" because they mistakenly believed that it was the site of an ancient Greek colony, Odessos. (In the Ukrainian language, Odesa is spelled with only one *s*.)

Because of its strategic location, Russia considered Odesa "the southern window to Europe," and developed it as a port and as a planned administrative center. Its duty-free status in the early part of the 19th century encouraged imports, and by 1850 Odesa was the largest wheat exporter in the Russian Empire. The city grew rapidly; in 1861 it was the largest city on Ukrainian lands with 116,000 inhabitants. Fewer than half were Ukrainian or Russian; about 25 percent were Jewish, and over 25 percent were Bulgarian, Greek, French, Italian, German, Polish, and

Moldovan. Nevertheless, in the second half of the 19th century a Ukrainian cultural movement gathered momentum; the city's Jewish and German communities also developed their own distinctive cultural forms.

By the 1880's Odesa was the second biggest port in the Russian Empire after St. Petersburg. Its primary exports were grain, sugar, and other agricultural products and its imports were tea and coal. The railroad stimulated further growth. The first industries processed agricultural products and imported raw materials.

Unemployment in years of bad harvest led to unrest. Odesa became a hotbed of political ferment. It was one of the chief centers of the 1905 workers' revolts, but demonstrations were ruthlessly suppressed. During 1917 to 1920, many factions struggled to control Odesa — Bolsheviks, Whites, Ukrainians, Germans and Austrians, French and allied forces. The city suffered heavier losses than any other in Ukraine.

Under the Soviet regime, foreign trade lost some importance while heavy industry was emphasized. In 1941, despite a heroic resistance, Odesa was captured by the Germans and administered by Romanians. Before it was recaptured by the Soviet Army in 1944, it suffered heavy loss of life and property. It did not regain its pre-war population of more than half a million until 1956.

ORIENTATION TO THE CITY AND SIGHTSEEING

Odesa is one of the few planned cities in Ukraine. The central core is laid out on a grid whose spacious avenues are paved with granite and lined with acacia trees. The area contains a number of lovely Classical early 19th-century two-storied limestone buildings that house cultural and scientific institutions and governmental offices. The main street, with plenty of shops and pubs, is Derybasivska (Дерибасівська) Street, which was named after the Frenchman De Ribas, who led the capture of Odesa from the Turks in 1789. The focal point of the city center is **Prymorskyy** (Приморський) **Boulevard**, a shady seaside promenade with many historic landmarks, that offers an 180 degree panorama of the port. Odesa's most recognizable landmark, the great Potemkin staircase, descends from the Prymorskyy Boulevard to the port.

To the west of the city center is an industrial district. To the north — beyond a strip of dense railway and tram lines, ship repair yards, factories, and warehouses — are flat, sandy beaches. A plateau to the south and southwest of the port is covered with gardens and parks. Going south along the parkland on Proletarskyy Boulevard are hospitals, rest homes and sanatoria, educational institutions, and the botanical gardens. South and west of the city along the coast are the more picturesque beaches and resorts.

Maritime Stairs (Приморські Скгоди, *Prymorski Skhody*), popularly known as the Potemkin Steps, link Prymorskyy Boulevard to the port on the north edge of the city. The steps were immortalized by Sergei Eisenstein's 1925 film, *Battleship Potemkin*, which depicts the 1905 mutiny of the ship's crew, even though the crowd massacre that took place on them was cinematic invention. The steps were designed by architect F. Boffo and constructed from 1837 to 1842. The 192 steps are wider at the bottom than the top so that when viewed from the bottom looking up, they give an illusion of being steeper than they actually are.

At the top of the steps on Prymorskyy Boulevard, the toga-clad figure depicted on the monument is that of Armand-Emmanuel du Plessis, Duke of Richelieu. The French nobleman became governor of Odesa in 1805 and oversaw its transformation from a village to a modern city.

The Catacombs. Under the city are hundreds of kilometers of tunnels that were carved out in the 19th century when the sandstone beneath the city was quarried for use in construction. The tunnels and caves attracted those who needed a place to hide, both heroes and criminals. During World War II, anti-Nazi resistance fighters were headquartered in the caves. Navigating the network of tunnels without an experienced guide is not wise (and may be forbidden). Check at a hotel service bureau for a tour. Bus No. 84 from Odesa stops outside the catacombs — ask for *katakomby.*

Shevchenko Park occupies 91 hectares (225 acres) on a plateau to the south and southwest of the port. The park contains the monument to Taras Shevchenko, a sports stadium, open-air theater, and an observatory.

Museums in Odesa, while worth a visit, are not overwhelmingly large. **Odesa Art Museum** (Одеский Художній Музей, *Odeskyy Khudozhniy Muzey*) is at 5-a Korolenka (Короленка) Street. Founded in 1899, the museum has departments of medieval art, prerevolutionary art (18th to 20th centuries), Soviet era art, and decorative and applied arts. It's housed in the imposing Count Potocki's Palace, an 1805-1810 Classical-style building with decorated ceiling and parquet floors. The museum is open daily except Tuesday from 10 a.m. to 6 p.m.

Literary Museum (Літературний музей, *Literatyrnyy Muzey*), 2 Lastochkin (Ласточкін) Street, pays tribute to famous writers who lived and worked in Odesa — Pushkin, Gogol, Chekhov, Tolstoy, and Gorky. It's open daily except Monday.

Museum of Archeology (Одеский Археологічний Музей, *Odeskyy Arkheolohichnyy Muzey*), 4 Lastochkin (Ласточкіна) Street, is a major archeology museum with collections from regional expeditions as well as Egyptian, Greek, and Roman artifacts. On display are Trypilian and late Bronze Age artifacts, Black Sea Hellenic sculptures, and coins from many periods and places. A highlight is the Gold Depository (*Zolota Kladova*) with jewelry and coins from the early Greek Black Sea colonies to the 20th century. Museum hours are daily from 10 a.m. until 5:30 p.m.

Maritime Museum (Музей Морського Флота, *Muzey Morskoho Flota*), 6 Lastochkin Street, is housed in a beautiful 1842 Classical and Renaissance style building designed by G. Toricelli. Both the exterior and interior of the building have recently been completely renovated and new exhibition halls were built. On display are 10,000 exhibits, including paper and scale models that illustrate shipbuilding and navigation from ancient times through the Kozak era to modern nuclear-powered submarines. The museum is open daily except on Thursdays from 10 a.m. to 5 p.m.

Museum of Western and Oriental Art (Одеский Музеи Західного та Східного Мистецтва, *Odeskyy Muzey Zakhidnoho ta Skhidnoho Mystetstva*) 9 Pushkin Street, was founded in Odesa in 1920. It contains several diverse departments: ancient art; Greek and Roman sculpture, pottery, and glass; Western European masters; Oriental art; and applied art, including porcelain, glass, and tapestries. It's open daily except on Tuesdays from 10:30 a.m. to 5:30 p.m.

RECREATION AND SIGHTSEEING

Odesa has seven theaters, a philharmonic orchestra, opera and ballet theater, and circus. In addition, the city hosts many visiting theater companies, musicians, and performers. Gambling was not legal under Soviet rule, but now nightlife is more vigorous than ever with many hard currency casinos for roulette and blackjack.

Odesa Theater of Opera and Ballet (Одеский Театр Оперу та Балету, *Odeskyy Teatr Opery ta Baletu*), Tchaikovsky Lane, was built in 1884 to 1887 in the Viennese neo-Renaissance style, according to a design by H. Helmer and F. Felner, the same architects who designed the Vienna Opera. The rococo interior includes a ceiling decorated with scenes from the works of Shakespeare. The theater contains five tiers with 1560 seats. The Odesa Opera has always been one of the leading opera theaters of Europe; while the quality of performances is reputed to have declined in recent years, the beauty of the theater is not to be missed.

Philharmonic Hall, 15 Rozy Luxemburg Street, was designed by A. Bernardazzi and G. Lonsky and built from 1894 to 1899. Formerly the New Stock Exchange, the building's Florentine Restoration facade is decorated with ceramic plate, marble, and stained glass windows. Inside, there's a sculpted wood ceiling symbolizing trade and industry. The Philharmonic has an American conductor, Hobart Earle, whose enthusiasm and good humor have revived Odesans' interest in the orchestra. Home performances are a sell-out and the orchestra is frequently on tour.

Odesa Theater of Musical Comedy (Одеский Театр Музичноі Комедіі, *Odeskyy Teatr Muzychnoi Komedii*), 3 Chizhikova (Чіжікова) Street features the operettas of Ukrainian and Russian composers. This very popular company is directed by a gifted ballet-master who incorporates ballet stars in the performances.

Beaches. Odesa's beaches, stretching both to the north and the south, are very crowded. Luzanovka to the north, with its many amusements, is very popular. Ferries to Luzanovka leave every 20 to 30 minutes from Morskyy Vokzal. The southern beaches are more attractive. Particularly nice are Arkadiya (Аркадія), Velyka Fontanka (Велика Фонтанка), Zolotyy Bereh (Золотий Берег), and Chornomorska (Чорноморска). A nice skylift, Konatna Doroha (Конатна Дорога), at the corner of the street of the same name (formerly Sverdlova Street) and Pyrohovska Street, is a convenient way to get down to the beaches and back.

Odesa's reputation as a health resort dates back to the 1820's. Therapeutic ingredients in the waters and muds along with the mild climate and beautiful beaches attracted vacationers and patients seeking a cure from various ailments — from arthritis to tuberculosis to skin disorders. Today numerous resorts, beauty spas, and sanatoria dot a 50-mile stretch of coast from the village of Fontanka north of Odesa to Lebedivka to the south. They attract hundreds of thousands of vacationers and medical patients yearly who seek health and beauty in hydro and mud treatments.

ACCOMMODATIONS

Hotel Londonskyy (Лондонський), 11 Prymorskyy (Приморський) Boulevard, is a hotel with some wonderful 19th century features — wide corridors, grand marble staircase, charming courtyard, large rooms with view of the harbor. Recent renovations have made it one of the best in all of Ukraine. It offers good services for businesspersons.

Hotel Krasnaya (Красная), 15 Pushkin (Пушкінска) Street at the corner of Rozy Luxemburg, is not far from the harbor. This is another elegant 19th century building converted from a private mansion. Its Russian name, "red," comes from the rose-colored sandstone. Classical statuary and white marble columns add to the grandeur. It offers good business facilities and contains the main Intouryst travel bureau.

Camping Delfin (Кемпінг Делфін), 299 Kotovskoho (Котовского) Road, 11 km (7 miles) north of the center, is a huge campground with campsites and bungalows, restaurant, bar, sauna, beach, and English-speaking service bureau. Camping Delfin is open June through September.

Chorne More (Чорне Море), 52 Rishelevska Street, is a nine-story 1970's Inturyst hotel near the city center. Amenities include an air-conditioned restaurant and many English-speaking services.

SHOPPING

With its mild climate and its entrepreneurial spirit, Odesa has always encouraged street vendors. New freedoms have brought even more shopping, so that an ambience of an open air bazaar pervades the whole city. The city does not offer much in the way of traditional crafts, however. On the western edge, south of Ovidiopilska (Овідіопільска) Road, shortly before the ring road, is an enormous weekend flea market where you can find all sorts of western goods. On sunny days, there's an open air souvenir market on Derybasivska (Дерибасівська) Street, in the park adjacent to Preobrazhenska Street. At *Pryvoz*, the central produce market on Pryvozna (Привозна) Street at the south end of Prospekt Myra (проспект Мира), you're likely to find grapes as large and luscious as any you've ever seen as well as all sorts of exotic fruits and vegetables.

Although the most interesting merchandise is sold on the street, there are a number of shops centered around Derybasivska Street, which is largely a pedestrian mall. At number 16, *Ukrayinski Suveniry* (Українскі Сувеніри) has a good selection of pottery and rugs. The biggest book store, *Dom Knihi* (Дом Кніги) at 25 Derybasivska also has a good music department, and there's also a book market in Gretchevska Square. At number 33 Derybasivska is *Pasazh*, an arcade with some fashionable shops. Around the corner on 33 Pushkin Street, the Kashtan no longer sells Ukrainian pottery but western food products, appliances, and lingerie. At 72 Pushkin is the *TSUM* or Central Department Store (Центральний Універмаг, *Tsentralnyy Univermah*). The street for art galleries is Lastochkin Street, and there's a nice art gallery at 45 Mala Arnautska, in the basement apartment.

USEFUL ADDRESSES

The main post office and telegraph office is at 10 Sadova (Садова) Street. MTTS, the inter-city telephone and telegraph station is at 100 Frunze (Фрунзе) Street.

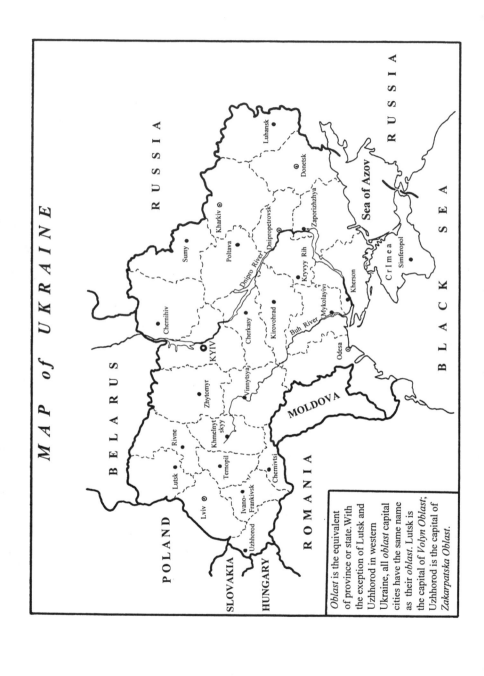

MAP of UKRAINE

RUSSIA

BELARUS

POLAND

SLOVAKIA

HUNGARY

ROMANIA

MOLDOVA

RUSSIA

Sea of Azov

BLACK SEA

Crimea

Luhansk

Donetsk

Zaporizhzhya

Kharkiv

Dnipropetrovsk

Kryvy Rih

Kherson

Simferopol

Sumy

Poltava

Dnipro River

Kirovohrad

Mykolayiv

Chernihiv

Cherkasy

KYIV

Buh River

Odesa

Vinnytsya

Zhytomyr

Khmelnyt-
skyy

Rivne

Ternopil

Chernivtsi

Lutsk

Lviv

Ivano-
Frankivsk

Uzhhorod

Oblast is the equivalent
of province or state. With
the exeption of Lutsk and
Uzhhorod in western
Ukraine, all *oblast* capital
cities have the same name
as their *oblast*. Lutsk is
the capital of *Volyn Oblast;*
Uzhhorod is the capital of
Zakarpatska Oblast.

CHAPTER 26.
FROM WEST TO EAST AROUND UKRAINE

Besides the better-known tourist destinations, there are many other historic, cultural, and recreational attractions in Ukraine that are worth a visit. From the beech and oak forests, across the broad plains, to the rocky coasts, there are ancient churches filled with stunning religious art, medieval castles, a wealth of museums with fine and folk arts, and a rich tradition of performing arts to be discovered. Ukraine is divided into 24 administrative oblasts or provinces. Going from west to east, here are some of the highlights.

Starting in the Drohobych district of the Lvivska region, is a charming memorial complex honoring Ukraine's second-greatest literary figure, Ivan Franko. Located in the village of Franko's birth, **Nahuyevychi** (Нагуєвичі -- also called Ivana Franka), the memorial consists of the restored homestead of Franko's parents, including farm buildings. Across the road is the Franko walk, consisting of a path through the woods past wooden sculptures carved with selections of his writings.

Carpathians The geographic center of Europe are the Ukrainian Carpathian Mountains (Карпати, *Karpaty*). Situated in the southwestern corner of Ukraine, they border on Romania, Hungary, Slovakia, and Poland. The most mountainous oblast in Ukraine is Transcarpathia (Закарпацька, *Zakarpatska*). Parts of the Ivano-Frankivska, Chernivetska, and Lvivska oblasts are also in the Carpathians.
    The Karpaty are medium-height mountains whose terrain ranges from hilly to mountainous. Deciduous and coniferous forests alternate with rolling hills and Alpine meadows that are dotted with charming villages. The climate, with its long spring, pleasant summer, warm fall, and mild winter, is a tourist's dream. The Karpaty's tranquil beauty, invigorating air, and natural mineral springs make it Ukraine's second resort and recreation area, after the Crimea. Hiking, fishing, and enjoying the therapeutic benefits of the waters are some of the main activities of the resort towns. There are good ski slopes, but snow melts quickly because of mild winter temperatures.
    Several Ukrainian ethnic groups are indigenous to the area. The Lemkos and the Boikos are agricultural people who built villages at low altitudes, while the Hutsuls, who occupied higher elevations, were traditionally engaged in cattle breeding and shepherding. The Hutsuls are noted for their rich cultural traditions and fine woodcrafts which are sold in the area's resort towns.

The Hutsul Alps, the most picturesque of the Ukrainian Carpathians, are a group of mountains between the Bila Tysa (Біла Тиса) and Ruskova (Рускова) river valleys in the Transcarpathian region. At the heart of the Hutsul region is **Rakhiv (Раків)**, a town of 16,000 on the Tysa River, that — according to a marker on the Uzhhorod-Rakhiv (Ужгород-Рахів) Autoroute — is the geographical center of Europe. Rakhiv was a major livestock trading center in the 17th and 18th centuries and is now a resort center. The Carpathian Nature Preserve, established in 1968, was Ukraine's first reserve for protection of the environment, plants, and animals. Its 18,000 hectares (54,700 acres) include the Karpaty's highest point, Mt. Hoverlya (Говерля), 2061 meters (6679 feet) high. Protected among the beech, fir, and spruce forests in the preserve are deer, mountain goat, lynx, and brown bears. There are stalactite caves in the reserve as well as an Alpine vegetation belt with a large rhododendron area. **Yasynya (Ясиня)** is a resort town of 8,000 situated in a broad valley on the Chorna Tysa (Чорна Тиса) River. In the town is an 1824 wooden church and a 200-bed hotel with a Hutsul craft shop.

In the Ivano-Frankivska region, the popular resorts are in the Prut (Прут) River Valley. **Yaremche (Яремче)**, set high in the mountains, about 500 meters (1650 feet) above sea level, is a very popular downhill ski resort. It has two tourist centers, a number of rest homes and sanatoria. A footbridge crossing the River Prut affords a view of a small waterfall; on the other side is *Hutsulshchyna,* a picturesque wooden restaurant that's a wonder of woodwork and design. Nearby are craft stalls. In the adjoining town of **Dora (Дора)** is a 17th century wooden Hutsul church, built without nails. Upstream, **Vorokhta (Ворохта)**, surrounded by coniferous and beech forests, has sanatoria, a sports base, and a wooden 18th century church.

Slightly east, about 70 miles from the city Ivano-Frankivsk, is **Kosiv (Косів)**. This town of about 10,000 is dotted with health spas and sanitoria. Its biggest attraction lies outside the town. At the bustling twice-weekly open market, you can buy anything from a pig to pastries to spare auto parts. This market is considered the best place to find Hutsul woodcrafts. Make your way past the mélange of colorful booths, to the rear through a wooden gate to the craft section. Market day is Saturday plus a weekday the town chooses, currently Tuesday.

Kolomyya (Коломия), a lovely small city at the southern entrance to the Carpathians in the Ivano-Frankivsk region, is famous for its wood carvers and master-ceramicists and weaving and embroidery. Its chief attraction is the very interesting **Museum of Hutsul Folk Art** at 25 Teatralna Street. On display are crafts from the 18th century, including woodcrafts, ceramics, pysanky, metal-, leather-, and fabric-work, and folk musical instruments. Museum hours are 10 a.m. until 6 p.m. Saturday through Thursday; it's closed on Friday. Going west on the main road, you'll come to a wooden Church of the Annunciation, dating from 1587. While the local hotel can't be recommended, you can find satisfactory lodging with interesting and hospitable local families through the **Kolomyya Bed and Breakfast Association.** Organized by an American Peace Corps worker, the association lists attractive and clean homes which provide good home cooking. Contact the Kolomyya Bed and Breakfast, c/o Luba Tomchuk, Staromyska 7, Kolomyya, 285200 Oblast Ivano-Frankivska, Ukraine. Tel. (3433073) 2-21-02 or Fax the city administration, (3433) 2-14-80, but beware that due to bad telephone lines, some faxes go through blank. The **Cafe Kaska** in town makes tasty tortes and various other pastries. It's located at 26 Renaissance Prospect and is open daily from 9 a.m. to 7 p.m.

Ivano-Frankivsk, the administrative center of the oblast, is a typical, pleasant city, where day-to-day life of ordinary Ukrainians can be observed. In the center of the city are some fine examples of 18th century baroque churches. There's also an art museum and a museum of regional history. In summers, international flights land at the city's airport -- formerly used by the military -- with its good runway.

Also in the summer, outdoor cafes spring up like mushrooms. **Slovan** (Слован), a new privately-owned Ukrainian restaurant at 4 Komarova Street in the center of town, offers a good choice of well-prepared food. It's open daily from 11 a.m. to 12 p.m. The **Hotel Roxolana** (Роксолана), a joint venture with American and Austrian partners, may well be the finest hotel in Ukraine. This small rebuilt hotel features large, comfortable rooms, a nice lobby with security cameras (although it doesn't seem to need this precaution) efficient staff, and an Austrian-inn-type breakfast buffet. Rooms cost about half that of the best hotels in Kyiv. Much of its clientele consists of tour groups sponsored by its owners, but rooms are often available and its good restaurant is open for three meals a day. Hotel Roxolana is at 7--9 Grunwald Street. Tel. (03422) 27949; fax (03422) 24769. In the U.S. call (800) 242-7267.

Heading east, in the Chernivetska oblast, is the town **Vyzhnytsya** (Вижниця) on the Cheremosh (Черемош) River. The Cheremosh Tourist Resort is open year-round. From there you can take a bus tour through the picturesque mountain roads or a walking tour in the footsteps of Oleksa Dovbush, an 18th-century local hero known as the Ukrainian Robin Hood.

There are several larger cities in the Carpathians that make a good base for excursions. **Uzhhorod** (Ужгород), population 125,000, is the center of the Transcarpathian province, the most south-western region of Ukraine. Its name literally means "city *(horod)* on the Uzh," because the serpentine River Uzh (Уж) descends from the mountains and winds through it from west to east. Once the westernmost outpost of the Kyivan state, Uzhhorod fell under the Polovtsi, a Hungarian tribe; was ruled by Transylvanian princes and Austrian Hapsburgs; and was part of Czechoslovakia in the 1920s and 1930s. It has a sizable Hungarian population.

Uzhhorod is a pretty city with a relaxed ambience. Cypress trees and iron-cast statues — an example of regional art — lend a touch of the exotic to this traditional center of pottery production. Autumns here are particularly pleasant with colorful trees and a grape harvest. A footbridge links the city center on the north side to the hotels, railway and bus stations on the south side. In the center are small privately run cafes that feature Hungarian or Slovak dishes. On the south edge of the city, the **Hungarian Restaurant**, one of several restaurants and coffee shops in the huge modern tourist hotel, **Zakarpattya** (Закарпаття), serves moderately spicy dishes accompanied by a band or floor show.

The castle-fortress on the hill at the end of Kapitolna (Капітольна) Street near the town center was built on the site of the earlier palace of the Ukrainian prince Laborets, who was executed by the Hungarian army in 896. The castle was in use between the 13th and 17th centuries. Inside is an art gallery and the **Museum of Regional Studies** whose area archeology exhibit includes a fine collection of Bronze Age objects. It also has a collection of folk art which shows the variation among different ethnic groups. Adjacent to the castle is the **Museum of Folk Architecture and Folkways,** a collection of several dozen old wooden buildings containing traditional furnishings, costumes, and crafts of the indigenous ethnic groups including Hutzuls, Romanians, Hungarians, and Boikos.

Not far to the south is **Mukacheve** (Мукачеве), the second largest city in the Transcarpathian region with a population of 90,000. Settled since prehistoric times, Mukacheve's strategic position on the Lyatorytsya (Ляториця) River near the border separating Ukrainians, Slovaks, and Hungarians resulted in a complicated political history.

The chief architectural monument is **Palanok** (Паланок) **Castle,** a huge fortress that stands on a hill high above the town. The fortress is rich with medieval architecture — thick walls, bastions and tower, a moat and two inner yards. Formerly a residence of Old Slavic, Hungarian, and Transylvanian knights, it served as a prison, an agricultural school, and a technical school during the Soviet period. The castle, which is being restored, today functions as a history museum.

Chernivetska Region The Carpathian mountains taper off into foothills in the Chernivetska oblast in southwestern Ukraine, eventually forming a broad plateau. This region, which borders Romania and Moldova, was historically known by its ethnographic name, Bukovyna. It's about 70 percent Ukrainian, with substantial numbers of Romanians, Moldovans, and Russians. The region is famous for its wood carvings, *kylym* weaving and embroidery.

The city of **Chernivtsi** (Чернівці), population 261,000, is the political and cultural center of the region. Situated on both banks of the Prut (Прут) River, the site was inhabited as far back as the Paleolithic period. Remnants of the Trypilian, Scythian, and early Slavic cultures have been uncovered. During its recorded history, Chernivtsi was ruled by half a dozen countries and acquired a cosmopolitan character from its ethnically diverse population. Chernivtsi has a university, a medical school, an art school, a theater, a philharmonic orchestra, many squares and parks, and a botanical garden.

Chernivtsi's old town is a blend of central European architecture, reflecting its century and a half as an outpost of the Hapsburg Empire. The theater of music and drama was designed by the two Viennese architects who built the Vienna and Odesa opera houses. The central street, vulytsya Kobylyanska (вулиця Кобилянска), named after the Ukrainian writer Olha Kobylianska, has charming shops and cafes.

East of the center, on Ruska (Рус'ка) Street, is **St. Nicholas Cathedral** (Миколаївська, *Mykolayivska*), built by the Romanians in 1939. A copy of a 14th century royal Romanian church, its four oddly twisted cupolas earned it the nickname "drunken church." Just north of the cathedral off Sahaydachnoho (Сагайдачного) Street is **St. Nicholas**

Church, a little wooden church dating from 1607 that was constructed without a single metal nail. Reputedly the oldest building in the Chernivtsi region, the church was restored in 1954. At the west end of town is the most impressive building in the city, the main building of **Chernivtsi University.** Built from 1864 to 1882 as the residence of the Bukovynian metropolitans, its Romanesque and Byzantine architecture is embellished with motifs of Ukrainian folk art, for example, tile roof patterns that duplicate the geometric designs of weavings.

　　The Chernivtsi Museum of Folk Architecture and Folkways, 2 Svitlovodska (Світловодська) Street contains examples of Bukovynian folk architecture.

Khotyn (Хотин), is northeast of Chernivtsi on the Khmelnytsky (Хмельницький) Road. The town is noted for a fortress the Genoese built on the steep right bank of the Dnister River in the second half of the 13th century. Rebuilt in the 15th and 16th centuries, the fortress has been the location of a number of films because of its classic castle appearance along with its remarkably good condition. The fortress complex includes defensive towers from 1480, a commandant's palace, and a church. Khotyn has changed hands many times over its long history; its most important struggle was the Khotyn Battle of 1621 when Zaporizhski Kozaks joined the Polish to defeat the Turks, thus checking the Turkish westward conquest of Europe.

Kamyanets-Podilskyy (Кам'янець-Подільський) in the Khmelnytska region, just 23 km (14 miles) north of Khotyn, has been continuously occupied since the Kyivan-Rus period. It's situated on a sheer rock bluff carved out of the steppe by the Smotrych (Смотрич) River below. An important commercial center on the route from Kyiv to the Balkans, it shows the influence of the four communities that settled it — Ukrainian, Polish, Armenian, and Jewish. The various powers that ruled over Kamyanets-Podilskyy over the centuries — including the Turks — also left their mark. The composer Mykola Leontovych, while a student at a theological seminary here, wrote his world-famous Epiphany carol *Shchedryk*, which, in English, is known as the "Carol of the Bells."

　　The Kamyanets-Podilskyy Historical Museum and Preserve contains almost 100 architectural monuments and other artifacts. The centerpiece of the preserve is the large stone citadel that guarded access to the city. Inside is a fine ethnographic museum with costumes from Bukovyna, embroidery, art and religious artifacts. The preserve covers about 30 hectares (12 acres) and includes seven towers, dungeons, turrets, and underground passages. The fortress represents military architecture of the feudal era and played a significant role in the complicated history of Kamyanets-Podilskyy. The fortress and other remnants of diverse cultures — a Polish town hall, a number of Roman Catholic monastic buildings, Armenian warehouses — provide archeologists with more than one field day. Layers of civilization in this ancient settlement are strangely juxtaposed. There's an Islamic minaret, for example, topped with a bronze statue of the Madonna. The historical sites are largely unrestored, but a team of Canadian archeologists has undertaken the study, preservation, and site-management of the Old City in Kamyanets-Podilskyy.

Pochayiv Monastery (Почаївьска Лавра, *Pochayivska Lavra*) is approximately 75 km (45 miles) north of the city Ternopil in the Ternopilska oblast. The monastery is the second largest Orthodox shrine in Ukraine, after the Kyivan Cave Monastery. Its first recorded history dates to 1527. Legend has it that it was founded by monks from the Cave Monastery who fled the Tatar invasion of Kyiv in 1240. In 1261 the monks saw an apparition of the Mother of God. From the imprint of her right foot on the rock on which she stood, there flowed an eternal spring with healing powers.

The monastery grew from the donation of benefactors. In 1597 a Ukrainian noblewoman, A. Hoyska, donated a large estate as well as a miraculous icon of the Mother of God which had been brought to the area by a Greek metropolitan. This icon reputedly healed many who prayed to God before it and it saved the monastery from an attack by Turks and Tatars in 1675. The complex flourished and grew despite a complicated history of being buffeted among churches and states. In 1730 it was transferred to the Ukrainian Greek Catholic Church, and under the Basilian monastic order became an important cultural and publishing center. In 1831 the Russian government gave the monastery to the Russian Orthodox church and in modern times the Soviet regime all but closed it. It's fully functioning again as a monastery, with about 70 monks in residence.

The most noteworthy building in the complex is the **Assumption Cathedral** (Успенський Собор, *Uspenskyy Sobor*), which was built on the cliffside terrace from 1771 to 1783 and renovated in 1876. The vast cathedral has eight large and seven smaller cupolas and can accommodate 6,000 people. Surrounding the cathedral are monks' cells, and nearby are a bishop's residence, a large bell tower, and several other churches of differing architectural styles.

Pochayiv is once again one of Ukraine's primary pilgrimage sites. Thousands of faithful come on August 5 to commemorate the anniversary of the deliverance from the Turks. Daily worshippers at the 5 a.m. service revere the miraculous icon, which -- draped with an embroidered towel according to Ukrainian custom -- is lowered for veneration; as well as the healing "footprint" spring, whose gold cloth is unveiled. Visitors coming later can receive a sample of the spring's holy water. The city of Pochayiv also contains an ethnographic museum; a wooden church dating from 1643, the **Church of the Holy Protectress** (Покровьска, *Pokrovska*) and **All Saints Church** (Всіхсвятська Церква, *Vsikhsvyatska Tserkva*), a baroque church from 1773.

Chernihiv (Чернігів), population 310,000, is the principal city of the Chernihivska oblast. Its position on the Desna (Десна) River north of Kyiv along the border of Russia and Belarus attracted settlers as early as 2,000 B.C., according to archeological finds. First historical mention of the city dates back to 907, when it was second in size to Kyiv. From a lookout point on **Boldin Hill** in this city rich with parkland and noted church architecture, you can see the beautiful golden domes among the chestnut and oak trees. Also visible in the skyline are smokestacks and pollution as Chernihiv is also an industrial city.

The city is noted for its monumental structures, particularly the churches, erected during the 11th and 12th centuries. Many are located at the **M. Kotsyubynsky Park of Culture and Recreation,** located at Chernihiv's early fortress settlement, the *dytynets*. The most notable structure in this area is the Spaso-Preobrazhenskyy Sobor or **Cathedral of the Transfiguration of the Savior**, one of the oldest churches of Kyivan Rus, built about 1017 by Mstyslav, the younger brother of Yaroslav the Wise. **St. Katherine Church,** on a hill opposite the *dytynets,* was completed in 1715 to commemorate the heroism of the Kozaks of Chernihiv in the storming of the Turkish fortress of Azov in 1696. It contains a museum of national decorative art of the Chernihiv region.

The Yeleskyy Monastery on Proletarska Street was founded by Grand Prince Svyatoslav in the mid-11th century. Its structures include the 12th century Uspensky (Dormition) Cathedral with a five-tiered iconostasis, one of the largest in Ukraine. **Trinity Monastery** on Tolstoy Street (вулуця Л'ва Толстого, *vulytsya Lva Tolstoho*), is one of the finest architectural complexes of its kind in Ukraine, with its churches, consistory, printing house, and monks' cells. It was founded by the monk Antoniy in 1069 and rebuilt in 1649 when it became a center of Ukrainian chronicle-writing. On the grounds are Antoniy's Caves, which contain three underground wooden churches. Two churches at the monastery are worth a visit: the Troyitsky Cathedral (1679-1695) and the 1677 Presentation (Введренска, *Vvedrenska*) Church with its five-tiered bell tower.

Pereyaslav-Khmelnytskyy (Переяслав-Хмелнитскии), in the Kyivska oblast, played an important role in history because of its location about 80 miles downriver of Kyiv. One of the oldest cities in Ukraine, it was a strategically important fortress in the defense of Kyiv Rus against the steppe nomads. Centuries later it was a center of the Kozak state. In addition to its political and military importance, many of Ukraine's greatest writers and thinkers found their inspiration in Pereyaslav and its neighboring villages.

Several churches were built during the Ukrainian Baroque period. St. Michael Church (1646-66) was constructed on the site of a medieval church of the same name that was destroyed by the Tatars; Ascension Cathedral (1695-1700) was financed by Ukrainian Kozak leader Ivan Mazepa; its bell tower was constructed from 1770 to 1776.

Today Pereyaslav-Khmelnytskyy is a museum town. Mykhailo Sikorsky, a museologist and historian (b. 1923), founded most of the town's 17 museums and personally collected a large proportion of their holdings. The **Pereyaslav-Khmelnytskyy Historical-Cultural Preserve** includes a historical museum with four branches whose huge collections range from a second century chess set to Bohdan Khmelnytsky's sword. Among the branches are an archeological museum, the H. Skovoroda Museum, and a diorama of the battles for the Dnipro in the Peryaslav-Khmelnytsky region in 1943. Set in former sacristy of the old Ascension Church, the lifelike diorama depicts the fierce battle in which some quarter million Ukrainian troops lost their lives in regaining a Nazi stronghold.

The Pereyaslav-Khmemnytskyy preserve also includes an open air museum of architecture and folkways. The museum displays a wealth of traditional rural architecture and features a museum of *kobza* (bandura) playing; a bread museum; a beekeeping museum; a folk-art museum; and a Sholom Aleichem museum.

Cherkaska Region The scenic Cherkaska oblast straddles the Dnipro in the forest-steppe belt in the heart of Ukraine. The first human settlement dates to the seventh to third century B.C. The region was part of Kyivan-Rus; was later devastated by the Tatars; was under Lithuanian rule in the second half of the 14th century; and served as an important Ukrainian political center in the Zaporizhskyy Kozak struggle against Poland between 1648 and 1654.

Kaniv (Канів), 162 km (100 miles) downriver from Kyiv, is a pilgrimage destination for those of Ukrainian roots because it's the burial place of the great poet and patriot, Taras Shevchenko. Area excavations have uncovered dwellings and artifacts of an ancient settlement of Slavic farmers and herders. Its recorded history dates to 1144. The construction of the Kaniv Hydro-Electric Power Station brought it into the modern era.

The **Kaniv Museum-Preserve** (Канівський Музей-заповідник, *Kanivskyy Muzey-zapovidnyk*), is located atop a high bluff overlooking the Dnipro. A climb up 400 steps leads to the burial place and monument to Taras Shevchenko, who expressed the wish in one of his most-loved poems, *Zapovit* ("Testament"), to be laid to rest above his beloved Dnipro river. Adjoining the gravesite is an interesting literary-memorial museum detailing his life and works.

The **Kaniv Nature and Historical Reserve** (Канівський Природничо-історичний Заповідник, *Kanivskyy Pryrodnycho-istorychnyy Zapovidnyk*) is about 16 km (10 miles) south of Kaniv. This forest-steppe preserve is approximately 2000 hectares (5000 acres) of forests and hills containing more than 5,000 different native plant species and a wealth of wildlife including 275 species of birds. Fossils and artifacts from the late Paleolithic and Neolithic eras and the Trypilian and Scythian cultures are noticeable.

Cherkasy (Черкаси), population 308,000, is a port city on the Dnipro, 240 km (150 miles) downriver from Kyiv. Originally an outpost on the southern frontier of the Kyivan State, it later became a Kozak defense point against Tatar and Turkish raids. Cherkasy is the home of many institutes of higher learning. It has a music and drama theater, a puppet theater, a philharmonic society, an ethnography museum, a planetarium, and a covered farmers' market. The **Regional Ethnography Museum** at the beginning of Slavy (Слави) Street, is over 75 years old and has more than 100,000 exhibits.

Uman (Умань), a city of 93,000, is about 188 km (117 miles) west of Cherkasy. During its centuries under Polish rule, the city received its outstanding landmark, **Sofiyivkyy Park** (Софіївкий Парк), built in 1796 by Polish Count Potocki in honor of his wife, Sofia, a former Turkish slave.

Sofiyivka is situated on a picturesque site on the outskirts of the city. The original landscape design included entrance grottoes, waterfalls, and a system of waterways and lakes with footbridges, fountains, and sculptures over 150 hectares (370 acres) of land. Over time, an assortment of pavilions and temples were added. The park was restored between 1966 and 1972 and now functions as an arboretum with nearly 500 varieties of trees and shrubs.

Also in Uman is the **Uman Regional Studies Museum** (Уманьський Крайезнавчий Музей, *Umanskyy Krayeznavchyy Muzey*). It has a large archeological and ethnographic collection ranging from prehistoric and Scythian cultures through the Kozak period.

Poltavska Region The Poltavska region is an area of lowland plain on the left (east) bank of the Dnipro. It was part of Kyiv Rus in the 10th to 11th centuries, belonged to the Pereiaslav principality in the 11th to 13th centuries, then controlled by the Tatars and later by Lithuania and Poland. A series of peasant-Kozak uprisings against the occupying forces culminated in 1648 in war. Under the leadership of Hetman Bohdan Khmelnytsky, the struggle for national liberation freed Ukraine of Polish rule.

The region was a battleground during the period of the Great Northern War between Sweden and Russia (1700 to 1721). The turning point of the war was the Battle of Poltava in 1709. After assurance that Ukraine would not be annexed to Poland in case of a Swedish victory, Hetman Ivan Mazepa and his troops sided with Charles XII of Sweden against Peter I. Their defeat resulted in Russian military rule in the Hetmanate and a decrease in its autonomy. Ultimately, serfdom was introduced into Ukraine.

The Poltavska region is particularly rich in Ukrainian culture. Taras Shevchenko lived here from 1843 to 1846. Nikolai Gogol, who is usually counted as one of the great Russian writers, was born Mykola Hohol (1809-52) in the village of **Velyki Sorochyntsi** (Велики Сорочинці) in the Myrhorod (Миргород) district. Gogol was an ethnic Ukrainian who wrote on Ukrainian themes and subjects, but worked in the Russian language in order to be published and recognized. The village contains a literary museum to Gogol and the 1732 baroque **Church of the Transfiguration** (Преображенська, *Preobrazhenska*) with a magnificent large carved wooden iconostasis.

Gogol spent his childhood and adolescence in the village **Hoholeve** (Гоголеве). His parent's estate was reconstructed in 1984 and today is a cultural preserve, including a house, pavilion, park and a museum. The philosopher and poet Hryhoriy Skovoroda was born in the village of **Chornukhy** (Чорнухи) in 1722. The estate of his parents was reconstructed and today houses a historical-ethnographic museum. The Ukrainian composer Mykola Lysenko (1842-1912) was born and spent his early years in the village **Hrynky** (Гринки). The Poltavska region also has several towns noted for their folkcrafts — **Opishnya** (Опішня) for ceramics, **Reshetylivka** (Решетилівка) for weavings and embroidery, and **Velyki Sorochyntsi** (Велукі Сорочинці).

The administrative center of the Poltavska oblast is the city of **Poltava** (Полтава), population 350,000. Situated on three hills on the Vorskla (Ворскла) River, Poltava is on the Kyiv-Kharkiv Road, about 333 km (207 miles) east of Kyiv and 135 km (84 miles) west of Kharkiv. Historically, the city has been an important cultural center with a long theatrical tradition and a prominent role in the 19th century Ukrainian literary renaissance.

All major streets of the city lead to a large, circular plaza, Round Square (площа Крула, *ploshcha Kruhla*) which is halfway up the main thoroughfare, **Zhovtneva** (Жовтнева) **Street**. At the south end of the street are several attractions:

The **Regional Studies Museum at Lenin Square** (площа Леніна, *ploshcha Lenina*), is housed in the provincial *zemstvo* (county council) building. Built from 1903 to 1906 in the Ukrainian Moderne style, it stimulated a revival of the national style in Ukrainian architecture. The building was destroyed during the Second World War and rebuilt in the 1960s. Its facade is embellished with crests of the region's towns and contains ceramics and majolica from historic area pottery factories. The museum is one of the largest in Ukraine with diverse collections from many sources. They include valuable archeological objects; historical documents and manuscript books; and folk arts, including *kylyms*, costumes, embroidery, woodcarvings, and ceramics. It also contains a diorama of the region's wildlife.

The **Savior** (Спаська, *Spaska*) **Church**, 1705-1706, is the only example of 18th century wood architecture in the Poltavska region. The **Poltava Art Museum**, 11 Spaska Street, features departments of 16th-to-19th-century European art and 17th century to contemporary Ukrainian and Russian art. Among the painters represented are E. Delacroix, L. Cranach, G. van Eyk, and I. Repin.

Poltava Battle History Museum is at Shvedska Mohyla (Шведська Могила) on the site of the battle, about 7 km (4 miles) north of the city center. Take Zhovtneva Street north from the Column of Glory and at the end bear right on Zinkivska (Зінківська) Street. The **Cathedral of the Elevation of the Cross** (Хрестовоздвиженський Собор, *Khrestovozdvyzhenskyy Sobor*) was built from 1689 to 1709 right outside Poltava near the village of **Chervonyy Shlyakh** (Червоний Шлях) It's the only existing seven-domed Ukrainian Baroque structure in Ukraine.

The restaurant *Poltava*, in the Motel Poltava, 6 km (3.7 miles) west of the center on Radnarkomivska Street, has an international reputation. Based on a survey of tourists' opinions, *Poltava* was named one of the 100 best restaurants in the world in an international gastronomic Grand Prix competition in Madrid in 1991.

Dnipropetrovsk (Дніпропетровськ) is the country's third largest city with a population roughly 1,175,000. It was founded in 1787 by Prince Potyomkin on the site of a Zaporozhzhian village of Polovysia. Industrial development began with the laying of a railroad line in the 1870s that linked the city with the industrial centers of the Donets Basin. Today it's one of the largest metallurgical and machine-building centers of Ukraine and an important river port and rail center.

Despite its pollution, Dnipropetrovsk is an attractive-looking city with its parks and green areas and beautiful stretch of river. It has a large university, an opera and ballet theater, several drama theaters, a philharmonic, an organ music hall, a circus, and a planetarium. Bisected by the river Dnipro, the city center is on the right bank. The main thoroughfare is the lively Avenue of Karl Marx, a beautiful wide street lined by acacia trees. At the east end is the **Yavornytsky Museum of History,** worth a visit. Highlights are its archeological department with its collection of stone *baba* figures; its Kozak-era objects; and its "Battle for the Dnipro" diorama. In a separate building are tapestries and paintings. **Shevchenko City Park** lies below on the slopes of the riverbank. A skylift links the city to the park and a large island in the river with its beach.

Zaporizhska Region The Zaporizhska (Запоріжська) oblast in southeastern Ukraine extends south to the Sea of Azov. The name comes from the phrase *za porohamy* (за порогами) or "beyond the rapids," referring to the spot past a series of rapids on the Dnipro where navigation was possible. The name also referred to the territory inhabited by a particular organization of Kozaks from the mid-16th century to 1775. The Zaporizhzhyan frontier grew as a result of Ukrainians fleeing serfdom. They established homesteads and built fortified camps called *sichi* (січі) to defend themselves against Tatar raids. The camps were later united to create a central fortress, the *Zaporizhska Sich* (Запоріжська Січ). The *Sich* was the embryonic form of the independent Kozak state.

As well as Kozak lore, the Zaporizhska region has some significant older items of interest. In **Melitopol** (Мелітополь), 110 km (67 miles) south of the city of Zaporizhzhya, a Scythian royal burial mound from the 4th to 3rd century B.C. was excavated in 1954. The remains of a noble couple and a slave as well as 4,000 artifacts, including much gold and silver, were uncovered. The collection is in the Museum of Historical Treasures of Ukraine in Kyiv. Across the Dnipro from Zaporizhzhya, heading west to the village of **Verkhnya Khortytsya** (Верхня Хортиця), is the site of a 700-year old oak tree that died in 1995. The historic tree stood about 36.5 m (120 feet) high with a trunk diameter of almost 7 meters (23 feet) and was said to have sheltered Bohdan Khmelnytsky and his Kozak troops while planning their battle strategy.

Zaporizhzhya (Запоріжжя), a city of 897,000 on the left (east) bank of the Dnipro, is the capital of the region. Rebuilt after World War II, the city has modern architecture and wide tree-lined wide streets. The city is an educational and research center and has an array of cultural facilities. Even with its scenic and cultural attractions, Zaporizhzhya's overwhelming impression is that of a dirty, polluted city, with huge smokestacks spewing out black clouds of smoke. The city's gigantic industrial complex owes its existence to the massive steel and concrete Dnipro Hydroelectric Station dam. Built from 1927 to 1932 with the help of Canadian and American engineers, the dam was the USSR's first hydroelectric dam and provided energy for Zaporizhzhya's extensive industrial growth. Partly destroyed in World War II, it was rebuilt and expanded. The area also has nuclear and fossil-fuel power plants.

Khortytsya (Хортиця) **Island,** southwest of Zaporizhzhya, is the largest island in the Dnipro River, covering an area of over 3,000 hectares (7,400 acres). The island was designated a historical-cultural preserve in 1965 for its important role in Ukrainian history. Attracted by the natural fortress formed by the island's steep and rocky perimeter, freedom-loving Kozaks established Khortytsya as their base camp against various invaders in the late 15th century. From here the Kozaks ruled south central and northeastern Ukraine for over 150 years. Hetman Bohdan Khmelnytsky launched his anti-Polish war from here in 1648 and in the 1660's and 1670's the otaman I. Sirko used Khortytsya Island as his military base. The Kozaks held the island until the *Zaporizhska Sich* was destroyed in 1775 by the Russian Army on orders of Catherine II.

The rocky north end of the island contains most of the Kozak remnants. Remains of the *Sich* fortifications include a fortress and a shipyard built in 1737 during the Russo-Turkish War. Natural formations on the island hold many legends: **Durna Skelya** (Дирна Скеля) is the cliff where Kozaks were punished; **Chorna Skelya** (Чорна Скеля) is a cliff where the Kyivan Prince Svyatoslav was killed by the Pechenegs in 972. On **Mala (Small) Khortytsya Island,** 10 km (6 miles) north, are remains of some of the earliest fortifications, dating from the 1550s.

The **Zaporizhski Kozaks Historical Museum,** on the site of the Kozak docks at the north end of Khortytsya Island, contains everyday items of the Kozaks. The museum is closed Mondays. Next to it is a recent memorial mound honoring all those who died for Ukraine's freedom. Other popular tourist attractions are gala traditional dinners with folk shows at the hotel *Zaphorizhzhya* in Zaphorizhzhya; a ride on a *chayka* (чайка), a canoe-like Kozak boat; a several-day excursion down the Dnipro on a large, motorized *chayka,* including fishing and visiting villages and historical sites; and a visit to the Orlovaky horse-breeding farm and a Kozak equestrian show.

Kharkiv (Харків) was founded in 1656 by the Zaporozhzhian Kozak, Kharko. Today it's Ukraine's second largest city with 1.6 million residents. Only 40 km (25 miles) from the Russian border, Kharkiv is a highly Russified city. About 94 percent of the residents speak Russian, while some 71 percent are fluent in Ukrainian. Russian is the language heard most often in public, although street signs are now mostly in Ukrainian. The city council approved many new street names, but the new street signs are going up slowly.

Although not a major tourist destination, Kharkiv is worth a visit. It's pleasant, spacious, and attractive. Its rich academic and cultural life earns it the nickname "the Boston of Ukraine." It has more than 20 institutes of higher learning, the most prominent being Kharkiv University, as well as outstanding professional theaters, museums, and scores of libraries. Within its 272 sq. km (105 sq. miles) are more than 100 parks. Compared to Kyiv, accommodations and shopping are a bargain. Hotels cost $35–$80 per night. Most are rather mediocre, but the **Hotel Kyivsky**, 4 Kultury Street, is topnotch. Prices, quality, and the selection of handicrafts in Kharkiv are better than in Kyiv. Domestic planes link Kharkiv with many Ukrainian cities, and the airport is under reconstruction to become an international one.

From 1919 to 1934, when it served as the capital of Soviet Ukraine, Kharkiv was intensely developed. Many industries were established, apartments built, and public transportation extended. Ukrainian academic and cultural life also flourished during this period: important scientific institutions were established; museums and theaters erected; and writers' and artists' associations formed. With the rise of Stalin, not only was Ukrainian cultural life suppressed in Kharkiv, a wave of persecution against the Ukrainian intelligentsia originated here. Much historic architecture, including many baroque churches, was senselessly destroyed to make way for government buildings. After the capital was transferred to Kyiv in 1934, Kharkiv lost much of its Ukrainian character.

During World War II, the city was hotly contested and suffered extensive damage. The Germans occupied it for 22 months, during which time they killed 100,000 people and forcefully sent another 60,000 to Germany as laborers. After the war, the city was rebuilt with broad streets, large apartment blocks, and massive administrative and office buildings

Kharkiv's main thoroughfare — and street to stroll — is **Sumska** (Сумська) **Street**, an old street with many beautiful buildings, lovely parks, lots of small cafes, some restaurants and souvenir shops. North of the city center and extending west to Klochkivska (Клочківська) Street is **Shevchenko Park**, which includes a zoo. The north edge of the park faces the massive **Independence Square** (площа Свободи, *ploshcha Svobody*), also known as *ploshcha Nezalezhnosti*. The huge crescent-shaped building that edges the north of the park facing the square is **Kharkiv University**.

While church architecture does not dominate Kharkiv, there are several noted churches. The **Cathedral of the Holy Protectress** (Покровська, *Pokrovska*) is at 8 Universytetska (Університецька) Street, through the arch entryway. The church and its bell tower were built in 1689 as part of the original fortress settlement. The white stone church is in the style of a typical wooden Ukrainian church. Adjoining the church is the former bishop's residence, built in the Classical style in 1820.

Farther down the street is a Kharkiv landmark, the 89 meter (292 feet) high bell tower of the **Uspensky Cathedral**. The golden-domed brick cathedral adjacent to it was built in the baroque style from 1771 to 1778. The church is now used for organ concerts.

Going west across the Lopan (Лопаи) River to Blahovishchenska (Благовіщенська, formerly Karl Marx) Square is the striking-looking principal Orthodox church in Kharkiv. **Blahovishchenskyy Cathedral** was constructed from 1881 to 1901 of dark red and cream bricks in an alternating striped pattern. Architecture and motifs were based on the Hagia Sofia Cathedral in Istanbul. The church is worth a visit for the beauty of its interior as well as its choir singing.

The **Kharkiv Art Museum**, located at 11 Radnarkomivska (Раднаркомівська) Street, is one of the most important in Ukraine. Founded in 1920, the museum has nearly 20,000 works exhibited in 25 halls. The painting division is the strongest: it encompasses medieval murals, 16th to 19th century icons, portraits, folk paintings, and 20th century painting. A self-portrait by Taras Shevchenko is on display. A gallery devoted to the works of late 19th century realist I. Repin, includes his famous work, *The Zaporizhski Kozaks Write a Letter to the Sultan*. The museum is open daily except Tuesday from 10 a.m. until 5.30 p.m.

Kharkiv Historical Museum, 10 Universytetska (Університетска) Street, has holdings of 200,000 items. Its exhibits include articles from archeological discoveries in eastern Ukraine and from the early history of Kharkiv, as well as numismatic, ethnographic, and weaponry exhibits. Open 10 a.m. to 6 p.m. daily; Fridays open noon to 8 p.m.

For the performing arts, there's the **Lysenko Theater of Opera and Ballet** at 31 Sumska (Сумська) Street; **T. Shevchenko Kharkiv Ukrainian Drama Theater**, 9 Susmka Street; and **Pushkin Russian Drama Theater** at 7 Skrypnyk (Скрипника) Street.

Kharkiv has some good shops for gifts, crafts and souvenirs. *Salon Arka*, 48 Sumska Street, has lacquer boxes, stacking dolls, painted eggs, rings, and earrings. *Salon Kramnytsya*, 52 Pushkinska Street, features wood carved boxes, paintings, traditional embroidery and knitware. *Vernisazh*, 11 Sumska Street, has lacquer boxes, miniature paintings, decorations, fancy earthenware, and paintings. *Ukrainskyy Suveniry*, 3 Moskovskyy Avenue, has a good selection of embroidery, wood carving, and painted boxes.

Donbas Area The Donbas, also called the Donets Basin, is an area about 60,000 square km (23,170 square miles) that contains one of the largest coal deposits in the world. The region is a vital fuel source for Ukraine, producing about half of its coal, and it is an important industrial region of Ukraine. Straddling the Ukraine-Russia border with two-thirds of it lying on the Ukrainian side, the Donbas region has been heavily Russified. **Donetsk** (Донецьк), population 1,121,000 is the primary city of the Donbas urban cluster and a regional center. It's the largest center of metallurgy and coal mining in Ukraine and has hundreds of industrial enterprises, primarily machine-building and chemicals. On its outskirts, the city doesn't seem very enticing with the huge pyramids of coal that surround it, but Donetsk is surprisingly one of the greenest cities in Ukraine with many thousands of acres of park land and gardens in the center, criss-crossed by wide tree-lined boulevards.

Donetsk is a large center of learning and culture. It has five institutions of higher learning, and several dozen specialized secondary schools. The main street, **Artem Street** (вулиця Артема, *vulytsy Artema*), is five miles long and contains the city's main administrative and cultural buildings.

Performing arts in Donetsk include the **Opera and Ballet Theater**, 72 Artem Street; **Ukrainian Theater of Music and Drama**, 74-a Artem Street; **Puppet Theater**, 18 Illich Avenue (проспект Ілліча, *prospekt Illicha*); **Philharmonic**, 117 Postyshev Street (вулиця Постишева, *vulytsya Postysheva*), and a circus. **The Museum of Fine Arts** is at 35 Pushkin Boulevard and there's a 280-hectare (692-acre) **Botanical Garden** near the city center.

Folk Art Centers

Ukraine is a treasure trove of folk arts, but two regions of the country are particularly renowned. In western Ukraine are several centers of Hutsul crafts: **Kosiv** (Косів) in is in the piney woods of the Carpathian Mountains about 115 km (71 miles) from the city Ivano-Frankivsk. In the 19th century Kosiv was noted for its production of painted tile stoves.

Today it's a center of Hutsul folk art, and has a technical school that trains artisans in applied folk handicrafts. Finely carved and inlaid wood, metal and leather works, weavings, embroidery, and pottery can be found in the huge open air market every Saturday and Tuesday.

Nearby is **Vyzhnytsya** (Вижниця) on the Cheremosh river, about 86 km (50 miles) west of Chernivtsi. The Applied Arts Building was founded at the turn of the century to teach wood carving. It's also a center for weavers, embroiderers, and designers.

In the Poltavska oblast, several small towns are noted for their folk crafts: **Velyki Sorochyntsi** (Великі Сорочинці) is a village of about 5,000 on the Psel (Псел) River in the Myrhorod district of the Poltavska oblast. Every year on the last weekend of August, embroiderers, carpet makers, wood carvers, and potters sell their wares at the famous Sorochynskyy Fair. **Opishnya** (Опішня), a village on the Poltava-Hadyach (Полтава-Гадяч) Road, 43 km (27 miles) north of Poltava, is famous for its earthenware. Archeological excavations have unearthed semi-pit dwellings with clay ovens dating from the late 8th to 9th century. A ceramics factory makes tableware with traditional decorations, animal figures, and clay toys. Every year the village sets aside a Sunday in June to celebrate the holiday of potters. Opishnya masters of the biligreed technique demonstrate the procedure to visitors. Articles of embroidery and other items are also on display. **Reshetylivka** (Решетилівка), a small town and district center on the Hovtva (Говтва) River is about 34 km (21 miles) east of Poltava on the road toward Kohrol (Когрол). Its factories specialize in traditional *kylyms*, woven cloths, embroidered shirts, blouses, tablecloths, napkins, and *rushnyky*, or towels. One of the factories has a museum and shop. In the Dnipropetrovska oblast, the village **Petrykivka** (Петриківка) was known since the 18th century for its distinctive paintings of stylized floral and plant motifs that decorated traditional stoves, whitewashed house walls, and door and window frames. Today, Petrykivka painting is applied to various forms of decorative arts by craftsmen of the Museum of Applied Art in Petrykivka.

CHAPTER 27: Crimea

CRIMEA   Крим   krihm

The Crimean Autonomous Republic occupies a peninsula about the size of the state of Maryland; geographically the land mass is an extension of Ukraine, while historically it has a greater association with Tatar peoples, and later, with Russia.

The northern three-quarters is semi-arid steppe land cultivated with wheat, corn, and sunflowers. South of Simferopol, the capital city, the plains rise into the high pastures and forests of the **Crimean Mountains**. These reach a height of 1500 meters (5,000 feet) before dropping away to a narrow coastal strip of stony beaches. Most of the two-and-one-half million inhabitants of the Crimean Peninsula live in the cities and towns that ring the Black Sea coast, especially along the peninsula's southern edge. Crimea is a major tourist resort, famous for its perfect climate, scenic vistas, clear sea and pretty forested mountains.

History: Crimea was dominated by Turkey for centuries until Russia annexed it in 1783. From 1854 to 1856 it was a battleground of these two imperial powers, with the British and French siding with Turkey. In 1921 Crimea became an autonomous republic under the Russian SSR even though it shared no border with Russia. At that time it was populated largely by Tatars. During World War II, heavy fighting took place on Crimea. Following the three years of German occupation, Stalin falsely accused the Tatars of collaboration, deported them, and transferred the area to the Russian S.F.S.R. In 1954 Crimea was awarded to Ukraine in commemoration of the 300th anniversary of Russian-Ukrainian unity. After the break-up of the Soviet Union in 1991, it became an independent state within the boundaries of Ukraine.

Language and Tourism: Ethnic Russians constitute a little more than two-thirds of the 2.7 million inhabitants of the Crimea. About 20 percent are Ukrainian. The number of Tatars, who have started to return following Ukrainian independence, is about eight percent and increasing. There are also Armenian, Greek, German, and Bulgarian communities. For the most part, Russian is the language spoken and seen in public. Skyrocketing inflation and Crimea's uncertain political climate have put a damper on tourism, so plenty of hotel rooms are available. The

Crimean Republican Council of Ministers adopted a resolution which introduces mandatory registration of all non-residents visiting the peninsula. The move is reportedly aimed at controlling migration processes and fighting organized crime, but no doubt will help bolster the Crimean treasury.

Crimean tours usually start and end with a visit to the area's regional capital and crossroads, **Simferopol** (Сімферополь), a city of 346,000 on the Salhyr (Салгир) River. Simferopol has a pleasing tropical ambience. Remnants of the old Tatar quarter with its narrow winding streets and Oriental buildings lend an exotic touch. There's a university, numerous research institutes, theaters of Ukrainian music and drama, Russian drama, a philharmonic orchestra, and a circus. Simferopol is a major rail and road junction, linked by train to major cities in Ukraine and Russia. In Simferopol, the main highway splits into scenic winding roads through the Crimean Mountains to the popular coastal resorts. A trolley, several cars long, runs frequently from Simferopol's railroad station to Yalta via Alushta. The trolley ride to Yalta takes about two and one-half hours.

Most of the shops, cafes, and tourist attractions are centered around Karl Marx and Pushkin Streets and Kirov Prospekt. Kirov crosses an attractive city park on the banks of the river. The leading attraction is **Neapolis,** a 20-ha (50 acre) excavation less than a mile southeast from the city center between Vorovsky and Krasnoarmeyskaya streets. Neapolis was a Scythian town from the 2nd century B.C. to the 4th century A.D. when it was abandoned after attacks by the Goths and Huns. Excavations starting in 1827 uncovered a thick-walled city containing stone buildings, some ornamented with tiles and frescoes. A royal mausoleum with burial chambers dug into the rock formations contains the graves of 72 Scythian noblemen with gold ornaments and weapons.

Bakhchysaray (Бахчисарай), 33 km (20 miles) southwest of Simferopol, is a small town that for centuries served as the capital of the Crimean Khannat (Tatar Moslem state). The **Khan's Palace** was constructed by Ukrainian and Russian captives in 1519, destroyed later by fire, and rebuilt in 1787 when Crimea was annexed to Russia. Now the center of the **Bakhchysaray Historical and Archeological Museum,** the palace complex includes the original harem, mosque, and cemetery and assorted structures. In the inner courtyard is the city's landmark, the white marble Fountain of Tears, built in memory of the last khan's lost love.

Several miles outside of Bakhchysaray, beyond the village of Staroselye, is one of the Crimea's largest cave settlements. **Chufut-Kale** was carved out of limestone bluffs, perhaps as early as the sixth century. Over the centuries it was inhabited by many different peoples. The name Chufut-Kale, Hebrew for city, comes from its last regular inhabitants, a dissident Jewish sect called the Karaites. The ruins are part of the Bakhchysaray Historical and Archeological Museum and include numerous cave dwellings, defensive walls, a Tatar mausoleum from 1437, the ruins of a mosque, and two temples, one with Hebrew inscriptions. Across the valley, the Monastery of Dormition, which flourished from the 8th to 19th centuries, shows the mystical element of Ukrainian Christianity. Both the churches and monks' cells were carved out of a sheer rock face. Some of the monks had themselves lowered into isolated caves to spend the rest of their days in silent prayer.

To the south is **Sevastopol,** a picturesque port city with white limestone buildings set on broad tree-lined avenues. After Russia annexed Crimea in 1783, Catherine II ordered the fortress and navel port built as a base for the Russian Black Sea Fleet. Ownership of the fleet — and control of the city — is claimed by both Ukraine and Russia. Its current sensitive political situation puts it off limits to casual tourists.

Just 16 km (10 miles) south of the city is **Balaklava** (Балаклава), site in 1854 of an indecisive battle of the Crimean War that English poet Alfred Lord Tennyson immortalized in his poem, "Charge of the Light Brigade." Balaklava is also officially closed to foreigners.

RESORT TOWNS

Crimea's main attraction is its Mediterranean-like coastal strip, particularly along the southeast. Here the Crimean Mountains culminate in their highest peaks and extend nearly to the Black Sea, a salt water sea that is clear and clean. (Both the shore and bottom are rocky, so swimmers need good foot protection.) The narrow strip (1 to 7 miles wide) of cypress-dotted lowland with interesting rock formations jutting out over the sea is interspersed with charming resort cities and towns, all linked by a main highway. The nucleus of the shoreline is **Yalta** (Ялта), and to its east and west are parks and gardens, palaces, and numerous resorts and sanataria for respiratory ailments.

Lower mountain slopes along the coast are covered with vineyards. This region produces some superb wines, and is especially renowned for its sweet and dessert wines. Muscat is the most important grape variety grown; others are Cabernet, Pinot Gris, and Reisling. Altogether 43 branded wines come from Crimea's southeastern coast, including reds, whites, rosés, and fortified wines. Other important crops are tobacco and flowers for local perfumeries.

The Simferopol—Yalta Road extends about 97 km (60 miles) through a scenic high pass in the Crimean Mountains. Near the halfway point on the road is **Alushta** (Алушта), the Crimea's second largest seaside resort. Alushta is an ideal base for those who want to explore the mountains. Accessible from here are Mount Demerdzhi, 1,219 meters (4,000 feet) above sea level, and the finest waterfall in the Crimean Mountains, the Dzhur-Dzhur Waterfall. Extending west toward the town of Masandra (Масандра) is Alushta's biggest attraction, the 30,000-hectare (70,000-acre) **Crimean National Nature Preserve**. Dedicated to protecting the forest and its native flora and fauna, the Preserve contains a variety of Crimean animals, such as mouflons, gazelles, and foxes.

Along the Yalta—Alushta Highway 18 km (11 miles) east of Yalta is **Hurzuf** (Гурзуф), a village of winding streets and old wooden houses that's a popular retreat of artists and writers. About 6 km (4 miles) east of Yalta on the outskirts of Masandra is the **Nikitskyy Botanical Gardens**. The Gardens were established in 1812 on a square mile of terraced hillside extending to the sea. There are 28,000 plant varieties. The view is most scenic from the Upper Park, which contains what may be the world's largest rose collection, with approximately 2,000 cultivars. **Masandra** is where Crimean wine production started in 1785. The Central Research Institute of Viticulture and Viniculture located here has worked to improve thousands of grape hybrids from Algerian, French, Italian, Hungarian, and Syrian vines. Connected with the institute is the main winery of the **Masandra Wine-Making Complex**, a combine of area wineries that produces 29 branded wines. Tastings can be arranged for tour groups.

Yalta (Ялта) was a Greek colony named Yalita in the first century B.C., and over the centuries passed through many hands. It came under Russian control in 1783 with the Russian annexation of Crimea. In 1823 Prince M. Vorontsov decided to build up Yalta as the major settlement of the Crimean south shore. The prince's choice was ideal. Yalta is situated on a gently curving bay that shields it from the north winds. Its swimming season lasts from June to October; summers are never uncomfortable, and winters are often mild enough for roses to bloom through December. The fragrance of magnolia and roses wafts among the palm trees and the slopes leading up to the mountains are ideal for vineyards and orchards.

The area's opulent summer estates and gardens were built by various noblemen. Artists and writers, attracted by the peaceful beauty, found their inspiration here. Anton Chekhov wrote *The Cherry Orchard* and *Three Sisters* here; Mark Twain found Yalta "a beautiful spot" that reminded him of the Sierras; Maxim Gorky, Leo Tolstoy, Sergei Rachmaninov spent time here, and noted Ukrainian poet Lesya Ukrayinka came here seeking a cure for her tuberculosis. The city isn't just a playground. It has research institutes for the study of grape growing and wine production and for the therapeutic properties of the climate. Wine-making, fruit-canning, and tobacco-processing are the chief industries.

As the nucleus of the resort area, Yalta is well-linked to neighboring towns by bus, trolleybus, or ferry. The main street of the tourist section, **Lenin Embankment** (Набережна Леніна, *Naberezhna Lenina*), is a seaside promenade with shops, restaurants, hotels, and the post office. Shops are typically small and sell a little bit of everything. Street vendors sell ice cream, post cards, flowers, and such local handcrafted items as scenic oil and watercolor paintings and wooden jewelry from native trees.

There are two outstanding hotels, the **Oreanda** and the **Yalta,** and a number of others that are less grand. Side streets lead up to the mountains. Litkens Street, near the motor boat harbor begins with a state wine-tasting establishment, nearby is the **Chekhov Theater** and the **Yalta Philharmonic.** A skylift near the center behind the **Solchi Cafe** gives a 10-minute ride over the rooftops to a mountain lookout.

Chekhov Museum, 112 Kirova (Кірова) Street, is the two-story white house which Chekhov built and in which he spent the final years of his life. On display are the house, garden, editions of his works, and personal effects. The **Armenian Church** on Zahorodna (Загородна) Street, built from 1909 to 1917, is noted for its medieval-style architecture.

Heading west on the Yalta — Sevastopol Highway are some of the area's main attractions. Three km (1.8 miles) from Yalta is **Livadiya** (Лівадія) where the Russian royal family first started building a summer retreat in

1860. Among the 60 structures, the centerpiece is the White or **Grand Palace** built for Nicholas II in 1911 in an Italian Renaissance style. The palace was the location of the 1945 Yalta conference in which Stalin, Churchill, and Roosevelt planned the post-war order of Europe. The palace is open for viewing and has a lovely park. Ten km (6 miles) west of Yalta at **Haspra** (Гаспра, formerly *Miskhor*, Мисхор) is that quintessential image of Crimea, **Swallow's Nest** (*Lastivchyne Hnizdo*, Ластівчине Гніздо). This scale model recreation of a medieval Danube castle was commissioned by a German baron in 1912. Sitting on top of a sheer cliff overlooking Ay-Todor Cape, Swallow's Nest contains a restaurant. Nearby are the ruins of a 2,000-year-old Roman fortress. Regular excursion boats to Swallow's Nest from downtown Yalta leave from the harbor by the Diana Casino-Hotel.

At **Alupka** (Алупка), 17 km (10 miles) west of Yalta, is Crimea's most spectacular estate, the **Vorontsov Palace and Park**. Designed by noted British architect Edward Blore for the immensely wealthy, English-educated Count Mikhail Vorontsov, the palace was built over an 18-year period starting in 1832. On the exterior, the palace is an odd conglomeration of styles — the entrance resembles a Scottish castle and the seaside facade is Arabic. Within its 150 rooms is a museum containing 19th-century furniture, porcelain and crystal, rare books, and paintings by western European, Russian, and Ukrainian masters. A 40-hectare (100-acre) hillside park with hundreds of exotic plants and trees surround the palace.

CHAPTER 28. REFERENCE SECTION

REVISED ENGLISH SPELLING FOR UKRAINIAN PLACE NAMES

In 1989 the Ukrainian Parliament adopted legislation to Ukrainianize the names of cities and towns, that is, to use their historic Ukrainian names. (Russian names are still generally used in Crimea.) The following English-language transliterations of the oblast capitals and other noted places have been adopted by the United States Board on Geographical Names, an official U.S. government body. All major map publishers are now using the US BGN transliterations in their new maps and atlases.

City Name (Former Name) *Ukrainian Spelling*

Country

Ukraine, Ukrayina (the Ukraine) Україна

Capital

Kyiv or Kyyiv (Kiev) Київ

Autonomous Crimean Republic Capital

Simferopol (Simferopol) Сімферополь

Capital Cities of Oblasts (Regions)

With the exception of Lutsk and Uzhhorod in western Ukraine, all oblast capital cities have the same name as their regions.

Name (Former Name)	Spelling in Ukrainian	Oblast Name
Cherkasy (Cherkassy)	Черкаси	Cherkaska
Chernihiv (Chernigov)	Чернігів	Chernihivska
Chernivtsi (Chernovtsy)	Чернівці	Chernivetska
Dnipropetrovsk (Dnepropetrovsk)	Дніпропетровськ	Dnipropetrovska
Donetsk (Donetsk)	Донецьк	Donetska
Ivano-Frankivsk (Ivano-Frankovsk)	Івано-Франківськ	Ivano-Frankivska
Kharkiv (Kharkov)	Харків	Kharkivska

Kyiv or Kyyiv (Kiev)	Київ	Kyivska
Kherson (Kherson)	Херсон	Khersonska
Khmelnytskyy		
(Khmel'nitskiy)	Хмельницький	Khmelnytska
Kirovohrad (Kirovograd)	Кіровоград	Kirovohradska
Luhansk (Lugansk)	Луганськ	Luhanska
Lutsk (Lutsk)	Луцьк	Volynska
Lviv (L'vov)	Львів	Lvivska
Mykolayiv (Nikolayev)	Миколаїв	Mykolayivska
Odesa (Odessa)	Одеса	Odeska
Poltava (Poltava)	Полтава	Poltavska
Rivne (Rovno)	Рівне	Rovenska
Sumy (Sumy)	Суми	Sumska
Ternopil (Ternopol)	Тернопіль	Ternopilska
Uzhhorod (Uzgorod)	Ужгород	Zakarpatska
Vinnytsya (Vinnitsa)	Вінниця	Vinnytska
Zaporizhzhya		
(Zaporozh'ye)	Запоріжжя	Zaporizhska
Zhytomyr (Zhitomir)	Житомир	Zhytomyrska

Other Noted Place Names

Bila Tserkva (Belaya Tserkov')	Біла Церква
Chornobyl (Chernobyl)	Чорнобиль
Dnipro (Dnieper)	Дніпро
Kolomyya (Kolomyya)	Коломия
Kaniv (Kanev)	Канів
Kryvyy Rih (Krivoy Rog)	Кривий Ріг
Mukacheve (Mukachevo)	Мукачеве
Sevastopol (Sevastopol)	Севастополь
Uman (Uman)	Умань
Yalta (Yalta)	Ялта

UKRAINIAN NAMES

While a last name does not positively reveal ethnic identity, and though there is some overlap between Ukrainian names and those of other Slavic groups, there are certain signs that a name may be of Ukrainian origin. Ukrainian names are often short and some have only one syllable. Names ending in *-ko* tend to be Ukrainian; in eastern Ukraine, many end in *-enko*. In western Ukraine, many names end in *-chuk* or *-iak* or *-iuk*.

Like English, Ukrainian names have their origin in occupations, and common objects or concepts such as colors. Thus Melnyk (Мельник) is miller; Chumak (Чумак) is carter; Bily (Білий) is white; and Svoboda (Свобода) is freedom. Animal names are also common surnames: Vovk (Вовк), sometimes spelled Wowk, is wolf. Generally, Ukrainian names are more fanciful than English surnames: Skovoroda (Сковорода), the name of the 18th century Ukrainian philosopher, means "frying pan;" Smetana (Сметана) — a name Ukrainians share with the Czech composer — means "sour cream," Mak (Мак) is "poppy," and we've even known a Neyizhsalo (Неїжсало) or "don't eat lard."

PUBLIC HOLIDAYS

On public holidays there is no school, and the post office and shops are closed. Only essential services such as medical and transportation services operate.

When the soviet period ended, a few of the traditional religious holidays became public holidays. The day on which Ukraine declared its independence in 1991 was also recognized. There's been some debate whether holidays that were established under soviet rule should still be observed, even though their meaning is not political. These are the current public holidays in Ukraine, but the list may still be amended:

January 1	New Year's Day
January 7	Christmas
March 8	International Women's Day
May 9	Victory in Europe Day
August 24	Independence Day

In addition, Easter and Holy Trinity are holidays that always fall on Sunday. Many celebrate the Orthodox New Year on January 14, but it's not an official national holiday. Note that the religious holidays are observed according to the Old Style or Julian Calendar, although in everyday life the Gregorian calendar is used.

NUMBERS

Cardinal Numbers

0	нуль	nool'
1	один (*m.*), одна (*f.*), одно (*n.*)	o-DIHN, od-NAH, od-NO

2	два (*m., n.*), дві (*f.*)	dvah, dvee
3	три	trih
4	чотири	cho-TIH-rih
5	п'ять	p'yat'
6	шість	sheest'
7	сім	seem
8	вісім	VEE-seem
9	дев'ять	DEHV'-yat'
10	десять	deh-SYAT'
11	одинадцять	o-dih-NAHD-tsyat'
12	дванадцять	dvah-NAHD-tsyat'
13	тринадцять	trih-NAHD-tsyat'
14	чотирнадцять	cho-tihr-NAHD-tsyat'
15	п'ятнадцять	p'yat-NAHD-tsyat'
16	шістнадцять	sheest-NAHD-tsyat'
17	сімнадцять	seem-NAHD-tsyat'
18	вісімнадцять	vee-seem-NAHD-tsyat'
19	дев'ятнадцять	dehv'-yat-NAHD-tsyat'
20	двадцять	DVAHD-tsyat'
21	двадцять один	DVAHD-tsyat' o-DIHN
22	двадцять два	DVAHD-tsyat' dvah
23	двадцять три	DVAHD-tsyat' trih
24	двадцять чотири	DVAHD-tsyat' cho-TIH-rih
25	двадцять п'ять	DVAHD-tsaht' p'yat'
26	двадцять шість	DVAHD-tsyat' sheest'
27	двадцять сім	DVAHD-tsyat' seem
28	двадцять вісім	DVAHD-tsyat' VEE-seem
29	двадцять дев'ять	DVAHD-tsyat' DEHV'-yat'
30	тридцять	TRIHD-tsyat'
31	тридцять один	TRIHD-tsyat' o-DIHN
32	тридцять два	TRIHD-tsyat' dvah
33	тридцять три	TRIHD-tsyat' trih
40	сорок	SO-rok
50	п'ятдесять	p'yat-deh-SYAT'
60	шістдесять	sheest-deh-SYAT'
70	сімдесять	seem-deh-SYAT'
80	вісімдесять	vee-seem-deh-SYAT'
90	дев'ятносто	dehv-ya-NOS-to
100	сто	sto
150	сто п'ятдесять	sto p'yat-deh-SYAT'
175	сто сімдесять п'ять	sto seem-DEH-syat' p'yat'

200	двісті	DVEES-tee
300	триста	TRIHS-tah
400	чотириста	cho-TIH-rihs-tah
500	п'ятсот	p'yat-SOT
600	шістсот	sheest-SOT
700	сімсот	seem-SOT
800	вісімсот	vee-see-SOT
900	дев'ятсот	dehv'yat-SOT
1,000	тисяча	TIH-sya-chah
1,100	тисяча сто	TIH-sya-chah sto
1,500	тисяча п'ятсот	TIH-sya-chah p'yat-SOT
2,000	дві тисячі	dvee TIH-sya-chee
5,000	п'ять тисяч	p'yat' TIH-syach
10,000	десять тисяч	DEH-syat' TIH-syach
100,000	сто тисяч	sto TIH-syach
1,000,000	мільйон	meel'-ŸON

Ordinal Numbers

Ordinal numbers are adjectives and change their endings according to gender, number, and case. Here are the forms for the nominative singular, for masculine, feminine, and neuter, respectively

first	перший, перша, перше	PEHR-shihў, PEHR-shah, PEHR-sheh
second	другий, друга, друге	DROO-hihў, DROO-hah, DROO-heh
third	третій, третя, трете	TREH-teeў, TREH-tya, TREH-tyeh
fourth	четверт(ий) (-а) (-е)	cheht-VEHR-(tihў), (-tah), (-teh)
fifth	п'ят(ий) (-а) (-е)	P'YA-(tihў), (-tah), (-teh)
sixth	шост(ий) (-а) (-е)	SHOS-(tihў), (-tah), (-teh)
seventh	сьом(ий) (-а) (-е)	S'O-(mihў), (-mah), (-meh)
eighth	восьм(ий) (-а) (-е)	VOS'-(mihў), (-mah), (-meh)
ninth	дев'ят(ий) (-а) (-е)	deh-V'YA-(tihў), (-tah), (-teh)
tenth	десят(ий) (-а) (-е)	deh-SYA-(tihў), (-tah), (-teh)
twelfth	дванадцят(ий) (-а) (-е)	dvah-NAHD-tsya-(tihў), (-tah), (-teh)
fifteenth	п'ятнадцят(ий) (-а) (-е)	p'yat-NAHD-tsya-(tihў), (-tah), (-teh)
twentieth	двадцят(ий) (-а) (-е)	dvah-TSYA-(tihў), (-tah), (-teh)
fortieth	сороков(ий) (-а) (-е)	so-ro-KO-(vihў), (-vah), (-veh)
hundredth	сот(ий) (-а) (-е)	SO-(tihў), (-tah), (-teh)

Other Numerical Expressions

once	один раз	o-DIHN rahz
twice	два рази	dvah rah-ZIH
three times	три рази	trih rah-ZIH
one plus three	один плюс три	o-DIHN plyus trih
nine minus six	дев'ять мінус шість	DEHV'-yat' MEE-noos sheest'
four times five	чотири помножити на п'ять	
	cho-TIH-rih pom-NO-zhih-tih nah p'yat'	
eight divided by two	вісім розділити на два	
	VEE-seem roz-dee-LIH-tih nah dvah	

TIME

Time Zones. All of Ukraine is in a single time zone, which is seven hours ahead of Eastern Standard Time in New York and Toronto and two hours ahead of Universal Time. Ukraine goes on daylight savings time starting the last Sunday of March and ending the last Sunday of October.

The 24 Hour Clock. Timetables, official notices, and tickets for events and travel in Ukraine use the European or military system of numbering the hours of the day from 0 to 24. Figuring 0 for midnight, noon is 12, 1:00 p.m. is 13, 2:00 p.m. is 14, etc. To convert the 24-hour system to the a.m.-p.m. system, to subtract 12 from the time. Thus a theater ticket that says 19:00 is for 7 p.m.

In common usage, Ukrainians divide the 24 hour day into four periods: morning, afternoon, evening, and night. The division between the periods is not absolute, and there may be a bit of overlap. Morning or ранку (RAHN-koo) starts at 3:00 or 4:00 a.m. and continues until 11:00 a.m. or noon. Afternoon or дня (dnya) is from 12:00 p.m. until 4:00 p.m. Evening or вечора (VEH-cho-rah) is from 5:00 p.m. until 11:00 p.m. and night or ночі (NO-chee) is from 12 a.m. or 1:00 a.m. until 3:00 or 4:00 a.m.

When verbally giving the time in Ukrainian, there are several ways to express a number, just as in English 2:45 can be "two forty-five," "quarter to three," or "fifteen minutes before three."

Here is the standard method of giving the hour and its divisions when speaking Ukrainian. Note that in some instances the words for "hour" or "minutes" are actually expressed, while in other uses they are implied.

1. For time on the hour, use the ordinals *first, second, third,* for *one, two, three,* along with the qualifying word for either "night, morning, day, or evening."

a.m.-p.m.	*24-hour time*	*Ukrainian term (24-hour system)*
1 a.m.	1.00	перша година ночі PEHR-sha ho-DIH-nah NO-chee
2 a.m.	2.00	друга година ночі DROO-hah ho-DIH-nah NO-chee
3 a.m.	3.00	третя година ночі TREH-tya ho-DIH-nah NO-chee (RAHN-koo)
4 a.m.	4.00	четверта година ранку cheht-VEHR-tah ho-DIH-nah RAHN-koo
5 a.m.	5.00	п'ята година ранку P'YA-tah ho-DIH-nah RAHN-koo
6 a.m.	6.00	шоста година ранку SHOS-tah ho-DIN-nah RAHN-koo
7 a.m.	7.00	сьома година ранку S'O-mah ho-DIH-nah RAHN-koo
8 a.m.	8.00	восьма година ранку VOS'-mah ho-DIH-nah RAHN-koo
9 a.m.	9.00	дев'ята година ранку dehv'-YA-tah ho-DIH-nah RAHN-koo
10 a.m.	10.00	десята година ранку deh-SYAH-tah ho-DIH-nah RAHN-koo
11 a.m.	11.00	одинадцята година (ранку) o-DIH-nahd-tsya-tah ho-DIH-nah (RAHN-koo)
12 noon	12.00	полудень po-LOO-dehn'
1 p.m.	13.00	перша година дня PEHR-shah ho-DIH-nah dnya
2 p.m.	14.00	друга година дня DROO-hah ho-DIH-nah dnya
3 p.m.	15.00	третя година дня TREHT-ya ho-DIH-nah dnya
4 p.m.	16.00	четверта година дня cheht-VEHR-tah ho-DIH-nah dnya
5 p.m.	17.00	п'ята година вечора P'YA-tah ho-DIH-nah VEH-cho-rah

6 p.m.	18.00	шоста година вечора
		SHOSH-tah ho-DIH-nah VEH-cho-rah
7 p.m.	19.00	сьома година вечора
		S'O-mah ho-DIH-nah VEH-cho-rah
8 p.m.	20.00	восьма година вечора
		VOS'-mah ho-DIH-nah VEH-cho-rah
9 p.m.	21.00	дев'ята година вечора
		dehv'-YA-tah ho-DIH-nah VEH-cho-rah
10 p.m.	22.00	десята година вечора
		deh-SYA-tah ho-DIH-nah VEH-cho-rah
11 p.m.	23.00	одинадцята година вечора
		o-DIH-nahd-tsya-tah ho-DIH-nah
		VEH-cho-rah
12 a.m.	24.00	північ
(midnight)		PEEV-neech

2. To express time from the exact hour to the half hour, the
construction literally means "number of minutes on the [next hour]" so
that 5:10 is "ten minutes on the sixth [hour]": (десять хвилин шостої,
DEH-syaht' khvih-LIHN SHOS-to-yee); 5:30 is expressed as "half on
the sixth [hour]" (пів шостої, peev SHOS-to-yee). The word "on" is not
expressed, but reflected in the case ending of the hour word. Here are
some other examples of telling time from the hour to the half:

1:05	п'ять хвилин другої	p'yat' khvih-LIHN DROO-ho-yee
2:05	п'ять хвилин третьої	p'yat' khvih-LIHN TREH-t'o-yee
3:05	п'ять хвилин четвертої	p'yat' khvih-LIHN
		cheht-VEHR-to-yee
4:05	п'ять хвилин п'ятої	p'yat' khvih-LIHN P'YA-to-yee
5:05	п'ять хвилин шостої	p'yat' khvih-LIHN SHOS-to-yee
6:05	п'ять хвилин сьомої	p'yat' khvih-LIHN S'O-mo-yee
7:05	п'ять хвилин восьмої	p'yat' khvih-LIHN VOS'-mo-yee
8:05	п'ять хвилин дев'ятої	p'yat' khvih-LIHN dehv'YA-to-yee
9:05	п'ять хвилин десятої	p'yat' khvih-LIHN dehs-YA-to-yee
10:05	п'ять одинадцятої	p'yat' o-dih-NAHD-tsya-to-yee
11:05	п'ять дванадцятої	p'yat' dvah-NAHD-tsya-to-yee

3. For time after the half hour but before the next exact hour, the
number of minutes until the approaching hour is expressed. Thus 5:35 is
expressed as "without twenty-five minutes of the sixth [hour]": (без

двадцяти п'яти шоста, behz dvahd-tsya-TIH p'ya-TIH shos-TAH). Note that this construction is the equivalent to the English language referring to 5:35 as "twenty-five minutes of six," or 6:50 as "ten minutes of seven." Here are some other examples of time before the hour:

5:35	без двадцяти п'яти шоста	behz dvahd-tsya'-TIH p'ya-TIH SHOS-tah
5:40	без двадцяти шоста	behz dvahd-tsya'-TIH SHOS-tah
5:45	без п'ятнадцяти шоста	behz p'yat-NAHD-tsya'-tih SHOS-tah
5:50	без десяти шоста	behz dehs-ya-TIH SHOS-tah
5:55	без п'яти шоста	behzh p'ya-TIH shos-TAH

4. For quarter past and quarter to the hour, чверть or "quarter" is often used.

quarter past two   чверть на третю ...
chvehrt' nah TREH-tyu
(literally, *"quarter on the third [hour]"*)

quarter to four   без чверті четверта ...
behz CHVEHR-tee cheht-VEHR-tah
(literally, *"quarter without the fourth [hour]"*)

5. For half past the hour, the construction is literally "half to the hour approaching."

half past three   пів четвертої
peevh cheht-VEHR-to-yee
(literally *"half to the fourth (hour)"*)

Other Points About Expressing Time

When you hear the time announced on Ukrainian radio or TV according to the 24-hour system, the number of the hour is simply followed by the number of minutes that have elapsed. Thus 7:35 p.m. will be announced as "nineteen hours and thirty-five minutes" (дев'ятнадцять годин тридцять п'ять хвилин). This is more direct and logical than the spoken vernacular; if you find it easier to express time by the official manner when conversing, go ahead and do so; while not idiomatic, it's perfectly acceptable and you will always be understood.

Note that when written numerically, a period is used rather than a colon to separate the minutes from the hours: 17.00, 17.12, 17.40, for example. Sometimes the minutes are written as a superscript and underlined: 17⁴⁰.

Basic Phrases and Questions Involving Time

My clock/watch stopped.
У мене зупинився годинник.
oo MEH-neh zoo-pih-NIHV-sya ho-DIH-nihk

I'm sorry I'm late.
Пробачте, я (запізнився, *m.*) (запізнилась, *f*).
pro-BAHCH-teh ya (zah-peez-NIHV-sya) (zah-peez-NIH-lahs')

What time is it now?	Котра тепер година? kot-RAH teh-PEHR ho-DIH-nah
It's (late) (early).	Це (пізно) (рано). tseh PEEZ-no (RAH-no)
This clock/watch is fast.	Цей годинник відстає. tsehў ho-DIHN-nihk veed-stah-YEH
My clock/watch is slow.	мій годинник спішить. meeў ho-DIHN-nihk spee-SHIHT'
What day is it today?	Який сьогодні день? ya-KIHУ s'o-HOD-nee dehn'
What's today's date?	Яке сьогодні число? ya-KEH s'o-HOD-nee chihs-LO

Hours and Minutes

hourly	кожну годину KOZ͡H-noo ho-DIH-noo
in ten minutes	через десять хвилин CHEH-rehz DEH-syat' khvih-LIHN
in a quarter of an hour	через п'ятнадцять хвилин CHEH-rehz p'yat-NAHD-tsyat' khvih-LIHN
in half an hour	через пів години CHEH-rehz peev ho-DIH-nih
in three quarters of an hour	через сорок п'ять хвилин CHEH-rehz SO-rok p'yat' khvih-LIHN

in an hour	через годину
	CHEH-rehz ho-DIH-noo
in two hours	через дві години
	CHEH-rehz dvee ho-DIH-noo
until what time?	до котрої години
	do ko-TRO-yee ho-DIH-nih

Days and Weeks

The names of the days are not capitalized in Ukrainian.

Today is ...	Сьогодні ...	s'o-HOD-nee ...
Monday	понеділок	po-neh-DEE-lok
Tuesday	вівторок	veev-TO-rok
Wednesday	середа	seh-reh-DAH
Thursday	четвер	cheht-VEHR
Friday	п'ятниця	P'YAHT-nih-tsya
Saturday	субота	soo-BO-tah
Sunday	неділя	neh-DEE-lya

I'll be going	Я їду....	ya yee-DOO
We'll be going	Ми їдемо....	mih YEE-deh-mo
on Monday	в понеділок	v po-neh-DEE-lok
on Tuesday	в вівторок	v veev-TO-rok
on Wednesday	в середу	v SEH-rch-doo
on Thursday	в четвер	v cheht-VEHR
on Friday	в п'ятницю	v P'YAT-nih-tsyu
on Saturday	в суботу	v soo-BO-too
on Sunday	в неділю	v neh-DEE-lyu

weekday	день неділі	dehn' neh-DEE-lee
weekend	вихідні	vih-kheed-NEE
today	сьогодні	s'o-HOD-nee
in the morning	вранці	VRAHN-tsee
this morning	сьогодні вранці	s'o-HOD-nee VRAHN-tsee
at noon	о полудні	o po-LOOD-nee
in the afternoon	після обіду	PEES-lya o-BEE-doo
this afternoon	сьогодні після обіду	s'o-HOD-nee PEES-lya o-BEE-doo
this evening, tonight	сьогодні ввечері	s'o-HOD-nee v-VEH-cheh-ree
at midnight	о півночі	o PEEV-no-chee

daily	кожний день	KOZH-nihў dehn'
during the day	напротязі дня	nah-PRO-tya-zee dnya
during the morning	напротязі ранку	nah-PRO-tya-zee RAHN-koo
during the evening	напротязі вечора	nah-PRO-tya-zee VEH-cho-rah
last evening	минулого вечора	mih-NOO-lo-ho VEH-cho-rah
last night	милнулої ночі	mih-NOO-lo-yee NO-chee
yesterday	учора	oo-CHO-rah
day before yesterday	позавчора	po-zahv-CHO-rah
three days ago	три дні тому	trih dnee to-MOO
last week	минулого тиждня	mih-NOO-lo-ho TIHZHD-nya
tomorrow	завтра	ZAHV-trah
tomorrow morning	завтра вранці	ZAHV-trah VRAHN-tsee
tomorrow afternoon	завтра після обіду	ZAHV-trah PEES-lya o-BEE-doo
tomorrow evening	завтра ввечері	ZAHV-trah v-VEH-cheh-ree
day after tomorrow	післязавтра	pees-lya-ZAHV-trah
next week	наступного тиждня	nahs-TOOP-no-ho TIHZHD-nya
in two weeks	через два тиждні	CHEH-rehz dvah TIHZHD-nee
every week	кожний тиждень	KOZH-nihў TIHZH-dehn'

Months and Years

The names of the months are not capitalized in Ukrainian.

January	січень	SEE-chehn'
in January	в січні	v SEECH-nee
February	лютий	LYU-tihў
in February	в лютому	v LYU-to-moo
March	березень	BEH-reh-zehn'
in March	в березні	v BEH-rehz-nee
April	квітень	KVEE-tehn'
in April	в квітні	v KVEET-nee

May	травень	TRAH-vehn'
in May	в травні	v TRAHV-nee
June	червень	CHEHR-vehn'
in June	в червні	v CHEHRV-nee
July	липень	LIH-pehn'
in July	в липні	v LIHP-nee
August	серпень	SEHR-pehn'
in August	в серпні	v SEHRP-nee
September	вересень	VEH-reh-sehn'
in September	в вересні	v VEH-rehs-nee
October	жовтень	ZHOV-tehn'
in October	в жовтні	v ZHOVT-nee
November	листопад	lihs-to-PAHD
in November	в листопаді	v lihs-to-PAH-dee
December	грудень	HROO-dehn'
in December	в грудні	v HROOD-nee

this month	цього місяця
	TS'O-ho MEE-sya-tsya
last month	минулого місяця
	mih-NOO-lo-ho MEE-sya-tsya
six months ago	пів року назад
	peev RO-koo nah-ZAHD
next month	наступного місяця
	nahs-TOOP-no-ho MEE-sya-tsya

for three months	три місяці	trih MEE-sya-tsee
year	рік	reek
last year	минулого року	
	mih-NOO-lo-ho RO-koo	
next year	наступного року	
	nahs-TOOP-no-ho RO-koo	
decade	декада	deh-KAH-dah
century	вік, століття	veek, sto-LEET-tya

It's the third of March.	Сьогодні третє березня.
	s'o-HOD-nee TREH-tyeh BEH-rehz-nya
It's the 29th of July.	Сьогодні двадцять дев'яте липня.
	s'o-HOD-nee DVAHD-tsyat' dehv'-YA-teh
	LIHP-nya

On June first ...	Першого червня
	PEHR-sho-ho CHEHRV-nya
On the 12th of August...	Двадцятого серпня
	dvahd-TSYA-to-ho SEHRP-ya
1996	тисяча дев'ятсот дев'яносто шостий рік
	TIH-sya-chah dehv'-yat-SOT dehv-ya-NOS-to
	SHOS-(tihў) reek

Seasons and Special Days

spring	весна	vehs-NAH
in spring	весною	vehs-NO-yu
summer	літо	LEE-to
in summer	літом	LEE-tom
fall/autumn	осінь	O-seen'
in fall/autumn	восени	vo-seh-NIH
winter	зима	zih-MAH
in winter	зимою	zih-MO-yu
last winter	минулої зими	
	mih-NOO-lo-yee zih-MIH	
next spring	наступної весни	
	nahs-TOOP-no-yee vehs-NIH	
every summer	кожного літа	
	KOZH-no-ho LEE-tah	
during the fall	цілу осінь	TSEE-loo O-seen'
working day	робочий день	ro-BO-chihў dehn'
day off	відгул	veed-HOOL
holiday/feast day	св'ятковий день	sv'yat-KO-vihў dehn'
vacation	відпустка	veed-POOST-kah
school holiday	канікули	kah-NEE-koo-lih
birthday	день народження	
	dehn' nah-ROD-zhehn-nya	

General References to Time

right away	зараз	ZAH-rahz
now	тепер	teh-PEHR
soon	незабаром	neh-zah-BAH-rom

any time	в любий час	v lyu-BIHY̆ chahs
recently	скоро	SKO-ro
later	пізніше	peez-NEE-sheh
earlier	раніше	rah-NEE-sheh
always	завжди	ZAHVZ̑H-dih
often	часто	CHAHS-to
sometimes	інколи	EEN-ko-lih
rarely	рідко	REED-ko
never	ніколи	nee-KO-lih
before	перед	PEH-rehd
after	після	PEES-ly̑a
for a long time	дуже довго	DOO-zheh DOV-ho
a long time ago	давно	DAHV-no

AGRICULTURE

What is that plant?   Яка це рослина?

ya-KAH   tseh   ros-LIH-nah

Plants and their cultivation are very important in Ukraine, not only because agriculture is an important part of its economy but because Ukrainians love nature and love to grow things. They enjoy plants for their beauty as well as value them for their usefulness.

A few basic concepts associated with Ukraine:

The *steppe* (степ) is the broad band of grassland covering almost the entire southern part of Ukraine up to the foothills of the Crimean Mountains. Like the American prairie, almost all of the steppe's wild grass vegetation has given way to cultivation.

Chornozem (чорнозем) is the rich fertile soil that covers almost half of Ukraine, primarily the steppe belt. *Chornozem* is a thick layer of dark grey soil with a definite granular-lumpy structure and a high content of decomposed matter. The *chornozem* layer is soft and absorbs water and air well, promoting bacterial development and plant nourishment. Deep plowing increases the fertility resulting in the highest possible yields of all types of agricultural crops.

Ukrainian agriculture is based on collectivization, which was forcibly introduced in the late 1920's and early 1930's as a means of providing the state with maximum cost-free capital for developing heavy industry, supporting the military, and maintaining the bureaucracy. A typical collective farm, a *kolhosp* (колгосп), has about 1000 hectares of land. The state farm or *radhosp* (радгосп), more common in southern and central than in western Ukraine, is a more socialist form of agricultural organization than the collective farm, with the state owning not only the land but the means of production as well. State farms tend to be larger than collective farms.

A hectare (гектар, hehk-TAHR) or 10,000 square meters is approximately 2.5 acres.

What's the land like here?	Яка тут земля?	
	ya-KAH toot zehm-LY͡A	
desert	пустеля	poos-TEH-lya
field	поле	PO-leh
forest	ліс	lees
meadow	луг	loo-h
mountains	гори	HO-rih
orchard	сад	sahd
marsh	болото	bo-LO-to
melon field	баштан	bahsh-TAHN
pastures	пасовище	pah-SO-vih-shche
steppe	степ	stehp
vineyards	виноградники	vih-no-HRAHD-nih-kih

What kind of vegetation grows here?	Які рослини ростуть тут?	
	ya-KEE ros-LIH-nih ros-TOOT′ toot	
annual plants	однолітні рослини od-no-LEET-nee ros-LIH-nih	
crops	сільськогосподарські культури seel′-s′ko-hos-po-DAHRS′-kee kool′-TOO-rih	
flowers	квіти	KVEE-tih
fodder	кормові рослини	kor-mo-VEE ros-LIH-nih
fruits	фрукти	FROOK-tih
grass	трава	trah-VAH
grains	зернові	zehr-no-VEE
hay	сіно	SEE-no
perennial plants	многолітні рослини mno-ho-LEET-nee ros-LIH-nih	

seed	насіння	nah-SEEN-nya
tree, trees	дерево, дерева	DEH-reh-vo, deh-REH-vah
vegetables	овочі	O-vo-chee
weeds	бур'ян	boor'-YAN

What is your main crop? Яку основну культуру ви вирощуєте?
ya-KOO os-nov-NOO kool'-TOO-roo vih
vih-RO-shchoo-yeh-teh

With Ukraine's reputation as the "breadbasket of Europe," it's not surprising that grains are the most important crops. Millet, spring wheat, and barley cultivation date back to the Trypilian period (4,000-3,000 B.C.), rye appeared a couple of thousand years later, buckwheat in the first century A.D., followed by oats. Corn cultivation dates to the eighteenth century and rice didn't come into use until after World War II. Today the total grain harvest ranges from 40 to 50 million tons per year.

The mainstay of Ukrainian grain crops is wheat, especially winter wheat. The black soil (*chornozem*) and the warm, moderately rainy summers, primarily in southern and eastern regions of the country, provide ideal conditions for its cultivation. Here are the major crops:

barley	ячмінь	yach-MEEN'
buckwheat	гречка	HREHCH-kah
corn	кукурудза	koo-koo-ROOD-zah
millet	пшоно	psho-NO
oats	овес	o-VEHS
rice	рис	rihs
sorghum	сорго	SOR-ho
rye	жито	ZHIH-to
wheat	пшениця	psheh-NIH-tsya
spring wheat	яра пшениця	YA-rah psheh-NIH-tsya
winter wheat	озима пшениця	o-ZIH-mah psheh-NIH-tsya

These crops are grown for food processing, fodder, or industrial use:

alfalfa	люцерна	lyu-TSEHR-nah
castor beans	касторові боби	kahs-TO-ro-vee bo-BIH
clover	конюшина	ko-nyu - SHIH-nah
flax	льон	l'on

hemp	конопля	ko-nop-LYA͡
hops	хміль	khmeel'
legumes	стрючкові	stry͡uch-KO-vee
soybeans	сойові боби	SO-y͡o-vee bo-BIH
sunflowers	соняшники	SO-ny͡ash-nih-kih
sugar beets	цукрові буряки	tsook-RO-vee boo-RY͡A-kih
tobacco	тютюн	ty͡u-TY͡UN

Which food crops do you grow? Які овочеві культури ви вир ощуєте ya-KEE o-vo-CHEH-vee kool'-TOO-rih vih vih-RO-shchoo-yeh-teh

beets	буряки	boo-ry͡a-KIH
cabbage	капуста	kah-POOS-tah
carrots	морква	MORK-vah
cucumbers	огірки	o-hihr-KIH
garlic	часник	chahs-NIHK
onions	цибуля	tsih-BOO-ly͡a
pepper	перець	PEH-rehts'
potatoes	картопля	kahr-TOP-ly͡a
tomatoes	помідори	po-mee-DO-rih

What fruits grow in this region? Які фрукти вирощуються в цьому регіоні? ya-KEE FROOK-tih vih-RO-shchoo-yut'-sy͡a v TS'O-moo reh-hee-O-nee

apples	яблука	YAB-loo-kah
apricots	абрикоси	ahb-rih-KO-sih
cherries, sweet	черешні	cheh-REHSH-nee
cherries, tart	вишні	VIHSH-nee
grapes	виноград	vih-no-HRAHD
melons	дині	DIH-nee
pears	груші	HROO-shee
plums	сливи	SLIH-vih

Which berries do you grow? Які ягоди ви вирощуєте? ya-KEE YA-ho-dih vih-RO-shchoo-yeh-teh

blackberries	ожина	o-ZH͡IH-nah
black currants	смородина	smo-RO-dih-nah
red currants	порічки	po-REECH-kih

gooseberries	агрус	AHH-roos
raspberries	малина	mah-LIH-nah
strawberries		
east Ukraine:	суниці	soo-NIH-tsee
west Ukraine:	трускавки	TROOS-kahv-kih

What is this herb Як називається ця рослина?
called? yak nah-zih-VAH-yeht'-sy͡a tsy͡a ros-LIH-nah

Many plants are grown for their culinary flavor, for their medicinal use, or for their yield of essential oils. Roots, leaves, blossoms, buds, berries, or seeds of the following are commonly used for cooking or healing.

basil	волошки	vo-LOSH-kih
belladonna	беладонна	beh-lah-DON-nah
blueberry	чорниці	chor-NIH-tsee
(its leaves are used for colds and sore throat)		
camomile	ромашка	ro-MASH-kah
caraway	кмин	kmihn
dill	окріп	ok-REEP
foxglove	наперсник	nah-PEHRS-nihk
lavender	лаванда	lah-VAHN-dah
mint	м'ята	M'Y͡A-tah
parsley	петрушка	peh-TROOSH-kah
poppy	мак	mahk
rose	роза	ro-ZAH
sage	шавлія	SHAHV-lee-ya
sorrel	щавель	shchah-VEHL'
valerian	валер'яна	vah-lehr'Y͡A-nah
wormwood	полин	po-LIHN

What kind of tree is that?
Яке це дерево?
ya-KEH tseh DEH-reh-vo

aspen	осика	o-SIH-kah
beech	бук	book
birch	береза	beh-REH-zah
chestnut	каштан	kash-TAHN
cottonwood	топіль	TO-peel'

fir	ялина	ya-LIH-nah
linden	липа	LIH-pa
maple	клен	klehn
oak	дуб	doob
pine	сосна	sos-NAH

Special Plants Plants figure in story, song, and legend. Here are a few that have special meaning for Ukrainians:

Chestnut (каштан, *kashtan*) is the symbol of Kyiv. Huge chestnut trees line the main streets and avenues of the city. The hard currency shops are named for the chestnut.

Cherry (вишня, *vyshnya*). The luscious, deeply-flavored tart sour cherry is one of the most popular fruits in Ukraine. The leaves are added to pickles to lend flavor. The beautiful tree is abundant throughout Ukraine and in early spring their blossoms make a spectacular show. The cherry orchard is the theme of a much-loved Shevchenko poem which was made into a popular song.

Garlic (часник, *chasnyk*) is undoubtedly one of the most important plants in Ukrainian folk medicine and a primary ingredient of Ukrainian cuisine. It is not eaten to cure any particular ailments, but to promote general good health and well-being, a practice supported by numerous 20th-century medical studies. Ukrainians usually don't cook garlic but enjoy it in its raw state, with bread, butter, and salt, or diced into salads.

Viburnum or guelder rose (калина, *kalyna*) is an attractive deciduous shrub. Ukrainians also call it the "red snowball tree" because of its cluster of red berries which hang on the tree throughout the winter. The berries have a very high vitamin C content and an infusion of the mature dried berries is used for coughs. Because of the staying power of the berries, the *kalyna* has become a metaphor for the survival of the Ukrainian nation. *Kalyna* is the subject of various patriotic songs and the name of various organizations.

Willow (верба, *verba*). Gracing ponds and riverbanks, the elegant willow lends charm to rural landscapes. At least 30 species grow in Ukraine. In olden days, fences and baskets were made of willow twigs and the soft, light wood is also used for hand-carved articles such as musical instruments, for example, the bandura. The branches of one species, the pussy willow, are used on Palm Sunday instead of palm fronds.

Beekeeping   Бджільництво   bdzheel'-NIHTST-vo

Some plants are important in Ukraine because their blossoms provide nectar for bees. Wildflowers, buckwheat, clover, and linden blossoms are the primary types of honey. Each has a distinct color and flavor, ranging from light and delicately flavored wildflower honey to the dark, strong tasting buckwheat.

Beekeeping or apiculture has been widespread in Ukraine since ancient times, but declined in the 17th and 18th centuries with deforestation, the cultivation of the steppes, and the prominence of sugar. In the first half of the 19th century apiculture was revived and entered a modern period with the invention of the first frame hive by Peter Prokopovych, a landowner in the in the Chernihiv area. By the eve of World War I, beekeeping was highly developed in Ukraine with about 2,000,000 hives. With collectivization, nearly all collective farms began to keep bees. While beekeeping still remained a popular individual enterprise, the collectives became the primary source of honey production in Ukraine. Apiculture is most developed in the forest-steppe region and in the steppe region.

Ukrainians value honey not only for its sweetening ability but also for its medicinal properties. Several books have been published in Ukraine about the use of honey as treatment for many diseases, especially those of the lungs, throat, and skin. The *propolis* (прополіс), a sticky substance bees collect from buds, is a powerful antibiotic against bacteria.

apiary	пасіка	PAH-see-kah
bees	бджоли	BDZHO-lih
beehive	вулик	VOO-lihk
honey	мед	mehd

SIGNS, ABBREVIATIONS, and ACRONYMS

Names on buildings:

Аптека	Pharmacy	ahp-TEH-ka
Банк	Bank	bahnk
Гастроном	Grocery	hahs-tro-NOM
Кафе	Cafe	KAH-feh
Лікарня	Hospital	lee-KAHR-nya
Медпункт	Nurse's Station	mehd-POONKT
Міліція	Police Station	mee-LEE-tsee-ya
Поліклініка	Clinic	po-lee-KLEE-nee-kah
Пошта	Post Office	POSH-tah
Продукти	Grocery	pro-DOOK-tih
Телеграф	Telegraph	teh-leh-HRAHF
Телефон	Telephone	teh-leh-FON
Школа	School	SHKO-lah

Signs posted indoors or around buildings:

Вихід	Exit
Відкрито	Open
Від Себе	Push
Вільно	Unoccupied
Вхід	Entrance
Вхід через Другі Двері	Entrance Other Door
До Себе	Pull
Ескалатор	Escalator
Зайнято	Occupied
Закривайте Двері	Keep Door Closed
Закрито	Closed
Закрито на Обід	Closed For Lunch
Закрито на Переоблік	Closed For Inventory
Закрито на Перерву	Closed For A Break
Ліфт	Elevator
Ласкаво Просимо	Welcome

(*literally, "We kindly ask," seen over the entrance of many businesses and schools*)

Не Входити	Don't Enter
Не Курити	No Smoking
Не Торкатись	Don't Touch
Не Фотографувати	No Photography
Не Шуміти	Don't Make Noise

Нема Виходу	No Exit
Нема Входу	No Entrance
Обережно Пофарбовано	Caution — Wet Paint
Пожежний Вихід	Fire Exit
Прошу Входити	Please Enter
Ремонт	Renovations
Ремонтні Роботи	Maintenance
Руками не Торкатись	Don't Touch (Hands Off)
Службовий Вхід	Employees' (Service) Entrance
Сходи	Stairs
Тихо	Quiet
Туалет	Toilet

Outdoor, street, and traffic signs

Висока Напруга	High Voltage
Идіть	Go
Небезпечно	Danger
Небезпечно для Життя	Life In Danger
Нема Ходу	Not A Thoroughfare
Нема Переходу	No Crossing
Нема Проходу	No Trespassing
Обережно	Caution
Обережно Газ	Caution Gas
Об'їзд	Vehicle Detour
Обхід	Foot Detour
Перехід	Crossing
Повільно	Go Slow
Прохід	Throughway
Стійте	Wait
Стоп	Stop

Abbreviated Signs

A	[автобус, автобусна зупинка]	bus, bus stop
Ж	[жіночий]	women's rest room
М	[метро]	subway
Т(м)	[трамвай, трамвайна зупинка]	streetcar, streetcar stop
Т(р)	[тролейбус, тролейбисна зупинка]	trolley, trolley stop
Ч	[чоловічий]	men's restroom

Abbreviations

авт.	автобус	bus
д., буд.	дім, будинок	building
г., год.,	година	hour
г.	гора	mountain
гр-н.	громадянан	Mr. or Mrs.
кар.	карбованець	karbovanets
кв.	квартира	apartment
корп.	корпус	corpus

(*part of a structure, for example, a particular building at a university*)

ім.	імені	named after ...
м.	місто	city
п., пн.	пан, пані	Mr., Mrs.
обл.	область	oblast (region)
оз.	озеро	lake
р.	ріка	river
р-н.	район	raion (county)
с.	село	village
сел.	селище	settlement
хв.	хвилина	minute

EMERGENCY PHRASES

HELP!	Допоможіть	do-po-mo-Z͡HEET'
STOP THIEF!	Зупиніть Злодія!	zoo-pih-NEET' ZLO-dee-ya
WATCH OUT!	Обережно!	o-beh-REHZ͡H-no
POLICE!	Міліція!	mee-LEE-tsee-ya
FIRE!	Пожар!	po-Z͡HAHR

[While the Ukrainian word for fire, пожежа (po-Z͡HE-zhah), is used in normal conversation, in times of emergency most Ukrainians will use the Russian word пожар.]

INDEX